Sanford M. Dornbusch
W. Richard Scott

with the assistance of
Bruce C. Busching and James D. Laing

▲▲

EVALUATION AND THE EXERCISE OF AUTHORITY

▲▲

Jossey-Bass Publishers

San Francisco · Washington · London · 1977

EVALUATION AND THE EXERCISE OF AUTHORITY
A Theory of Control Applied to Diverse Organizations
by Sanford M. Dornbusch and W. Richard Scott

Copyright © 1975 by: Jossey-Bass, Inc., Publishers
615 Montgomery Street
San Francisco, California 94111
&
Jossey-Bass Limited
28 Banner Street
London EC1Y 8QE

Library of Congress Catalogue Card Number LC 74-9344

International Standard Book Number IBSN 0-87589-247-7

Manufactured in the United States of America

JACKET DESIGN BY WILLI BAUM

FIRST EDITION
First printing: February 1975
Second printing: August 1977

Code 7436

The Jossey-Bass
Behavioral Science Series

▲▲

For Red
and Joy

Preface

▲▲

Evaluation and the Exercise of Authority reports the results of a decade-long research program in formal organizations. There are four noteworthy features of this effort:

First, we have developed a general formulation of evaluation and authority that is applicable to numerous types of organizations. To test the generality of our theory, we studied a football team, a hospital, an electronics plant, a physics research group, a student newspaper, numerous public schools and radical or alternative schools, a university (faculty), and a Roman Catholic archdiocese. From this research, we report empirical data on more than twenty different types of authority relations in diverse organizational settings.

Second, our theory has been developed in close connection with the continuing program of research. Our studies are cumulative in that all were guided by a set of core concepts and theoretical issues, with later studies taking earlier results into account. The interweaving of theoretical developments and empirical studies is symbolized by the organization of this book, which, after two introductory chapters, alternates theoretical presentations (Chapters

Three, Five, Seven, and Nine) with summaries of empirical findings (Chapters Four, Six, Eight, and Ten).

Third, our final chapter is not a conventional summary, but an attempt to draw together the many threads into a web of inter-related principles. We state there a relatively formal theory of evalu-ation and authority—a type of theory that is more often discussed than constructed. We publish these propositions, theorems, and corol-laries not to mark the conclusion of the quest, but rather so that others can use our work, conduct further tests, and move on to develop better theory.

Lastly, to our surprise and pleasure, our theoretical approach has had a practical payoff. Participants in the organizations we studied reported to us that our perspective helped them in identi-fying some of their problems and dealing with them. We believe that our theory can easily be applied to improve the functioning of many organizations.

Formal organizations may be viewed as structures devised to accomplish specified goals. General objectives are established from which more specific subgoals are derived. These subgoals are allocated as tasks to organizational participants. Goals are attained because participants carry out activities designed to realize them. Thus, in order to realize its goals, an organization must control the task performances of participants. It attempts to do so by distributing valued sanctions—rewards and penalties—to participants. The distribution of sanctions is vested in the hands of a subset of orga-nizational participants (superiors) who use them to control the task performances of other participants (subordinates).

In a rational system, evaluation is an indispensable process for controlling task performances. If evaluations were absent, re-wards and penalties would be distributed in a random or capricious manner. Therefore, it is fundamental to the control of performances that organizational superiors evaluate subordinates' performances, and that these evaluations help to influence the distribution of organizational sanctions.

Evaluation is a complex process, four components of which are distinguished: assigning a goal to a participant, determining criteria to be employed in evaluating task performances, selecting the sample of performances or outcomes that will be inspected, and assessing the sampled performances with the established criteria. Since in an organization each of these components of the evaluation process may be exercised by different participants, we must investigate the coordination of these various activities. That is, we consider the organization of control relations into control systems.

Our approach is not based on a rational model of organizational control systems because we believe that all control attempts in organizations are rationally based. We have much evidence to the contrary. Rather, we use a rational model as a means of detecting problems in existing control systems. Conflicts and inadequacies occur frequently and have important implications for system operation and maintenance. Four classes of problems are identified that produce low performance evaluations through no fault of the performer: situations in which the participant whose performance is to be controlled receives contradictory evaluations, or is evaluated for performances or outcomes over which he or she lacks control, or is unable to predict the relation between work performed and evaluations received, or is expected to meet unattainable standards. We explore these problems by examining the presence and frequency of such "incompatibilities" in control systems. We predict that incompatibilities tend to be associated with system instability, as reflected by participant dissatisfaction and attempts to change the system.

The stability of control systems is also affected by the type of tasks being performed. Control arrangements that would be suitable for some types of tasks may be quite inappropriate for others. Tasks are categorized along several dimensions—clarity of the goal pursued, efficacy of the procedures employed, predictability of the relation between task procedures and outcomes—as a basis for evaluating the appropriateness of control systems. Ill-suited systems are expected to be less stable.

Other factors which affect the operation and stability of control systems include the frequency with which performances are sampled by evaluators and evaluations communicated to performers, the visibility of task performances and outcomes to evaluators, and the extent to which there is agreement among evaluators concerning the criteria to be employed in evaluating performances. These and similar factors affect participants' perceptions as to whether the

evaluations which they receive are soundly based and hence affect
their reactions to control systems.

Control systems regulate task performances but by what
means are control systems themselves regulated? The distinction
between a power system and an authority system is employed to
enable us to discuss one important arrangement by which control
systems are regulated. While power is the ability of some participants
to distribute valued sanctions to other system members, authority is
the normative regulation of this relation. Although such regulation
may occur in a variety of ways, emphasis is placed here on the
regulation of the power wielder by participants superior to him in
the power structure, participants in a position to "authorize" his
control attempts.

Evaluation processes play a double role in our conception of
control systems. Evaluation is fundamental to the regulation of task
performances of participants in organizational systems; and evaluation processes are essential to the regulation of the control systems
themselves, as arbitrary power is domesticated to become regularized
authority.

Evaluation and the Exercise of Authority reports a conceptualization of and develops a theory concerning authority systems
in formal organizations. Evidence bearing on this theory is drawn
from field studies carried out in a number of diverse organizations.
These studies began with an examination of selected organizational
positions in five very different organizations: a large teaching hospital, a basic research facility, an assembly line at an electronics
plant, a student newspaper, and a university football team. Virtually
identical questions were posed in studying authority systems in each
of these settings. We refer to this first investigation as the Five
Organizations study. Subsequent investigations took our collaborators and us into still other settings where we attempted to replicate
previous findings and follow up new leads. Organizations studied
included a university faculty, public elementary schools, nursing
units in general hospitals, radical and alternative schools, and
parishes in a Roman Catholic archdiocese.

That we were led into such a diverse collection of organizations is partially attributable to the skills and interests of our col-

leagues and collaborators. We are pleased to be able to acknowledge their many contributions to this project.

The origin of this enterprise was a faculty seminar in the Department of Sociology at Stanford University. Joseph Berger, Santo F. Camilleri, Bernard P. Cohen, and Morris Zelditch, Jr., sat with us for long hours discussing the nature of evaluation processes. Our four colleagues gradually concentrated their effort on a set of experimental studies, focused on evaluation processes in small groups. Together we received a grant from the National Science Foundation which supported the Five Organizations study, out first set of field studies (Grant G23990).

Working with us at this time were Bruce C. Busching and James D. Laing. They were carrying out Ph.D. dissertations under our direction, but that bald description completely misstates the nature of our interaction. Busching and Laing were colleagues in every way and played an equal role in the development of our research. They not only influenced the first tests of our ideas, but also helped to shape much of our conceptual apparatus. Our listing them on the title page is one way of saying that we cannot determine which ideas were ours and which were theirs. We had a true intellectual partnership.

In addition to Busching and Laing, other graduate students at Stanford elected to collaborate with us as they carried out their dissertation research. Warren F. Bryld, Robert Crawford, Robert R. Hind, Leonard Magnani, Gwen D. Marram, Brian McCauley, June E. Thompson, and Donald Turner provided empirical tests of various aspects of our formulation. Thomas R. Burns obtained his doctorate with us by extending and revising our formulation.

Three other graduate students, Patricia Barchas, Katherine Ullman Barchas, and Marjorie Seashore helped in our interviews at the hospital. Even more important, their assistance with the pretesting of our instruments as well as their independent but related studies made a major contribution. They also provided a continuing flow of friendly criticism, as did Karen Cook, Connie J. Evashwick, Ann D. Flood, James C. Moore, Jr., Andrew Paoli, Inger Sagatun, Claudia K. Schoonhoven, Sandra Smith, and David G. Wagner.

Many other Stanford students—undergraduate as well as

graduate—helped at some stage in the research program. Two small classes helped us gather data for the Five Organizations study. The following students in a freshman seminar at Stanford interviewed football players and the staff of a student newspaper: Karin Bjorkland, Gretchen Carter, Gary Goedecke, Paul Goldman, Michael Lindeman, Richard Shockley, and Richard Spier. A graduate class in field methods also helped gather data from the electronics assembly line and the physics research group. Its members were Ronald E. Anderson, Perry Birchard, Peter Ekeh, Ann D. Flood, David Gustafson, Patricia Kariel, Paul D. Reynolds, John H. Simpson, Barbara Sobieszek, Timothy Wirth, and Judith Young.

In addition to these persons, Michael Berkowitz, David Gonzales, and Judith Hanks assisted in the interviews in public schools. Russell Endo carried out a separate study of task evaluation in the student newspaper. Freda F. Eisenson provided an important resource in the early stages of our school studies by sharing with us her varied experiences in public schools. Amitai Etzioni gave us friendly criticism of the early conceptualization of authority rights. Leora Herrmann and Steven S. Dornbusch helped with late stages of the analysis.

As we concentrated our research efforts on schools, our colleagues at the Stanford Center for Research and Development in Teaching provided guidance and support. Criticism and help came from Elizabeth G. Cohen, coordinator of the Environment for Teaching Program, C. Norman Alexander, John W. Meyer, and the late Paul Wallin. The U.S. Office of Education (Project 5-0252-0307) and the National Institute of Education (Contract NE-C-00-3-0062) have provided financial support for some of our studies. We are indebted to Robert N. Bush and Terence E. Deal for creating a favorable organizational climate at the center.

We also must acknowledge the generous assistance of the many organizations that let us study in detail their ongoing operations, placing no restriction on eventual publication of our findings. Preserving their anonymity prevents our thanking them publicly.

Finally, since this project has lasted so long, we have to thank a parade of secretaries who have typed numerous versions of questionnaires and drafts of chapters. Suzanne Ayala, Karin Inge, Margaret Montgomery, Linda D. Rechtin, Rosalind Revelle,

Catherine Ruck, and Sandra P. Williams helped us meet numerous deadlines.

This long list of co-workers and associates indicates the extent to which, with their help, we kept applying and redefining our basic ideas in a host of large and small studies. Even our last theoretical effort in Chapter Eleven was aided by our colleagues Bernard P. Cohen and James C. Kimberly. The final result, although their product, is our responsibility.

Stanford, California   SANFORD M. DORNBUSCH
December 1974   W. RICHARD SCOTT

Contents

▲▲▲

Preface   vii

1. Descriptive Account of the
        Research Program   1

2. Power and Authority   29

3. Goals, Tasks, Sanctions   65

4. Goals, Tasks, Sanctions:
        Empirical Studies   100

5. Evaluation Process   134

6. Evaluation: Empirical Studies   163

7. Authority in Formal Organizations   192

8.   Authority: Empirical Studies   209

9.   Incompatibility and Instability
        of Authority Systems   243

10. Incompatibility and Instability:
        Empirical Studies   283

11. Theory of Evaluation and Authority   332

     Bibliography   359

     Name Index   374

     Subject Index   376

Evaluation and the Exercise of Authority

A Theory of Control Applied
to Diverse Organizations

▲▲

Chapter 1

Descriptive Account of the Research Program

▲▲

The research reported in this volume had its origin more than ten years ago when we met together weekly in an informal seminar with several of our colleagues in the Department of Sociology at Stanford University. At first the discussion was wide-ranging and unstructured. Little by little a set of common interests began to emerge as we considered such problems as the following: If a hierarchically organized team does well, are rewards distributed according to the status or responsibilities of participants? If a team does poorly, how is blame distributed? How does a general conception of the performance capacities of a participant affect the evaluations made of a particular performance? When is it appropriate to evaluate each step of a performance and when is it appropriate to evaluate the outcome? Eventually a research proposal for the investigation of "authority and evaluation structures" was written by the group, and funding was obtained from the National Science Foundation.

From the earliest stages of our collaboration in the research

1

seminar, we expected to organize ourselves into two teams, one to carry out laboratory experiments, the other, field investigations. However, as the two teams worked separately to develop and implement their research strategies, their substantive interests also began to diverge. Both teams continued to pursue the problems of evaluation and control, but with different emphases. The laboratory group focused attention on the ways in which the performance expectations associated with certain status characteristics affect performance evaluations, control attempts, and responses to control attempts. (See Zelditch, Berger, and Cohen, 1966; Berger, Cohen, and Zelditch, 1966; Camilleri and Berger, 1967.) The field team concentrated on the evaluation process itself and on the various problems associated with attempts to assess directly the quality of performances and their associated outcomes. (For an early statement of our interests and approach, see Scott, Dornbusch, and others, 1967.) In short, the laboratory team increasingly turned its attention to how *expectations* about task performances structure the ensuing behavior and the evaluations of that behavior, while the field team focused on arrangements devised for evaluating the *actual* performances of organizational participants and on the problems associated with those arrangements. Unless otherwise indicated, from this point we restrict attention to the activities of the field team.

At the outset of our research, we carried out informal interviewing and nonparticipant observation in two wards of a large hospital. Both nursing teams and physician groups were observed across a range of tasks, and, over a period of more than a year, we attempted to move from relatively unstructured recording of task-related activities and interactions to more structured observations. Much time and energy were invested in observing interactions. However, we soon discovered that often we could not make the distinctions required by our theoretical interests without asking participants to tell us what meaning they assigned to particular events. For example, sometimes the superior's silence was perceived as a strong negative evaluation by subordinate workers. Many statements which subordinates took to be directives or orders from superiors sounded to us like requests or suggestions, for example, "I'd check on that." And questions like, "Have you considered disease X?" were sometimes considered negative evaluations by interns, although the evaluative component was missed by the observer.

Consequently we decided that our research interests would be better served by directly questioning organizational participants. Hence, following the exploratory phase of field work, which relied very heavily on observation, all our systematic data were gathered via questionnaires or interviews with organizational participants either in their role as subordinates (evaluatees) or superiors (evaluators). Nevertheless, the early months of observation helped us become more aware of some of the complexities of organizational control systems, suggested a number of specific propositions and interesting problem areas for study, and provided our research group with a common body of descriptive information relevant to our theoretical interests.

Five Organizations Study

Our early field interviews were designed to achieve two purposes. First, we wished to operationalize our conception of authority. Second, we sought to test our predictions relating conflicts or inadequacies in the evaluation process to instability of the authority system. Both kinds of data were gathered in an interview held with an organizational participant in his role as a subordinate. That is, the interview focused attention on the respondent as a recipient of evaluations rather than as an evaluator attempting to control others. Further, the interview focused on the evaluation of a single organizational task performed by the respondent. (Criteria employed in selecting the task are described in Chapter Four.) We restricted attention to a single task because of the assumption that authority systems for the same performer can vary markedly from one task to another. Also, given the desired level of detail concerning the exercise of authority rights and problems of evaluation, time limitations prevented questioning the subject about more than one of the tasks performed. Interviewing time ranged from 45 minutes to as long as two and a half hours, but averaged about 75 minutes.

Data were collected from respondents in sixteen different positions located in five organizations: a large teaching hospital, a basic research facility, an assembly line at an electronics plant, a student newspaper, and a university football team. The primary selection criteria were diversity and proximity. All the organizations studied were in the San Francisco Bay Area within easy commuting distance of Stanford University. In some types of research, gathering data from a single geographical region would seriously affect the generalizability of findings, but we do not believe that the principles we tested here are much affected by geography. We sought diversity of organizations so as to maximize the variety of contexts within which to examine our predictions. We sought—and found—organizations varying greatly in such important characteristics as size, complexity, professionalization of the work force, mechanization of technology, height of the official hierarchy, and specificity of goals. Our small set of five organizations was also sufficiently large to include both profit and nonprofit firms, and two organizations in which financial incentives were not employed. We were fortunate that the first five organizations we approached were willing to cooperate with us.

Although we refer here and elsewhere to this research as the Five Organizations study, we did not study these organizations as a whole but concentrated on the analysis of selected positions and their associated authority systems within each organization. Several criteria were employed in selecting the sixteen positions studied. First, in order to maximize diversity along a number of dimensions which organizational researchers often regard as salient, we selected positions which varied greatly in terms of location in the hierarchy, educational requirements for incumbents, supervisory responsibilities, complexity of work performed, and whether they were typically staffed by males or females. Second, we attempted to select positions including large numbers of occupants so that we could learn about factors characteristic of the position and not peculiar to a particular incumbent. We found this to be a difficult criterion to meet in the two highly professionalized organizations, the teaching hospital and the basic research facility. In spite of their large size, we had difficulty in locating positions for which there were a sizable number of occupants since a very specialized work force is present in these settings. "Many positions, few incumbents" appears to be the principle of organization here. Third, we selected only those positions which were clearly defined, for which there was an atmosphere of established practice. Thus, we attempted to avoid positions which were undergoing rapid change or were newly established.

Once the positions to be studied were selected, we attempted to interview all occupants of the position who had been incumbents long enough to be familiar with their job situation and with their associates. Usually, we were able to spot and eliminate newcomers in the early reconnaissance phases of our investigation. Questions early in each interview sought to identify the respondent's particular work group. All subsequent questions concerned the situation in that work group. If no such work group could be identified, the respondent was thanked and the interview terminated.

We now turn to a brief description of each organizational position examined in this first study.

The positions selected in the teaching hospital were nurse's aide, nursing team leader, clinical clerk, intern or junior resident physician, and senior resident physician. All these positions functioned primarily in the context of the hospital ward as opposed to some more specialized unit. Data were collected in three types of wards: internal medicine, pediatrics, and surgery. The hospital used a nursing team arrangement in which one registered nurse served as team leader with one or more nurses or nurse's aides serving as team members. Under this arrangement, nurse's aides spent more time in direct contact with patients while registered nurses assumed a more supervisory role. The house staff physicians also were organized into teams which assumed responsibility for the care of specified groups of patients under the direction of attending physicians. A typical house staff arrangement placed a chief resident (a physician in training at least three or four years beyond the MD degree) in charge of several medical teams, each of which was headed by a senior resident (a physician two or three years beyond the MD). Each senior resident supervised the work of two or three junior residents or interns (physicians one or two years beyond the MD). Attached to each medical team were one or two clinical clerks (medical students in their third or fourth year of training for the MD degree). In all, ninety-five hospital participants were interviewed. The positions studied are summarized in Table 1. The specific tasks on which the interview focused for these positions are described in Chapter Four.

Table 1.

FIVE ORGANIZATIONS STUDY:
DISTRIBUTION OF RESPONDENTS BY POSITION AND ORGANIZATION

Organization	Number of Organizational Units	Number of Respondents	Position of Respondents
Hospital	3 (departments)	25	Nurse's Aide
	5 (wards)		
	3 (departments)	29	Nursing Team Leader
	5 (wards)		
	2 (departments)	9	Clinical Clerk
	3 (departments)	21	Intern
	3 (departments)	11	Senior Resident
Research Facility	2 (departments)	7	Engineer
	2 (departments)	6	Draftsman
	1 (department)	5	Storekeeper
	1 (department)	4	Technical Typist
Electronics Firm	4 (benches)	25	Assembly Line Worker
Student Newspaper	3 (shifts)	15	Desk Worker
	3 (shifts)	14	Copy Editor
Football Team	4 (strings)	20	Member of Defensive "Front Eight"
	3 (strings)	5	Member of Defensive "Back Three"
	4 (strings)	15	Member of Offensive Line
	4 (strings)	13	Ball Carrier

The basic research facility, like the teaching hospital, provided us with a considerable variety of positions in terms of complexity of the tasks performed and the educational requirements for occupants. Because of the difficulty of finding sufficient occupants for a given position, we did not attempt to study the upper-level scientific personnel within this organization. Rather, we concentrated on middle-level and support personnel. The positions investigated were engineer, draftsman, storekeeper, and technical typist. The engineers and draftsmen were located in two departments, mechanical engineering and electrical engineering. The engineering groups were responsible for designing and testing various kinds of components to meet specifications established by research physicists within the facility. Engineers within each department were primarily responsible for designing components, draftsmen for developing the design idea and preparing layout drawings of the components. The two positions worked in close cooperation on these tasks. The stores section was responsible for inspecting, cataloging, and shelving some 6000 items required for the operation of the research facility. A team of storekeepers worked under the supervision of a manager in carrying out these tasks. Technical typists were located in the reports section of the technical and public information division. Their work consisted primarily of preparing draft and final versions of the many technical reports produced by the scientific personnel of the facility. In all, twenty-two respondents were interviewed in the scientific research facility; their distribution by position and department is indicated in Table 1.

The electronics plant was added primarily to remedy a deficiency noted in the course of our studies at the hospital and the basic research facility. These two organizations were so highly differentiated in their structure and so fluid in their personnel practices that we sought an organization having more workers in stable situations performing comparable tasks. The assembly line at the electronics plant fulfilled this requirement. All the workers interviewed were in the manufacturing division of the firm and performed similar tasks at four assembly benches. The tasks involved wiring components on printed circuit boards by selecting and soldering wires and attaching other prefabricated components. Conveyor belts formerly used in this plant were no longer in operation, and the workers operated at their own pace. None of the workers in these positions belonged to a union. Twenty-five assembly workers were interviewed within this organization. (See Table 1.)

The student newspaper was selected to introduce an organization having little power over participants. All workers were volunteers, and it was expected that many would have relatively low commitment to the organization. The two positions selected for examination in this organization were desk worker and copy editor.

Desk workers were chiefly responsible for preparing and editing news releases and for copy reading. Copy editors were engaged almost exclusively in copy reading and final editing of the materials prepared by desk workers. Participants spent only a few hours per week in these positions. Fifteen desk workers and fourteen copy editors were interviewed, these positions organized by shift as indicated in Table 1.

The final organization included within the study was a university football team. Like the student newspaper, lower-level participants in this organization were volunteers. Unlike the newspaper organization, however, we expected student participants to exhibit relatively high commitment to this organization and to place considerable importance on the sanctions dispensed by it. Probably the most important reward at the disposal of the football team was playing time in the intervarsity contests. Players were expected to place great value on this reward. Further, perhaps more than in any other organization we examined, we found the football team placed great emphasis on the evaluation of performance of participants, with great care being taken to detect and correct players' errors. To this end a large coaching staff was present and observing performance at all practice sessions and games. Filming of these events provided further opportunities to review the performance of individual participants—in slow motion if desired.

Four types of player positions were distinguished after discussions with coaches and players: member of the "front eight" (defensive lineman or linebacker), member of the "back three" (defensive back), ball carrier (quarterback, runningback, fullback, flanker back, or split end), and offensive lineman (offensive center, guard, tackle, or tight end). Fifty-three football players were interviewed, as noted in Table 1.

In the Five Organizations study a total of 224 respondents located in sixteen positions gave us information. Each participant was interviewed to discover the nature of the authority structure to which he or she was subject in the performance of a single, important organizational task. The same basic questionnaire was employed in interviewing all respondents, producing systematic, comparable information on 224 authority systems. The basic proposition tested in this study was that incompatibilities—conflicts or inadequacies—in authority systems would give rise to instabilities—dissatisfaction, nonconformity, change attempts—in authority systems. The salient material is reported in this volume, but the technical details are best seen in Laing (1967) and Busching (1969).

Studies of Professional Organizations

After completing the Five Organizations study, we began a series of additional studies of authority and evaluation in organizations. These studies were carried out over a number of years in a variety of settings, and each was directed to a different research issue. Yet all these studies bear an important family resemblance. Before describing each in detail, let us identify their common features.

The Five Organizations study provided what appeared to be rather conclusive evidence in support of the predicted relationship between incompatibility and instability of authority systems. Hence, in our subsequent research we turned to other facets of authority relations and to other factors affecting system stability.

From the outset of our research program, we believed that authority systems are often task-specific—that is, that occupants of organizational positions frequently participate in more than one authority system depending on which task they are engaged in. We acted on this assumption in the Five Organizations study by specifying just one task in terms of which each respondent was asked to describe the authority system. Since we asked each respondent about only one task, however, we were not able to test our assumption that authority systems vary by task. In all our subsequent research, we took care to distinguish the different tasks performed by respondents and, with the exception of one study, gathered data from each respondent pertaining to authority systems for several tasks. The number of tasks examined varied from one study to another, but all studies included the investigation of more than one task.

When we were dealing with a single task for each respondent in the Five Organizations study, it was possible to obtain considerable information from respondents on the details of the process by which their performances were evaluated. Thus, we were able to investigate which persons were perceived to be carrying out particular components of the evaluation process. We distinguished in that study four types of evaluation activities that, if authorized, were regarded as exercised authority rights. As we began to investigate multiple tasks, however, it was necessary for the sanity of the respondent to sacrifice much of this more detailed information. Rather than distinguishing types of authority rights, we focused on a generalized right to evaluate organizational performance on a given task.

A second feature shared by these later studies is that they all focused on participants carrying out professional tasks in a professional organization. Many investigators have pointed to the special circumstances surrounding the professional worker employed in an organization and their relation to evaluation and control. The professions are occupations whose practice involves the application of highly technical skills based on a body of abstract principles arrived at by scientific research or logical analysis. Practitioners have undergone long periods of socialization in which they are expected not only to acquire the requisite knowledge and skills but also to internalize a set of normative codes and standards which will govern their performance. Because of their special competence, the professions demand, and are normally granted, the right to regulate their own practice by controlling the quality of training institutions (for example, by accreditation procedures), the access to practice (by examination, licensure, and certification procedures), and quality of performance (by the use of review boards and committees to police ethical conduct). Professional practitioners demand autonomy in carrying out their performance of specialized tasks. They expect to be protected from lay (nonprofessional) evaluation and to be subject only to the standards and codes of their professional group as enforced by colleague surveillance.

This somewhat idealized description of the structure and operation of the professions must be modified by the long-term trend in modern societies in which independent and entrepreneurial practice has gradually given way to organization-based practice for most professional workers. Associated with this change in the locus of practice is a change in the patterns of evaluation and control. As Etzioni (1961, p. 259) asserts: "A large amount of control over professional performances has been transferred from the professional community to the professional organization." If this is the case, the question remains as to what types of evaluation processes and authority relations operate with respect to the work of professionals in organizations.

Previous research suggests that professional organizations may be usefully categorized into *autonomous* and *heteronomous* organizations (Hall, 1967; Scott, 1965). In the former, professional participants enjoy a relatively high degree of autonomy from administrative control. Organizational officials delegate to the group of professional employees considerable responsibility for defining and implementing their goals, for setting performance standards, and for seeing to it that standards are maintained. For this purpose, professional participants typically organize themselves—as a staff in hospitals, as an academic council or senate in universities—to assume these responsibilities. Colleagues acting through a variety of committee and departmental structures are expected to maintain professional standards of practice. Administrative structures in such organizations are parallel to these professional units and are expected to exercise control only over administrative (nonprofessional) matters. Professional organizations which are likely to conform to the autonomous pattern include general hospitals, therapeutic psychiatric hospitals, medical clinics, elite colleges and universities, and research organizations devoted to basic research.

In the heteronomous professional organizations, by contrast, professional employees are clearly subordinated to an administrative framework and are granted less autonomy, although still more than is traditional in bureaucratic structures. An elaborate set of rules and a system of routine supervision control many aspects of the tasks performed by professionals in these settings. Examples of professional organizations often corresponding to this type include many public agencies—libraries, public schools, social welfare agencies—as well as such private organizations as religious colleges and firms engaged in applied research.

The studies described below were conducted in both autonomous and heteronomous professional organizations. Although we know from previous research something of the broad patterns of authority and control typically employed in these settings, we know relatively little in detail about their evaluation processes and authority systems. Our research provides data on these matters. We have tended to concentrate on heteronomous organizations, in part because of their special significance for our research interests in the stability of authority systems. If professionals believe that their knowledge and skills entitle them to regulation by a type of authority system different from the one used in their organization, this belief should have important implications for the stability of the organization's systems. This interest is pursued in our analysis of differing task conceptions and in our examination of discrepancies between actual and preferred control arrangements.

A final characteristic of our second set of studies is that each study reflects an increasing amount of attention devoted to two factors of critical importance for the evaluation process: the clarity of the standards used by evaluators and the extent to which these standards are known to performers; and the degree to which task performance or outcomes are visible to evaluators.

Each of the several studies of evaluation and authority in professional organizations can now be briefly described. Table 2 summarizes the distribution of respondents by position and organization.

University Faculty. Our first study in this series was an investigation of authority relations and evaluation processes in a university faculty. This research was carried out by Robert R. Hind under our supervision. A detailed report of the study is contained in Hind (1968), and a summary of the procedures and selected findings are reported in Hind (1971) and in Hind, Dornbusch, and Scott (1974). All data were collected in a large, private, research-oriented university—an autonomous professional organization. This research afforded us the first opportunity to explore the extent to which authority systems vary as a function of the type of task being performed.

Using criteria described in Chapter Four, four tasks typically performed by faculty were selected: classroom teaching, research and scholarship, university service, and service external to the university. An interview schedule was developed to collect systematic information from each faculty member as to how authority relations were perceived to vary by task. Because of the nature of this organization, we expected respondents to perceive their professional colleagues both within and outside the university as important evaluators, al-

Table 2.

STUDIES OF PROFESSIONAL ORGANIZATIONS:
DISTRIBUTION OF RESPONDENTS BY POSITION AND ORGANIZATION

Professional Group	Number of Organizational Units	Number of Respondents	Position of Respondents
University Faculty	1 (University) 6 (disciplinary areas)	100	Professor
Diocesan Clergy	1 (archdiocese) 101 (parishes)	101 106	Pastor Assistant Pastor
Public School Teachers	1 (district) 6 (schools)	131	Teacher
Principals	3 (districts) 33 (schools)	33	Principal
Nurses and Teachers	3 (hospitals) 32 (nursing units) 1 (district) 15 (schools)	194 244	Nurse Teacher
Alternative and Public School Teachers	24 (alternative schools) 2 (districts) 5 (schools)	100 100	Teacher Teacher

though we expected that the degree of importance attributed to evaluators would be affected by the type of task.

Data for this study were gathered in structured interviews with a random sample of one hundred faculty members in the School of Humanities and Sciences (liberal arts) stratified by rank. The respondents were selected in approximately equal numbers from each of the three professorial ranks. For some analyses, respondents were grouped into six disciplinary areas: natural sciences, mathematical sciences, social sciences, humanities, languages, and arts. Roughly equal numbers of respondents were contained within the three sciences and the three humanities areas. All interviews were conducted by Robert Hind, who at the time of the study was serving as staff director for a university committee appointed to investigate undergraduate teaching at the university. Individual respondents were assured anonymity, and data were grouped to prevent the identification of responses pertaining to particular departments or chairpersons.

Diocesan Clergy. Our second investigation took us into the oldest and one of the least studied professional organizations in the world: the Roman Catholic Church. We did not, of course, attempt to examine authority systems within the Church as a whole. Our focus was on the authority relation between the parish pastor and his assistant pastor(s) within one archdiocese. This research was conducted by Father Donald E. Turner, S.J., under our direction. (See Turner, 1971.)

Unlike our approach in all the other studies within a professional organization, we did not explore variations in authority by task within this setting. The authority exercised by pastors over assistant pastors is very comprehensive and diffuse (this was believed to be the case before the study but is reinforced by our findings), and so it did not seem useful to examine such variations as might occur among tasks. The specific tasks performed by assistant pastors which were expected to be evaluated by parish pastors were determined—some twenty-two of them—but were put to a different purpose. The twenty-two tasks were roughly categorized as professional activities (for example, hearing confessions, counseling, preaching) and as bureaucratic activities, including domestic activities (for example, keeping parish records up to date, handling door and telephone duty at the rectory). We were interested in investigating two issues: the extent to which pastors (evaluators) and assistant pastors (evaluatees) placed the same degree of importance on these various tasks in judging the performance of the assistant pastor; and the extent to which the assessment of task importance by assistant pastors varied by length of service in a parish organization. By inference, the latter question sought to throw some light on whether assessments of task importance by assistant pastors tended with time to resemble more closely their superior's rankings of task importance. Conceptions of task importance were expected over a period of time to be affected by the evaluation process. We also, of course, were interested in examining the extent to which importance was placed by pastors and their assistants on the more professional, as compared to the more bureaucratic, tasks.

The study population was restricted to full-time pastors who enjoyed the services of one or more full-time assistant pastors, and to those full-time assistants in a single archdiocese. The study was carried out with the active cooperation of the Archbishop. Several eligible pastors refused to participate and others were unavailable at the time of the study. The sample was composed of 101 pastors and 106 assistant pastors (see Table 2). All data were gathered by means of structured interviews conducted by Donald Turner, S.J. It is important to point out that the interviewer was a priest and therefore inside the church organization, and also a Jesuit and therefore outside the diocesan system. Such a combination of credentials seemed optimal for research in this setting.

Public School Teachers. Our first study of authority and evaluation within the public school system was carried out in a small school district in Northern California. Collaborating with us on this study were Karen C. Cook, Connie J. Evashwick, Leonard L. Magnani, and Inger Sagatun. A more detailed discussion of the setting and research procedures and a presentation of selected findings is contained in Magnani (1970).

Our interest in the public school as an organization was generated by a combination of factors. First, we had been invited to become Research Associates of the Stanford Center for Research and Development in Teaching and to use the resources of the Center for continuing and extending our research on authority systems in the public school system. Second, upon being enticed into this research setting, we quickly realized the advantages it afforded in terms of presenting large numbers of comparable position occupants in similarly structured organizations. Also, having completed the investigation of teachers in an autonomous professional organization—the university study—we were anxious to explore a heteronomous professional organization, in which participants, having a less secure claim to professional status, were regulated to a greater degree by administrative control.

Our study of the university faculty had revealed that authority relations indeed vary according to the task being performed: professors reported differing sets of evaluators with varying amounts of influence for each of the four tasks considered. Having discovered and described these variations, we wanted to explain them. In order to do so, we moved from a content-oriented typology of tasks to a more analytical approach to explain why, for example, teaching subject matter for elementary school teachers was subject to authority relations different from those for record-keeping. To approach this type of question, we described tasks by their location on each of the following dimensions: task clarity, task predictability, and task efficacy. They were defined at a level sufficiently abstract to be applicable to any task. These particular dimensions were selected, of course, because we expected them to help us predict variations in authority relations. Thus, while in our university study we had been content to show that authority relations varied as a function of task, we hoped in the school district study to understand more precisely what type of authority relation is associated with what type of task. In general, we expected that the greater the clarity of goals associated with the task, the higher the predictability of the relation between means or activities and ends or goals, and the greater the efficacy of the task activities in realizing objectives, the more routinized the task would be and the more standardized the task procedures would become, with little autonomy or discretion granted to performers.

A seemingly straightforward set of predictions relating the characteristics of the task to the nature of the authority system which controls task performance is complicated by the fact that organizational participants do not always agree on the nature of the task being performed. Some view a given task as high on predictability, for example, while others see the same task as low on predictability. In our view, these varying conceptions give rise to differing expectations as to what are the most appropriate authority relations for controlling performances.

In the school district study and in subsequent research, we attempted to examine varying task conceptions and the implications for work arrangements generally and authority relations specifically. Teachers, for example, hold differing conceptions of the various tasks they perform, and with these conceptions are associated differing expectations as to what organizational arrangements are appropriate for controlling task performances. Task conceptions differ not only among performers but also between performers and other participants in the organization, for example, between teachers and administrators. Since administrators often establish work arrangements, performers may not always have their expectations realized. Hence, in this study we not only examined the actual work arrangements but also determined what work arrangements were preferred by performers. We expected discrepancies between actual and preferred working arrangements to be characteristic of heteronomous professional organizations, in which professional performers are expected to have less power to determine their work arrangements. We expected that the greater the discrepancy between preferred and actual work arrangements as perceived by performers, the greater would be the instability of their authority systems.

In short, two very important changes in our theoretical approach began to take place at this juncture in our work. First, we began to concentrate on the development of an abstract set of task dimensions in terms of which differing types of work could be examined and compared. It should also be noted that our focus shifted from an objective to a subjective view of tasks. Perceptions can vary among participants as, for example, between administrators who design work arrangements and performers who carry out the work within these arrangements.

The second change directed our attention from authorization, as a source of support for norms, to propriety, which focuses on the attitudes of participants toward the authority norms to which they are subject. We expected impropriety to be an important source of system instability—that is, to cause dissatisfaction with the authority system and attempts to change it.

Our first study in the public schools was initiated by a request for assistance from the superintendent of a nearby district. He had recently appointed a district-wide committee of teachers to examine current arrangements for the evaluation of teachers and to develop recommendations for better procedures. He encouraged us to carry on our studies of authority and evaluation within his district in collaboration with the committee of teachers. Working in conjunction with this committee we developed, criticized, pretested, and revised a questionnaire. Our entry into the system to gather systematic data was under the auspices of this committee, and research personnel were introduced into each school by individual committee members.

With the assistance of the committee, we chose for analysis four tasks performed by teachers: teaching subject matter, maintaining control, character development, and record-keeping. These four tasks, with attendant explanatory material, appeared to communicate effectively to the teachers which aspects of their role performance were under discussion.

Teachers from all six schools within the district participated in the study. For the first time in our research, structured questionnaires to be filled out by respondents were used instead of interviews. The questionnaires were group administered, however, with members of the research staff present to provide orientation and to clarify questions. Administration of the questionnaire took place at a school-wide meeting called by each principal in which a member of the teachers' committee introduced the research group and explained the purpose of the study. Teachers were told that the research group was there to gather information for use by the teachers' committee, as well as attempt to develop general knowledge on the organization of the public schools. Individual respondents remained anonymous, and care was exercised in our reporting of information to the school district to ensure that no individual teacher or group of teachers could be identified. In this fashion, data were gathered from 131 teachers in six schools, approximately 85 percent of teachers in the district (see Table 2).

Principals. In our previous research on schools, data had been collected from teachers in their role as subordinates—as recipients of evaluations from organizational evaluators. We were understandably anxious to extend our knowledge of these organizational control systems by gathering data from respondents occupying supervisory positions, both in order to examine the authority system from their vantage point and to compare their perceptions of the operation of the system with those of their subordinates. To this end, a study was designed to focus on the role of the public school principal as an organizational evaluator of teachers' task performances. This research was conducted by June E. Thompson under our direction. (See J. E. Thompson, 1971.) Whenever possible, questions asked of principals were phrased so as to be comparable with questions asked of teachers. The same four teaching tasks were distinguished in the expectation that principals' views of their authority would vary according to the type of task being supervised. In many cases, principals were queried not only about their own conceptions of teacher tasks and authority relations, but also about their perception as to how teachers viewed these matters. The theoretical issues pursued in this study were the same as those governing the school district study: variations in task conceptions, the relation between task conceptions and work arrangements, discrepancies between actual and preferred working arrangements, and the relative influence of teachers and administrators in establishing work arrangements.

The six principals from the original school district study were obvious candidates for this study. Because of the small number of schools involved in this district, however, we decided to augment our study by including principals from two other districts in the same geographical area. These districts were similar in that they were located in the same part of the state and were engaged in the same general tasks. However, one of the districts included was considerably larger and incorporated a more diverse group of students in socioeconomic terms. The three districts together included forty-one schools. Thirty-three principals composed our study population. The remaining eight principals were eliminated from our study because they were serving their first year as principal (see Table 2).

A combined questionnaire and interview approach was devised for this study. Participating principals were sent a brief questionnaire containing background information and other items which we believed could be more efficiently obtained in this manner. An appointment was then made with each principal at which time the questionnaire was retrieved and an interview conducted. All interviews with principals were conducted by one of three researchers carefully selected to ensure their ability to communicate with and be accepted by the school administrators. All were advanced students in educational administration at Stanford who possessed considerable administrative knowledge and experience in the public schools.

We had planned to administer our teacher questionnaire in the appropriate schools within the two new districts, but competing demands rendered this desirable objective unfeasible. Hence, we did not have data from teachers to match our principals in the two new districts, and were forced to make our comparisons between the views of principals located in three districts with the views of teachers located in a single district. Although later comparisons with teachers in other districts generally support our findings, all conclusions drawn from such a sample must be viewed as highly tentative.

Nurses and Teachers. As we have seen, professional workers expect to enjoy considerable autonomy in carrying out tasks for which they are specifically trained. Even in their normative prescriptions, however, professionals do not expect to be completely free from control and surveillance. Ideally, they are governed by a system of colleague review and control. Our previous research on the university faculty gave evidence that while organizationally designated superiors (for example, deans, department chairmen) were perceived to exercise considerable authority over task performance, the evaluation of colleagues both within and outside the university was viewed as having substantial influence. Further, the data indicated that visibility of task performance was an important determinant of evaluation importance. Departmental colleagues were perceived as more important evaluators for the task of teaching than colleagues located in other universities. The importance attributed to the evaluations of nonorganizational colleagues increased substantially for the task of research. Clearly, teaching performance is much less visible to one's colleagues located at other universities than is published research.

Since the university is an example of an autonomous professional organization, we expected to find control arrangements that were compatible with professional norms, including a substantial role for peers in the evaluation process. This is what we found. As our research efforts moved into the public school system, an instance of a heteronomous professional organization, we expected to find more bureaucratized authority systems in which administrators exercised a higher degree of control and the evaluations of one's colleagues were viewed as less important. Again, our data were consistent with this expectation. Public school teachers do not have sufficient power to establish professional control systems.

Perhaps, however, it is not simply a matter of the relative power of professionals versus administrators. We conjectured that one reason why teachers in our school district study did not attribute great importance to the evaluations of their peers was that conditions in traditionally structured schools did not allow for visibility of teachers' performances to their colleagues. Teachers in the conventional school carry out their task performance in relative isolation from their peers who may have little basis for evaluating the work of their colleagues.

A good many schools are now experimenting with new teaching arrangements in which small teams of teachers are formed to carry out teaching tasks jointly. Such arrangements allow for some differentiation in teaching roles, so that a teacher better qualified in certain tasks can concentrate on these while other team members focus on complementary tasks. Teaming also permits greater flexibility of student groupings and frees the time of one teacher to engage in planning and preparation while others manage the class. From our point of view, however, the most significant effect of teaming is its impact on the visibility of teacher performance to colleagues. Our question is: Will teachers who regularly perform in teams attribute greater importance to the evaluations of their peers than teachers who teach in isolated classrooms? More generally, we would expect that the greater the visibility of performance to evaluators, whether peers or superiors, the more likely performers would view these evaluations as accurate, as soundly based, and hence the more importance they would attribute to these evaluations.

The effect of teaming on visibility of performance and on the authority system was examined in a study of public school teachers and hospital nurses. This research was conducted by Gwen D. Marram under our supervision. (See Marram, 1971.) Our discussion to this point has been focused on teachers, but nurses are in a highly comparable situation. For physicians the hospital is typically an autonomous professional organization since physicians in most hospitals develop arrangements in which members of their own profession assume substantial control over the performance of professional tasks. For nurses, however, the hospital is a heteronomous professional organization in that nurses are to a greater extent subordinated to administrative control. Like teachers, nurses sometimes perform their tasks as individual practitioners and sometimes operate as members of a team. Our comparative study allowed us to examine the effect of teaming on visibility and control arrangements in two organizational settings, as well as explore differences in the team structure in the two situations.

In addition to its concern with the effects of teaming on visibility in two settings, this study was also the first in which we employed the concept of soundly based evaluations. This concept was intended to include but be broader than our earlier focus on incompatible evaluations. Evaluations are soundly based to the extent that the direction and level of effort by performers affects the quality of their performance or outcomes and that better performances or outcomes receive higher evaluations. When these two conditions are met, we have one way that performers through their own task efforts are able to affect the evaluations they receive.

We wished to retain our task-specific approach to the study of evaluation and authority relations in schools and hospitals. The previously developed classification of teacher tasks was used in this study, but it was necessary to devise a comparable set of tasks for characterizing the work of nurses. This classification was developed by Gwen Marram, a registered nurse and nursing educator. The tasks selected were: carrying out doctors' orders, ward management, providing comfort and support to patients, record-keeping, and observation and assessment of patients.

Data for this comparative study were collected through the use of a questionnaire filled out by 194 staff nurses located in three general hospitals and 244 teachers located in fifteen elementary schools in one district, a district not previously studied (see Table 2). Virtually all teachers and nurses in the organizations studied agreed to cooperate: only twelve teachers and three nurses eligible to participate refused. Arrangements were made through school principals to administer questionnaires to teachers on a group basis. Nursing schedules did not permit this convenience, and each nurse was individually contacted. The selection of hospital units and schools was governed by our desire to have roughly equal proportions of respondents from team and nonteam situations. Four of the schools in the study were of open-space design and used team teaching almost exclusively; six of the schools contained traditional classrooms and did not use teams; and five schools were of mixed design, employing both team and nonteam approaches to teaching. Approximately twenty nursing units within the three hospitals used the team approach to nursing exclusively; ten units did not use team nursing; and two employed a mixed approach. Hospital units and schools were categorized as having a team approach if they had formalized teams and afforded the performers an opportunity to see each other as they performed their tasks. By these criteria, approximately eighty-one nurses were classified as participating in a team, eighty-nine as not in a team, and twenty-four in a mixed situation. In the schools, fifty-six teachers worked in a team situation in open-space schools, one hundred six worked in schools with only isolated classrooms, and eighty-two worked in mixed schools (see Table 2).

Alternative and Public School Teachers Study. In our previous studies conducted within the public school system, we had examined the extent to which the conceptions of the task held by performers (teachers) differed from those held by administrators (principals). We believed that an important determinant of such variations was distance from the actual setting in which the work was performed. For example, we expected performers who carried out a given task would be more inclined to emphasize the lack of predictability of the problems they encountered, while administrators who were more distant from the work setting would see the tasks as more predictable, unless the administrators were from the same professional group as the performers.

In addition to possible variations in task conceptions between performers and administrators, task conceptions may also vary among performers. Workers performing ostensibly similar tasks may differ greatly in their perceptions as to the clarity, predictability, and efficacy of their tasks. Variance in task conceptions may be a function of many factors, including amount of training, previous experience, and personality characteristics.

We did not attempt in our research to explore the effects of such individual characteristics and experiences on task conceptions. Rather, we chose instead to focus on those factors which create among a set of performers a common or shared conception of the tasks they perform—a conception shared by performers in one setting, but differing from that held by similar performers in other settings. One such factor is probably the level of professionalism, which can be relatively consistent for workers in a given setting but vary greatly across settings. Professionalism is an important variable in this connection because professional training involves more than the acquisition of knowledge and skills: professional schools attempt to inculcate in their trainees particular views as to the nature of the work being performed. In short, professional socialization is directed at ensuring the acquisition of particular conceptions of the task being performed by the professional group.

Another factor which may influence the conceptions of tasks performed is general philosophy or ideology. From time to time there occurs among all occupational groups performing complex tasks a reevaluation of conventionally held views of the nature of the work being performed. Underlying assumptions are questioned, existing goals are challenged, and current practices are criticized as being ineffective or misdirected. Such ideological critiques are currently creating waves in such occupations as law (Ginger, 1972) and social work (Piven and Cloward, 1972), but nowhere is there as much ferment as in the occupation of teaching. Numerous and highly vocal critics have assailed the public school system and its participants both for failing to perform effectively the tasks it was established to carry out and for pursuing the wrong goals (Dennison, 1969; Goodman, 1965; Holt, 1964; Jackson, 1968; Silberman, 1970). Such critiques may be inducing change in the public school system. But social reformers have not been content to wait for the slow and uncertain process of changing existing institutions; they have encouraged and participated in the creation of alternative school organizations to bring about the redefinition of the tasks to be performed by teachers.

Our research team viewed the alternative school movement as providing an opportunity to investigate the relation between varying conceptions of similar tasks on the one hand, and preferred and actual working arrangements on the other. We decided to compare the conceptions of teaching tasks held by public school teachers with those held by teachers in alternative schools and to examine work arrangements and authority systems within the two settings. The study was conducted by Brian L. McCauley under our direction. (See McCauley, 1971; McCauley, Dornbusch, and Scott, 1972.)

A new public school sample of one hundred teachers was drawn from five schools in two districts. The alternative school sample was made up of one hundred teachers in twenty-four San Francisco Bay Area alternative schools. These teachers were hostile to the idea of organization, but we knew they would necessarily have some form of organization in order to cope and survive. We had to persuade each of these teachers individually to answer our questions. Most participated reluctantly. We expanded our descriptions of the teaching tasks to meet their resistance (see Chapter Four).

Diversity of Settings. We would like to call attention to a common characteristic displayed by our second group of studies. In every case, our collaborators brought to our research specialized competence in the particular organization under study. Thus, Robert Hind, who carried out the study of the university faculty, in addition to being a doctoral candidate in higher education, had many years of experience as a university administrator and at the time the research was being carried out was staff director of a research program on undergraduate education. Donald Turner, S.J., had numerous years of service in the Roman Catholic Church. June Thompson and those who assisted her in the study of principals were doctoral students in educational administration with considerable experience in school teaching and administration. Gwen Marram, who conducted the comparative research on nurses and teachers, was a registered nurse with broad experience in patient care in hospitals and in teaching nurses and, at the time of her research, was completing her studies in educational administration. And Brian McCauley who carried out the research on public and alternative schools, was a former teacher, who, as a student in the School of

Education, had developed close personal ties with educators working in alternative schools.

The specialized abilities and backgrounds of our several collaborators helped us to be sensitive to salient differences in these varied settings as we designed our research and prepared our data-collection instruments. Their intimate knowledge of the research situation helped protect us from the danger of employing inappropriate or blunt instruments that could do damage to the differing realities of each setting. In each case, research instruments were revised and adapted so as to be comprehensible and acceptable to respondents and to exploit differences among these organizations. However, our concern for sensitivity and variety did not detract from our larger purpose of gathering comparable data allowing us to test and revise our developing theory of authority and evaluation in formal organizations.

Table 2 presents in summary form the number and types of organizational units and respondents studied in all research conducted since the earlier Five Organizations study. Including both the Five Organizations study and the studies of professional organizations, the total number of respondents who contributed to our research is 1333. Although the settings in which these respondents were located vary and the issues explored differ from one study to another, the leitmotiv guiding our research has remained the exploration of evaluation and authority systems within organizational settings.

Statistical Tests of Our Theory

We believe in a model of scientific investigation which is often endorsed by behavioral scientists but seldom practiced by them. We have not published piecemeal the results of each study. Rather, we have sought to develop a theory, a set of interrelated principles, and to test that theory.

Most of the data we gathered concern some aspect of an individual's authority system. We define an authority system as the authority rights, based on evaluation processes, exercised over and by an individual in the performance of a specified task. In the Five Organizations study we focused on the validity and propriety of authority systems and on the relationship between incompatibility and instability in those systems. In our later research in professional organizations, we gradually extended our analyses to include relationships among other aspects of evaluation systems, such as the impact of conceptions of the task upon work arrangements and the relation of visibility of performances to the soundness of evaluations.

Therefore we do not have a single dependent variable whose variation is to be explained. We have not added variables to build a model of causal influences that can explain much of the variation in that single dependent variable. Nor do we test isolated hypotheses, each to be confirmed or disproved independently. Our attempt to develop a theory of evaluation and authority in organizations requires a different style of presentation of our empirical findings.

We agree with Lipset, Trow, and Coleman (1956) that statistical tests of significance, which serve to reject chance as the basis for each finding, are inappropriate in testing a set of interrelated propositions. First, although we studied samples of respondents in many organizational settings, our organizational units were not randomly selected from any clearly defined universe of organizations. Second, each organizational context affects the authority relations embedded in it, so that authority systems in an organization cannot provide data which are truly independent tests of a hypothesis.

The third and most important reason for not using statistical tests of significance is that our hypotheses are related. Each empirical result confirms or refutes a network of hypotheses. We cannot perform a test of significance on a set of interlocking results gathered from diverse organizations. Like Lipset and his colleagues, we have concentrated on the pattern of our findings rather than focusing on isolated statistical results.

Accordingly, we have tried to simplify the presentation of our findings by always using the same statistical measure, gamma, to express the relationship between two variables (Goodman and Kruskal, 1954). Gamma is a nonparametric measure, meaning that it makes no assumptions about the distribution of the variables being related. Gamma may be interpreted as a measure of proportionate reduction in error. Suppose one tried to order pairs of cases on the second variable, knowing nothing about the first variable. Then one might use a pattern of random assignment, letting chance processes determine one's prediction of which case in each pair will be higher or lower. But if the second variable, whose ordering one is trying to predict, is closely related to the first variable, one can make fewer errors in ordering pairs of cases on the second variable by knowing their order on the first variable. The absolute value of gamma measures the proportionate reduction in error when one shifts from a strategy of random assignment in ordering each pair of cases to a strategy based upon knowledge of the order of the pair on the first variable. The greater the strength of relationship between the two variables, the larger the absolute value of gamma (Costner, 1965).

Very often we will dichotomize our data into just "high" and "low" scores. Then gamma simply measures the extent to which knowing that a case was high or low on the first variable reduces error in predicting whether that case will be high or low on the second variable.

Gamma may assume values from -1.00 to $+1.00$. A negative gamma indicates that the order on one variable is inversely related to the order on the other; high value on one variable is likely to be associated with a low value on the other variable. A positive gamma means that the order on one variable is similar to the order on the other variable. The magnitude of gamma, whether positive or negative, indicates the amount that errors in predicting the order of cases on the second variable are reduced by knowledge of their order on the first variable.

Our presentation of results in terms of a single statistic, gamma, is intended to help the reader in interpreting the pattern of our findings. We believe that detailed presentation of diverse statistical measures would hinder communication of the extent to which our empirical studies support or refute the set of interlocking principles which form our theory.

Chapter 2

Power and Authority

▲▲

The reader who is eager to get to the systematic presentation of our theory can skip this chapter and proceed immediately to Chapter Three. The intent of the present chapter is to compare and contrast our conception of power and authority with that of others, both predecessors and contemporaries. There has been no dearth of attempts to capture and domesticate the concept of authority, and we would be less than honest were we not to record the ways in which we have benefited from the efforts of others, even when we disagree with them.

Power is a significant and pervasive social phenomenon which can be fruitfully studied in a large variety of social settings; our explicit comments and our data are restricted to this single context. Before discussing power we define formal organizations and briefly comment on some of their salient characteristics.

Formal and Informal Organizations

Formal organizations are most easily discussed in contrast with informal systems. The term *organization* in its general sense is defined as a network of social relations which orients and regulates the behaviors of a limited set of individuals in the pursuit of relatively specific goals. The phrase *limited set of individuals* implies the existence of participation boundaries, including rules for specifying who is and is not a member. While we will concentrate on participants identified as organizational members, the proposed definition does not restrict consideration to this group; individuals other than members often participate in organizations and for many analytical purposes must be considered a part of the organization.

Social relationships among members of organizations attempt to shape member activities toward the attainment of established objectives. There is an emphasis on goal attainment and, hence, on member performances as contributions to goal attainment. Finally, the goals pursued are relatively narrowly defined and limited. This last criterion is admittedly vague, for organizations vary considerably in the specificity of the goals they pursue, but it is meant to exclude collectivities where the goals pursued tend to be extremely diffuse, such as families, communities, and entire societies.

An organization is said to be *formal* to the extent that the normative expectations shared by participants prescribe appropriate behavior for the occupant of a given organizational position regardless of the identity of the particular individual occupying the position. A position is simply a location in a system of social relations whose characteristics are defined by expectations directed at the location by occupants of related positions. Formalization functions to standardize behaviors, to make the actions of position occupants more predictable. Also, because formalization makes the recurrent behaviors of participants and their relationships more explicit, it encourages the deliberate construction and reconstruction of the organizational system and so facilitates, but by no means guarantees, rationality of design. The term *rationality* is used in a narrow sense indicating only that "a series of actions is organized in such a way that it leads to a previously defined goal" (Mannheim, 1950, p. 53). To say that an organization is formal, however, says nothing about the specific form assumed by the system; a formal organization may have, for example, a high or low degree of specialization, a broad or tall hierarchy, and elaborate or simple communication channels.

Formalization is a variable; we may speak of organizations or segments of organizations as being more or less formalized. Nevertheless, by *formal organizations* we indicate that class of organizations which has undergone considerable formalization relative to others, which are designated *informal*. Once formal organizations have been distinguished from other types of collectivities, however, we will be concerned with all their aspects, not just with those portions that have been formalized.

Power

Concept of Power. There are many conceptions of power (Cartwright, 1959, 1965; Schopler, 1965). For present purposes, it will not be necessary to undertake a painstaking review of these various viewpoints, but only to indicate the general foundation of our own approach. We will begin with a brief consideration of three definitions of power. These definitions span half a century, and one could wish for stronger evidence of progress made in clarifying this concept.

Certainly, Weber's definition of power has had the greatest influence on the work of social scientists in this century. For Weber: "Power (*Macht*) is the probability that one actor within a social relationship will be in a position to carry out his own will despite resistance, regardless of the basis on which this probability rests" (1947, p. 152). Weber's definition includes interpersonal power where one actor exercises control over another, although it is not restricted to this case. Dahl's definition, on the other hand, is restricted to the interpersonal situation: "*A* has power over *B* to the extent that he can get *B* to do something that *B* would not otherwise do" (1957, pp. 202–203). Yet another closely related definition is furnished by Emerson, who also focuses on interpersonal power: "The power of actor *A* over actor *B* is the amount of resistance on the part of *B* which can be potentially overcome by *A*" (1962, p. 32). Emerson's approach differs from Weber's and Dahl's but is similar to that proposed by Thibaut and Kelley (1959), in its emphasis on the basis of power, as follows: "The power of *A* over *B* is equal to, and based upon, the dependence of *B* upon *A*" (1962, p. 33). The dependence of one actor on another, hence the power of one actor over another, varies, according to Emerson, as a function of two factors. *B*'s dependence on *A* is directly proportional to *B*'s motivational investment in goals mediated by A; and inversely proportional to the availability of these goals to B outside the A-B relationship (Emerson, 1962, p. 32).

These influential students of power with their slightly different emphases agree on certain basic features. First, all conceive of power as a property of a social relation, not as an attribute of an actor; that is, they suggest that it is vacuous to assert that a given individual has power without specifying over whom this power is held. This point is made most explicitly by Emerson, who argues that A's power is based on B's dependence. B is dependent on A to the extent that B aspires to goals mediated by A. (See also Thibaut and Kelley, 1959, pp. 100–125.) Thus, B's dependence—and hence A's power—is a function of both B's and A's characteristics. Who has power over a given individual will depend on what that individual values. To use an extreme example, a gunman has no power over an individual who places no value on his life; nor does a rich person have power over one who scorns money and the things it can provide. It is always a simplification to speak only of A's power, and to do so is to court danger, although the danger may be minimal when the basis of A's power allows A to mediate widely shared goals, such as money.

Second, Weber, Dahl, and Emerson agree that the bases of power are diverse and vary from one situation to another. This characteristic is made explicit by Weber and has been elaborated in a typology proposed by French and Raven (1959). The variety of power bases can be illustrated by two examples. If the members of a work group value solutions to technical problems, as was the case with the federal law enforcement officials studied by Blau (1955), then expertise in solving these problems can become an important basis of power in such groups. And if boys prefer to avoid black eyes and like to be associated with winning teams in athletic events, as was the case in the camping situation studied by Lippitt, Polansky, and Rosen (1952), then such characteristics as strength and athletic prowess will become important bases of coercive and reward power in such situations. Which characteristics in fact function as the bases of power in a given situation depends on a number of factors, including the nature of group goals, the values held by individual group members, and the distribution of valued characteristics within the group.

A third feature shared by these three definitions is that power is defined in terms of its results, in terms of what changes its exercise brings about. Power is defined as A's ability to succeed, to win, to overcome even in the face of resistance, or as the probability that A will do so. In the case of interpersonal power, the resistance comes from another actor, and power is deemed to be present to the extent that A can successfully get B to do something that B would not otherwise do or that for some reason B resists doing. In short, power is measured in terms of interpersonal control or influence.

Our own definition of power shares with the definitions just reviewed the first two characteristics: a focus on power as an attribute of a relationship, and a recognition that power may rest on quite varied bases. However, we do not subscribe to the third characteristic. Taking our cue from Emerson's discussion (rather than from his definition) and from the work of Thibaut and Kelley, we prefer to define power exclusively in terms of the dependence of B upon A rather than in terms of the degree to which A is likely to to be successful in controlling B. That is, rather than discussing power in terms of the results which may be obtained by its use (what A can get B to do), we prefer to describe power in terms of the amount of force or pressure A can bring to bear on B (what A can do to or for B), regardless of B's response to this pressure.

Returning to Emerson's discussion, the power of one actor over another "resides implicitly in the other's dependency" (Emerson, 1962, p. 32). Thus, the amount of power that A has over B is quantitatively equal to the dependence of B on A. This dependence may be described in terms of the resources A has which make B dependent upon A. We refer to resources used by A with the intent of rewarding or punishing B as *sanctions*. And, accordingly we will define *power* as the ability and willingness of one person to sanction another by manipulating rewards and punishments which are important to the other.

After we define the concept of sanction in more detail, we will consider the ways in which differential power—that is, differential ability to manipulate sanctions of importance to others— emerges in informal groups and formal organizations.

Sanction. A sanction is any act performed with the primary intent of providing or withholding gratifications or deprivations for an individual or set of individuals. We employ the adjective *primary* to acknowledge the complexity of motivation behind actions (Gross, Mason, and McEachern, 1958, p. 65). Sanctioning often entails the distribution of valued objects or the granting of access to desirable situations. Examples of positive sanctions are awarding a salary bonus, giving the Nobel Prize, and removing a person from an undesirable assignment. Examples of negative sanctions include demoting people, giving them poor recommendations, not increasing their salaries, and hurting them physically. As should be clear from these examples, actions intended to provide gratifications or withhold deprivations are viewed as positive sanctions, while actions intended to withhold gratifications or apply deprivations are viewed as negative sanctions.

It is important to note that the definition of sanction focuses on the intent of the person carrying out the action, not on the reaction of the recipient to the action. The sanctioner, *A,* attempts to behave in ways believed to furnish gratifications or deprivations to some other person, *B.* Because values and interests vary among individuals, however, not all actions intended as sanctioning by *A* will be perceived as such by *B.* For example, a study of nurses by Bennis and colleagues (1958) found that supervisory nurses inaccurately perceived which rewards were desired by staff nurses, and, for this reason, were often unsuccessful in attempting to regulate their behavior by the manipulation of sanctions. Conversely, behavior not intended by *A* to have significance as a sanction may nevertheless be perceived by *B* as rewarding or punishing. For example, a supervisor planning the vacation schedules of subordinates may unknowingly be distributing rewards or penalties to them.

Just as *A* and *B* may differ on whether a given behavior has gratificational significance, so they may differ in their assessment of how much importance to attribute to a specific sanction. *A* and *B* may agree that gratifications or deprivations are being dispensed, but yet disagree about the value or importance of the sanctions.

Because *B*'s perception of *A*'s action may differ from *A*'s intent, we need to speak not only of sanctions—actions intended to have gratificational significance—but also of valued sanctions or sanctions important to *B*—actions both intended to have gratificational significance by *A* and perceived to have such by *B*. Our definition of power takes account of both initiator's intent and recipient's perception by speaking of *A*'s sanctions (initiator's intent) which are important to *B* (recipient's perceptions).

Informal Groups. In recent decades a large number of studies have examined the operation of power in informal groups. For our purposes, one of the most interesting research foci in this setting has been a concern with the emergence of power differences in previously undifferentiated task groups. These studies have illuminated how dependence and power relationships come to be built up over a period of time and also how authority systems emerge out of power relations. The latter process will be described in a later section of this chapter. The emergence of power differences has been explored in field studies (Lippitt, Polansky, and Rosen, 1952; Sherif and Sherif, 1953), as well as in the laboratory (Bales, 1952; Bales and Slater, 1955; Levinger, 1959). These studies describe the way in which certain personal qualities or characteristics which differ among members become the basis for differences in sanctioning ability.

As analyzed by Homans (1961) and Blau (1964), the process of differentiation occurs through a series of exchanges among group participants. Over a period of time, some members who are both willing and able to make important contributions to goal attainment, whether goals of individual members or of the group as a whole, come to hold power over others who are less willing or less able. Briefly, the process by which differences in power emerge is as follows: A given member *A* furnishes assistance to another member *B*, who, if unable to reciprocate with equally valued services, can respond with thanks and gratitude. For a time, this sort of exchange may be satisfactory to both parties: one value—assistance—is exchanged for another—thanks or praise. There are a number of reasons, however, why we would not expect such an exchange of values, if long continued, to be satisfactory for *A*. First, the skills which enable a person to furnish assistance to others are comparatively rare, whereas approval or gratitude is less so. This means that *B*'s contribution will tend to be less highly valued than *A*'s.

There is likely to be a larger market (other group members) for A's contributions than for B's. Second, marginal utility functions which affect the value placed on additional units of assistance and gratitude are likely to be favorable to assistance; that is, second, third, and fourth units of gratitude are likely to be less valued by A than second, third, and fourth units of assistance are valued by B. In short, if A continues to provide assistance to B, B will become increasingly dependent on A, but A will not become more dependent on B. And, as noted above, B's dependence is the basis of A's power.

Sanctioning differences between A and B increase the probability that A can influence or control B. Because A can manipulate sanctions valued by B—specifically, in this case, A can furnish or withhold assistance—this ability can be a basis for attempting to force B to do things. Since we define power in terms of the application of valued sanctions rather than in terms of response to their exercise, our definition of power allows us to separate these variables: we can view the amount of power as an independent variable and the amount of control over behavior as a dependent variable.

Formal Organizations. Hierarchy is not an inevitable characteristic of formal organizations. It is possible to conceive of a formal organization whose positions are not differentiated with respect to such factors as status and power; a collegial body perhaps comes closest to this form of organization. However, given the need for mechanisms to regulate and control the behavior of participants in the pursuit of specific goals, hierarchy, as one such mechanism, is a pervasive feature of formal organizations. An organizational hierarchy is, among other things, a power system. (A hierarchy is also a status system involving the differential allocation of power and prestige, a vertical division of labor with different task assignments, and an arrangement for grouping positions.) Built into the definitions of positions and the specification of relations among positions is differential access to rewards and penalties which can be used to attempt to influence the behavior of others. That is, a differential ability to sanction can be made a characteristic of the position regardless of the characteristics of the person occupying the position. For example, a supervisory position may be defined in such a manner that the occupant is allowed to determine who will carry out undesirable tasks in a given work group or who will receive a higher rate of pay. These powers are designed to be exercised by the office incumbent regardless of personal qualities. In this manner, power and dependence relations are built into the formal system of most formal organizations.

Formal power systems are expected to be more stable than informal power systems. Because formal power is attached to relationships between positions rather than to relations between specific persons, it tends to persist in spite of the comings and goings of particular occupants. Interpersonal power, however, is wedded to relationships among specific participants. It is unlikely to survive changes in actors, as Weber (1946, pp. 245–252; 1947, pp. 363–373) notes in his discussion of the inherent instability of charismatic leadership, leadership based on the possession of rare and highly valued personal attributes. Also, reliance on formal power partially frees the organization from the necessity of finding natural leaders to fill its leadership positions; individual office holders receive an allowance of rewards and penalties with which to influence subordinates and are not required to rely exclusively or even primarily on the development of informal power over subordinates.

The formal power system within an organization is not the only locus of power in such settings. There are many sources of power and no organization can hope to control all of them (Mechanic, 1962a). On the other hand, it should not be supposed that the formal power system is of little or no consequence in determining the activities of organizational participants. In many, if not most, formal organizations, it is of primary importance.

Authority

Thus far we have talked only about power. What of authority? Most social scientists define authority as *legitimate power*. Legitimacy is an exceedingly complex concept, and many competing and overlapping definitions have been proposed. We adhere to the Weberian view (1947, p. 124) that one can appropriately speak of the presence of a legitimate order "only if action is approximately or on the average oriented to certain determinate 'maxims' or rules." In more modern language, we may say that legitimacy refers to the existence of norms which govern action. Social norms legitimate action by defining it as correct, or appropriate, or permissible. Here we are concerned only with the legitimation of power relations. Thus, two elements must be present before we can speak of authority or legitimate power: There must be a set of persons or positions linked by power relations, and a set of norms or rules governing the exercise of power and the response to it.

Virtually every sociological treatment of authority focuses attention on the subordinates in the power relation. It is their beliefs and attitudes toward the exercise of power and their norms which are often viewed as critical in defining authority. The view of authority to be developed here permits consideration of the norms and beliefs of groups other than subordinates. For the present, however, let us restrict our attention to subordinates in the power relation.

Limiting attention to the beliefs and attitudes of subordinates, several dimensions of authority may be identified, all of which modify the power relation and are expected to affect the response of the subordinate to the exercise of power. These dimensions will be briefly introduced at this point, to be amplified later in this chapter as we review some of the previous discussions of authority in informal groups and formal organizations.

Validity vs. Propriety. The first dimension of authority is one which Weber clearly recognized but which has not been systematically exploited by later students of authority. This dimension concerns the validity of the norms underlying the power relation, defined by Weber (1947, p. 124) as follows: "such [a legitimate] order will only be called 'valid' if the orientation to such maxims includes, no matter to what actual extent, the recognition that they are binding on the actor." Whether a given subordinate complies with the norm was viewed by Weber (1947, p. 125) as immaterial to the question of validity: "Even in the cases of evasion of or deliberate disobedience to these prescriptions, the probability of its being recognized as a valid norm may have an effect on action. This may, in the first place, be true from the point of view of sheer expediency. A thief orients his action to the validity of the criminal law in that he acts surreptitiously. The fact that the order is recognized as valid in his society is made evident by the fact that he cannot violate it openly without punishment." Further, whether the subordinate agrees with or approves of the legitimate order has no effect on its validity, as Weber (1947, pp. 148–149) points out in his discussion of legitimate orders of the legal type. Thus: "The legally established order of an associative relationship may originate in one of two ways: by voluntary agreement, or by being imposed and acquiesced in . . . The system of order of a corporate group may be imposed, not only on its members, but also on nonmembers who conform to certain criteria . . . Even in cases where there is formally 'voluntary' agreement, it is very common, as is generally known, for there to be a large measure of imposition." In short, Weber attempted to distinguish between recognition of a normative order regarded as binding on participants, and the participant's willing acceptance and approval of the order. The validity of the normative order depends exclusively on the first criterion.

The distinction just made constitutes the basis for our second dimension of authority. We are also interested in the subordinates' evaluation of the normative order since this will undoubtedly have an impact on their behavior with respect to it. Hence, we may identify the dimension of the perceived propriety of the norms supporting the exercise of power. Validity refers to whether subordinates acknowledge the existence of a normative order; propriety has reference to whether they themselves approve of this order.

Cohen (1966, p. 17) has applied precisely these distinctions in his analysis of general norms and rules. His discussion helps to pin down the dimensions we propose for the study of authority relations (emphasis in original):

> Much of the disputation about rules is over the question of what the rules *ought to be* rather than over what they *are*. We may disagree on the *propriety* of a rule—that is, on whether it is a good, fair, reasonable rule—but agree on its *validity*. This is not a trifling distinction. To concede the validity of a rule is to concede that people have a right—even an obligation—to use it as a 'standard of judgement and to apply sanctions to those who violate it. I may think that the speed laws in my city, or the rules about smoking in classrooms on my

campus are silly, but I recognize that they are valid rules;
this recognition implies at least that the 'proper authorities' have the right to enforce them if I violate them.

The distinction between valid and proper exercise of power
has not been made in discussions of authority systems, but it points
to a source of ambiguity in some definitions of authority. Thus,
French and Raven (1959, p. 159) state that "In all cases, the
notion of legitimacy involves some sort of code or standard, accepted
by the individual, by virtue of which the external agent can exercise
his power." Ambiguity arises because of the varied possible interpretations of the phrase "accepted by the individual." Similar terminology appears in many other proposed definitions. Simon (1952, p.
1133) in his discussion of authority appears to move in the direction
of using propriety as his criterion for authority. He suggests that
legitimacy should be viewed as a psychological rather than a legal
concept—a concept having reference to the subordinate's internalized attitudes toward superiors which provide the motivation for
accepting the relationship. Verba (1961, p. 170) also moves in this
direction, stating that "arbitrary interpersonal influence exists when
the recipient of the influence attempt does not consider that attempt
legitimate—i.e., when the recipient does not feel that the leader
should perform the acts he does perform" (emphasis in original).

We believe, then, that it is important to distinguish between
the following two questions which might be asked of a subordinate:
Does A have the right to exercise power over you? and *Should A*
have the right to exercise power over you? Since one may often get
different answers to these two questions, they should not be confused.

Authorized vs. Endorsed Power. Underlying these dimensions
of authority is a question of central importance for our conception of
authority: namely, whose norms—that is, the beliefs of what set of
participants—serve to legitimate the exercise of power? Gouldner
(1954, pp. 181–228) has raised this question about organizational
rules in general, and he has used it to suggest a typology of forms of
organization. The "punishment-centered" type of organization is
one in which rules are initiated and enforced by one set of participants on another, for example, by superiors (management) on subordinates (workers) or by subordinates (workers acting through

their unions) on superiors. The "representative" type occurs when superiors and subordinates act in concert to initiate and enforce rules. And the "mock" type exists when rules are imposed on organizational participants (both superiors and subordinates) by some outside agency but neither superiors nor subordinates act to enforce them. For our purposes Gouldner's typology is of less interest than his general thesis that various participants in an organizational hierarchy may initiate and enforce divergent sets of rules.

It is usually possible to identify a large number of groups and subgroups in a formal organization who hold certain beliefs or norms about how power should be exercised and how to respond to it. To simplify what can be a very complex situation, we will focus attention on the norms of two important groups: those who are superior to and exercise power over A, the power-wielder, and those who share with B the situation of being subordinate to A and subject to A's power. Examination of the beliefs of these two groups concerning A's exercise of power over B suggests the two new dimensions of authority. We will say that A's power over B is *authorized* to the extent that beliefs held by groups superior to A legitimate A's power over B; and we will say that A's power over B is *endorsed* to the extent that beliefs held by B's colleagues who are also subject to A's power legitimate A's control over B. These two dimensions are conceptually independent in that authorized power may or may not be endorsed, and endorsed power may or may not be authorized.

We can focus on the attitudes and beliefs of subordinates, and yet distinguish between authorized and endorsed power. Thus, we may say that power is authorized to the extent that B believes that A's exercise of power is viewed as legitimate by A's superiors; and power is endorsed to the extent that B believes that A's exercise of power is viewed as legitimate by B's peers or colleagues.

We have, then, two sets of distinctions which may be applied to the study of authority relations. First, subordinates may believe certain norms governing power relations to be valid in the sense that they acknowledge that the norms do exist, and subordinates may view certain norms governing the power relationship to be proper in that they believe that these norms are as they should be. Subordinates may view norms as valid but not proper, or as proper but not valid, or as both proper and valid. Where power relations are viewed as neither proper nor valid, there is by definition no authority relation because of the absence of any normative support.

The second set of distinctions refers to the source of norms supporting the power relation. Power may be authorized by norms enforced by persons superior to the power-wielder; or it may be endorsed by norms enforced by colleagues of the subordinate. Power becomes authority when it is authorized, or when it is endorsed, or both; but persons either superior or subordinate to the power-wielder must initiate and enforce norms regulating the exercise of power if we are to speak of authority. We return to this distinction later in this chapter and throughout this volume. It occupies a central place in our conception of authority.

We hope the reader will not be confused by the necessary use of two similar sounding terms to refer to separable phenomena. We have used the term *authority* to refer to legitimate power. This usage is necessary in order to discuss previous theory and research. In the course of our discussion of authority, we have distinguished between authorized power and endorsed power. It should be clear that authorized power is not the only form of authority analyzed by our predecessors. Later in this volume, we will define authority only in terms of authorized power, so that the confusion in terminology is only temporary.

Formal and Informal Authority. A third set of dimensions which may be employed in the examination of authority relations is much more familiar to sociologists. This is the distinction between formal and informal authority. This distinction was first explicitly described by Roethlisberger and Dickson in their classic study, *Management and the Worker* (1939, p. 558): "the patterns of human interrelations, as defined by the systems, rules, policies, and regulations of the company, constitute the formal organization . . . It includes the systems, policies, rules, and regulations of the plant which express what the relations of one person to another are supposed to be in order to achieve effectively the task of technical production. It prescribes the relations that are supposed to obtain within the human organization and between the human organization and the technical organization." By contrast, these authors describe the informal organization as follows: "Many of the actually existing patterns of human interaction have no representation in the formal organization at all, and others are inadequately represented by the formal organization . . . Too often it is assumed that the organization of a company corresponds to a blueprint plan or organization chart. Actually, it never does . . . The formal organization cannot take account of the sentiments and values residing in the social organization by means of which individuals or groups of individuals are informally differentiated, ordered, and integrated" (1939, p. 559). In short, Roethlisberger and Dickson employ these terms to distinguish between the rules and regulations—the official blueprint—on the one hand, and the actual sentiments and behavior of organizational participants on the other.

A related, but somewhat distinctive, definition of these concepts is supplied by Litterer (1963, p. 10), who suggests that: "By formal is meant those aspects of organizations which have been, or possibly might be, consciously planned . . . The informal organization is conceived of as being the aspects of organization that are not formally planned but that more or less spontaneously evolve from the needs of people." Thus, Litterer suggests that the appropriate distinction is not that between official rules or prescriptions for behavior on the one hand and actual behavior on the other, but between two types of behavior distinguished by their origins: formally planned and relatively spontaneous behavior.

Both of these conceptions of the distinction between formal and informal are different from the one we propose. Consistent with our earlier definition of formal organizations, formal authority is viewed as authority attached to a position in an organization—that authority which exists regardless of the characteristics of individual position occupants. Informal authority, then, is that authority which is based on the personal characteristics or resources of an individual. Thus, in distinguishing formal from informal authority, we are not primarily concerned with the source of legitimating values on which authority rests. The formal authority associated with a given position in an organizational hierarchy might have its historical roots in the value systems of subordinate groups and have emerged spontaneously only to become institutionalized later. The important point is that, whatever its original source, the authority now resides in the position so that it is available to all its occupants. And we do not, like Roethlisberger and Dickson and many other sociologists, define formal authority as that authority which is specified by the table of organization or by the written job definitions of positions. Such blueprints specifying prescribed authority relations may have little or no effect on the actual behavior of participants. Formal authority is not to be equated with officially defined authority. Our view of formal authority appears to be generally consistent with that of Blau (1964, pp. 205–206), Davis (1948, p. 95), Evan and Zelditch (1961, p. 884), and Raven and French (1958), although the terminology sometimes varies. For example, Raven and French (1958, p. 83) use the term *legitimate power* in the same way in which we propose to use the term *formal authority:* "Legitimate power in formal organizations is largely a relationship between offices rather than between persons. Assuming that the factory worker accepts the right of his supervisor to hold his position, that supervisor will, by virtue of this occupancy, have the legitimate right to prescribe behavior for his worker; the worker will, in turn, feel obligated to accept these orders."

The distinction between formal and informal authority cuts across the other dimensions. Formal authority may be valid or proper or both. It may be authorized or endorsed or both, although, as we argue below, formal authority is more likely to be authorized than endorsed. Similarly, informal authority may be valid or proper or both, and may be authorized or endorsed or both. Some think of informal authority as only endorsed, resting on personal and specific relations that develop between a leader and his subordinates. But authorized power can also be informal, as we have defined the latter concept. Thus, French and Raven (1959, p. 160) have pointed out that an individual may possess certain characteristics such as age (being older) or sex (being male) "which are specified by the culture as giving him the right to prescribe behavior" for others. The cultural values specifying such control as appropriate may be highly specific: for example, an individual's specialized technical skills may become the basis for authorized, informal authority in a limited context.

A review of the literature on authority in both informal groups and formal organizations suggests that sociologists have tended to define power as legitimate—hence, as authority—to the extent that norms held by the group subordinate to the power-wielder define his exercise of power as acceptable or appropriate. In our terms, the emphasis has been on endorsed power. Further, attention has been directed in most past studies to informal rather than formal authority, even when the research has been conducted in a formal setting. We will briefly review this literature and then attempt to develop an alternative conception of authority which we believe to be better suited to the study of authority in formal organizations.

Informal Groups. We have described above the manner in which power differences may emerge in informal group settings as a consequence of exchange processes occurring between participants. Status processes are also at work in these settings and they have an important part to play in transforming power into authority. As exchanges go on between actors A and B, to the extent that B comes to recognize the greater value of what is offered by A in comparison with what B has to offer in return, B will become increasingly obligated to A for the assistance rendered. Such differential social obligations constitute the basis for differential status as B comes to recognize and acknowledge A's superiority and hence B's own inferiority. As Homans (1961, p. 298) explains: "A man earns high esteem by providing for others services they cannot provide nearly so easily for themselves. At least for the time being they cannot make him a return in kind, as fair exchange would require, and so they become his debtors. True, they do render him esteem, which by making him superior makes them by the same token inferior. But from this point of view esteem is a token of unpaid debt: it is a promissory note. What it promises is that at some later occasion they will redeem the pledge by doing what the creditor asks of them, by submitting, that is, to his authority." What needs to be added is the statement that, in general, individuals will be more willing to follow the advice or be subject to the control of others whom they regard as superior to them. They are more likely to regard it as right or appropriate when a person whom they acknowledge to be superior attempts to control them. In this manner, differentiation of status serves to legitimate differences in the distribution and exercise of power.

From Homan's point of view, for one to speak of authority it is sufficient for B to approve A's exercise of power. Blau and Scott (1962) have argued, however, that it is inappropriate to speak of authority emerging in a pair relation. Social norms supporting the exercise of power can only arise in a group context involving two or more subordinates. They argue: "Authority relations can develop only in a group or larger collectivity, and not in isolated pairs, because only group values can legitimate the exercise of social control and only group norms can serve as an independent basis for enforcing the pattern of compliance. Once an authority structure has become institutionalized, however, it can find expression in apparently isolated pair relationships" (1962, pp. 29–30). The presence of more than one person in the subordinate position is critical because subordinates as a group have an important role to play in an authority system. "Given the development of social norms that certain orders of superiors ought to be obeyed, the members of the group will enforce compliance with these orders as part of their enforcement of conformity to group norms. The group's demand that orders of the superior be obeyed makes obedience partly independent of his coercive power or persuasive influence over individual subordinates and thus transforms these other kinds of social control into authority" (Blau and Scott, 1962, p. 29).

Homans (1961, pp. 294–295) describes in his own terms the development of this kind of control system in which subordinate members participate in the control process, but he does not make this a defining criterion of authority, as do Blau and Scott.

Like Homans, Blau (1964) uses an exchange framework to describe the differentiation of power relations in informal groups and the emergence of authority, but his perspective permits a more adequate description of the problems associated with the transformation of power into authority in informal groups. According to Blau, power relations may develop into authority under the condition that the power-wielder acts so as to make compliance with demands generally rewarding to subordinates. He argues: "If the benefits followers derive from a leader's guidance exceed their expectation of a fair return for the costs they have incurred, both by performing services and by complying with directives, their collective approval of his leadership legitimates it. Their joint obligations

for his contributions to their welfare and their common approval of his fairness, reinforced by their consensus concerning the respect his abilities deserve, generate group pressures that enforce compliance with his directives" (1964, p. 202).

This argument helps explain why an authority system does not invariably develop in an informal group context. It is not always possible to exercise power over others and at the same time give them rewards. Let us return for a moment to the situation where leaders have not yet emerged in a group, to the time when power and status differences among members have not developed. Members may desire power, but they will also want to gain the approval of their fellows. As Bales (1953, pp. 140–143), Blau (1964, pp. 33–50), and a number of other social analysts have noted, the attainment of power and the gaining of social approval sometimes make incompatible demands on an individual. The road to power is taken by attempting to make contributions to goal attainment, which in turn entails making suggestions, evaluating the contributions of others, and attempting to control and mobilize members to work on task solutions. However, these activities may not elicit the approval of others. It is not particularly gratifying to be dependent on another for help, nor is it pleasant to have one's task contributions evaluated and criticized by another, even if the criticisms are justified.

These problems are particularly acute if group members initially perceive themselves to be status equals. This is often the case where new groups are forming in natural situations and where *ad hoc* groups are brought together in a laboratory. For example, the members of Bales' groups—Harvard male undergraduates—undoubtedly perceived themselves initially to be status equals (Berger, Cohen, and Zelditch, 1966, p. 30). Hence, we would expect, and Bales' research documents, fierce status struggles (Heinecke and Bales, 1953). Further, in groups such as those studied by Bales, it is difficult for one member to find ways of rewarding others. The task has been set by the experimenter, with little reason for participants to be too concerned about the quality of the outcome. When the collective goals are not highly valued by participants, the contributions of would-be leaders to their attainment are not perceived as gratifying by individual members (Verba, 1961, p. 169). Leaders working on the task do not mediate between members and valued

goals; hence, members are less willing to acknowledge their dependence on these leaders.

It is, perhaps, because of such special circumstances that Bales' laboratory groups sometimes developed a differentiated leadership structure. There emerges a "task specialist," who concentrates on solving the problems confronted by the group members at the cost of arousing their resentment and hostility, and a "socioemotional specialist," who is concerned with providing gratifications to members and boosting their morale (Bales and Slater, 1955; Slater, 1955). In our view, this type of role differentiation occurs in response to a particular set of conditions and should, therefore, not be regarded as a universal tendency in all task groups, as has sometimes been suggested (for example, Etzioni, 1965).

This brief discussion suggests that power is not easily transformed into authority in informal groups, and that, when it is not, special structural arrangements may be necessary to prevent the group from being torn by struggles for status and power. When there is a mobilization of social norms in support of a particular distribution of power, it becomes possible for leaders to lead and followers to follow without generating disruptive emotional responses. Such norms foster the development of stable expectations concerning the role one is to play in the group structure. Further, the emergence among subordinates of social norms which support the power structure helps render power relations more impersonal and, hence, reduces the tensions associated with the exercise of interpersonal power. As Thibaut and Kelley (1959, p. 129) suggest: "Nonadherence is met with the use of power to attempt to produce conformity, but the influence appeal is to a supra-individual value ('Do it for the group' or 'Do it because it's good') rather than to personal interests ('Do it for me' or 'Do it and I'll do something for you')." Finally, because the norms distribute responsibility for surveillance among all group members, the control system operates effectively even when superiors are temporarily absent.

In sum, from this perspective, authority, in contrast to nonlegitimate or illegitimate power, provides the basis for a more stable and effective control system. Whyte (1955), in his analysis of the leadership structure of the Norton Street gang, provides a detailed

description of the operation of such a legitimate power structure in an informal group.

Formal Organizations. We have stated that organizations are systems of power in that differential control of rewards and penalties is typically built into the definitions of organizational positions. But in few formal organizations are participants content to rely on power alone as a basis for control. Weber (1947, p. 325) notes that in his experience no organization "voluntarily limits itself to the appeal to material or affectual motives as a basis for guaranteeing its continuance. In addition, every such system attempts to establish and to cultivate the belief in its 'legitimacy.' " Caplow (1964, p. 82) comes to the same conclusion: "Despite sanctions and penalties at critical points, almost every organization depends more upon consent than force to accomplish its objectives." In short, most formal organizations attempt to legitimate their power systems, and any attempt to understand the control system in formal organizations must deal with authority as well as power.

Sociological studies of authority in formal organizations may be characterized as having five central foci: one set of studies examines subordinate belief systems which legitimate existing distributions of power; a second deals with the attempts of organizational superiors to influence the belief systems of subordinates; a third briefly characterizes the blueprints for formal authority arrangements but concentrates attention on informal departures from these planned control systems; a fourth describes and analytically examines authority systems as they operate in specific contexts; and a fifth group of studies has attempted to examine the relation between various characteristics of authority structures and other structural features among a series of organizations. As a means of placing our own approach to the study of authority in formal organizations in perspective, let us briefly summarize each of these approaches.

SUBORDINATE BELIEF SYSTEMS. Weber's (1947, pp. 324–423) justly famous typology of authority (traditional, charismatic, and rational-legal) may be viewed as an attempt to identify different types of subordinate beliefs, which in turn can be related to variations in "type of obedience, kind of administrative staff de-

veloped to guarantee it, and the mode of exercising authority."
Weber used historical materials to develop and refine his categories
of analysis. Other studies focusing on subordinate belief systems, almost without exception, use Weber's typology as a point of departure. Empirical studies in this tradition include those of Gouldner (1954), who analyzed variations in beliefs and attitudes toward
rules among workers in a gypsum plant; Harrison (1959), who examined member beliefs underlying the authority exercised by leaders and officers of the American Baptist Convention; and Peabody
(1964), who surveyed worker norms supporting compliance in a
local police department, a welfare agency, and an elementary school.

ATTEMPTS BY SUPERIORS TO INFLUENCE BELIEFS OF SUB-
ORDINATES. Broadly speaking, organizational superiors can follow
two kinds of strategies in attempting to influence the belief systems
of subordinates as these relate to the distribution and exercise of
power. They may be designated as the *ideological* and the *interpersonal* strategies.

The ideological approach involves an attempt on the part of
power-wielders to manipulate directly the values or beliefs of those
subject to the power system so that they will come to view the existing distribution of power as legitimate. The top management of
organizations often combines with other elite bodies in the society
to develop and sustain culture-wide ideologies which defend current
power arrangements as morally justified. An early and pervasive
ideology of this type was the "divine right of kings"; a contemporary
example is the "equal opportunity" ideology which posits a positive
correlation between position in a hierarchy and the merit of the
occupant of the position. The most complete analysis of such managerial ideologies is provided by Bendix (1956), who has examined
the belief systems supporting organizational arrangement during
the early phases of industrialization in England and Russia, in the
recent industrial history of the United States, and in the Soviet Zone
of East Germany. Hartmann (1959) has provided an empirical
study of the ideologies which support the *Unternehmer* (owner-en-
trepreneur) position in German management. And, as has been frequently noted, some industrial sociologists and social psychologists,
whether consciously or not, have contributed to the development of
new managerial ideologies. (See, for example, Baritz, 1960; Bendix

and Fisher, 1949; Kerr and Fisher, 1957; Perrow, 1972, pp. 61–95; V. Thompson, 1961, pp. 114–137; Wolin, 1960, pp. 407–429.)

In addition to participating in the development of such culture-wide ideologies, management groups also expend considerable energy in maintaining support for their positions within their organizations. Barnard (1938, p. 279) has discussed this executive function in the following terms: "The distinguishing mark of the executive responsibility is that it requires not merely conformance to a complex code of morals but also the creation of moral codes for others. The most generally recognized aspect of this function is called securing, creating, inspiring of 'morale' in an organization. This is the process of inculcating points of view, fundamental attitudes, loyalties to the organization or cooperative system, and to the system of objective authority, that will result in subordinating individual interest and the minor dictates of personal codes to the good of the cooperative whole." Selznick (1957, pp. 90–100, 150–154) has also placed considerable emphasis on the engineering of consent and the creation of "socially integrating myths" by organizational leaders. Such leadership is exercised in the drafting of company policy statements, in the preparation of propaganda for internal as well as external consumption, and in the development of orientation and training programs for fledgling participants.

The interpersonal strategy also aims at the development of social norms which will justify and support the power hierarchy, but its approach is less direct than that represented by the ideological strategy. And, unlike the ideological approach, interpersonal techniques are used primarily in situations involving face-to-face interaction of a superior with subordinates. Perhaps the most widely employed techniques are those which develop the social obligations of subordinates to superiors by exchange processes similar to those characterizing the emergence of power differences in informal group settings. Superiors attempt to act so that their behavior provides gratifications to subordinates. Subordinates become dependent on their superiors for these services and, with time, these joint obligations come to be expressed in social norms justifying the superiors' special position and enforcing compliance to their directives (Blau and Scott, 1962, pp. 140–145). A great many studies focusing on the leadership behavior of persons occupying superior positions in an organizational hierarchy, such as the series conducted by the Survey Research Center of the University of Michigan (Likert, 1961), or those carried out by the Personnel Research Board at Ohio State University (Stogdill and Coons, 1957), may be viewed as attempts to describe and analyze the characteristics of superiors who are more or less successful in using interpersonal strategies to develop and extend their authority over subordinates. Emphasis is placed in this literature on superiors' special skills, such as degree of technical competence, which enable them to render valued services to subordinates; on their human relations attitudes, such as degree of employee-orientation or consideration, which render them attractive to subordinates; or on their ability to defend the interests of their work group in negotiations with higher management (Bowers and Seashore, 1966; Pelz, 1952; Wager, 1965).

It has been recognized, however, that the position of the superior in a formal organization is not exactly comparable to that of an informal group leader because of the former's access to organizational sanctions. As Blau (1964, p. 210) notes: "Although managerial authority in organizations contains important leadership elements, its distinctive characteristic, which differentiates it from informal leadership, is that it is rooted in the formal powers and sanctions the organization bestows upon managers."

Organizational superiors enjoy distinct advantages over their informal counterparts, as has been noted in our earlier discussion of formal, as compared with informal, power. For example, formal leaders can more easily concentrate on the discriminating use of the power they have, being freed to a considerable extent from the necessity of competing with others for its possession. More obviously, the powers bestowed upon superior officials assist them in providing services to subordinates, such as channeling needed information, supplies, and equipment to subordinates. Another rather clever tactic available to the formal office holder has received considerable attention. Since formal sanctions are placed at the disposal of superiors, they are able to court the favor of subordinates by judiciously refraining from using these sanctions (Blau, 1955, p. 169; Gouldner, 1954, p. 173). Such strategic leniency generates social obligations and collective approval, which nourish the development of social norms legitimating the existing distribution of power.

In addition to those interpersonal tactics which are expected to create social obligations among subordinates, a set of dramaturgical techniques employed by superiors to support their positions has been discussed by V. Thompson (1961, pp. 138–151). Thompson's thesis is that with the growth of specialization, managers are increasingly unable to exercise intelligently their right to command. Lacking a real function, managers devote more and more attention to keeping up the appearance of performing one, engaging, in Goffman's (1959) terms, in "impression management." In this vein, Thompson (1961, p. 142) argues: "The dramaturgical management of impressions about hierarchical positions and roles is no longer a sporadic affair depending upon the accidents of personality. It appears to be institutionally organized. That is to say, opportunities for hierarchical success in modern bureaucracy depend to a very large extent upon the ability and willingness to engage in impression management. Our contention is that this kind of behavior is essential as a device for maintaining the legitimacy of hierarchical roles in the face of advancing specialization." One need not completely agree with Thompson's premise concerning the loss of managerial functions to accept as valid his argument that dramaturgical techniques help some superiors to defend the legitimacy of their positions *vis-à-vis* subordinates.

DEPARTURES FROM FORMAL BLUEPRINTS. A large number of empirical studies begin with a cursory discussion of the organization's blueprint or model of authority as embodied in its table of organization, but concentrate on informal and idiosyncratic departures from it. Two subcategories of research may be identified here. First, there are those studies which attempt to describe the actual, as contrasted with the prescribed, distribution of power or authority in the organization. Dalton's (1959) comparative analysis of power relations among line and staff officers in a number of firms follows this approach, as does J. Thompson's (1956) study of authority and power in two ostensibly identical air force wings. In addition, the attempt by Tannenbaum (1968) to summarize the amount and distribution of power within formal organizations by construction of control graphs contrasts the actual distribution of power with the prescribed distribution.

A second group of studies surveys a set of officeholders in

identical organizational positions in order to describe and analyze
the bases of their differential authority or power. That is, an attempt
is made to examine positions with similar levels of formal authority
and power in order to investigate the ways in which the personal
characteristics and behaviors of officeholders contribute to an aug-
mentation or erosion of their formal authority or power. The Ohio
State Leadership studies are often of this type (for example, Halpin, 1956; Shartle, 1951) as are those conducted by the Survey
Research Center of the University of Michigan (for example, Kahn
and Katz, 1953; Katz and others, 1950, 1951). Many of the other
studies which examine leadership behavior in supervisory positions
also fall within this category. (For summaries of such research, see
Blau and Scott, 1962, pp. 140–164; Etzioni, 1961, pp. 89–126;
Likert, 1961, pp. 5–25, 89–96; Likert, 1967; Perrow, 1972). An
experimental approach is taken by Evan and Zelditch (1961), who
control the formal position while varying the competence of the
occupant in order to determine the effect of competence on subordinates' conformity and perceptions of legitimacy.

SPECIFIC CONTEXTS. The empirical literature on authority
also contains several good descriptive-analytical studies examining
the operation of authority systems within specific organizational
contexts. For example, Janowitz (1959a, 1959b) has analyzed the
changing patterns of authority in the military; Goss (1961) has
studied influence and authority within a hospital out-patient clinic;
Bucher (1970) has described power processes in a medical school;
Freidson and Rhea (1963) have examined control processes in a
medical group; Clark (1963), Hill and French (1967), and Gross
and Grambsch (1968) have examined faculty power in universities;
Kaufman (1960) has described the remote-control systems devised
to regulate the behavior of rangers in the United States Forest Service; Kornhauser (1962) has analyzed the professional and administrative arrangements for controlling the work of scientists employed
in industrial organizations; and McCleery (1957, 1961) and Cloward (1960) have examined the formal and informal power and
authority arrangements operating in a prison. Such descriptive accounts of the operation of power and authority systems in particular
types of organizations are very useful; it would be well to have many
more of them. However, in such accounts (and this criticism applies

to many of the studies discussed in the other categories) one is never entirely certain as to which assertions are applicable to authority or power systems in general and which apply only to the particular occupational group or situation under analysis. Only comparative studies which use similar concepts to investigate authority systems across a broad range of organizations can furnish the basis for generalizations concerning authority systems.

STRUCTURAL ELEMENTS. The decade of the 1960s saw the emergence of an important new strand of empirical research on authority structure. Unlike previous studies which have tended to concentrate on authority norms or practices as they operate in a single organization, this group of studies explores the interrelation of structural features across a sample of organizations. In this research, the authority structure is taken as one among several structural features to be examined in relation to other structural characteristics. For example, the size or shape of the authority hierarchy may be examined as a function of the organization's size or its technological features. Also, unlike most previous research, these studies have concentrated on formal, rather than informal, authority structures.

A large number of dimensions of formal authority structures have been identified and explored in these studies. For example, Pugh and his colleagues (1968) distinguish between the dimensions of centralization and configuration in examining organizational authority structures. Centralization refers to the locus of authority to make decisions affecting the organizations—whether it occurs higher or lower in the hierarchy for particular decisions—whereas configuration refers to the shape of the role structure and includes such variables as the "height" of the hierarchy and the span of control. Blau and Schoenherr (1971) distinguish four aspects of the authority structure: differentiation, indicated by the number of hierarchical levels in the organization; management overhead, measured by the proportions of managerial and staff personnel; span of control of managers; and decentralization of responsibilities as measured by the level at which a variety of decisions are made. Both of these studies, as well as others of the same type, demonstrate that authority structures in organizations vary as a function of other structural and environmental features, and that it is necessary to distinguish

several dimensions of authority structures because they are differentially affected by these other features. While there is the promise
of cumulative findings and some convergence in theoretical frameworks, there is little consensus at present on the dimensions to be
employed and even less on the specific indicators to be used in measuring them. (See Pennings, 1973.) Nevertheless, we view this line
of research as extremely promising, both because it has reasserted
the importance of formal structural features of organizations and
because it views these features as problematic, as something to be
explained.

What are we to conclude from this review of the literature
on authority in formal organizations? Viewed in terms of our dimensions of authority, it appears that: first, the distinction between
valid and proper authority has not been made, and it is often difficult to tell which usage is intended; second, the emphasis has been
on norms enforced by the subordinate group, that is, on endorsed
as opposed to authorized power; and third, while the distinction between formal and informal authority is frequently employed (with
varying meanings), more attention has been devoted to the analysis
of informal than formal authority systems. Thus, from our point of
view, although the distinctive feature of authority in formal organizations is the reliance placed on valid, authorized, and formal
power, all but the most recent sociological literature has emphasized
proper, endorsed, and informal power. In the final section of this
chapter, we begin the construction of an alternative conception of
authority designed to correct this imbalance.

Alternative Conception of Authority

Normative Regulation of the Power-Wielder. Following the
lead of previous sociologists, we have defined authority as legitimate
power. Power is legitimate to the extent that there exist social norms
which govern the exercise of power and the response to it. Our review of the sociological literature on authority in informal groups
and formal organizations suggests that more attention has been
given to the regulatory effect of the norms on the behavior of subordinates than to their effect on the behavior of the power-wielder.
As we have seen, emphasis has been placed on the ways in which

norms constrain and support the behavior of those subject to the exercise of power by harnessing peer group forces to support the control attempts of the power-wielder. Norms operate in such a way that conforming behavior of subordinates is encouraged and rewarded, while deviant behavior is discouraged and punished.

Our view of legitimate power suggests that the norms operate in two directions: to constrain and support the behavior of those who are subject to the power; and to constrain and support the exercise of power by the power-wielder. Little attention has been directed to the latter, although we believe that it is the more significant consequence of the operation of authority norms. The critical difference between power and authority, in our view, is that authority, but not power, is subject to normative constraints; the behavior of the parties involved, both power-wielder and recipient, is to some degree constrained and supported. In short, authority is a form of legitimate power, and *legitimate power is normatively regulated power.*

We have already considered.the way in which the norms regulate the responses of subordinates to the exercise of power in informal groups. Let us now consider how norms also regulate the behavior of the power-wielder. As we have noted, power differences are generated in informal groups by means of exchange processes, and authority emerges as joint obligations give rise to collective norms legitimating the exercise of power. Emerson (1962), however, presents a slightly different view of the emergence of authority in such a situation, a view consistent with the earlier formulation but containing an emphasis relevant to this discussion. He argues that persons in dependent positions *vis-à-vis* others will attempt to increase their own power so as to offset or balance the influence of the more powerful members. One important technique available to groups of persons dependent on some other is coalition formation: joining forces to act in concert when dealing with the power-wielder. The consolidation of such coalitions is viewed as identical with the process of norm formation. "Such norms are properly viewed as the 'voice' of the collective actor, standing in coalition against the object of its demands" (Emerson, 1962, p. 38). These norms are used by the coalition to limit and regulate the power exercised over them. Thibaut and Kelley (1959, p. 134), in their discussion of norms, have also described how norms seek to limit power: "Norms are, in the first place, rules about behavior. They tell each person what is expected of him in certain situations, and in so doing they indirectly indicate requests that others may not properly make of him. In this way he is protected from subjugation to another's whimsically exercised power."

Hence, the emergence of group norms with respect to the exercise of power cuts both ways. By legitimating the power of the dominant member it mobilizes group support, making subordinate members co-participants in enforcing directives. On the other hand, these same norms specify the area within which power may be exercised, identifying which power acts are to be supported and which are not, and, in this manner, regulating and constraining the exercise of power.

The discussion by Emerson (1962) and Thibaut and Kelley (1959) most clearly applies to the situation in which power is legitimated by endorsement; subordinates acting in coalition restrict the power of their common leader. But the general phenomenon described need not be restricted to situations involving two parties. As Caplow argues in his analysis of three-person systems: "In a brilliant essay Nadel (1957) points out that the interaction of any pair of complementary roles in an institutional system is generally witnessed by related third parties. These witnesses have a personal stake in the outcome of the interactions which they observe (for example, a parent is legitimately concerned with the relationships between his children). Such witnesses may be said to monitor relationships on behalf of the larger social system, maintaining a link between social norms and private relationships" (Caplow, 1964, p. 9). We, of course, are especially interested in the intrusion of the third parties who monitor the power relationship.

Let us turn our attention to formal organizations. Parsons, among others, has recognized that the social norms legitimating the exercise of power are directed at the power-wielder as well as toward the recipient of the exercise of power. He writes: "The concept of compliance should clearly not be limited to 'obedience' by subordinates, but is just as importantly applicable to observance of the normative order by the high echelons of authority and power. The concept of constitutionalism is the critical one at this level, namely that even the highest authority is bound in the strict sense of the concept bindingness used here, by the terms of the normative order under which he operates, e.g., holds office. Hence binding obligations can clearly be 'invoked' by lower-order against higher-order agencies as well as *vice versa*" (Parsons, 1963, p. 243).

Parsons points to the double-edged nature of legitimacy norms, while retaining the view common to most sociologists that it is the subordinate group which invokes and enforces norms on the power-wielder. This may sometimes be the case, but we should not overlook the possibility that norms may be enforced on the power-wielder and recipient by persons in positions superior to that of the power-wielder. In short, the exercise of power may be regulated by authorization rather than (or in addition to) endorsement.

Authorized Power. The view of authority as authorized power is not without precedent in the literature. Looking first at theoretical statements, the concept of a hierarchy of offices, basic to every treatment of formal organizations, explicitly points to the control of lesser officials by higher officials. As Weber (1946, p. 197) states: "The principles of office hierarchy and of levels of graded authority mean a firmly ordered system of super- and subordination in which there is a supervision of the lower offices by the higher ones." Weber also points to the use of rules to govern the exercise of sanctioning powers by officials: "The authority to give the commands required for the discharge of these [official] duties is distributed in a stable way and is strictly delimited by rules concerning the coercive means, physical, sacerdotal, or other—which may be placed at the disposal of officials" (1946, p. 196). Weber does not say so, but presumably these rules are enforced at least in part by persons in positions superior to that of the power-wielder.

Barnard's (1938) perspective also suggests an interest in authorized power, but his discussion of authority appears to mix authorization and endorsement. On the one hand, he argues that authority resides in the authenticated, authorized communications stemming from the occupant of an office (1938, p. 180); but he includes an emphasis on endorsement when he discusses the role of the subordinate's peer group in defining the boundaries of the "zone of indifference" within which orders will be accepted (1938, pp. 167–170).

Finally, Bierstedt's theoretical discussion of authority in formal organizations appears to be consistent with our view of authorized power. He writes: "It is in the formal organization of associations that social power is transformed into authority. When social action and interaction proceed wholly in conformity to the norms of the formal organization, power is dissolved without residue into authority. The right to use force is then attached to certain statuses within the association, and this right is what we ordinarily mean by authority (Bierstedt, 1950, p. 734). Authority is always a power phenomenon. It is power which confers authority upon a command. But it is sanctioned power, institutionalized power" (Bierstedt, 1954, pp. 79–80). Or, in our terms, it is authorized power both circumscribed and backed up by those in the organization superior to the power-wielder.

Two experimental studies indirectly support our distinction between endorsed and authorized power. In the first, Raven and French (1958) reported that whether or not a superior was perceived as the legitimate occupant of an office (elected to office vs. usurping office) did not affect the degree of public conformity exhibited by subordinates. In the second, Evan and Zelditch (1961) found that variations in the perceived competence of the supervisor did not significantly affect subordinates' felt obligation to obey. In our terms, the compliance reported in these experiments was little affected by the manipulation of perceived propriety of the authority relation and may be interpreted to rest on perceived authorization. In the Raven and French experiment, authorization could stem from the inaction of the experimenter, who did not attempt to control or remove the usurper, and in the Evan and Zelditch study, from the presumed organizational support for the office holder's decisions.

In a power hierarchy, the control attempts of one individual may be limited and regulated by the normative restrictions imposed by superiors. Like endorsement, authorization supports and constrains the power-wielder. It is the process that links control attempts to the power system of the larger organization. A control attempt authorized by superiors is one which will be backed up by them, if necessary, by the use of sanctions. The fundamental process which underlies both the control attempt and its authorization is that of evaluation, as will be discussed in succeeding chapters.

The distinction between authorization and endorsement can be illustrated by the following situations which might be found in specific organizations. First, authority which is endorsed but unauthorized is exemplified by the authority of an informal leader among the inmates in a prisoner-of-war concentration camp, where such leaders are removed as soon as they are detected by the administration. Such leadership among the inmates may be authorized by the prisoners' parent military organization, if, for example, the informal leader is also the officer of highest rank. This suggests that such concepts as endorsement and authorization are relative ones dependent on which organizations are being analyzed and on the boundaries for the organizational systems. Second, authority which is authorized but not endorsed may be illustrated by the authority of guards in the concentration camp who are acting in accordance with the regulations established by their superiors. In most cases, their authority will not be supported by the norms of the captive group. Concentration camps may seem to be a special case, but one can certainly find many instances in which officials are authorized to exercise certain kinds of power over their subordinates regardless of the norms of the subordinates. And one can also find instances in which a given official, perhaps because of exceptional competence or unusual interpersonal skills, can exercise power over subordinates greater than that authorized by superiors. Such power, while not authorized, may be legitimated by the norms shared by those subordinate to it. Finally, power in formal organizations may be both authorized and endorsed. There will be many instances within organizations where the authorized power of officials is reinforced by the norms held by those subordinate to such power. In fact, it may safely be asserted, as Weber (1947, p. 325) does, that virtually every organization attempts "to establish and to cultivate the belief in its 'legitimacy'."

It must be emphasized that by including within the general concept of authority, power which is authorized by persons superior to the power-wielder, the range of phenomena encompassed is extended considerably over that included under the more traditional conception. Industrial and professional organizations fall within this rubric, as do less traditional relations. To adopt our position is to view as authority the authorized exercise of power by a prison guard, taking no account of the norms of prisoners with respect to such behavior. And police officers acting in accord with rules enforced by their superiors are said to have authority when operating in lower-class neighborhoods, where their acts may not be endorsed, as well as in middle-class districts, where the norms of residents are more likely to support their exercise of power.

Nevertheless, all power does not become authority under our conception. Power which is neither regulated by norms enforced by persons subordinate to the power-wielder nor by norms enforced by persons superior to the power-wielder remains simply power, not authority. In our view, unauthorized power is always problematic and troublesome in a social relation just because it is unregulated and, hence, unpredictable. Power which is not supported and constrained by norms often gives rise to conflict and opposition, as Blau (1964) has observed. Thus, the charge of "police brutality" normally means that in the view of client or citizen groups, the police have used power beyond that authorized by the rules of their organization, and superiors are called upon to regulate their behavior more closely. In this instance power is alleged to be exercised beyond authorized limits.

This example, however, raises a very important general issue. Sometimes the charge "police brutality" refers not simply to the conduct of an individual officer who has exceeded his authority, but implies that the entire police apparatus, from the review board and chief administrative officer down to the cop on the beat, is corrupt or an agent of class oppression. The issue is no longer the conduct of an individual participant but of an entire organization. In such a case, can we speak of the officer having exercised authority? Fortunately, our earlier distinctions prove helpful in interpreting this case. We can argue that as long as the officer is behaving in accord with the rules of his organization as interpreted by his superiors, he is exercising valid, authorized power, a form of authority. But if he and his organization are neither supported nor approved by the client groups over whom power is exercised, then his power is neither endorsed nor proper. Thus, his authority is only partially legitimated.

In all the studies reported in this volume, we are dealing with employees or volunteers within organizations. We would expect this type of respondent to be generally more supportive of the norms of the overall organization than, for example, selected client or citizen groups who may be less identified with and less trustful of the organizations with which they come in contact. Hence, the type of situation represented by this example hardly appears in our empirical materials.

Formal and Informal Authorized Power. As indicated in our review of the literature on authority in formal organizations, more attention has been focused in past studies on informal than on formal authority. We believe this to be one consequence of the emphasis on endorsement of power by subordinates. The endorsed power approach is most typically used to examine a set of position occupants in order to differentiate among them with respect to their power to influence. That is, formal authority rights are held constant in order to examine differences in power and authority resulting from the personal resources of the occupant or the kind of relationships established with a particular subordinate group. The endorsed power approach could also be employed to discern those rights held in common by position occupants, but it is not particularly well suited to answer this kind of question.

The authorized power approach is, we believe, somewhat better suited to elicit information on rights held in common by position occupants. By focusing on those control attempts of position occupants which are normatively regulated by their superiors, we are more likely to find rights which are associated with the position and are available to all occupants. Because organizational superiors are often concerned with the consistency and predictability of behavior, and because they must be able to replace one position occupant with another, we would expect considerable similarity in the authority rights exercised by a given set of position occupants. The extent of consistency is, however, always an empirical question.

Our conception of authority is not restricted to the analysis of formal power systems but is applicable to informal systems as well. To the extent that informal groups are complex enough to have a multiple level leadership structure, the behavior of persons in the middle layers may be regulated as much by the reactions of superiors as by the normative boundaries enforced by subordinates. Thus, for example, in the street corner gang studied by Whyte (1955) the power exercised by Doc's lieutenants would be regarded as authorized to the extent that it was seen to be authorized by Doc, the informal leader.

Within formal organizations, informal arrangements may arise whereby particular position occupants, because of their superior abilities, political skills, or other reasons, may be supported by their superiors (authorized) in exercising power over their subordinates in a manner not permitted typical position occupants. It may be that such special authorizations often follow from successful attempts by the position occupant to extend legitimate power over subordinates through the direct or indirect manipulation of subordinate values. In such a case, authorization serves primarily to consolidate the gains won by a broadening of the base of legitimacy. On the other hand, special authorizations to particular incumbents may be made without regard to the norms of the subordinate group.

In this chapter, we have developed the distinction between power and authority and our emphasis upon authorized power. But that theoretical analysis is necessarily distant from the on-going activities of participants in formal organizations. To get the work of the world done, the goals of organizations have to be translated into the tasks of organizational performers, and systems of control must be developed. Our next chapter shifts our discussion of authority in formal organizations to this level.

Chapter 3

Goals, Tasks, Sanctions

▲▲

Before systematically developing our conception of authorized power, we need to define some more basic concepts upon which our analysis of authority systems will rest. This chapter will lay part of the necessary foundation by introducing the concepts of organization goals, tasks, sanctions, and evaluators. Chapter Five will complete this introduction by specifying components of the evaluation process, components that will serve as the basis for our discussion of authority systems.

Goals

Concept of Goal. The concept of organizational goal is among the most slippery and treacherous of all those employed by the analyst of organizations. One source of difficulty is that investigators have in mind differing analytical objectives when they employ the term. Some analysts emphasize that goals serve as a source of identification and motivation for participants (Barnard, 1938; Clark and Wilson, 1961). Others point out that goals may be employed as ideological weapons with which to overcome opposition and obtain support from the environment (Parsons, 1960, pp. 44–47; Selznick, 1949). Still others emphasize the way in which goals function to orient and constrain the behavior of participants in organizations (Simon, 1964). The first two uses of the concept focus on the cathectic (emotional) properties of goals as they serve as bases of attachment for both organizational participants and the relevant public. The third use directs attention to the cognitive aspect of goals as they provide orientation and guidance for participants in the system. Employing system descriptions first suggested by Gouldner (1959), it is our observation that the cathectic properties of goals are more likely to be singled out for attention by those viewing the organization as a natural system, the cognitive aspects by those viewing the organization as a rational system.

It is important to realize that a description of goals which is satisfactory for analysts concerned with cathectic properties of goals may be unsatisfactory for analysts interested in the cognitive contributions of goals. Vague and general descriptions of the goals of an organization may suffice for motivational analysis but are less satisfactory for investigations focused on cognitive effects. Thus, to say that the goal of a hospital is to "care for and cure patients" may be sufficiently precise for examining its motivational significance for participants or the public. Such a general description, however, may serve only as a point of departure for the cognitive analyst interested in the effects of goals on the day-to-day activities of organizational participants. While it is true that some participants orient their behavior in terms of quite general goals, others are guided by much more specific and limited objectives. Our major interest is in the cognitive functions of goals in guiding the behavior of organizational participants, so that we will need to develop a relatively precise formulation of the concept of goal.

A *goal* may be defined as a conception of a desired end state of an entity. Such a definition may appear both complicated and vacuous, but we will attempt to demonstrate its utility. The final term *entity* is deliberately vague because goals can refer to conceptions of the desired end state of either objects or activities. Since it is easier to illustrate our ideas when objects serve as entities, we will briefly postpone discussion of activities as entities. Objects serving as entities may be either material or symbolic. A person, an engine, a set of ideas, all are examples of the large variety of objects which may serve as entities under appropriate circumstances.

The end state of an entity is determined by the values or magnitudes exhibited for selected properties. The properties or dimensions of an entity are simply certain of its characteristics which are singled out for attention. For example, properties which might be identified for a person include weight, race, body temperature, and appearance. To say that a given person weighs 150 pounds and is a Caucasian is an assertion about the values exhibited by a person on two selected properties, weight and race.

Goals select certain properties of entities for attention and, further, specify values desired for these properties. A physician confronted by a febrile patient may take as a goal the reduction of the patient's body temperature to a normal level. In this simple example only one property—body temperature—is identified, and approximately 98.6F specifies the desired value on that property. A physician is rarely confronted by patients exhibiting a single symptom; ordinarily, patients present a more complex set of symptoms. In such cases, a physician might identify numerous properties, and the goal would be expressed in terms of the relative importance of each property and the values to be achieved with respect to each of them. This set of values describes the desired end state of the entity.

Turning to another example, a parishioner's soul might be the entity of interest to a minister, the latter singling out for attention such properties as love of God, concern for others, and devotion to the church. In addition to identifying several properties, a minister would be concerned with the range of possible values along each dimension or property as well as with its relative importance. Both the minister and the physician would hold conceptions as to the relative importance of some properties and the relative desirability of some values (or states defined by a set of values); that, for example, a state of grace is preferable to sinfulness, or a state of good health accompanied by a common cold is to be preferred to a serious illness. Such conceptions of desired end states are what we mean by goals.

Implicit in the preceding discussion are two ideas which should be made explicit. First, conceptions of desired end states vary enormously in clarity and precision. Electronics firms may be able to specify with great precision the values to be attained with respect to specified properties of an electronic instrument, whereas a university may desire to produce educated graduates but be uncertain about which of their properties are most important and which values on the selected properties are the most desirable. Second, it is possible to identify both highly general and very specific goals. Since specific goals are often subsumed under general goals, it is often difficult to decide which goal to examine. For example, students may desire A's in a course because they desire high grade point averages because they desire admission to graduate schools because they desire to enter a profession. It is fruitless to attempt to determine in such a case which is the real goal of each individual. It is the analyst who must decide which is the goal of interest, as determined by the purposes of the investigation. Regardless of the level of generality of the goal selected for study, we should recognize that a selected goal may be composed of specific subgoals which we may want to study, and that the goal selected may itself be viewed as a subgoal of some more general goal. These comments have implications for our conception of the desired end state. The end state on which we choose to focus may represent only a proximate end which, once achieved, will give way to another more ultimate objective, or it may represent a final end state. The concept of end state is meant to include both proximate and final ends.

Goals may also be conceptions of the desired end state of an activity or set of activities. Examples of activities which might function as entities under appropriate circumstances are performing a surgical operation, reading proof on a newspaper, or tackling an opposing football player. The properties for these activities are dimensions along which the activities may be described, including such variables as speed, accuracy, and judgment. A range of values is associated with each property, and some values may be designated as preferable to others.

Thus, where the entity involved is an object, such as a human body, the goal is a conception of the desired end state of that object, specifying what values are to be achieved on selected properties of that object. And when the entity involved is an activity or set of activities, the goal is a conception of the desired end state of these activities, specifying what values are to be attained on selected properties of the activities. However, whether the entity is conceived of as an object or as a set of activities is only a matter of perspective, of how the entity is viewed. A goal may be set in terms of desired values on properties of an object (a lower body temperature of a patient), or desired values on the properties of a set of activities (correctly selecting and administering medications in order to reduce body temperature). In the first case the focus is on the object which is to be affected or transformed to attain some specified state; in the second, the focus is on a set of activities designed to bring about the change. This distinction is employed later when we distinguish between the two ways in which tasks are allocated.

Goal-Setting and Assignment. Having determined what is meant by the concept of goal, we turn our attention to the more specific topic of organizational goals. Clearly, a danger to be avoided is the reification of the organization—its treatment as a collective actor which in some metaphysical manner arrives at a definition of its objectives and mobilizes energy for their attainment. The opposite extreme is also unacceptable; we do not want to conclude that the goals of the organization are the sum total of the goals of its individual members. It will help us avoid both dangers if we continually emphasize the question: Which participants set the goals toward which the efforts of other participants are directed? (Cf. Gross, 1968.) This question reminds us that while organizational goals are set by individuals, individuals in the organization may not participate equally in the goal-setting.

The location of organizational goal-setters will vary with the type of organization, although most organizations can be characterized as adhering to one of three patterns. Goals may be set by a small entrepreneurial or managerial elite, as in some industrial and commercial firms. By contrast, goals may arise from some set of values shared by rank-and-file participants who found or join organizations as a means to realizing their objectives. Such organizations usually develop mechanisms for determining and expressing the will of the majority, although the presence of such democratic machinery does not guarantee the preservation of this pattern (Michels, 1949). This pattern is most likely to occur in smaller, often short-lived, voluntary organizations.

Neither of these patterns seems to describe realistically the goal-setting process in the majority of organizations. A small elite is rarely powerful enough to impress its conceptions of desired end states on all other participants, and seldom do we find organizations in which rank-and-file participants share equally in goal-setting. Rather, as Cyert and March (1963) have suggested, goal-setting in organizations is often accomplished through a continual bargaining process among shifting coalitions of the more powerful participants. The number of participants included in these inner circles of decision-making is undoubtedly increasing. Power is shifting from generalists to a growing body of specialists. In addition, entrepreneurs often give way to an elite corps of managers supplemented by a large staff of technical experts, a phenomenon which Galbraith (1967) has termed the "technostructure." Lower-level participants also organize into unions whose spokesmen may demand a voice in goal-setting activities. When the interests of these various individuals and groups diverge, coalitions are formed and bargains struck, the resulting agreements defining the desired end states.

We conclude that organizational goals are conceptions of desired end states determined by members in dominant coalitions. This definition encompasses all three patterns of goal-setting in that a managerial elite or a majority of participants may constitute the dominant coalition in some organizations. The goals so defined may be transitory or poorly integrated or actually conflicting. Organizations, like individuals, may be more or less rational in their goal-setting processes.

Organizational goals are only conceptions of desired end states. As such they may have little effect on the behavior of participants. (See, for example, Perrow, 1961; Selznick, 1943.) Goals are more likely to have behavioral consequences when they guide the behavior of specific participants by specifying desired end states for the activities they perform or for the objects on which they work (cf. Simon, 1964). In short, goals are most likely to have consequences for the behavior of participants when they are assigned to specific participants. General organizational objectives must typically be divided into minor goals, and minor goals into subgoals, before assignment to specific participants. In the rational case, these goals and subgoals are interrelated so as to constitute "means-end chains," the achievement of one goal serving as the means to the attainment of the more general objectives (Simon, 1957). But we do not restrict our attention to systems whose goals are rationally articulated. We shall include in our formulation cases of inconsistent or conflicting goal assignments.

Those who assign goals in organizations are not necessarily the same individuals who define goals, and to the extent that goals are seriously modified in the process of assignment, goal assigners may be said to participate in the goal-setting process. Disagreements over the degree to which goal assigners modify goals lie at the heart of the controversy in public administration concerning the usefulness and validity of the traditional distinction between policy and administration. For our purposes, we must be able to identify the goals of an organization, but we need not ascertain how or by whom they are set. In our discussions we will be more concerned with goal assigners (task allocators) than with goal-setters.

Tasks

Allocation. A task is any activity or set of activities carried out by a person or persons to attain a goal. An organizational task is a set of activities carried out to attain an organizational goal. To assign a goal to an organizational participant is to allocate a task to that person.

Like goals, tasks vary in their specificity, more specific tasks often serving as subtasks within more general tasks. Consider, for example, the activities performed by an intern in diagnosing a patient's illness. This set of activities is composed of a number of subactivities, for example, obtaining a medical history, conducting a physical examination, ordering laboratory tests, and recording notes in the patient's chart. The set of diagnostic activities may also be viewed as a subactivity in the larger set directed toward curing the patient. Which of these sets of activities is to be viewed as the task must be decided by the researcher's scientific objectives, although in making this decision the researcher may wish to take into account the perceptions of the task performer or task allocator.

Decisions and implementations are two distinct types of activities which can be associated with the carrying out of a task. Decisions may be generally defined as the making of choices which significantly affect future courses of action. One set of important decisions are those which define the goals of action, those which determine the desired end states. But at present we are concerned only with decisions made within the confines of an allocated task. We assume that the goal has already been selected and assigned to an actor as a task and focus only on decisions made in connection with carrying out the assigned task. Someone must determine how the task is to be carried out—what course of action is to be followed in pursuing the goal. Within the confines of a given task, then, decisions refer to the primary mental activities which select a path to be followed which significantly affects subsequent activities. By contrast, implementations are those activities entailed in executing the chosen course of action. Some choice is necessarily involved in any kind of behavior, but by definition, choices made in implementing a course of action do not significantly alter the path already chosen.

An actor who has been allocated a task may or may not have the responsibility for making decisions as to how the goal is to be pursued. Such decisions may be made elsewhere in the organization, and the task given the actor may be simply to carry out a prescribed course of action. We will say, by definition, that an actor who is assigned a goal and allowed to make at least some nontrivial decisions regarding course of action has received a delegation. For example, a quarterback on a football team may be told by his coach: "Pass or run, but get that first down." The quarterback in this situation has been delegated the responsibility of choosing which set of task activities he and his team members will execute on the next play.

By contrast, a directive presumes the previous selection of a path and tells the actor to carry out a prescribed course of action. No decisions significantly affecting path choice are allowed to the actor receiving a directive. Thus, to continue with the football example, the coach's instructions to the quarterback might have been: "Call play G-8 on third down," with the quarterback thus prevented from selecting the path and told simply to carry out a previously determined course of action.

There appears to be a close empirical association between these two types of task allocation, directives and delegations, and the two types of entities, activities and objects. In our earlier discussion, it was concluded that an allocator may supply either a conception of the desired end state of the activities to be carried out; or a conception of the desired end state of the object on which the activities are to be performed. In general, it appears that a directive is more likely to specify the desired end state of activities, while a delegation is more likely to specify the desired end state of objects.

Let us suppose, for example, that a superior wanted to restrict the discretion exercised by a subordinate and simply have an order carried out. The most restrictive kind of command which could be given would specify in detail the activities to be performed. Such a directive is exemplified in the instructions given to hospital technicians conducting laboratory tests. However, if a superior wished to assign a goal but permit the performer a great deal of freedom, the superior would tend to describe the desired characteristics of the object on which the activities were to be performed rather than the characteristics of the activities themselves. Thus, an engineer may be told to design an efficient wave guide or a reporter told to produce a 200-word human-interest story. March and Simon (1958, p. 147) come to a similar conclusion, allowing for differences in vocabulary: "The amounts and kinds of discretion available to the organizational participant are a function of his performance program and in particular the extent to which the program specifies activities (means) and the extent to which it specifies product or outcome (ends). The further the program goes in the latter direction, the more discretion it allows for the person implementing the program to supply the means-ends connection."

Although this association between delegation and the specification of characteristics of objects, and between directives and the specification of characteristics of activities, appears strong, exceptions are not rare. Allocations specifying desired properties of activities vary greatly in the precision and detail with which such activities are specified. For example, a medical resident may be told to diagnose accurately the condition of a patient. Although this allocation specifies the desired end state of an activity, it is clear that many critical decisions will be made by the resident in carrying out this task. Similarly, allocations describing the end state of an object may permit relatively little discretion if the desired properties to be realized are specified in detail and if the repertory of techniques for achieving the prescribed ends is limited.

Performances and Outcomes. We have defined goals as conceptions of desired end states of entities, with the entities being viewed either as activities or objects. Regardless of how entities are conceived by the allocator or by the performer, carrying out a task always results in changes in the end state of the activities and usually results in changes in the end state of the objects on which the activities are performed. It is obvious that the carrying out of a set of task activities always results in changes in the values of the properties of the activities themselves. The number of mistakes, strength exerted, or speed are examples of properties along which values are changing as the task is being executed. The actual values achieved by the participant in carrying out the task activities may be termed the performance. The values characterizing a given performance may not have been specified by the goal assigned to the performer (because the goal may focus attention on the object rather than on the activities) and, even if specified by the goal, often may not correspond closely with the desired performance values.

Carrying out a set of task activities usually, but not inevitably, results in changes in the task object. The final values on the properties of the task object following the execution of the task activities may be termed the outcome of the task. For example, the outcome of an engineer's activities may be correctly installed magnets, and the outcome of writing a newspaper article may be changes in the state of knowledge or opinions of the readers. But it is also possible that the end state exhibited by a given task object may be the same state exhibited by the object prior to the performance; activities were performed which did not succeed in bringing about changes. We still regard such an unchanged end state as an outcome, although it will usually be regarded as an unsuccessful outcome by the performer or the task allocator.

It is always possible to identify both a performance and an outcome in connection with the carrying out of any task, although some kinds of tasks might appear to lack an object that is distinguishable from the activities themselves. For example, a ballet dancer may be allocated the task of dancing a particular number. Carrying out the specified activities clearly results in a performance which may be described in terms of the values attained on some of its properties (for example, adherence to dance routine, grace, balance). But is there also an identifiable outcome which can be distinguished from the performance? We would argue that there is if the dance was allocated as a task. Activities carred out for their own sake are not here regarded as tasks—they are not work but play. Outcomes which might be identified if the ballerina were allocated the task of dancing might be the increased proficiency, strength, or self-confidence resulting from the practice, or changes in the state of the audience viewing her performance, described in terms of such properties as its esthetic satisfaction or mood.

In short, carrying out a set of task activities always results in a performance and an outcome. However, both are to be distinguished from a goal. A goal is a conception of some *desired* end state of an entity, while both the performance and the outcome are descriptions of the *actual* end state of an entity following the carrying out of the task activities. The basic distinctions suggested by the preceding discussion are summarized in Table 3.

Let us summarize the discussion to this point. Organizational goals are typically discussed in terms of the organization as a whole. Our conception includes this level but also allows the analyst to move to the level of the individual actor, to determine the extent to which organizational goals affect the actor's behavior as an organizational participant. Goals are conceptions of desired end states of entities, the entities consisting of either activities to be carried out or objects to be affected. Organizational goals are such conceptions as determined by members in dominant coalitions. To view organizational goals from the standpoint of a particular performer is to see assigned goals as setting tasks for each participant. Tasks may be allocated by delegation, permitting the performer to make decisions as to path choice in realizing the goal, or by directive, permitting the performer no significant choice as to the path to be followed but requiring that the performer implement the selected path.

When tasks are allocated by directive, the entities specified by the goal are usually conceived as activities, while tasks allocated by delegation typically involve entities conceived as objects. Carrying

Table 3.

TYPES OF ALLOCATIONS AND TYPES OF RESULTS OF TASKS

TYPE OF ALLOCATION

1. DIRECTIVE
   (e.g., "Execute play G-8")

RESULT OF TASK ACTIVITIES

a. *Performance:* The actual activities carried out in implementing the directive (e.g., the quality of the blocking or ball-handling)
b. *Outcome:* The condition of the task object following the carrying out of the activities (e.g., changes in the position of the football)

TYPE OF ALLOCATION

2. DELEGATION
   (e.g., "Get that first down")

RESULT OF TASK ACTIVITIES

a. *Performance:* (1) the actual decision activities carried out in connection with delegation (e.g., the astuteness of play selection); (2) the actual activities performed in implementing the decisions (e.g., the quality of the blocking, ball-handling)
b. *Outcome:* The condition of the task object following the carrying out of the activities (e.g., changes in the position of the football)

out a set of task activities always results in both a performance and an outcome. Both performance and outcome refer to the actual values attained on selected properties of an entity—the former referring to the end state of the task activities, the latter to the end state of the task object. The actual result of carrying out a set of task activities, the performance or the outcome, may differ from the desired result of the assigned task.

Task Conceptions and Work Arrangements. We have suggested that tasks differ in the manner in which they are allocated to performers. Tasks also differ in another important respect which has lately been summarized under the general rubric, "technology." This concept directs attention to such matters as the nature of the activities to be carried out in performing the task, the characteristics of materials being processed, and the state of current knowledge used in the work process (Hickson and others, 1969). Recent work—in particular, empirical research by Udy (1959b, 1970) and Woodward (1958, 1965, 1970a) and the theoretical writings of Perrow (1967, 1970) and J. Thompson (1967)—argues for the importance of technological variables as determinants of the structure of organizations.

One of the major differences between these efforts and our own is the level on which the analysis is conducted. Most previous work has attempted to relate the characteristics of technology to the characteristics of organizational structure at the level of the organization as a whole. This requires what we have elsewhere labeled an "assumption of homogeneity," which posits that the technology employed by an organization is essentially similar across tasks and occupational groups and that the social structure of the organization is uniform across work units (Scott, Dornbusch, and others, 1972). We resist this assumption and insist that many organizations employ technologies which vary in important respects across departments, across occupational groups within departments, and across types of tasks performed within occupations. We prefer to focus on the possible variations in technologies associated with different tasks performed by participants in a given position. For example, the technologies used by school teachers would be expected to vary across such diverse tasks as teaching subject matter and record-keeping.

In the same manner, and for the same reasons, we prefer not to characterize the structure of an organization as a whole but to allow for the possibility of multiple structures with varying characteristics within a single organization. Indeed, we will entertain the possibility that a single participant may be involved in multiple structures, each varying somewhat according to the task to be carried out. Obviously, the tasks performed by many classes of participants are sufficiently similar so that they all may be conducted within a single work structure. But other participants may carry out tasks associated with quite diverse technologies. We will explore the possibility that this technological variety is accompanied by a parallel diversity in organizational structure. Since we do not focus on the structure of the organization as a whole, but only on that limited part of the structure which impinges on a specific participant, we replace the term *organizational structure* with the more modest *work arrangements*. In sum, we propose that the problems raised by the assumption of homogeneity can be largely removed by changing the level of analysis to examine the relation between the technologies associated with particular tasks (rather than technology in general) and work arrangements (rather than organizational structure in general).

Task Conceptions. In the early stages of our work, we employed the distinction between "active" and "inert" tasks (Scott and others, 1967). We argued that carrying out a set of task activities always entails overcoming some kind of resistance. For example, resistance may refer to the inertia of an object which is to be moved, the opposition of a competitor, or the complexity presented by a problem to be solved. Resistance is always encountered in the attempt to change the values of the properties of an entity, and it is to overcome this resistance that energy is applied in the performance of task activities. We also argued that the amount of resistance to be overcome was not so critical as its variability. Using this criterion, two polar types of tasks were distinguished. If the resistance to a given task was known to be relatively constant from performance to performance, then the task was said to be inert. For example, a mile is to be run along the school track; grades are to be transcribed in a permanent record file. If the resistance was known to vary from performance to performance, then that task was considered to be active (cf. Perrow, 1967; Thibaut and Kelley, 1959, pp. 150–152). We believed that whether a task was active or inert had important implications for work arrangements, in particular for the way in which tasks are allocated and evaluated.

This distinction between active and inert tasks soon led to conceptual and empirical problems. What we began by viewing as an objective phenomenon—whether or not variable resistance is encountered—we came to regard as more subjective in character— how the resistance is viewed by organizational participants. Other studies of technological variables, perhaps because they do not focus on the situation of the individual task performer, assume that organizational participants agree on the characteristics of the technology being employed—that is, on the basic nature of the materials being processed, the techniques being employed, or on the utility of the available technical knowledge. We question this "assumption of consensus" and propose that these technological characteristics are more controversial than they at first appear. They are to an important degree subjective and, hence, subject to dispute and dissensus. In recognition of the fact that various classes of participants may not agree on the nature of the technology being employed, or on the characteristics of the tasks they perform, we speak not of technology *per se*, but of task conceptions.

Task conceptions are the ways that certain categories or groups of organizational participants view the attributes of their tasks. The term *conception* was chosen as representing a compromise between the notion of task characteristic, which sounds too objective, and the notion of task perception, which places too much emphasis on differences among individual participants. We expect task conceptions to vary as a function of such factors as the current state of technical knowledge, the reference groups used by participants, and the organizational location of participants. The effect of these variables will be amplified after we consider another problem associated with the distinction between inert and active tasks. The first problem led us to develop the notion of task conception; the second led us to elaborate the original distinction by developing more precise task dimensions.

Task Dimensions. The original distinction between inert and active tasks was developed to help us deal with such questions as: What makes a task routine? Why is it that certain tasks can be handled adequately in a standard, programmed fashion whereas others require the exercise of much discretion in the choice of appropriate activities? Why is it that some kinds of tasks can always be successfully performed while others often fail through no fault of the performer? In order to be able to explain differences in work arrangements, we focused on differences in the nature of the work being performed.

As we have seen, the distinction between active and inert tasks first centered on the amount of variability in resistance encountered by the performer. Further analysis suggested, however, that variability was not as critical as was the predictability of resistance. Some tasks are performed against variable resistance which is predictable, the resistance varying in a patterned or regular fashion. For example, a disease may pose a variable but patterned resistance and hence allow for a relatively high degree of predictability. We argue that the more predictable the resistance encountered, the more the associated work arrangements can be made routine.

But predictability is but one condition for routinization. One can accurately predict the problems to be encountered in a task performance and still not necessarily be able to handle them so as to secure a successful outcome. Predictability does not ensure efficacy, as is illustrated by a surgeon operating on a cancer patient. Further, neither predictability nor efficacy is likely unless the goals to be realized by the task performance are clearly specified, and tasks performed within organizations vary greatly in the clarity of their goals. What had been regarded as a single dimension—variability of the task resistance encountered in the course of a task performance— became elaborated into three dimensions. The active-inert distinction refers to predictability, efficacy, and clarity. These three task dimensions appear closely related but are conceptually distinct. Also, what had been regarded as an objective characteristic of tasks—variability of resistance encountered—came to be increasingly viewed as, at least in part, a function of the characteristics of the performer. That is, predictability, efficacy, and clarity are affected both by the characteristics of the work to be done and by the performer's knowledge, capabilities, and goals. Having described their emergence, let us more carefully define each of the three task dimensions of the active-inert distinction.

In attempting to reach a goal, the task performer undertakes a set of activities which may be described as a path leading to task completion. Each path choice has some probability of success associated with it which may or may not be known. The first dimension, predictability, refers to the extent to which the performer has knowledge of which path is most likely to lead to success. We expect the degree of predictability to be affected by the general state of knowledge concerning the resistance of the particular class of task objects and by the specific knowledge and experience of the performer.

The second dimension, efficacy, is defined as the probability of successful attainment of the goal. Operationally, efficacy may be viewed as the proportion of task performances which lead to a successful outcome. High efficacy implies the availability of a set of activities that makes a successful outcome likely. Such activities may be the result of theoretical knowledge of cause-effect relations (J. Thompson, 1967, p. 85), habitual skills, or consistent good luck. Like predictability, efficacy varies as a function of both the general state of knowledge and the knowledge and skills of a particular performer.

The third dimension, clarity, refers to the extent to which it is possible to specify analytically the desired properties on performances or outcomes to be attained. We have noted that goals vary enormously in clarity and precision. Since tasks are allocated goals, lack of clarity in goals affects the degree of specificity of the properties to be attained by the task performance. Contributing to the dimension of clarity are such factors as the number of subgoals which are identified, the precision with which properties are specified, and the types of scales along which they can be measured. The task dimension of clarity-vagueness is somewhat similar to J. Thompson's (1967, p. 85) distinction between "crystalized" and "ambiguous" standards of desirability, except that Thompson is describing differences among assessment or evaluation systems while our dimensions are designed to describe differences among allocated tasks.

Clarity differs from goal consensus. Consensus on goals is a measure of the amount of agreement among participants on statements describing goals. Clarity refers to the type of statements made, to whether the language is relatively precise or vague. Sometimes goals are purposefully stated vaguely in order to achieve higher consensus.

Like the other task dimensions we have considered, clarity is affected by the state of theoretical and technical knowledge in the area of concern. Where one has greater knowledge, the desired properties will be more visible and better understood and, hence, can be more clearly specified. Thus, physicians today can more clearly specify the desired properties associated with the state of good health than they could fifty years ago, although even today there exists much vagueness and lack of specificity in descriptions of this state.

To summarize, working at the level of a specific task isolated for analysis, we have defined the active-inert distinction in terms of three dimensions of task conceptions. We suggest that tasks vary in the extent to which the goals to be realized are clearly specified (clarity), the materials to be processed behave as anticipated (predictability), and the means have been developed for achieving desired outcomes (efficacy). We believe these dimensions are helpful in predicting work arrangements.

Task Dimensions and Work Arrangements. We expect there to be a relation between conceptions of task dimensions and organizational work arrangements. That is, for a specific task, we expect that participants' views of the nature of that task will be associated with their views concerning the work arrangements which are—or which they believe should be—established for that task.

By work arrangements we simply mean those features of the work setting that govern the manner in which participants carry out the tasks in question. Thus, allocation by directive or delegation, arrangements for the evaluation of performance, the manner in which work is divided and subdivided among performers, and the number and specificity of rules governing task activities are examples of important components of work arrangements. Our own emphasis will be on the arrangements by which task performances are controlled: on the structures for allocating and evaluating task performances.

There appears to be a relatively clear connection between the type of task to be performed and the work arrangements appropriate for regulating a task. Generally, in the interests of organizational effectiveness and efficiency, we would expect tasks which are high on clarity, predictability, and efficacy to be allocated by directive; tasks low on these three dimensions we would expect to be allocated by delegation. In its simplest terms, the argument is that, given high clarity as to the objectives to be attained, high predictability of the resistance to be encountered, and established procedures for successfully handling this resistance, it is efficient to develop standardized, routine procedures which performers are directed to follow. High clarity contributes specific success criteria for use in designing sequences of activities. When the resistance confronted is predictable, it is possible to specify in advance the appropriate task activities to perform. When highly efficacious sequences of activities have been developed, performers will be expected to follow these set routines.

Sometimes the entity as it comes to an organization is unpredictable, but it can be transformed at an early stage in the production process so that it will exhibit greater predictability. Industrial concerns do this when they remove impurities in their raw materials and achieve the desired consistency prior to stages of fabrication (Perrow, 1967; J. Thompson, 1967, p. 20). And some kinds of person-processing institutions (such as military academies, custodial prisons, and monasteries) attempt to increase predictability by systematically de-individualizing their recruits, removing or ignoring their distinctive characteristics and emphasizing their common features (Dornbusch, 1955; Goffman, 1961, pp. 12–48; Wheeler, 1966). To the extent that the desired uniformity of materials is not achieved, later routinized procedures for dealing with these entities will be ineffective.

In developing efficient work arrangements for inert tasks that are high on clarity, predictability, and efficacy, there are important economies to be realized by centralizing decisions concerning appropriate task activities and assigning specific sequences of standardized activities to individual performers. Directed tasks, designed and coordinated from above, are more readily subdivided so as to gain the advantages associated with extensive specialization. Among the efficiencies realized by subdividing tasks and assigning specific performance programs to workers are short training periods, replaceability of participants, increased skills through frequent repetition of activities, and ease of observation and control (Gulick, 1937). Of course, there is a price to pay. The problems associated with such work arrangements include the fatigue associated with performing repetitive tasks, lack of involvement, relative inflexibility of the structure, and high interdependence in that problems at one work station may ramify through a large portion of the production apparatus.

Let us consider very briefly the effects of this type of task on the structure of the organization as a whole. To do so, we explicitly assume that the tasks performed by the organization are predominantly inert. Extensive specialization would lead to a high division of labor for the organization as a whole, and many explicit rules for performers would result in a high level of formalization at the organizational level of analysis. In addition, we would expect organizations performing these types of tasks to develop a sizable administrative component to parcel out the tasks; design the performance programs; recruit, train, and supervise the work force; handle unusual problems falling outside the routinized sphere of activities; direct the flow of materials; and coordinate the contributions of the lower-level participants. In short, a high level of bureaucratization would also be expected.

Returning from the organizational level to the level of a single task, let us now consider the appropriate work arrangements for the processing of tasks which are low on clarity, predictability, and efficacy. For such active tasks, it is more effective to allow the individual performer to assess the amount and type of resistance confronted at any particular time and to adjust the activities accordingly. Since activities to be performed cannot be specified in advance without a high risk of error, such tasks are better delegated than directed. The allocator allows the performer to determine the most effective means for pursuing the objective. It is also more appropriate for performers in this situation to participate in goal-setting in the sense that conceptions of desired outcomes may be adjusted to suit specific circumstances.

To the extent that individual workers are permitted to exercise discretion in handling tasks allocated to them, the subdivision of tasks is less feasible. Since problems cannot be predicted in advance, arrangements for dividing labor on these tasks cannot be predetermined. Because choice of later activities is affected by the success or failure of earlier activities—feedback from the task object—a single performer, or a set of performers working in concert, is better able to carry out the entire sequence of required activities. If work must be passed on to others, a bulky record detailing the previous history of task activities—such as the patient's chart in a hospital—usually accompanies the transaction.

The greater discretion permitted workers confronting active tasks must usually be coupled with greater individual competence, requiring longer training periods, if the discretion granted is to be effectively employed in guiding the selection and sequencing of task activities. This in turn means, at the organizational level, a smaller

administrative component since less planning, supervision, and coordination are required. In short, we would expect active tasks to
be carried out under work arrangements in which there is less formalization of rules for task activities, less minute specialization of
personnel, and less centralization of decision-making.

To this point we have discussed the relation between work
arrangements and task conceptions only in those situations in which
the three dimensions vary together. We have done so because we
believe that each of the three dimensions is positively correlated
with the others and that their effects on work arrangements are, in
general, mutually reinforcing. Without undertaking a systematic discussion of the relation between work arrangements and other possible combinations of values on these dimensions, let us attempt to
illustrate some of the issues raised by considering each of these dimensions separately. Most of our examples will concern professionals.

Let us begin with the dimension of efficacy. While many
would regard the average professional, such as a physician or scientist, as having high efficacy in carrying out those tasks which are
central to role performance, we would argue that professionals are
only moderately high in efficacy. Indeed, those tasks on which professionals become routinely successful probably get shifted to ancil-
lary personnel, such as technicians. As the risk diminishes, so does
the appeal of the task (Leavitt, 1962). As the task moves in the direction of becoming routine, it is sloughed off as not being worthy of
the true professional (Hughes, 1958).

On the other hand, very low efficacy constitutes a problem for
the organizational analyst in that there is no clear basis for predicting
organizational arrangements. Freidson (1967, p. 498) illustrates
this problem in comparing mental hospitals with general hospitals:
"It seems no accident that the most marked variations in organization and in staff-patient and staff relations are to be found in
mental rather than general hospitals. It is not in general hospitals
that conditions can so easily vary from those of a concentration
camp to those of a partially self-governing community. The organization of mental hospitals can vary so markedly because there is no
clearly efficacious method of 'curing' the mentally ill." There can be
enormous differences in the work arrangements associated with
tasks low on efficacy since the basis for their organization appears

to be ideology rather than technology, and there are fewer constraints on variation in ideology (Perrow, 1965).

It is our impression that on core tasks most professionals are moderately high on efficacy and low to moderate on predictability. That is, professionals are to be found in situations in which success is not automatic or even highly probable—although it is believed that the probability of a professional's succeeding is much greater than that of a nonprofessional—and in which it is not clear what is the best course of action. Freidson (1970, p. 164) emphasizes the lack of predictability which characterizes diagnostic tasks for physicians: "Probabilities can only guide the determination of whether a patient does or does not have a disease. Thus, even when general scientific knowledge may be available, the mere fact of individual variability poses a constant problem for assessment that emphasizes the necessity for personal firsthand examination of every individual case and the difficulty of disposition on some formal, abstract scientific basis." As we have already stated, such situations are most appropriately handled by the delegation of decision-making rights to the performer, who is in the best position to be knowledgeable about the specific type and amount of resistance encountered.

Finally, clarity and efficacy are related in interesting ways. Obviously, a clear view of the goals to be attained may enable workers to improve their performance by helping them focus attention on the relevant attributes of the task object and by providing a clear set of criteria for selecting among alternative activities. Less obviously, the direction of the association may be reversed: ability to produce certain effects or readily to measure changes in certain properties of the task object may cause participants to concentrate attention on these aspects of the work process, even though this may result in a substantial narrowing or distortion of the original goals. They come to define what they can do as what they should be doing. Here we have a goal displacement process in which the original, broader, and more vague goals are supplanted by a narrower set of specific objectives. This process is illustrated by a social work agency that emphasizes the number of casework visits to clients per month rather than the types of services offered clients by workers or the progress of clients from a dependent to a more independent status (Scott, 1969). More generally, the increasing clarity of tasks that is associated with a narrowing of objectives appears to be a characteristic of semiprofessional occupations in contrast with fully professional ones.

Semiprofessionals such as nurses, engineers, and secondary school teachers, and full professionals, such as physicians and scientists, appear similar in being moderately high on efficacy and relatively low on predictability for many of their tasks. What may differentiate them is the level of goal clarity. The goals for semiprofessionals are relatively high in clarity, we argue, largely because the organizations by which they are employed assume the right to set goals to govern their task performance. This is one of the important senses in which these types of professionals are "heteronomous" or externally controlled (Scott, 1965). By contrast, full-fledged professionals, enjoying greater autonomy, conceive of their central tasks as relatively low on clarity, insisting on their right to participate in goal-setting and to adjust the desired end states according to changing views of the situation, new possibilities, and special circumstances.

This argument implies not only that task conceptions shape work arrangements but also the reverse, that work arrangements can shape task conceptions. An important issue then becomes: Who establishes the work arrangements?

Power, Propriety, and Instability. In attempting to explain the relation between technology and structure or, for our level of analysis, the relation between task conceptions and work arrangements, one might posit a form of technological determinism: the technical requirements of the task to be performed force certain regularities upon the behavior of participants. However, few sociologists are consciously willing to embrace such a deterministic framework; indeed, one leading advocate of the technology approach, Joan Woodward, has explicitly rejected it (1970b, p. 23). Instead, most analysts in this tradition prefer to assume that arguments relating technology to structure are valid only "under the assumption of rationality." We are asked to assume that participants in organizations will be motivated to devise and establish the most effective and efficient arrangements for task performance. Thus, in the midst of developing his arguments relating technology to structure, Perrow

(1970, p. 80) reminds us: "We must assume here that, in the interest of efficiency, organizations wittingly or unwittingly attempt to maximize the congruence between their technology and their structure." And J. Thompson (1967) prefaces all his specific propositions linking technological and structural variables with the elusive phrase: "Under norms of rationality."

How plausible is this assumption? We have known since the work of Roethlisberger and Dickson (1939), if not long before, that the logic of efficiency is not the only logic used by organizational participants. Constraints on rationality are a pervasive theme in the work of analysts like Selznick (1943, 1948, 1949) and M. Dalton (1959), who emphasize such motivational factors as self-interest, identification with subunits, and commitments which bind actors to particular skills or work arrangements. And Simon (1957) reminds us that the rationality exercised in organizations is bound by cognitive constraints, including selective routing of information and selective attention to information received. It should not be necessary to persuade social scientists that assumptions about the rationality of human action should be reluctantly embraced, and, whenever possible, relaxed or discarded.

We have previously questioned the assumption of consensus —the assumption that organizational participants will invariably hold the same or similar task conceptions. Disagreements concerning task conceptions may occur among various sets of organizational participants, but in our view two sets are of critical importance. First, we must be concerned about those higher-level participants whose responsibility it is to devise and establish work arrangements for the tasks. Such administrators must have conceptions of these tasks in order to design appropriate structures. It is among this group, if anywhere, that one would expect to find some concern for developing effective and efficient work arrangements. Perhaps such administrative decisions "under norms of rationality" are the implicit mechanisms involved in the conventional arguments linking technology with structure.

The other important set of participants is composed of those who carry out the tasks. Performers can surely be expected to hold conceptions of the clarity, efficacy, and predictability of the various tasks on which they work. Whether the conceptions held by administrators and performers converge for a task is a matter to be empirically determined, although it appears that there are important systematic factors at work to help us predict the result.

Among the most important determinants of task conceptions, we believe, are the work arrangements themselves. In particular, we expect the task conceptions of performers to be affected by the specific working arrangements within which they are expected to carry out their tasks. Methods of task allocation and evaluation are, among other things, messages concerning the nature of the tasks from those who control to those who perform. Thus, if workers are told to follow a standard operating procedure in carrying out a particular task, they are being told something about the predictability of that task as conceived by their superior. In general, we believe that existing work arrangements do affect the task conceptions held by both administrators and performers, and that they operate to increase consensus on tasks between these groups.

Other factors, however, operate to reduce consensus on task conceptions between performers and administrators. We expect that the closer a participant is to the task performance, the more unpredictable and demanding the task will appear to be. To take a simple example, a nursing supervisor may well conceive of bedmaking as a clear and predictable task, but the aide who has to do the bedmaking may emphasize the unpredictable resistance offered by shrunken or torn bed sheets and by uncooperative patients. In general, we expect administrators' conceptions of the tasks performed by their subordinates to be higher in clarity, predictability, and efficacy than the performers' views of the same tasks. Empirical evidence will later lead us to add an important limitation to this generalization.

In addition to distance from the task, performers and administrators often differ in their view of both the level and scope of the task. Performers are more apt to concentrate on individual task objects, while administrators will be concerned more with the set of task objects. For example, a classroom teacher may view the task of teaching as reacting appropriately to the differing needs and problems of each student. School administrators, however, are more likely to be concerned that all students perform sufficiently well to enable them to move from class to class and from school to school

(Bidwell, 1965). Again, the tendency is for the performer to focus on variability, while the administrator focuses on uniformity, the characteristics that task objects share as a class.

Further, performers may differ from administrators in their reference groups—the groups to which they look for orientation and guidance—and these groups may in turn hold differing task conceptions. We believe that such reference group processes operate within many occupational groups. However, they are particularly visible and, hence, more easily studied, in organizations employing professional or semiprofessional employees. Professional groups are particularly likely to develop task conceptions which diverge from those of administrators. These conceptions are transmitted by external socializing organizations and reinforced by peer group pressures. Because alternative task conceptions are collectively held, these shared conceptions and expectations concerning appropriate work arrangements become important unifying forces for occupational groups across varying settings.

What happens when the task conceptions of administrators and performers diverge? We do not, of course, expect to find more than one set of work arrangements. We do expect the actual work arrangements to be imposed on the less powerful by the more powerful group. The more powerful group will usually be the administrators, although in some situations performers may have sufficient power to determine the nature of the arrangements under which they work (Scott, 1972). One way in which to examine these processes would be to note what task conceptions are held by varying groups of participants at a particular time and to note at a later time what work arrangements seem to be in force. However, we have not attempted to carry out such a longitudinal study.

Another approach is to distinguish between participants' descriptions of *actual* working arrangements and participants' views of *preferred* working arrangements. For example, performers are asked first to describe the arrangements under which they perform a specified task. They are then asked to report their beliefs as to what arrangements ought to be in effect. This distinction has some similarity to our earlier contrast between validity and propriety. Insofar as the existing work arrangements involve power and authority relations to which participants are subject, the distinction is identical.

Participants confronted by an improper control system can react in one of three general ways, which will be described in detail in Chapter Nine. First, they may choose to leave the system, a response which is greatly affected by the availability of relatively desirable alternatives. Second, they may change their task conceptions so as to view the control system as more proper. We believe that if participants are subject to an existing set of work arrangements for a longer period of time, they are more likely to believe that the existing work arrangements are proper.

The first two responses—withdrawal from the existing system and conversion to it—act to conserve the control system without altering its configuration. Our primary interest centers upon a third response, which we label *instability*, the creation of pressure for change in an existing system. The following kinds of reactions are taken as direct evidence for the existence of instability: (1) dissatisfaction with some specific component of the control system (for example, with the way tasks are allocated) or with the control system as a whole; (2) the communication of dissatisfaction with the system to others in the organization; (3) the suggestion of changes in the system to others in the organization as a consequence of dissatisfaction with the system; and (4) noncompliance to the control system as a consequence of dissatisfaction with the system. We believe that if a system is unstable, its instability will be expressed by the regular occurrence of at least one of these kinds of responses.

Our basic prediction is that control systems that are viewed as improper by participants are more likely to be unstable. Unstable systems are, by definition, in tension and highly susceptible to change.

Sanctions and Evaluations

Early in the chapter we described the goal-setting processes in organizations and the way in which goals are allocated as tasks to individual participants. However, the allocation of a task does not automatically guarantee that the recipients will shape their efforts toward the attainment of the assigned goal. Participants must be motivated to pursue assigned goals. The usual organizational solution to the problem of motivating participants is the creation of a power structure. In an organization, some participants are granted differential access to sanctions which are used to motivate other participants. Among the rewards and penalties frequently dispensed by organizations are salaries, promotions, shift assignments, diplomas, titles, vacation schedules, and office furnishings. We need now to examine the ways in which sanctions may be employed to motivate participants to pursue organizational goals.

Sanctions, Control, and Evaluation. "Power is the resource that makes it possible to direct and coordinate the activities of man" (Blau, 1964, p. 199). We have said that power represents the ability and willingness to manipulate sanctions of importance to another. However, the ability to reward and punish another does not inevitably confer control over the other's behavior, as Thibaut and Kelley (1959) have argued. If A is to use power over B as a resource for attempting to control B's activities, then A's sanctioning behavior toward B must be contingent upon the nature of B's behavior. Alternatively, if B is to be motivated by dependence upon A to perform certain activities, then B must perceive a relationship between these activities and the sanctioning behavior of A.

Thus, in order to talk of power as the basis of a control system, one must link A's sanctioning behavior to the behavior of B which calls forth the sanction. The sanctioner must selectively employ sanctions to reward or punish certain types of behavior. This connection is made quite explicit in two of the better-known examinations of organizations as systems of control. The most important postulate of the contributions-inducements scheme initiated by Barnard (1938, pp. 139–160) is that each organizational participant receives inducements (valued sanctions) in return for making contributions to the organization. And Etzioni (1961, p. 11) describes the power system of organizations as including: "(1) the directives the organization issues, (2) the sanctions by which it supports its directives, and (3) the persons who are in the power positions." The process by which sanctioning power becomes translated into a control attempt is made even more explicit by Thibaut and Kelley (1959, pp. 240–241, emphasis in original): "converting fate control in order to get a person to perform a specific behavior requires three different kinds of activities: (1) *stating a rule* as to the desired behavior and the consequences (of doing it or not); (2) *maintaining surveillance* over the person . . . and evaluating the degree to which his behavior meets the normative criterion; and (3) *applying sanctions* to produce the predicted consequences." This statement anticipates the basic components of our theory, which emphasizes the crucial role played by the evaluation process in translating power into control. In terms of our own approach, goals are set and tasks are allocated, and sanctions are made contingent upon task performance. But the mediating set of activities that links performances to rewards and penalties is the evaluation process—a process which will be carefully examined in Chapter Five.

Rewarding and punishing individuals on the basis of evaluations of them or their activities is not, of course, the only way by which power can be translated into control. It is possible to punish individuals indiscriminately, regardless of their qualities and actions, and through this "random terror" gain some measure of control over all participants (Arendt, 1958, pp. 419–437; 460–479). It is equally possible to reward individuals indiscriminately, passing out benefactions to all or to some selected by whim or chance. An extreme example is the "caucus race" of *Alice in Wonderland,* in which it is decided that "All have won, so All must have prizes."

A less extreme but nonfiction example is provided by Abegglen's (1958) study of a sample of Japanese factories. More recent studies (for example, Marsh and Mannari, 1971) indicate that Abegglen probably exaggerated the difference between the behavior of Japanese and factory employees in other countries. Nevertheless, the pattern he described is of sufficient theoretical interest to merit brief consideration. In many of the firms studied by Abegglen, once workers were accepted for employment there were few attempts to evaluate them or their contributions. Sanctions were distributed equally among participants in similar positions, with minor adjustments based on the employee's education and size of family. Abegglen emphasizes that these Japanese workers are bound to their organizations by diffuse reciprocal ties, workers accepting a lifetime commitment to their employers and vice versa. It may be that such diffuse commitments partially account for the absence of specific evaluations; they imply an unconditional acceptance of participants, an unwillingness to distinguish between them with respect to their contributions to the organization. Another type of organization combining diffuse commitment with the absence of specific evaluations controlling the distribution of sanctions is one which is organized on egalitarian principles. Thus, in some utopian communities, rewards are evenly distributed among all participants even to the extent of establishing a regular rotation of offices among members. But in these groups, as in the Japanese factories surveyed by Abegglen, participants are often carefully screened and evaluated before being admitted to membership.

While such exceptions may be found, we would argue that the vast majority of organizations distribute sanctions to their participants on the basis of evaluations made of them or their behavior. Such practices allow organizations to teach participants which behaviors or characteristics are desired and which are not, to reinforce preferred behaviors and to penalize undesirable behaviors, and to provide a continuing basis for motivation of participants.

Importance of Evaluations to Participants. Evaluation is a pervasive social process; everyone evaluates everyone else a great deal of the time. We need to differentiate those evaluations which participants consider important from those which they may safely choose to disregard.

Individual participants ultimately decide which evaluations and evaluators are important to them, but organizations attempt to influence participants as they make this decision. Most organizations specify in advance that a group of participants will evaluate other participants. To ensure that the evaluations of members of this group will be deemed important, they are allowed to influence the distribution of organizational sanctions to back up their evaluations. Participants whose evaluations are perceived as determining the distribution of organizational sanctions are termed *organizational evaluators.*

Organizational evaluators vary in their ability to determine the distribution of sanctions, and the sanctions they control vary in importance to participants. Bendix (1956, pp. 213–216), for example, cites data to show that first-line supervisors in industry, whose evaluations formerly had a crucial bearing on important organizational rewards and penalties received by workers, now control fewer sanctions of importance to workers. We will consistently employ the term *influence* to refer to the amount of control which evaluators have over the distribution of organizational sanctions. And we will employ the term *central* to refer to those evaluations which are believed by participants to affect the distribution of those organizational sanctions they consider of value. In some cases, no sanctions of value to a given participant will be controlled by the organization. Usually, however, organizations will control at least some sanctions valued by participants. We would expect that the more the participant values the sanctions controlled by the organization, and the more influence an organizational evaluator has on the distribution of these sanctions, the more importance the participant will attach to the evaluations made by that organizational evaluator.

Organizational evaluators are not, we should add, the only evaluators of importance to participants in an organizational context, although they play a central role in our conception of authority structures. Evaluators may also be regarded as important for reasons other than their ability to direct the flow of organizational sanctions. This may come about in several ways, of which we will briefly discuss three.

First, participants who are committed to the goals of the organization or to the subgoals toward which their efforts are directed may value evaluations of their performance because of their concern for the quality of work rather than because of an association between evaluations and organizational sanctions. Such commitment fosters concern with evaluations of performance insofar as these are believed to provide feedback on the quality of the performance. Evaluations which we shall term *soundly based* are important to participants who care about the quality of their task performances. In order to be soundly based, evaluations must meet several conditions: first, the performer's efforts must affect the quality of performances or outcomes in such a manner that more or better effort produces performance or outcome values regarded as more desirable; second, higher quality performances or outcomes must receive higher evaluations. If the first two conditions are met, then so is a third: the efforts of the performer must be reflected in the evaluations received. Participants who care about organizational goals or subgoals will care about the soundness of the evaluations they receive. And such participants will regard as important evaluations they perceive to be soundly based even if these do not come from evaluators having influence on organizational sanctions but from colleagues, or clients, or others in a position to provide accurate feedback on quality.

Professional participants are often highly motivated to carry out their tasks, as we have noted, but the views of professionals as to which tasks are important or what constitutes proper procedure may differ in important ways from those of their organizational superiors. The most important evaluators for such professionals may be those who share a commitment to the same goals and who possess similar kinds of skills. Such persons are as likely to be located outside the employing organization as within it and, even if inside, may not hold high positions in the power structure of the organization. In such situations, the organizational evaluators may not be the most important evaluators. Hence, the organization may exercise relatively weak control over the task performances of such professional participants. To the extent that the goals pursued by professionals coincide with those set by an organization, the organization's lack of control may not be a problem; the organization can rely on professional evaluators to maintain performance standards. Problems arise, however, when professional and organizational objectives diverge. In such cases, organizational representatives may be unable to exercise effective control over professional participants.

In sum, high commitment to work goals causes participants to consider important the evaluations of persons capable of making soundly based evaluations with respect to these goals, even when these individuals have little or no influence on the distribution of organizational sanctions.

A second basis for the importance of nonorganizational evaluators may be briefly noted. Some evaluators in an organization will be regarded as important because they help to determine the acceptability and relative status of a person in the eyes of fellow workers. Colleagues or peers usually determine informal status, although in some organizations a person's standing in a social group may be in part a reflection of the evaluations made by organizational evaluators (Blau, 1955).

Third, some evaluations received by a participant may be regarded as important because of their relevance for his or her self-conception. The evaluation process has long been regarded by social psychologists as fundamental to the development and maintenance of self-conception (Mead, 1934; Miyamoto and Dornbusch, 1956; Reeder, Donohue, and Biblarz, 1960). Hence, participants in an organizational context who view certain persons as constituting a salient reference group will regard their evaluations as important regardless of their association with organizational sanctions.

While the evaluations of many persons in an organizational setting may be regarded by a given participant as important for one or other of these reasons, our focus will be on those evaluators empowered to administer organizational sanctions—that is, on the organizational evaluators. The evaluations made by these individuals are backed up by the sanctioning power of the organization and, for this reason alone, will be important to most participants in the organization. In addition, their evaluations may be regarded as important for other reasons: organizational evaluators may be perceived to be competent at attaining goals to which participants are committed; or they may be valued because their evaluations help to determine the informal status or self-esteem of participants. While organizational evaluators are not presumed to have any monopoly in these latter areas, social psychological studies suggest that power figures do tend to be perceived as more competent than persons lacking power and that their evaluations may have a considerable impact on both the informal standing and the self-esteem of those whom they evaluate. (See, for example, Hurwitz, Zander, and Hymovitch, 1953; V. Thompson, 1961, 58–80.)

Qualities vs. Activities. We shall now turn our attention to the object of evaluation—the participant and the performance. Having decided that participants are to be evaluated, evaluators must also decide which aspects of participants are to be selected for evaluation. Generally speaking, two classes of properties may be used as the basis for evaluating participants in an organization: qualities and activities.

Qualities are characteristics of persons which are singled out for attention. Individuals may be described in terms of certain values (or states) of the characteristics they possess or have attributed to them. Examples of qualities include: age, sex, manual dexterity, height, skin color, intelligence, education, and color of eyes. Some qualities are highly specific, denoting only one ability or attribute (for example, hair color, ability to add a column of figures); others are general, denoting many abilities or attributes (for example, intelligence, or social class). (See Berger, Cohen, and Zelditch, 1966, pp. 29–39.) Having a high or low state (or value) on some quality may come to be positively evaluated in a given situation, often because expectations about how well a person will perform under given circumstances tend to become associated with either high or low states on certain qualities. When certain expectations about performance come to be associated with a given state on some quality, we may speak of the development of a *status characteristic*. For example, it might be expected that a person possessing a high degree of manual dexterity would perform better in a task involving mechanical skills than another person having little or no dexterity, or that a person with considerable education would perform intellectual tasks with greater facility than a person with little formal education. To the extent that such expectations are held, manual dexterity and education function as status characteristics, the former fairly specific, the latter more diffuse.

While some status characteristics, such as intelligence and manual dexterity, may be directly related to quality of task performance, and others, such as possessing a college education or having seniority, are the result of past performances, we regard all such characteristics as qualities, not as activities. Achieved characteristics, no less than ascribed ones, are regarded as qualities of participants.

In some instances, the evaluation of organizational participants is based largely on status characteristics. For example, in his study of production organizations in nonindustrialized societies, Udy (1959b, pp. 100–110; 1961) reports that in many of these organizations evaluations of workers were based primarily on kinship or political status rather than on task performance. Hughes (1949), Collins (1946), and Dalton (1959, pp. 148–193), among others, have noted the effects of such status characteristics as ethnicity, education, and membership in external associations (for example, Masonic groups) on hiring practices and promotion opportunities in industrial organizations. Crozier (1964, pp. 63, 70ff.) reports that the distribution of sanctions to employees of the French tobacco monopoly was based to a considerable extent on seniority.

Organizations employing professionals are especially likely to rely heavily on qualities rather than performances in assessing participants. Degrees and certificates of past achievements are interpreted as licenses permitting the holder a large measure of discretion and autonomy and freedom from systematic performance evaluation. More generally, it is a well-established practice in many organizations to reward participants differentially on the basis of past achievements, for example, years of schooling, number of degrees held, years of experience. Such practices may be justified as an inexpensive substitute for complex and costly information on current performance. Status characteristics create presumptions about future behavior, sometimes based on past performance. However, we must not forget that they are only presumptions. As Barnard (1946, p. 49) notes: "It is the presumption of capacities and limitations without necessary regard to the immediate concrete activities of the individual that is the essential feature of systematic status. The emphasis is on the potentialities of behavior, not necessarily upon the immediately observable behavior."

The other important basis on which participants may be evaluated is, of course, their activities. An activity is simply an action carried out by an individuual or a set of individuals. We limit our attention to those actions involved in carrying out organizational tasks. Such activities or set of activities have previously been termed *performances*. Examples are typing a letter, operating on a patient, preaching a sermon, and selling a product. The evaluation of task performances—whether by directly evaluating the activities themselves or the outcomes associated with the activities—is a crucial area for our theory. This topic is considered in Chapter Five.

Chapter 4

Goals, Tasks, Sanctions: Empirical Studies

▲▲▲

Although the principles we seek to test are general, the data which support or refute them are necessarily specific. All the hypotheses in this set of studies are examined in specific situations. We believe that one of the most crucial ways in which situations are defined in formal organizations is by the specification of tasks. Rights, responsibilities, relationships, activities—all may vary for the same participant or class of participants as different tasks are performed. Therefore, in all our studies, particular attention was paid to specifying the task or tasks in terms of which respondents were to describe their situations. Finally, in our research in professional organizations we were able to study performers as each performed diverse tasks.

Selecting Tasks

In early stages of our research, we interviewed 224 respondents occupying sixteen positions in five organizations. By operating in this number of contexts and organizational positions, we sought to increase the reliability and the generalizability of our findings. For these early studies, we focused on one task for each position, a task for which we identified the system of authority and evaluation.

The choice of task was crucial for us. We carried out field observations, discussed various tasks with superiors and participants, and then held preliminary interviews. We were seeking a single task of medium complexity for which the occupants of each position received an important evaluation. The tasks selected needed to be general enough to be nontrivial and constitute a significant portion of the participant's work, and yet be specific enough so that we were not dealing with global evaluations of the performer. Based on these criteria, a single task was selected for each position, as described in Table 4.

Table 4.

FOCAL TASKS IN FIVE ORGANIZATIONS STUDY

Organizations and Positions	Number of Respondents	Tasks
HOSPITAL		
Nurse's Aide	25	Carrying out special orders for patients.
Nursing Team Leader	29	Carrying out the doctor's orders (in caring for assigned patients).
Clinical Clerk	9	In the Department of Pediatrics
Intern	21	and Internal Medicine: Diagnostic workup and formulation of the therapeutic plan for the treatment of assigned patients.
		In the Department of Surgery:
Senior Resident	11	Patient care and treatment.
RESEARCH FACILITY		
Engineer	7	In the mechanical design divisions: Working on the design of (Component X).
Draftsman	6	In the electrical engineering department:

Table 4. (Cont.)

		Working on the (Component X) contract package.
Storekeeper	5	Waiting on customers.
Technical Typist	4	Typing technical publications.

ELECTRONICS FIRM

Assembly Line Worker	25	Working on "runs" (wiring components on printed circuit boards).

STUDENT NEWSPAPER

Desk Worker	15	Editing news releases and copy reading.
Copy Editor	14	Copy reading.

FOOTBALL TEAM

Member of Defensive "Front Eight"	20	Tackling.
Member of Defensive "Back Three"	5	Ball reaction.
Member of Offensive Line	15	Blocking.
Ball Carrier:	13	
Split End or Flankerback		Receiving.
Offensive Halfback		Carrying the ball.
Quarterback		Passing.

Descriptions of the authority systems associated with some of these tasks are presented in Chapter Eight, and analyses of problems —incompatibility—and reactions to problems—instability—associated with the evaluation of performance on these tasks are described in Chapters Nine and Ten.

In this chapter, however, we explore the effect of differing tasks and task conceptions on organizational work arrangements. For this purpose it is obviously desirable to have more than one task associated with each position. This allows us to separate uniformities in work arrangements based on the characteristics of performers (in which we are not interested) from those based on the characteristics of the tasks themselves (in which we are interested). We should add that, as well as testing our explicit hypotheses relating task characteristics to work arrangements, these studies can test our implicit assumption that the various tasks carried out by a given occupant of a position can vary as to their characteristics and in the work arrangements under which they are performed. Data on multiple tasks were collected in our studies of professional organizations—university faculty, teachers in public and alternative schools, nurses in hospitals, and priests in an archdiocese. To select these tasks, additional criteria were employed to augment those used in earlier studies of single tasks. We attempted to select a set of tasks at approximately the same "level," for example, level of complexity, number of subtasks, and time devoted to them. In addition, we attempted to select tasks which differed in their dimensions, for example, some relatively high on goal clarity and some relatively low on goal clarity. In all cases, in selecting the tasks, we worked closely with informants who were members of the appropriate occupational group: sometimes we relied on pretests with follow-up interviews; and sometimes we combined informal interviewing and observation.

Using these criteria and selection processes, multiple tasks were selected for the various positions as follows:

Tasks for the 100 university professors were: Classroom Teaching; Research and Scholarship; University Service, including committee service, administrative work, advising, and other non-instructional student contacts; and External Service, including consulting, service to professional organizations, membership on government boards.

Tasks for the 475 public school teachers (in three studies) and the 100 alternative school teachers were:

> Teaching Subject Matter: including, for example, leading (and participating in) discussions; preparing lesson plans; (stimulating student interests in learning); lecturing; (acting as a guide and/or facilitator in student learning activities); examining and grading students on their knowledge of subject matter.
>
> Teaching and/or stimulating citizenship, socialization, and character development (abbreviated as Char-

acter Development) : including, for example, social skills;
(guiding the student toward or providing an environment where student and staff understanding of themselves and each other can develop) ; manners; morality;
(helping the individual develop his full human potential) ;
interpersonal relations.

Maintaining Control: including, for example, preventing interference with other classes; keeping down
the noise level; (helping students find ways of achieving
individual freedom without placing restrictions on the
freedom of others) ; keeping the attention of the class on
their work; (helping students work out for themselves
the consequences their actions hold for others).

Record-Keeping: including, for example, reporting absences and/or latecomers; maintaining administrative records; turning in grades accurately and on time;
(fulfilling record-keeping tasks required by state laws) ;
taking attendance; (setting up a system that attempts to
measure the growth of student potential).

The phrases in parentheses were added for the study comparing
teachers in public and alternative schools.

Tasks for the 194 nurses were:

Carrying Out Doctor's Orders: including, for
example, administering treatments; giving medications;
instructing patients in pre- or postoperative care; etc.

Ward Management: which would include all activities necessary to manage or coordinate patient care,
such as supervision of personnel; making patient assignments; holding staff conferences; planning with auxiliary
staff; etc.

Providing Comfort and Support: including any
action or nursing approach which would serve to make
the patient more comfortable, give him emotional support,
or raise his morale (for example, listening to his fears
and concerns about a forthcoming operation or procedure).

Record-Keeping: which includes charting; trans-
ferring doctor's orders; keeping up the kardex; filling out
order forms for medications and procedure kits; etc.

Observation and Assessment: which would include any nursing care directed at diagnosing or evaluating patient illness (for example, checking patient progress or evaluating his overall adjustment to treatment and, if indicated, reporting back to the physician).

Finally, in the study of assistant pastors in a Roman Catholic archdiocese, we were particularly concerned to assess the impact of the organizational evaluation system on the level and direction of the performers' effort. It was, therefore, important to have a much more detailed breakdown of the tasks performed by assistant pastors so that fairly small and subtle shifts of work effort could be detected. Also, because we wished to analyze shifts between bureaucratic or domestic tasks and professional tasks, both types needed to be well represented in the task selection. For the study of the 106 assistant pastors, twenty-two tasks were selected:

Professional Activities:
    (1) Hearing confessions
    (2) Having personal social relations with people in the parish
    (3) Counseling
    (4) Teaching catechetics
    (5) Preaching
    (6) Reading in theology and related fields
    (7) Attending institutes and lectures in theology and related fields
    (8) Giving marriage and convert instructions

Bureaucratic (and Domestic) Activities:
    (9) Maintaining good relations with the housekeeper
    (10) Keeping parish records up to date
    (11) Being generally available to people in the rectory
    (12) Handling door and telephone duty at the rectory
    (13) Making sick call and hospital visits
    (14) Conversing with the pastor at meals and on recreational occasions
    (15) Moderating parish clubs and organizations
    (16) Wearing clerical dress at expected times
    (17) Maintaining good personal relations with the pastor
    (18) Youth work

(19) Saying mass and administering the sacraments
(20) Abiding by curfew
(21) Being generally available to the pastor at the rectory
(22) Being present and on time for meals at the rectory

It would be most unfortunate for the reader to conclude from our listing of tasks that assistant pastors carry out more subtasks than engineers or senior residents. We repeat that both the level at which tasks are identified and the number of tasks isolated for analysis are matters which depend entirely upon the analytical objectives of the investigator.

Task Conceptions and Work Arrangements

Our theoretical formulation states that there is a tendency for organizational work arrangements to reflect the characteristics of tasks which are allocated to organizational participants. Our studies of teachers and nurses tested this proposition. We operationalized three dimensions of the task conceptions of participants and hypothesized that these task conceptions would be associated with their preferred work arrangements and, to a lesser extent, their actual work arrangements. When clarity, predictability, or efficacy were low, we predicted that more freedom to choose appropriate paths would be expected and provided. To measure perceived clarity of the assigned goals, we asked, "How vague or undefined do your goals for each task appear to you?", with the following response categories: Extremely Vague, Very Vague, Moderately Vague, Slightly Vague, and Not At All Vague. For predictability, we asked, "For each task, how often can you predict which way of doing things is most likely to reach your goals?", with eight response categories: Always, Almost Always, Usually, Fairly Often, Occasionally, Seldom, Almost Never, and Never. The question for efficacy was, "For each task, how often are you successful in reaching your goals?", with the same eight response categories. Each of these questions on clarity, predictability, and efficacy was asked four times for teachers and five times for nurses—once for each task studied.

Our theory indicates that tasks characterized by high clarity, predictability, or efficacy should be assigned by directives rather than delegations. Since directives limit choice of task activities and the freedom of the performer, we used questions on perceived autonomy and freedom to indicate whether, from their viewpoint, performers had received directives or delegations.

To measure actual delegated autonomy for each task, we asked, "Think of the way each task is organized. In general, which of the following describes the way you usually do each task?" The response categories included:

> There is a standard operating procedure you are supposed to follow;
> Someone tells you how to do the task;
> You consult with others and decide together the way the task will be done;
> You consult with others and then you decide how to do the task;
> You alone decide the way the task will be done.

After answering these questions, respondents were asked to indicate their preferred degree of delegated autonomy for each task as follows: "Think of the way you believe each task should be organized. In general, which of the following best describes the way you should usually do each task?" The response categories were identical with those for the previous question, except that the word *should* was inserted in each possible response. For example, "There should be a standard operating procedure you are supposed to follow."

As an alternative measure of delegation, we sought to determine the existing and preferred degree of freedom in performing each task as perceived by the respondent. To determine the existing degree of freedom to make decisions, we asked, "Under present arrangements, how much freedom do you have to determine how each task is done?" The response categories were: A Great Deal of Freedom, Considerable Freedom, Some Freedom, Little Freedom, and No Freedom. The corresponding question for the preferred amount of delegated freedom was, "In this organization, how much freedom *should* you have to determine how each task is done?" All the response categories were identical with those for the previous question.

For most of our analyses we dichotomized the data into high

and low responses, using the median of the responses as the point of separation. However, it seemed to us that some of our response categories could be identified as clearly high or clearly low with respect to their intrinsic meaning; we did not allow any distribution of the data to cause the median to be inserted between these categories. For example, both Extremely Vague and Very Vague were considered high in vagueness, therefore low in clarity, regardless of the distribution of responses. If more than 50 percent of the respondents said that their goals were Extremely Vague, we still regarded those persons who stated that their goals were Very Vague as scoring low in clarity. For efficacy and predictability, similar guidelines were used. The responses Always and Almost Always were defined as high, just as Never and Almost Never were uniformly considered as low. The intrinsic or face-value response was taken into account in all dichotomies and corresponding statistical analyses, and we were faithful to these rules throughout our studies.

With these questions used to operationalize our task conceptions and the degree of actual or preferred delegations of autonomy and freedom in task performance, we could test hypotheses derived from our formulations. For these tests we required information from individuals occupying the same organizational position who performed several tasks and could report on the differing characteristics of these tasks. We obtained the necessary data from three studies of teachers and from a study of registered nurses. (See Magnani, 1970; Marram, 1971; McCauley, 1971.) We used the median response for each task dimension to measure the task conceptions among teachers and nurses. Since the median is a measure of central tendency that is relatively unaffected by extreme or unusual responses, it seemed well calculated to operationalize our notion of task conception. Each task could be given its median score on clarity, efficacy, and predictability, and these scores could be related to the amount of actual and preferred delegation.

We then had an unpleasant surprise. Among the four tasks for teachers and five tasks for nurses, those highest in clarity were also highest in both predictability and efficacy. Although we believed that these three dimensions were positively correlated with each other, we did not expect that we would be unable to disentangle their impact upon organizational arrangements. Unfortunately, for most of our analyses we are able to study only their combined impact upon actual and preferred work arrangements.

In each of our three studies of teachers, the task of Record-Keeping differed greatly from the other three tasks. Record-Keeping had the highest median score in clarity, in predictability, and in efficacy when contrasted with the three other teaching tasks. For nurses, the tasks of Record-Keeping and Carrying Out Doctor's Orders were reported to be highest in clarity, predictability, and efficacy. One way to test our formulation, therefore, was to see whether these more clear, predictable, and efficacious tasks were associated with less delegated autonomy and freedom for performers.

The data from the three studies of teachers and the study of nurses all supported our hypothesized relationship. In each study of teachers, Record-Keeping was the task with the least actual autonomy, least preferred autonomy, least actual freedom, and least preferred freedom. Among nurses, Carrying Out Doctor's Orders and Record-Keeping were, as predicted, the two tasks lowest in delegated autonomy and freedom, actual and preferred. Tasks high in clarity, predictability, and efficacy tended to be allocated by directive, and this arrangement was also the one preferred by performers.

No matter how we analyzed these task differences, we found the same consistent patterns. For example, if, instead of using the median for preferred freedom, we looked at the proportion of respondents in the three studies of teachers who wanted "a great deal of freedom," we recorded .66, .65, .63, and .30 respectively, for Teaching Subject Matter, Character Development, Maintaining Control, and Record-Keeping. Once again Record-Keeping was markedly different from the other three tasks.

Let us briefly look at comparative data for alternative schools. We asked teachers in alternative schools the same questions about the same four tasks that were used in our studies of public schools. In general, teachers in alternative schools viewed all their tasks as lower in clarity, predictability, and efficacy than teachers in the public schools conceived these same tasks. More concretely, alternative school teachers believed that they did not know as much as public school teachers believed they knew with respect to the specificity of their goals, their ability to choose the best route to success, and the likelihood of success in meeting their goals. Since, the median scores for teachers in alternative schools were lower in clarity, predictability, and efficacy, we expected teachers in alternative schools both to want and to receive higher levels of autonomy and freedom. For each task, this was indeed the case. Thus, task conceptions did seem to relate to differences in work arrangements for the same tasks for different types of organizations. The differences were found to be in the predicted direction for all four tasks.

A similar analysis contrasted nurses and public school teachers. Here we were dealing with different tasks, with the exception of Record-Keeping, and so a direct comparison was not possible. However, the average scores on clarity, predictability, and efficacy across all tasks did show that nurses perceived themselves as higher on all these dimensions than teachers perceived themselves. Accordingly, we predicted that nurses would get and desire less autonomy and freedom than would teachers. The data on actual and preferred delegation supported this hypothesis when summarized across five tasks for nurses and four tasks for teachers.

A final note should be of interest. We found that alternative schools, with a largely anti-organizational ideology, were organized in ways that were closely related to the task conceptions of their teachers. In alternative schools the rank correlation between the clarity, predictability, and efficacy of the four tasks and the preferred and actual delegation of freedom and autonomy was always -1.00. Although the magnitude of these correlations is very misleading, based as they are on a ranking of medians which sometimes varied little among tasks, our formulation does successfully predict the differences among tasks in alternative schools where concern for organizational efficiency is regarded as "a middle-class hang-up."

Although we emphasize a task-specific conception of organizational structure, we do not wish to suggest that comparisons cannot be made between occupants of different positions, combining the data across specific tasks. In her study of nurses and teachers, Marram (1971) found that for teachers in public schools the three most important tasks—Teaching Subject Matter, Character Development, and Maintaining Control—were approximately equal in delegated autonomy and freedom. For each of these three tasks the teachers had considerable autonomy and freedom, although for the fourth and least important task, Record-Keeping, delegated autonomy and freedom were low. Marram contrasted this relatively high autonomy for most teacher tasks with the much greater variability of the work situation for nurses. Nurses reported two tasks as their most important, Carrying out Doctor's Orders and Observation and Assessment, with Providing Comfort and Support only slightly behind. Looking at their most important tasks, we found that delegated freedom and autonomy were very low for Carrying out Doctor's Orders and very high for Observation and Assessment. Thus, the two most important tasks for nurses were quite different in their degree of delegation. Just using these data to report descriptively on the work situation of teachers and nurses, teachers seemed to have a high degree of delegated freedom and autonomy for all their tasks, save the least important task, while nurses perceived both directives and delegations among tasks which were most important. We can speculate, as does Marram, that the hospital structure provides more variability in the work arrangements for nurses because the tasks are regarded as crucial, and mistakes can often be devastating and not correctable.

At this point, we can report one of our failures. We expected that the evaluators of a task performance, who are typically more distant from the scene, would be more likely than the performer to emphasize the predictability of resistance to the achievement of task goals. We hypothesized, therefore, that principals would see a teacher's tasks as less active than would the teachers, who would stress the active, unpredictable quality of their work. Similarly, we compared the task conceptions of nurses and their supervisors. Although there were difficulties in the way we measured perceptions of superiors and subordinates, we found no reliable differences between evaluators and performers in their views of tasks as active or inert. It is possible that shared professional socialization, common backgrounds of training and experience, links supervisors to performers among teachers and nurses, overcoming the relationship we predicted. But for whatever reason, there was no tendency for evaluators, more than performers, to see tasks as inert.

Having tested our predictions for groups of performers, we can now shift our level of analysis to that of the individual respondent. If there were almost perfect consensus on task conceptions, differences among individuals would be reflections of chance processes. But, since respondents varied in the ways in which they viewed the same task, we can use our formulation to predict preferred arrangements from the individual's view of the task. Thus, at this point, our interest shifts from task conceptions to differences in the perceptions of a task by individual performers. For example, we predicted that persons who viewed a given task as having a more diffuse goal for that task would desire more autonomy than those who viewed their task goals as relatively clear and specific. For each task performed by teachers we computed gammas, nonparametric measures of the association of clarity with preferred autonomy and with preferred freedom. Computing gammas separately for each of the three studies of teachers produced three sets of four gammas to measure the relation between task clarity and preferred autonomy, and three sets of four gammas for the relation between clarity and preferred freedom. Of the resulting twenty-four gammas, seventeen were in the expected direction. However, the median gamma was only $-.21$, indicating that individual differences in the perception of task clarity were only slightly related to preferred delegation of autonomy and freedom.

We employed the same technique to examine the impact of individual differences in perception of the other task dimensions. Our results for predictability and efficacy were similar. Of the twenty-four gammas, nineteen were in the expected direction when predictability was used as the independent variable, and seventeen were in the expected direction when efficacy was used to predict preferred autonomy and freedom. The median gamma relating predictability to preferred autonomy and freedom was $-.16$, and the median gamma relating efficacy to preferred autonomy and freedom was $-.12$.

To summarize our analyses of the relationship between our dimensions of task conceptions and preferred work arrangements, differences among tasks with respect to clarity, predictability, and efficacy were related to preferred delegation of autonomy and freedom. Using the median response on each of these three dimensions as a single number to characterize each task, we found that there was a consistent negative association when clarity, predictability, and efficacy were related to preferred and actual delegation of autonomy and preferred and actual delegation of freedom. However, the correlations among the three task dimensions were sufficiently large to preclude our separating out the effects of each dimension on work arrangements. The same negative relationship reappeared when we focused on individual differences among participants, testing whether participants who were above average in their perception of a task as clear, efficacious, or predictable preferred less autonomy and freedom than those who viewed the task as less clear, efficacious, or predictable. However, the results were much weaker and much less consistent when we based our analyses on such individual differences in perception than when we analyzed task conceptions using medians for a set of position occupants. Organizational arrangements, both preferred and actual, were more likely to reflect average conceptions of the task dimensions than to be based on individual perceptions.

As is clear from our results, the three dimensions of task conception are positively correlated with each other. For example, Magnani (1970) found that teachers who reported higher clarity of their tasks tended to report higher efficacy and predictability, with gammas of .48 and .43 respectively. The relationship between efficacy and predictability was even closer. Since predictability refers to the best route and efficacy is concerned with the likelihood of success, many respondents gave identical answers to the questions on these two dimensions. In this study we made the mistake of placing the questions next to one another, so that about three-fifths of the teachers gave identical answers for the predictability and efficacy of a task, producing a gamma of .88. These results raise questions as to the utility of using three dimensions of task conception.

An earlier theoretical paper suggested inert-active as a single dimension on which tasks differ (Scott, Dornbusch, and others, 1967). Essentially we were talking about predictability, for we defined active tasks as those facing considerable unpredictable resistance to achieving the allocated goal. Analysis of the relative utility of our three dimensions suggests that predictability is indeed the best single measure, although it is only marginally better than efficacy as a predictor of preferred and actual work arrangements. We cannot expect predictability to be much more closely related to work arrangements than efficacy, given the high correlation between reported efficacy and predictability. Nevertheless, comparisons of these correlations usually indicate that the gamma between predictability and the dependent variable is sligthly stronger in the expected direction.

We also must note that, somewhat to our surprise, clarity is often reported as so high that it does not differentiate well among tasks. Most teachers, for example, believed their goals, even on Character Development, were Not At All Vague. Assuming that our measures are valid, it is such findings that led us to conclude that clarity of goals is an important basis for differentiating between semiprofessionals and the more fully developed professional occupations. As noted in Chapter Three, the goals for semiprofessionals are relatively high in clarity largely because the organizations by which they are employed assume the right to set the goals. Vague goals are displaced by more specific goals. Thus, Character Development comes to be interpreted as the inculcation of speciflc skills, for example, training students to respect authority and rules, to take turns, and to be courteous.

Finally, combining the three dimensions to predict preferred freedom and autonomy did not produce gammas that were appreciably higher than those for predictability or efficacy considered alone. To sum up, although the differences are not sufficiently great to permit us to be confident of our choice, we would select predictability as the single dimension of task conceptions which is most powerful and reliable in predicting differences in preferred and actual work arrangements.

Propriety and Stability. Our formulation states that control systems which are viewed as improper by participants are more likely to be unstable. We can use discrepancies between performers' reports of actual and preferred working arrangements as indicators of the propriety of the control system. Magnani tested our prediction that the more performers perceived their current work arrangements as improper—that is, reported the greatest difference between their actual level of autonomy and their preferred level of autonomy—the more they would engage in instability behavior—express dissatisfaction, suggest changes, and not comply with control attempts.

Chapter Five discusses the evaluation process, breaking it down into four components: allocation, criteria-setting, sampling, and appraisal. Magnani (1970) measured actual and preferred autonomy for the first three components of the evaluation system. He discovered that teachers were more aware of the extent to which they had autonomy with respect to allocation than of their autonomy with respect to other parts of the evaluation process. Teachers had little knowledge of what criteria were used or what information was collected to evaluate them. We present here Magnani's findings (1970) for the combination of all three forms of autonomy, but we look in detail only at autonomy with respect to allocation, the most reliable measure.

To measure the propriety of existing arrangements, Magnani measured the difference between the actual and preferred level of autonomy on allocation, criteria-setting, and sampling for each of four teaching tasks. He developed an ordinal scale to measure the level of propriety. Three levels of propriety were determined by comparing responses. The lowest level represented a difference of three or more response categories between the levels of preferred and actual autonomy; the middle level of propriety represented a difference of two response categories; and the highest level of propriety indicated identical responses to the two questions or a difference of only one response category. The three kinds of autonomy and the four teaching tasks thus provided us with twelve measures of autonomy for each of 131 teachers.

To measure instability behavior, part of the more general concept of instability, Magnani used four measures of the frequency of instability responses: expressing dissatisfaction to others in the organization, suggesting changes to others in the organization, not complying when told what to do or delaying in carrying out orders, and preventing evaluators from receiving information about performances. The last two measures are both forms of noncompliance to the structure of control. The specific questions were: "How frequently do you tell others in the school, publicly or privately, that you are dissatisfied with the way each task is assigned or evaluated?"; "How frequently do you suggest changes to others in the school because you are dissatisfied with the way each task is assigned or evaluated?"; "How frequently do you decide not to do all or part of what you are told, or decide to delay in doing it?"; "How frequently do you prevent information from being obtained on how you are doing on each task or any part of it?" The four measures of instability behavior were applied to each of the twelve measures of autonomy, providing forty-eight gammas representing the relationship between impropriety and instability behavior. The measures are, of course, not independent, and we used them only to obtain a general picture supporting or refuting our hypothesis.

The data strongly supported our formulation relating propriety to stability. Forty-one of the forty-eight gammas were positive, six were negative, and one was zero. Five of the six negative gammas occurred when the two measures of noncompliance were related to impropriety. Since other data in Magnani's study indicated that teachers rarely were given direct orders or were in a position to prevent information from being obtained by their principal, the weaker relationship for the noncompliance measures may be a function of existing work arrangements. But even for noncompliance, nineteen out of twenty-four gammas were positive.

If we limit our attention to autonomy with respect to allocation, the form of autonomy of which teachers were most aware, the relationship between impropriety and instability is clear. When expressing dissatisfaction in the measure, the gamma between impropriety and instability behavior ranges from .58 to 1.00 for the four tasks. For suggesting changes, the gammas are only slightly lower, ranging from .41 to .82. The eight gammas for the two measures of noncompliance are much lower, ranging from −.15 to .58, but even for noncompliance, the mean gamma is .18. In general, therefore, every analysis supports the hypothesis that work arrangements considered improper tend to be unstable.

Influence and Importance

It is central to our theory of authority within organizations that perceived influence upon organizational sanctions will lead to perceived importance of evaluations and evaluators. Evaluations which can affect the rewards and penalties of the organization are likely to be important to the person evaluated. Using data from the

Five Organizations study we have chosen several different ways of testing this relationship; all give strong support to it.

Importance of Evaluations. A prerequisite for the use of evaluations to control the behavior of organizational participants is that they care about the sanctions controlled by the organization. To test the scope of our theory, we purposely selected two volunteer organizations: the student newspaper and the varsity football team. These organizations were expected to differ from each other on the importance attached by participants to organizational sanctions. They did, indeed, differ on this dimension. We inquired about sanctions by asking participants in the student newspaper and the football team the question: "How important to you are the organizational rewards and penalties which the (organization) offers?" The five response categories were: Not at All Important, Slightly Important, Moderately Important, Very Important, and Extremely Important. The proportion of football players viewing sanctions administered by their organization as Very or Extremely Important was 85 percent compared with only 14 percent for workers on the student newspaper. These data can be put into perspective by noting that 66 percent of nurses, 45 percent of public school teachers, and 25 percent of the teachers in alternative schools viewed their organizational rewards and penalties as Very or Extremely Important.

Unfortunately, we chose too well in selecting the organizations within which to examine the relationship between the importance of sanctions and the importance of evaluations. The differences in responses between the student newspaper and the football team were great, but the variability within each organization was slight. To measure the importance of evaluations we asked: "How important to you are the evaluations you receive for your performance on (this task)?" Response categories were identical to those employed for the question on importance of sanctions. The questions on the importance of evaluations and of sanctions were widely separated in the interview. We hoped that this separation would reduce the likelihood of any respondent providing us with an artifically strong association between sanctions and evaluations.

The difference between the student newspaper and the

football team can be demonstrated by simply recording the proportion of persons viewing evaluations and sanctions as Very Important
and Extremely Important. For the desk workers, five out of fifteen
saw evaluations as Very or Extremely Important, and three out of
fifteen saw sanctions as Very or Extremely Important. Similarly, for
the copy editors, three out of fourteen saw evaluations as Very or
Extremely Important, and only one viewed sanctions as Very or
Extremely Important. The picture for the football team was reversed. Forty-five out of fifty-three saw their sanctions as at least
Very Important, and forty-eight out of fifty-three saw their evaluations as at least Very Important. Of course, there is a real difficulty
in interpreting the link between higher importance for both evaluations and sanctions for football players compared with workers on
the student newspaper as evidence of a link between evaluation processes and sanctions. We believe that the importance of the sanctions
caused the evaluations to be more important; but there were many
other ways in which these two organizations differed.

In order to control for this contextual problem we tried to
see what relationship there was between the importance of sanctions
and the importance of evaluations for individuals within the student
newspaper and within the football team. Unfortunately, although
the relationships tended to be in the predicted direction, they were
based upon a ludicrously small number of cases. A shift of one or
two cases would reverse the direction. The best we could do was to
combine the data from the student newspaper and the data from
the football team. Of course, this masked the differences between
the two organizations, but it did introduce, in the combined sample,
sufficient variability so that we could assess the power of the predicted relationship between the importance of sanctions and the importance of evaluations for individuals. When we dichotomized responses so that high importance for sanctions was Extremely or
Very Important and so that high importance for evaluations was
Extremely or Very Important, we found a strong relationship in the
predicted direction. Twenty-one of the thirty-three persons who attributed low importance to sanctions perceived their evaluations as
low in importance, while only five out of forty-nine persons who
attributed high importance to sanctions perceived the importance of
evaluations as low. The gamma for this relationship was .88. The

relationship was indeed very powerful, although we must remember that the data came from combining responses from two very different organizations. Once again, if sanctions were important to performers, then the evaluations that affect those sanctions were also important to them.

Importance of Evaluators. Although we obtained data on the overall importance of evaluations from only a subset of our respondents in the Five Organizations study, we have data from all respondents on the importance which they attached to specific categories of evaluators and on the extent to which they saw those evaluators as having influence over organizational sanctions. For this analysis, we considered only those respondents who reported more than one evaluator and who assigned differing levels of influence and importance to them. Among our 224 respondents were 103 individuals who reported multiple evaluators and reported variation on both variables.

To test the prediction that perceived influence over sanctions leads to perceived importance as an evaluator, we obtained a list of organizational evaluators from each respondent and then asked: "How important to you is (each specific evaluator's) evaluation of how well or poorly you are doing on (this task)?" Our scale of importance contained five response categories: Extremely Important, Very Important, Moderately Important, Slightly Important, and Not At All Important. To determine how much influence each evaluator was perceived to have on sanctions, each respondent was asked later in the interview: "How much influence do (each specific evaluator's) evaluations of your work as a (position) have on your organizational rewards and penalties?" The same categories were employed for this question, except that Important was replaced by Influential.

With appropriate data available for 103 individuals located in many differing positions within five quite different organizations we found strong support for our prediction. Dichotomizing influence and importance at the median for each respondent, persons perceived as having more influence on organizational sanctions were more likely to be perceived as being important evaluators. For ninety-three independent tests, the data were in the predicted direction. For only ten individuals out of 103 was the hypothesis not supported.

Our emphasis upon sanctions as the basis for importance of evaluators would no doubt be challenged by those who perceive many types of workers, but especially professionals, as having internalized standards, depending upon colleagues for evaluations, and thereby excluding themselves from concern with anything so crass as organizational rewards and penalties. We do not doubt that such occupational socialization does take place. But many organizations give professionals some control over meting out rewards and penalties to their peers. In this manner, professional standards can affect the distribution of sanctions, and the possession of internalized professional standards need not run counter to a general relationship between the influence of evaluators upon sanctions and their perceived importance as evaluators. Indeed, we found that the relation between perceived influence on sanctions and perceived importance of evaluators was just as strong for respondents in professional positions as for nonprofessionals. And even the ten "failures" in the 103 individual tests of our hypothesis were not more likely to be found among professional respondents. Nevertheless, internalized standards remain a significant variable affecting the importance of evaluations.

We argued in the previous chapter that evaluators may be regarded as important for reasons other than their control over organizational sanctions. To explore these areas, toward the end of our interview we stated: "Earlier you told me how important to you are the evaluations from each of your evaluators," and we summarized the previous responses at each level of importance. We then asked, "Are there any other people or groups of people connected with (the organization), or outside of (the organization) whose evaluations of you as a (position) are important to you?" If the respondent gave any nonorganizational evaluators, we then asked, "Why is (this evaluator's) evaluation of you as a (position) important to you?" This gave us the basis for the perceived importance of the nonorganizational evaluators who were named.

We hypothesized that those in professional positions would be more likely than nonprofessionals to report evaluators who were important even though they had no influence upon organizational sanctions. The data strongly supported this prediction. When we computed the mean number of nonorganizational evaluators for each occupational position, senior residents were highest at 2.7, followed by clinical clerks at 2.4, interns at 2.3, nursing team leaders at 2.1, and engineers at 1.9. The top five groups in number of nonorganizational evaluators reported were our five most professional positions. They usually named colleagues or clients as those persons who were important to them even without influence on organizational sanctions.

When we examined the reasons which were given for considering as important an evaluator who did not influence organizational sanctions, we again found a strong relationship to professionalism. The reasons given were classified into six categories: competence of the evaluator, improving the task performance, responsibilities and obligations to others, potential influence on nonorganizational sanctions, interpersonal relations, and a residual category. The first three categories would be, we hypothesized, related to professionalism, for each represented an internalized concern with proper performance.

Combining these three types of performance-oriented reasons for the importance of a noninfluential evaluator, we expected that the more professional positions would be more likely to emphasize them than would the nonprofessional respondents. Indeed, for nursing team leaders, 64 percent of all such responses fell within these three categories, and the corresponding percentages for clinical clerks were 50 percent, for interns, 58 percent, and for senior residents, 52 percent. These were the only groups in which the majority of the reasons for the importance of a nonorganizational evaluator fell within these three categories.

One professional position, that of engineers, was surprisingly low in selecting nonorganizational evaluators for professional reasons. Only 21 percent of the reasons for importance of noninfluential evaluators given by engineers related to competence, improving performance, or responsibilities and obligations. One basis for the apparent failure of our prediction became obvious when we looked at the reasons that engineers did give. They emphasized control over important future sanctions, in particular, the ability of others to aid them in getting another job. This type of reason suggested the presence of a high level of job insecurity among engineers in the research facility we studied. Because of basic changes in the operation of the facility at the time of our study, many engineering jobs were being terminated, and hiring patterns were changing. Examination of the responses for draftsmen in the research facility revealed the same high level of anxiety, with corresponding attention to others who might be brokers for new positions. Other research suggests that engineers lack some of the important qualities of the full-fledged professions and that, in general, they are beset by job insecurity (Perrucci and Gerstl, 1969). In any case, our own small sample revealed important differences between engineers and various categories of physicians and nurses with respect to the bases for selecting nonorganizational evaluators.

In summary, for all types of positions examined there was a strong positive relationship between perceived ability to influence the distribution of organizational sanctions and perceived importance as an evaluator. Respondents in professional as well as nonprofessional positions adhered to this general pattern. However, those in professional positions were more likely than others to perceive nonorganizational evaluators as important.

Importance of Tasks. So far, all our analyses relating influence on sanctions to importance have been based on data gathered from position occupants who each responded in terms of a single task. We can further examine this relationship by turning to those studies in which we asked participants about several of their tasks. Instead of focusing on evaluators, we can test our prediction by using tasks as the basis of comparison. Our new hypothesis is that those tasks whose evaluations are regarded as more influential in determining rewards and penalties will be considered more important by performers. Data for these tests come from our studies of public school teachers and nurses.

To measure the influence and importance of each task, very early in the questionnaire, immediately after the tasks were first introduced and defined, both teachers and nurses were asked: "How important to you are each of these tasks?" Response categories ranged from Extremely Important to Not At All Important. Toward the end of the questionnaire, nurses and teachers were told: "Evaluations of tasks may differ in their influence upon organizational rewards and penalties. The evaluation of one task may influence your rewards greatly, while the evaluation of other tasks may have no influence." Following this statement, the question was put: "How much influence do evaluations of your performance on each task have on your organizational rewards and penalties?" The four teaching tasks or the five nursing tasks were then listed with response categories ranging from Extremely Influential to Not At All Influential.

For both nurses and teachers there was a positive association between the ranking of tasks in terms of their perceived influence on sanctions and their ranking on perceived importance. The relation was stronger for teachers in public schools, with a gamma of .67, than it was for nurses, where the gamma was .40. Those tasks for which evaluations were greater in their impact upon sanctions were perceived to be more important by both sets of respondents. This relation is consistent with our view that, where sanctions are important, influence upon sanctions helps to determine perceived importance. Even in free schools there was a positive association between the importance of tasks and their influence on the distribution of sanctions. Of course, the causal direction of the association is left in doubt by correlational data, and there are good reasons for believing that these two variables are mutually interdependent.

The study of teachers and nurses provided an opportunity for a further refinement of our analysis. There are many factors which can affect subjective feelings of task importance in addition to the evaluation process. But, we would expect that, given a task which is considered to be important for any reason, the performer will want the evaluation of that task to have an impact upon organizational rewards and penalties. We would, therefore, predict that the correlation between the *desired* influence of evaluations on a given task and its importance should be higher than the correlation between *actual* influence and importance for this same task. After respondents had reported their perceptions of the actual influence of task evaluations for each task, they were asked: "How much influence *should* evaluations of your performance on each task have on your organizational rewards and penalties?" The same response categories were employed as for the question on actual influence.

The data were generally consistent with our expectation. For teachers, the gamma relating importance with desired influence was 1.0, compared with .67 with actual influence. For nurses, the gamma was .80 for desired influence, compared with .40 for actual influence. Minimally, we can conclude that performers want the distribution of sanctions to reflect in a balanced fashion the relative importance of tasks as they perceive them.

Before leaving the topic of influence on sanctions and importance of tasks, we feel compelled to comment more generally on the situation in public schools as revealed by our three studies. Many observers of the American public school system have noted the lack of control exercised by appropriate school officials over classroom teachers and have suggested that the heart of the problem resides in the lack of value attached by teachers to organizational rewards and penalties. We have already noted that the teachers in our studies did not place particularly great importance on organizational sanctions when compared with nurses, for example, although teachers did place some importance on them. We believe that, to the extent that there is a failure in the control system within public schools, it may not be so much a function of schools lacking a set of valued rewards and penalties as, rather, that the evaluation system used to assess task performance does not have sufficient impact on the distribution of these sanctions.

Nurses reported that evaluations of their task performances had greater influence upon sanctions than did teachers. Only one teaching task, Teaching Subject Matter, fell within the range of the five nursing tasks with respect to the influence that evaluations of each task had upon rewards and penalties. Principals agreed with teachers that evaluations of teachers' tasks had a low level of influence on sanctions. In fact, we found no significant difference between principals' and teachers' perceptions of the influence of evaluations of each task upon sanctions.

Given that teachers perceive their current task evaluations as having a relatively low impact on organizational rewards and penalties, we can examine their perceptions as to what would be desirable. We found that teachers wanted evaluations to have a greater influence on sanctions than they currently reported, and, in accordance with our previous findings, they desired the greatest increase in influence for the evaluations of Teaching Subject Matter and Character Development, the two tasks that were regarded as most important by the average teacher. These data indicate that increased control via the evaluation process is considered appropriate by performers when the structure of control is in accord with performers' perceptions of the relative importance of their tasks.

We have shown that there is a relation between the influence which evaluations of task performances have on the distribution of organizational sanctions and the importance which is attached to those tasks. Indeed, performers strive for balance between the importance of a task to them and the influence of evaluations of their performance on that task.

Direction of Causation Between Influence and Importance. To conclude this discussion, we turn our attention to data collected by Turner (1971) on the evaluative relation between pastors and assistant pastors in 101 parishes within a single archdiocese of the Roman Catholic Church. These data allow us not only to replicate portions of the preceding analysis using a much more detailed categorization of tasks performed, but also help us attack the problem of interpreting the direction of causation between influence on sanctions and importance. Ideally, we would like to test our formulation longitudinally, observing how organizational evaluations and sanctions shape over a period of time the views and behavior of individuals as they work within the archdiocese. Instead, we have used cross-sectional analysis as an imperfect substitute for the passage of time, comparing the responses of younger to older priests, or examining the effect of length of service since ordination. Either length of tenure or age, highly correlated with each other, provides a basis for discerning the way in which the evaluation process becomes a basis for social control. Obviously, cross-sectional analysis does not permit us the degree of control that one would obtain by employing a longitudinal design. It does not, for example, eliminate the effects of a changing environment or altered recruitment patterns. But it does provide some additional types of data to test our hypotheses and, for the first time, provides some evidence relating to the direction of causation.

As was the practice in the studies previously reported, each assistant pastor was asked to identify his evaluators and then asked: "How important to you personally are the evaluations of each of those you mentioned?" Again, the five response categories ranged from Extremely Important to Not At All Important. Similarly, later in the interview, after we had determined the personal importance of each evaluator named, we inquired about each evaluator's influence upon sanctions, using the same question employed in previous studies.

Using these cross-sectional data, we tested the hypothesis that importance ascribed to an evaluator would tend with time to reflect more and more closely the influence that evaluators had on organizational sanctions. Specifically, we expected that the older assistant pastors, compared with younger assistants, would report greater convergence in their ratings of an evaluator's influence on sanctions and his importance. Let us briefly summarize the findings for four classes of evaluators: the bishop, the pastor, peers (other assistant pastors), and parishioners (clients). Gammas were computed within dichotomized age groups of assistant pastors to express the relationship between the assistant pastor's perception of the evaluator's influence and the importance attached to his evaluations. We did, indeed, find that the gammas between influence and importance for young assistant pastors, aged twenty-six to thirty-five, were markedly less positive than the gammas for assistant pastors aged thirty-six and older.

For the bishop, the gamma between influence on sanctions and importance was $-.41$ for young assistant pastors, and it was a striking 1.00 for the older assistant pastors. There were only a few older assistant pastors who perceived the bishop as low in influence, and every one of these exceptional older assistants, in accordance with our hypothesis, considered the bishop low in importance. For the pastors as evaluators, the result was equally strong. The gamma for young assistant pastors relating influence to importance was $-.08$, and for older assistant pastors it was .79. The findings for peers and parishioners also strongly confirmed our hypothesis. For peers, the gamma between influence and importance was $-.29$ for young assistant pastors, and .45 for older assistant pastors. For parishioners as evaluators, the gamma moved up from $-.32$ for young assistant pastors to .12 for older assistant pastors. We therefore found, for every set of evaluators, that older assistant pastors, compared with younger assistant pastors, showed a much closer relationship between influence upon sanctions and importance of the evaluator.

The preceding analysis was based on individual differences among 106 assistant pastors in their perceptions of their evaluators. We can also aggregate the data for all assistant pastors and see if older assistant pastors, compared with younger assistant pastors, reduce the difference between the average perception of influence and importance. Two evaluators, the bishop and the pastor, were perceived by younger assistant pastors as high in influence and not as high in importance to them. Two other sets of evaluators, peers and parishioners, were perceived by younger assistant pastors as high in importance and low in influence. For older assistant pastors, the importance of the bishop was, in accordance with our theory, markedly higher. The proportion considering the bishop high in importance rose from 11 percent for younger assistant pastors, to 52 percent for older assistant pastors. The importance of pastors was not higher for older assistant pastors, but this may be partially explained by the fact that pastors were the only evaluators whom older assistant pastors considered less influential than did younger assistant pastors. Similarly, the predicted decline in importance for peers and parishioners was found among the older assistant pastors. In general, older assistant pastors as a group viewed the importance of a set of evaluators as more closely associated with the influence of those evaluators than did younger assistant pastors as a group.

We have been looking at evaluators to see whether differences in their influence on sanctions are related to differences in their importance as evaluators. We have shown that more influential evaluators tend to be perceived as more important evaluators. Let us now turn our attention to an analagous relationship for tasks, to see whether those tasks whose evaluations are perceived to be more influential in determining the distribution of sanctions tend to become the more important tasks. It will be recalled that we have rather detailed data on tasks performed by assistant pastors in the parish—in all, twenty-two tasks were examined in this study.

Relying on his own knowledge of parish tasks, Turner categorized these twenty-two tasks into two broad types: primarily professional tasks and primarily bureaucratic tasks, which included domestic activities. The tasks are listed earlier in this chapter. For present purposes, we need not be particularly concerned with the accuracy of the assignment of each task by this classification, but only need to assume that in general the two types of tasks were appropriately distinguished.

To facilitate their responses to a set of questions about parish tasks, all assistant pastors interviewed were presented with a list of these twenty-two tasks. Each assistant pastor was first asked: "How important is it to you personally that you do well on each of these activities?" Following his response to this question for each of the tasks, he was asked: "How important is it to your pastor that you do well on each of these activities, in determining his total evaluation of you as an assistant pastor?" The same scale of importance was used for both questions. Also, since the list of tasks was long, to eliminate the possibility that ordinal position on the list could bias responses, three different lists were employed with the order randomly determined on each list. No effect of order on importance was discerned when the particular list was cross-tabulated against the degree of importance assigned to each task.

Let us first examine the views of assistant pastors on the importance attributed by superiors to the tasks they perform. We found that assistant pastors perceived pastors as placing more importance than they themselves did on thirteen of the fourteen bureaucratic tasks. Conversely, assistant pastors perceived that pastors placed less importance than they themselves did on seven of the eight professional tasks. Given this information as to the perceived interests of these highly influential evaluators, we would expect that, with time, assistant pastors would come to reflect the evaluations of task importance of the pastors. (Again, since we lack longitudinal data, differences among respondents in length of tenure are employed to represent changes with time.) The data are consistent with this prediction. Assistant pastors ordained for a period of more than ten years placed greater importance on the bureaucratic tasks than did assistant pastors ordained for less than ten years. More precisely, only two of the fourteen bureaucratic tasks were viewed as more important by the more recently ordained assistants than by those whose ordination occurred more than ten years ago. Similarly, those assistants who were recently ordained gave higher importance ratings to six of the eight professional activities than did assistants who were ordained more than ten years ago. In sum, to the extent that we can interpret differences among respondents in length of tenure to represent changes in individual attitudes over a period of time, it appears that the longer these assistant pastors remain in this control structure, the more nearly their own views of task importance coincide with those of their closest influential evaluator, the pastor.

All pastors were once assistant pastors, and they had probably felt similar pressures during their tenure as assistants. We therefore sought an analogous set of influences in the careers of pastors. Experience within the parish is not the only conceivable source for increased sensitivity to hierarchical evaluations. It is quite possible that other work experiences in which bureaucratic evaluations are emphasized could have consequences for pastors similar to the effects of long tenure within a parish setting for assistant pastors. To test this reasoning, we classified all nonparochial job experiences reported by pastors into two categories: settings placing great emphasis on hierarchical evaluation and those placing relatively less emphasis on such evaluations. In the former category were such work experiences as holding positions in Chancery Office, or being a military, hospital, or prison chaplain. In the latter category, we placed jobs in schools and diocesan jobs performed away from the Chancery Office. This categorization produced approximately equal numbers of the 101 pastors in each of the three categories: primarily hierarchical, primarily nonhierarchical, and no experience outside the parish. We could then test our general expectation regarding the impact of various types of outside experiences on perceived importance of tasks.

The most obvious test of the impact of these outside experiences was to compare the importance assigned to the assistant pastor's tasks by pastors with considerable hierarchical experience and by pastors with little hierarchical experience. Considering first the eight professional tasks, pastors with little hierarchical experience viewed seven of them as more important in the work of the assistant pastor than did pastors with primarily hierarchical experience. Among the fourteen bureaucratic tasks, pastors with considerable hierarchical experience viewed ten of them as more important than did pastors with little hierarchical experience.

Another way of examining the same data regarding the impact of outside experiences was to analyze the pastors' choices of the five most important tasks for the assistant pastors. Among pastors with little outside hierarchical experience, 55 percent of the tasks selected by them as the five most important were professional tasks, while for pastors with considerable outside hierarchical experience, professional tasks constituted 44 percent of their choices of the five most important tasks. In addition, the impact of outside experiences was reinforced by the fact that persons with considerable hierarchical experience perceived the influence of parishioners and peers as lower, and that of the bishop as higher, than did pastors with little outside hierarchical experience. For this test, as for all but one of the preceding comparisons, the data showed that pastors with no non-parochial experience fell between the measures for those with little and those with considerable hierarchical experiences. The data almost invariably support the proposition that the nature of nonpastoral experience retards or reinforces the process of bureaucratization in the Church.

Finally, we examined the impact of agreement on task importance between the assistant pastor and his pastor. Here we examined the pastor and the assistant pastor as a pair, using each pair as a unit of analysis to predict the frequency of dissatisfaction of the pastor with the performance of the assistant pastor, and the satisfaction of the assistant pastor with the evaluations made by his pastor. We asked each pastor, "How frequently are you dissatisfied with your assistant pastor in his performance of those tasks which you or he consider important?" And we asked each assistant pastor, "In general, how satisfied are you with the evaluations made by your pastor regarding your performance as an assistant pastor?" Both assistant pastor and pastor were asked to choose the five most important tasks of the assistant pastor. We predicted that a state of agreement between pastor and assistant pastor on the importance of tasks would result in lower frequency of dissatisfaction by the pastor, and a higher level of satisfaction with the pastor's evaluation on the part of the assistant pastor. The data confirmed our expectations. The greater the actual overlap between assistant pastor and pastor on choice of important tasks, the lower the frequency of the pastor's dissatisfaction, with a gamma of −.36, and the higher the satisfaction of the assistant pastor with the pastor's evaluations, with a gamma of .32.

We next tested a series of hypotheses relating dissatisfaction of the pastor and satisfaction of the assistant pastor, not to the actual agreement between pastor and assistant pastor in their choice of the latter's five most important tasks, but to their perceptions of the situation. Each pastor was asked his perception of which five tasks were most important to the assistant pastor. Similarly each assistant pastor was asked his perception of which of his tasks were considered most important by the pastor. We predicted that the perception of agreement—high overlap between a respondent's choice of the five most important tasks and his perception of the five tasks most important to the other—would lead to a higher level of satisfaction for the respondent as well as for the other. This perception of agreement, it was argued, would influence the interaction itself, and so produce a favorable image in both parties.

The data supported our hypotheses relating the perception of agreement on the importance of tasks to the pastor's dissatisfaction and the assistant pastor's satisfaction. The greater the pastor's perception of overlap, the lower his dissatisfaction, with a gamma of −.20, and the higher the assistant pastor's satisfaction, with a gamma of .46. The greater the assistant pastor's perception of overlap, the lower was the pastor's dissatisfaction, with a gamma of −.52, and the greater the assistant pastor's satisfaction, with a gamma of .62. Thus, the perception of agreement by either party to the interaction was associated with more satisfaction for both parties.

Could this impact of the perception of agreement merely be a product of the actual overlap between pastor's and assistant pastor's choices? We controlled for the level of actual overlap and still found a strong relationship between the perception of agreement and satisfaction. Similarly, we found that accuracy of perception did not relate to satisfaction. It is the *belief* in agreement that has the most powerful effect. If evaluator and performer believe that they agree on which tasks are important, they are both likely to be more satisfied even when their belief is wrong. This finding is probably related to our earlier finding that performers want the structure of control to be consistent with the perceived importance of their tasks.

Summary

Using task-specific data, we first showed a relationship between task conceptions and organizational work arrangements. Tasks which were perceived as lower in clarity, predictability, and efficacy, were more likely to be delegated, giving autonomy and freedom to the performers, and such arrangements were more likely to be preferred for these tasks. We were unable to separate the impact of these three dimensions of tasks, nor could we demonstrate that superiors were more likely than subordinates to view tasks as inert. But we could show that work arrangements which were perceived as less proper were more unstable. The greater the difference between actual and preferred work arrangements, the more frequently performers engaged in instability behaviors.

We next showed that influence over the distribution of organizational rewards and penalties was related to the importance of evaluations and evaluators. Where organizational sanctions were less important, evaluations were regarded as less important. Using each individual respondent as a separate test of our hypothesis, we found strong evidence that evaluators who were perceived as higher in influence over sanctions were perceived as more important evaluators. This relationship was also present for professionals in our studies, although we did find that professionals were more likely to report some evaluators who were important to them even though they had no influence upon organizational sanctions. Just as the influence of evaluators was shown to be related to their importance, so we found a relationship between the influence of evaluations of each task upon rewards and penalties and the importance of the task to the performers. In addition, performers wanted the distribution of sanctions to reflect in an even more balanced fashion the relative importance of tasks as they perceived them.

Finally, we used data on the age and tenure of pastors and assistant pastors in a Roman Catholic archdiocese to provide a cross-sectional substitute for a longitudinal study. We found that there was a closer match between organizational influence of evaluators and their perceived importance for older assistant pastors than for younger assistant pastors. Similarly, since pastors emphasized bureaucratic tasks and assistant pastors emphasized professional tasks, we found that assistant pastors with longer tenure more nearly resembled pastors in viewing bureaucratic tasks as more important and professional tasks as less important than did assistant pastors with shorter tenure. Analysis of data from pastors also showed that the more or less hierarchical nature of experiences which they had in a nonpastoral context reinforced or retarded the process of bureaucratization in the Church. The direction of causation was clear: influence led to importance, both for tasks and for evaluators.

Analysis of the dyadic relationships within each parish, one pastor and one assistant pastor, showed that actual agreement on the importance of tasks was related to a lower frequency of dissatisfaction expressed by the pastor and a higher level of satisfaction for the assistant pastor. Perceived agreement, as distinguished from actual agreement, had the same effect. Controlling for the level of actual agreement, we found that accurate perception of task importance for the other was not a good predictor, but that the perception of agreement remained highly associated with less dissatisfaction by the pastor and more satisfaction of the assistant. Believing that there was agreement affected the interaction and had real consequences for both the believer and his associate.

Chapter 5

Evaluation Process

▲▲

Organizations are power structures in which some participants are given differential access to organizational rewards and penalties in order to control other participants. Evaluation is required if power is to be employed to control behavior. If A has power over B and wishes to use this power to control B's behavior, A must indicate to B what he or she wants B to do, determine what criteria to employ in judging B's success or failure, and make some attempt to ascertain the extent to which B's behavior conforms to these criteria. A may then sanction B, rewarding conformity or success, or punishing nonconformity or failure. Evaluation is one of the most commonplace of human acts. Each of us evaluates many things and many others, and each of us is evaluated many times a day by others. Our concern with evaluation, however, is restricted to evaluations (1) of organizational participants (2) by organizational evaluators—those whose evaluations help to determine the distribution of organizational sanctions—(3) which represent attempts by evaluators to assess participants' performances on organizational tasks. The end product of this assessment or evaluation process will be termed a *performance evaluation.*

134

We emphasize that a performance evaluation always entails the evaluation not only of a performance but of a performer as well. A performance, as we use the term, is never a disembodied or wholly mechanized set of activities but is always capable of being attributed, at least in part, to some individual or set of individuals. Thus, a performance evaluation is, by definition, an evaluation of a person.

We must also emphasize the great variety of performance evaluations encompassed by our perspective. There are, at one extreme, those official occasions, often annual or semiannual, when a general or global performance evaluation is made and communicated to the performer. Such evaluations often entail the use of a standardized evaluation schedule or form and the holding of a conference at which the performance evaluation is discussed. Very often too, important organizational sanctions are directly tied to these evaluations so that performers' salaries or promotions are determined by their attainment of a prescribed level of performance. At the other extreme are those occasions when an evaluator casually wanders into the work area, momentarily observes an ongoing performance or quickly scans the outcome, and indicates an evaluation to the performer with either a smile of approval or a frown of displeasure. We mean the term *performance evaluation* to encompass both these extremes as well as the many gradations between. Whenever participants learn in any way, indirectly or directly, how well or poorly their evaluator thinks they are doing on an organizational task, they have received a performance evaluation.

Analytical Model

What is the process by which a performance evaluation is reached? We suggest that it is both possible and useful to break down the evaluation process into a set of analytical components, each of which constitutes an essential part of the whole. Our identification of the evaluation components parallels to some extent previous attempts to distinguish between the several parts of the evaluation process. Discussions of the components of evaluation are particularly characteristic of works concerned with industrial administration (Bethel and others, 1954, pp. 229–251; Vance, 1959, pp. 460–490), but also appear in more general treatments of the management of organizations (Koontz and O'Donnell, 1955, pp. 545–567; Litterer, 1965, pp. 233–255). In the interests of clarity, we shall not concern ourselves at this point with the numerous complexities which may enter into evaluation processes but will concentrate on relatively simple situations. In the second section of this chapter, some of these complexities will be considered.

Our model of the evaluation process presumes the presence of at least two actors in an organizational context: the performer, who carries out the task activities, and the evaluator, who performs the activities necessary to arrive at a performance evaluation. We may note here, but will ignore for the present, that several different actors may play the role of evaluator, each performing one or more of the component activities necessary for the determination of the performance evaluation.

Four components of the evaluation process are identified: allocating, criteria-setting, sampling, and appraising. Each will be considered in turn.

Allocating. Before a task performance can be appraised, it must first have been assigned to someone. Someone must have been given the responsibility for performing the task or there will be nothing and no one to evaluate. Allocating is the act which determines who is to perform a given task and, hence, specifies who is to be evaluated for it. Since to allocate a task is to assign a goal, allocation may also be viewed as the act of deciding who is to pursue which goal. In actual practice, a broad range of decisions is included in the process of allocation. Subsumed under this component of evaluation are general decisions, such as the determination of the division of labor in the organization, as well as more specific decisions, such as which participant is to perform which task, or when or for whom or how it is to be done.

To speak of the evaluation of a task is to be somewhat inaccurate. Tasks as such are not evaluated; rather, the values attained on certain properties of the task performance or outcome are evaluated. Clearly, one property on which any task performance may be evaluated, for it is always imposed on a performer by an allocation, is conformity: the extent to which the performer has attempted to carry out the task activities to attain the specified goal. The receipt of an allocation notifies performers that they will be subject to evaluation with respect to whether or not they have attempted to attain the prescribed goal. Whether tasks are allocated by directive ("Carry out these activities as prescribed") or by delegation ("Do whatever is necessary to achieve these results"), the act of allocation notifies performers that they are subject to evaluation on the basis of conformity to the allocation.

The allocation of tasks to participants not only notifies the performers that their performances on those tasks are subject to evaluation, but also communicates to them at least some of the criteria on which the evaluation may be based. The assignment of a goal informs performers that they are expected to achieve certain values on selected properties of an entity. In the rational case, the properties identified and the values specified in the allocation will be among those considered in the evaluation of the task performance. Our conception of the evaluation process, however, is not restricted to the rational case. The act of setting criteria for task evaluation should take into account the information communicated to the performer when the task was allocated, but it often does not in this imperfect world. We must, therefore, consider criteria-setting as a seprable and distinct activity.

Criteria-Setting. Conformity to a task allocation is only one of the dimensions along which the performance of a task may be evaluated. Ordinarily, evaluators in organizations are concerned with more aspects of task performance than whether an attempt was made to carry out the task. Specifically, they are interested in assessing the effectiveness or the efficiency of a given task performance. In order to make such assessments, criteria must be established. The criteria which can be employed in the evaluation of a performance are almost infinite, but in the rational case they are in large measure determined by the goal toward which the performance is directed. That is, the only rational way to ascertain how far a performer has progressed is first to have some conception of where you want the performer to go. A goal is a description of such a desired destination and it is, hence, the logical source of criteria for assessing progress toward the goal. However, behavior is not always rational and logical. There may be discrepancies between the criteria implied by the allocation of a task and those criteria actually used in the evaluation of the performance.

Three distinguishable types of decisions must be made in establishing criteria for performance evaluation. First, the evaluator must determine which task properties should be taken into account in making the evaluation. It should be recalled that evaluations may be based on either the performance itself or on outcomes associated with that performance. Consider, for example, the evaluation of the work of a research physicist. Focusing on performance properties, an evaluator might consider the number of hours worked, the number of pieces of equipment used in an average day, the number of consultations with others, or the neatness of the work area. On the other hand, looking at the properties of the outcomes, the evaluator might focus on the inventiveness of the solutions of problems, the proportion of unsuccessful experiments, or the potential cash value of discoveries. With even this partial list, it is obvious that all task properties cannot be considered in arriving at an evaluation; there must be some selectivity. The goal toward which the task activities are directed indicates which task properties are most salient and will, in the rational case, suggest which attributes and properties will be emphasized in the performance evaluation. But, even in the nonrational case, some set of attributes or properties must be selected before a task performance can be appraised.

A second type of decision involved in the setting of criteria is closely related to the selection of task properties and performance attributes. If more than one property is selected for a given task evaluation, a decision must be made as to the relative weight to be assigned to each in arriving at an evaluation. The selection of weights determines the relative importance of the various task properties as they are combined to produce a performance evaluation. Sometimes equal weights are assigned to each of the properties. Thus, a typist may be evaluated on both speed and accuracy with each of these performance attributes given equal importance. Very often, however, some properties are singled out as more crucial than others. For example, a medical intern is evaluated on both the adequacy and the cost of the diagnostic procedures for a patient, but more importance is attached to the former in assessing the task performance. Just as the goal toward which a performance is directed usually indicates which task properties are of interest, it often also suggests their relative importance.

Before we discuss the third type of decision associated with criteria-setting, the concept of performance value must be introduced. Task properties constitute a set of dimensions along which a given performance may be located. Each dimension may be viewed as consisting of a continuum of all possible values along which a set of performances may vary. Thus, "speed" is an example of a continuous dimension which comprises all the possible degrees or amounts of "fastness" in performing a particular activity or set of activities. The continuum ranges from "extremely fast" to "extremely slow." Other dimensions may allow the identification of only a few values. For example, one task property associated with the performance of a surgical operation is whether or not the patient survived. Such a property identifies a dimension with only two values: either the patient lived or did not. A central part of any evaluation process is the act of determining what particular value has been attained on a given task dimension in a given performance. To determine a performance value is to locate the relevant aspect of a given performance on a specified dimension.

The setting of criteria for task evaluation does not require determining the values attained on task performances. These activities are associated with the act of appraising, and will be considered below. However, the concept of performance value is useful for understanding the concept of standard setting, and the latter is an important ingredient of criteria-setting.

Given that a performance value has been determined in connection with a particular performance of a task, that value is not directly interpretable but must be considered in the light of some standard. That is, a given performance value located at some point on the dimension of speed tells the evaluator how fast the performer is working but does not indicate in itself whether the performer is working too slowly or too rapidly. To make such a determination, the performance value attained must be compared with some standard which specifies the appropriate degree of speed. A standard, then, is an evaluative scale whose intervals constitute degrees of acceptability or preference, the scale typically ranging from low scores indicating "totally unacceptable" values at one end of the continuum to high scores indicating "highly acceptable" or perhaps "exceptional" values at the other end. A standard may consist of a single point on the evaluative scale separating acceptable from unacceptable values. More typically, however, a standard consists of a set of points distinguishing various levels of acceptability or nonacceptability. In addition to the scale itself, the standard also includes a set of rules to transform values on the performance dimensions into scores on the evaluative scale. The transformation rules specify, for example, how many shirts a tailor must cut out to merit a rating of "excellent" in the garment factory or how many client visits are required for the social worker to perform at an acceptable level in managing her case load or how many points a student must compile in a course to receive a grade of B.

The determination of standards and transformation rules is the third and final aspect of the criteria-setting component of the evaluation process. As in the selection of task properties and the determination of their weights, the standards to be used are often suggested by the goal of the task activities, since goals specify which values of the properties are more or less desirable.

Collecting the major points of our discussion, we see that the criteria-setting component of the evaluation process encompasses the following· types of decisions: the specification of the set of task properties to be considered; the assignment of weights to the several properties selected; and the setting of standards and the development of transformation rules for changing values on performance dimensions into scores on an evaluative scale.

Sampling. To arrive at a performance evaluation requires the identification of the value attained on one or more selected properties of the task. The identification of such a performance value requires that information be gathered on the task performance which is to be evaluated. The decision concerning which information will be used in order to arrive at a performance evaluation is termed the "sampling" decision. It is the third major component of the evaluation process. There are two separable aspects to the sampling decision: first, the choice of indicators for ascertaining the performance value attained, and second, the selection of the sampling technique for gathering the relevant information.

The first type of sampling decision attempts to determine what kinds of indicators will provide the most accurate information as to the value attained on a selected property during a given performance. This decision determines what is to be sampled, the primary consideration being the validity of the information gathered. Perhaps the most crucial decision here is whether to examine the performance itself, or the outcomes of the performance, or both. Thus, to determine the value achieved on a property during a given task performance, one may look at the properties of the task activities during the course of the performance (for example, one may watch an offensive lineman block an opponent), or one may look at the properties of the task object at the conclusion of the performance (was the opposing football player removed from the play), or one may do both.

Since we are concerned with the determination of a *performance* evaluation, it is important to note that the examination of performance properties provides direct evidence on which to base a performance evaluation, whereas the examination of outcome properties provides only indirect evidence as to the quality of the performance. To move from an inspection of a task outcome to statements about characteristics of the performance involves inferences about the relation between performance and outcome. The most frequent assumption underlying such inferences is that the values attained on outcome properties are a regular function of the values achieved on performance properties, but this assumption is not always justified.

Whether the decision is to examine performances or outcomes, an evaluator must still determine what specific indicators to employ in measuring the performance value. Defining a property dimension says nothing about how information relevant to that dimension is to be gathered; the latter problem is dealt with by selection of appropriate indicators. Some indicators can be reasonably direct, as when an evaluator uses the number of units produced in a given time as an indicator of speed of performance. Other indicators may be indirect. For example, the creativity of scientists may be measured by the number of scholarly papers published. Of course, the more indirect the measure, the more questionable is its validity.

It should be noted that two levels of the directness or indirectness of the indicators employed to assess performance values have been described. First, all indicators based on measures of outcomes constitute indirect indicators of performance values because assumptions must be made to translate measures of outcomes into measures of performance. On the second level, indicators of either performance or outcome values may vary in the extent to which they directly measure the value on the property.

After decisions have been made on the choice of indicators, the evaluator must still decide on the sampling techniques to be used in gathering the required information. This decision determines which specific performances or outcomes are to be examined and attempts to ensure the reliability of the information. Thus, in order to gather information relating to a teacher's performance, an evaluator might decide to make an unannounced visit to the classroom twice a year. Or a manager in charge of an electronic assembly line might determine that it was necessary to inspect every tenth unit produced. Elaborate sampling procedures are frequently developed in industrial systems where it is possible to specify with exactness the "extent to which defective items can be tolerated in products which are accepted" (Vance, 1959, pp. 460–490).

Appraising. To appraise a performance is to assign an evaluation to it. In general, the appraisal of a performance requires that information obtained on a given performance and the criteria established for the evaluation of that kind of performance be brought together in order to arrive at an evaluation. More precisely, the act of appraisal involves using information on the sampled indicators to determine values to be attributed to selected properties of a particular performance, employing the standards established for each of the properties to translate the observed values into scores, and, taking into account the weights assigned to each of the properties, combining the scores to arrive at a performance evaluation.

Several kinds of decisions enter into performance appraisal. One set of decisions has to do with how the levels of performance values are to be inferred from the magnitudes exhibited on the sampled indicators. In some situations the laws of probability can be used as the basis for these inferences, but, in the absence of controlled sampling procedures, the evaluator must rely on past experience or on rules-of-thumb. Thus, a foreman on an assembly line may know how many defective items will show up by chance in a sample of work taken; only if this number is exceeded does he conclude that the work is not up to standard. By contrast, a school principal examining student reading scores may have no systematic way to decide whether students in a particular teacher's reading class are performing up to their capacity. Another type of decision concerns how the standards are to be applied to a particular performance. The application of standards in specific situations is rarely a simple or straightforward procedure. It requires judgment with respect to the comparability of the performance situation and the situations for which the standards are considered applicable. Similar kinds of judgments are required in employing the specified property weights in combining scores to produce a performance evaluation. In short, appraisal is seldom a mechanical procedure. Moreover, task appraisal entails deciding how to interpret a low or high performance score. Accurately appraising a task performance requires knowledge of extenuating circumstances, whether it be the inexperience of the task performer, the lack of facilities, or assistance received from a more skilled co-worker. Such information is of critical importance in determining what, if any, message is to be communicated to the performer concerning the quality of his or her task performance.

A few general comments are now in order on this scheme for describing the evaluation process. The arbitrary character of our four-component division should be readily apparent. A host of decisions are involved in arriving at a performance evaluation, and we have merely organized these into rough groupings. The four components identified do appear to us to represent reasonably "natural" groupings of these decisions, but these are not exhaustive and other groupings can satisfy other purposes.

At the beginning of this discussion, we stated that we would start by analyzing relatively simple situations. Some readers may be somewhat dismayed by the complexity of these simple situations. We would point out, however, that the major components of the process are, in fact, quite simple: for a person's task performance to be evaluated, the performer must be told what to do (allocation), criteria must be set in terms of which the work will be assessed (criteria-setting), decisions must be made as to which aspects of the performance will be examined (sampling), and information about the performance must be compared with the performance standards (appraising). These activities are diagramed in Figure 1, which serves as a concise summary of our model of the evaluation process.

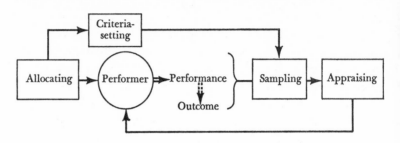

FIGURE 1.   A model of the evaluation process.

Readers familiar with systems analysis will recognize that our model of evaluation bears a strong family resemblance to a servo-mechanism arrangement in which the behavior of a system component is monitored and regulated by means of a feedback loop (Beer, 1959; Buckley, 1968; Kast and Rosenzweig, 1970). In our view, the melding of the traditional sociological approaches to the study of power and authority with the newer approaches to control developed by the systems analysts is one of the strengths of this model.

We do not distinguish the four components of the evaluation process as merely a logical exercise, but because in many situations, particularly in formal organizations, they are often assigned in varied combinations to different participants. For example, in an industrial plant, a superintendent may allocate the tasks to workers, engineers may set the criteria for acceptable tolerance limits, inspectors may select the sample of work to be evaluated, and a foreman may act as the appraiser, comparing the sample of work with the established standards. Figure 1 suggests that the four components cannot be randomly exercised but must be interrelated in a particular way if they are to comprise an evaluation system. Especially where the components are distributed among different persons, it is important not only that each actor make the required decisions, but that there be some coordination of their activities. Many of the problems which beset the evaluation process are due to problems of coordination of the various components. We shall discuss these problems in more detail in Chapter Seven.

We have identified the four components of the evaluation process and, as will be described in succeeding chapters, these components are central elements in our conception of the authority system. Before returning to the problem of authority, however, the remainder of this chapter will be devoted to a brief description of some of the problems and complexities which may affect the evaluation process. The present discussion will focus on those kinds of problems which beset evaluators or which interfere with the functioning of the larger organization. We will reserve for Chapter Nine our consideration of certain evaluation problems which impinge on the performer—on the person being evaluated. Of course, these two topics are not completely distinct but primarily reflect differences in the focus of attention.

Factors Affecting Evaluation Process

In his summary of the literature on organization design and systems analysis, Haberstroh draws two major conclusions from a review of those studies concerned with performance measurement: "First, performance reporting is omnipresent and necessarily so. Second, almost every individual instance of performance reporting has something wrong with it" (1965, p. 1182). Without completely embracing this pessimistic conclusion, we agree that there are many complex factors which need to be taken into account in designing appropriate systems to control task performance. We discuss these factors under three broad groupings: task characteristics, organizational arrangements, and problems affecting individual components of the evaluation process.

Task Characteristics. (1) Task Complexity: In general, the more complex the task, the more complex is the evaluation process required. If the task entails many activities and there are numerous properties of interest in connection with the activities or outcome, then the process of arriving at a valid and reliable performance evaluation is likely to be complicated. Say, for example, that an intern is to be evaluated for a diagnostic workup and formulation of a therapeutic plan for a patient. This task consists of many subtasks, each of which is composed of numerous activities: the taking of a medical history, the administration of a physical exam, the conducting of laboratory tests, the interpretation of these tests, the supervision of auxiliary personnel, etc. A number of attributes of importance to the evaluation process can be identified in connection with the performance of each subtask. Thus, history-taking might be assessed in the light of the following properties: thoroughness, speed, accuracy, clarity, and rapport with patient. According to our analytical model, the evaluator, having identified these properties, would attempt to sample the intern's performance in such a way as to determine the value achieved on each property. Armed with this information the evaluator would then consult a set of standards—one scale for each property identified—and, applying the prescribed rules, convert each value into a score. In order to obtain a general measure of the intern's history-taking performance, the evaluator might then combine the several property scores into an overall score, multiplying each by its assigned weight before combining. This or a related process would need to be repeated for each of the subtasks identified. And if an evaluation for the entire diagnostic and therapeutic performance was desired, the further step of combining the weighted performance evaluations for each subtask into an overall score would be required.

Admittedly, this description of the process by which performance evaluation is developed is an idealized one. All the steps in the process are never carried out in the evaluation of a complex task; the costs in time and effort are prohibitive. Nevertheless, if a serious attempt is made to evaluate performance, then each of the four evaluation components must be considered in some manner, however rough or slipshod. Given the requirement that a performance evaluation be made, the question is not whether the various components will be present. Rather we may ask how carefully, how self-consciously, and with what degree of validity and reliability the evaluation process is built on these components.

(2) Goal Clarity: Goals are defined as conceptions of desired end states of either activities or objects. These conceptions may vary enormously along the dimensions of specificity-diffuseness.

Specific goals are conceptions of desired end states which are formulated with sufficient precision so that they provide useful guidelines for the selection and organization of activities designed to achieve them. Specific goals lend themselves to being operationalized: it is possible to observe and test how well they are being achieved (March and Simon, 1958, pp. 155–157). In terms of our conception, operational goals are those which: allow for the clear specification of the relevant set of performance or outcome properties on which evaluations will be based; identify performance or outcome properties which permit direct or indirect observation of the performance values attained; and establish a set of standards the scales of which are ordered so as to reflect proximity to the desired end states.

Diffuse goals, by contrast, do none of these things. They provide at best only vague notions as to which properties and attributes are relevant, the values attained on the properties they do specify are not always readily observable, and the standards suggested are likely to be either unclear or conflicting. For example, the lack of specificity of goals appears to be a major source of the difficulties reported in evaluating and controlling research and development personnel in industry. Rubenstein (1957, pp. 98–99) summarizes these difficulties as follows: "management's attempts to control and evaluate research and development frequently bog down because there is no clear picture of the process and its products. Also, there is little agreement on the criteria and procedures necessary."

Attempts to evaluate the performances of participants in organizations serving diffuse objectives may have serious, negative consequences for goal attainment. Over-zealous evaluators may focus on those components of the task which are most easily measured while those aspects of the task which are less readily assessed may be ignored. Some participants, noting which aspects of their performances are evaluated, will concentrate their energies on the subset of task components that will immediately affect these short-run evaluations and neglect other aspects. (See Ridgeway, 1956.) This tendency results in a transformation of goals. As Haberstroh (1965, p. 1184) has noted: "performance measures should reflect real goals, for they surely will become operational goals in the day-to-day work patterns of affected personnel." A specific illustration of how choices in evaluative criteria lead to a transformation of goals is reported by Blau (1955, p. 43) in his study of an employment agency: "An instrument intended to further the achievement of organizational objectives, statistical records, constrained interviewers to think of maximizing the indices as their major goal, sometimes at the expense of these very objectives. They avoided operations which would take up time without helping them to improve their record, such as interviewing clients for whom application forms had to be made out, and wasted their own and the public's time on activities intended only to raise the figures on their record." Other case studies reporting similar results include those of Berliner (1957) and Dalton (1959). It appears that when organizational objectives are diffuse, a rigid, quantitative approach to evaluation may create as many serious problems for goal attainment as a lax procedure in which few serious attempts are made to evaluate the contributions of participants.

(3) Unpredictable Tasks: Performance evaluations may be based either on an assessment of the characteristics of the task performance itself (the activities) or on an assessment of the characteristics of the task outcome resulting from the completed performance. Let us consider first evaluations based on outcomes. In the case of a predictable task, the nature of the outcome is a regular function of the quality of the performance. Making a bed, adding a column of figures, baking a cake, painting a house—these and similar tasks confront the performer with a relatively predictable amount of resistance. For such tasks, the inspection of the characteristics of the outcome allows one to make reasonably accurate inferences as to the care, the speed, or the accuracy with which the activities were performed. By contrast, lack of predictability of the resistance encountered makes it more difficult to infer the characteristics of the performance from the nature of the outcome. For example, one physician may be able to restore the health of a patient while a second cannot achieve a comparable degree of success. Who is the better physician? Knowledge of the outcomes may give little indication as to the quality of the performances of the two individuals, for the one with the poorer outcome may have been confronted with a little understood disease. Thus, in the case of unpredictable tasks, an evaluator who has information only on the nature of the outcome

achieved may draw incorrect inferences as to the quality of task performances.

Further, low task predictability may also affect the characteristics of the performance. While some performance values may be unaffected by the amount of resistance encountered and so are a direct function of the performer's effort or skills, others may be affected. The amount of care exercised or the thoroughness with which the performer carries out tasks may be unaffected by the level of resistance encountered, but other attributes, such as speed or energy expended, are likely to be a function both of the performer's qualities and the level of resistance. Thus, the characteristics of performances themselves are not immune to the effects of unpredictable tasks. However, evaluators focusing on performances may be more aware of, and hence be more likely to take into account, the nature of the resistance confronting the performer than is the evaluator focusing on outcomes.

These brief comments should indicate the importance of two dimensions of the active-inert task distinction as they affect the evaluation of task performances. We return to these matters below in our consideration of problems affecting the individual evaluation components, as well as in Chapter Nine, where we consider evaluation problems in the authority structure.

Organizational Arrangements. (1) Visibility of Task Performance: One way in which it is possible for an evaluator to gather information relevant to making an evaluation is to observe the task performer in the act of carrying out task activities. However, there are usually a variety of limitations imposed on one person's attempt to observe directly the performance of another.

Merton, (1957, p. 343) has discussed in general terms one basis for the resistance of performers to attempts at routine observation of their activities.

> Resistance to full visibility of one's behavior appears . . . to result from structural properties of group life. *Some* measure of leeway in conforming to role-expectations is presupposed in all groups. To have to meet the strict requirement of a role at all times, without

some degree of deviation, is to experience insufficient allowances for individual differences in capacity and training and for situational exigencies which make strict conformity extremely difficult.

Resistance to full visibility of activities is, of course, accentuated by an (assumed or actual) cleavage of interests between authoritative strata and governed strata. The strong hostility toward 'close supervision' in business and industry evidently express this doubly reinforced objection to the surveillance of role-performance.

These and related considerations frequently give rise to work group norms which attempt to regulate the access of evaluators to the work place.

In addition to such norms, which may develop in any type of work situation, more elaborate and restrictive norms often arise among professional workers to protect their work from "outside interference." For example, physicians employed by clinics have as one aim of their norms the protection of the rights of each practitioner to make decisions for patients and, specifically, to ensure that nonmedical criteria are not allowed to intrude into the decision-making process (Freidson, 1970; Goss, 1961, pp. 44–48). Another factor supporting the development of such norms is the active nature of many of the tasks performed by professionals. Consider the case of a physician employed by a clinic. Confronted with the active task of curing or helping a patient, a physician will want to be free to select that set of activities best suited to achieve a successful outcome. Were the physician subject to episodic or routine performance inspection, however, and expected to be able to defend each decision whenever challenged, he or she might be constrained to select those activities that could be readily justified (conventional procedures) or gave the appearance of effecting immediate progress, rather than concentrating attention and energies on attaining a successful outcome in the long run. In fact, most workers will resist attempts by evaluators to monitor constantly their performances, and some professionals will object to virtually any attempt to observe them in the act of performing their work.

Observations of performance are not only restricted by the defensive tactics of performers. Many kinds of work performances occur under circumstances which render the regular inspection of worker activities impossible or impractical. For example, the nature of the work performed by sales personnel, social workers, and other groups who must visit clients in their homes or places of business militates against routine surveillance of their performance. Kaufman (1960) has described what must constitute almost a polar case of this situation in his analysis of the working conditions of forest rangers, who perform their task activities in areas far removed from the eyes of their superiors.

Some types of performances, such as those emphasizing mental activities, are by their nature very difficult to observe. Then too, most work situations contain numerous physical barriers of one type or another which prevent easy inspection. For example, the work of most public school teachers in conventionally structured class-rooms physically isolates them and prevents easy surveillance by either superiors or peers. For many types of work, accuracy of evaluation is predicated on sustained observation of the entire sequence of activities which constitutes a performance. In such cases, evaluators are understandably reluctant to jump to conclusions on the basis of information occasionally obtained on performance values. For example, in the group-practice medical clinic studied by Freidson and Rhea (1963, pp. 123–124), the colleague group was expected to evaluate the technical aspects of a physician's perfor-mance. Yet contacts among physicians were typically so selective and fragmentary that many physicians were either reluctant or completely unable to evaluate the performance of their fellow physicians.

A final set of basic limitations imposed on the direct observa-tion of performance may be considered under the general rubric of "costs." First, there is, of course, economic or financial cost. As Koontz and O'Donnell (1955, p. 548) note, "Any control device must meet the standard of economy, must, in other words, be worth its cost." Generally speaking, the routine, direct observation of one person's performance by another is undoubtedly one of the most expensive methods by which information on work activities can be acquired in that it requires the expenditure of large amounts of time by evaluators. There are also important psychological costs involved in systems based on the routine surveillance of performance. For the performer these may entail the oft-reported tensions associated with working under conditions of close supervision. (See, for example, Argyle and others, 1958; Gouldner, 1954, pp. 159–162; Kahn and Katz, 1953; Day and Hamblin, 1964.) Psychological costs may also be visited upon evaluators who, being in a position to observe many kinds of deviations, must determine which are critical under the given circumstances and which should be ignored. "It is in this sense that authorities can have 'excessive knowledge' of what is actually going on, so that this becomes dysfunctional for the system of social control" (Merton, 1957, p. 343).

Some of the problems which have been described in connection with the direct observation of performance are reduced if evaluators are willing to settle for occasional samples of performances. However, the infrequent sampling of behavior may also be resisted by performers, most often because of their fear that such samples will provide an unreliable basis for evaluation. Performers may become so concerned about the samples taken of their performance that they develop elaborate group warning systems: word is passed along the line that the inspectors are on the way. And since evaluations of performers often reflect upon their immediate supervisors, it sometimes happens that both supervisors and performers enter into collusive agreements for their mutual benefit but to the detriment of the larger organization. Dalton's (1959) case studies of several industrial firms provide numerous examples of such practices, of which the following account is but one instance:

> To limit the evasion, the Office notified Taylor that his job would now include surprise inspections and count of parts in each department. He and Bingham were alarmed by this new directive for neither had the front or address to carry out the order as intended. After conferences with the executives, their solution was not to make unannounced counts, but to telephone various heads before a given inspection telling them the starting point, time, and route that would be followed. By varying these conditions on successive tours, Taylor and Bingham made each inspection *appear* to catch the chiefs off guard [1959, p. 47].

Assuming, however, the absence of such alliances between evaluators and performers, and a concern on the part of the evaluator with the accurate measurement of performance values, the decision as to the size and frequency of the sample should take into account the nature of the tasks performed. Inert tasks require smaller samples of performance than do active tasks.

There are fewer problems for evaluators in obtaining access to the outcomes of performances compared with access to the performances themselves. As a basis for inferring the performance values, however, task outcomes are beset by two major problems. One of these has already been described: namely, the difficulties inherent in making inferences from outcomes to performances when the tasks are unpredictable. When the task performers do not have full control over the results of their efforts, so that a "poor" outcome can result from a "good" performance, then performers are less apt to view as soundly based those performance evaluations which are based on outcome measures.

A second source of difficulty associated with the evaluation of outcomes arises when more than one performer has contributed to the outcome. This problem occurs when workers are interdependent with respect to a given task performance. Since interdependence is an important structural feature of organizational work settings, we shall consider it below as a separate source of evaluation difficulties.

The frequency with which performances or outcomes are sampled varies greatly among organizations as well as among positions within organizations. For example, in assembly line situations, work may be constantly monitored through the use of automatic testing devices or full-time inspectors. In other situations, task performances may be only rarely reviewed. Jaques (1956) has conducted a systematic study of 300 individuals employed in an industrial firm and reports that the higher the grade of personnel, the less frequently performances are reviewed. He proposed that the time span between reviews of performance may be used as an indication of the length of discretionary freedom which, in turn, provides a measure of the amount of responsibility exercised.

In an attempt to reflect accurately previous ideas and research findings on visibility, we have emphasized the problems associated with and the restrictions placed on full visibility of performances and outcomes. These problems are real, but their importance has perhaps been exaggerated; or, at least, there may be equally important and pervasive offsetting forces which deserve consideration. Thus, while most performers might resist *full* visibility of work activities, as Merton suggests, we would also expect most performers to be equally uncomfortable with arrangements that completely concealed their performances and outcomes from inspection by others. After all, these others are often expected to distribute sanctions to performers based on these evaluations.

Rather than focusing on the need for privacy and for protection from close surveillance, our approach emphasizes the contributions which visibility of performances or outcomes makes to the receipt of soundly based evaluations. That is, while performers may not value visibility for its own sake, they may tolerate or even welcome it because of the contribution which this condition makes to accuracy of performance evaluations. The more possible it is for an evaluator to observe task performances and outcomes, or the larger the proportion of outcomes and performances observed, the better able the evaluator will be to formulate soundly based evaluations of the performer's work. Performers who are committed to the goals associated with their tasks, or who wish to do well in the eyes of others, or who value the sanctions associated with performance evaluations, are expected to desire soundly based evaluations.

The concept of work visibility sounds so clear and straightforward that we feel compelled to note its complexities. First, different aspects of the task may vary in visibility. One sequence of task activities may be relatively visible while another is much less so, or the performance of task activities may be difficult to observe, but the outcomes associated with those performances be relatively accessible. Second and even more common, the various tasks performed by a particular performer vary in visibility. For example, social workers are under closer surveillance by their supervisors when they are calculating clients' budgets in the office than when they are visiting clients in their homes. Third, tasks very greatly in their visibility to different sets of evaluators. For example, the scholarly work of professors may be visible to their colleagues but not to their students, while their teaching activities are visible to their students but often not to their colleagues.

The fact that evaluators differ in their ability to observe different tasks is in part due to the nature of the tasks, but it is also affected by the mode of organizing work. For example, Freidson (1960) and Freidson and Rhea (1963) have described how variations in the organization of medical practice affect visibility of work, and consequently, the relative importance of clients and colleagues as evaluators. Similarly, Meyer and Cohen (1971) have documented the impact of team teaching and open-space architecture on teachers' perceptions of the influence of colleagues. Our own research with Marram, reported in the next chapter, pursues these interests by examining the impact of teaming in two organizational settings, schools and hospitals. Team arrangements appear greatly to increase the visibility of performers' work to their colleagues. We expect that the greater the visibility of performances to evaluators, whether clients, peers, or superiors, the more likely performers are to view these evaluations as soundly based and the more importance they will attribute to these evaluations.

(2) Frequency of Communicated Evaluations: Another structural feature having important consequences for the evaluation process is the frequency with which performance evaluations are communicated to participants. This is to be distinguished, of course, from the frequency with which performances are sampled. It is at least theoretically possible for sampling to be quite frequent but communication of evaluations to be infrequent, and vice versa. We would expect that one of the significant ways in which organizations and work situations within organizations vary is in the frequency with which evaluations are communicated to participants.

Situations involving either very frequent or very infrequent communication of evaluations would appear to pose problems for performers. When evaluations are very frequent, performers are receiving maximum feedback as to how their performances are regarded and should be better able to adjust their performance levels to achieve desired standards. However, frequent evaluations are often perceived as close supervision, allowing little leeway for discretion or even for "breathing space." By contrast, very infrequent evaluations connote maximum discretion and autonomy of operation, and this situation is often desired by performers. Nevertheless, even participants who are accustomed to exercising great autonomy in the conduct of their task activities often desire some feedback to provide general guidelines for decision-making and as a means of testing their own judgements. The desire to escape from complete freedom is not pathological, at least not in an organizational setting where one's decisions and activities have consequences for the work of others.

(3) Complexity of Authority System. In this chapter we have introduced the four components of the evaluation process and have alluded to the fact that each of these components may be assigned to a different person. We will expand upon this notion in Chapter VII where we present our conception of the authority system. At this point, we simply wish to record the observation that many people may be involved in the authority system by virtue of exercising one or more of the evaluation components, and that the greater the number of persons involved, by definition, the greater the complexity of the authority system. Complex authority systems pose problems of coordination among those who carry out the evaluations, so that we would expect that more complex systems are more likely to be beset with problems—misunderstandings, communication failures, and other types of errors.

(4) Task Interdependence: Because of the widespread use of functional specialization, in which performers specialize in carrying out one set of activities rather than in producing one type of product, interdependence of task activities is a widespread phenomenon in complex organizations. Evaluators are confronted with the difficult problem of determining how a single outcome is to be differentiated so as to permit discriminant samplings of the contributions of each performer. Sometimes the outcome is a product which can be factored so that it becomes clear whose performances have affected which values on the outcome properties. But often such differentiation of the outcome is not possible. Then the evaluator who wishes to assign performance evaluations to individuals must fall back on the direct inspection of performance values, or attempt to redefine the task so as to examine earlier outcomes which reflect the efforts of individuals before their work is combined. We have more to say about task interdependence and outcome evaluation in our discussion of the various types of incompatibilities in evaluation in Chapters Nine and Ten.

(5) Power Differences: It is important to understand that our general conceptual framework focuses attention on the authorized use of power to control task performances by the distribution of organizational sanctions. In a sense our attention is concentrated on "domesticated power," on power harnessed in the service of organizational goals.

We should remember, however, that the power systems we are attempting to study are themselves established and maintained by power differences. They are frameworks established by the outcomes of a larger power contest that may involve many participants, past and present, within and outside the study organizations. Thus, as discussed in Chapter Three, different categories of participants—administrators and performers, for example—may disagree over the types of work arrangements to be established. Such disagreements are resolved by power, and the work arrangements established reflect these power differences.

We have indicated that organizational control is mediated by evaluation processes. Among the most important features of any organizational work arrangement, then, is the extent to which performers are able to influence the evaluation process directly, by having some say in the manner in which tasks are allocated, criteria are set, or samples of work are drawn. We have already described examples of performers' influence on sampling in our discussion of variations in the visibility of task performances. We can now state more directly that some differences in work visibility can be attributed to differences in the power of performer groups. Some workers are in a sufficiently powerful position to be able to have great influence on the manner in which their work is inspected. Similarly, work arrangements vary in the degree to which performers have power to influence the selection of the criteria in terms of which their work is evaluated or the manner in which tasks are assigned to them.

We consider these differences in performer power to be characteristics of the organizational arrangements within which work is evaluated and controlled. Such differences may have a variety of sources: the activities of professional associations or unions, or specific historical circumstances. Our theory does not attempt to explain these differences in power among performer groups, but we do expect them to have an impact on the operation of evaluation processes and on the stability of control systems.

Individual Components. As noted above, we reserve our more comprehensive and systematic discussion of problems in evaluation systems for Chapter Nine. Here we comment briefly on some prevalent problems besetting evaluators as these relate to each of the four components.

(1) Allocating: Allocation determines who is to be evaluated for what. Probably the most common type of problem in allocation involves a failure of communication between the allocator and the performer. For example, if the allocator is somewhat nondirective in the assignment of tasks, performers may not be aware of the fact that they have been given a task for which they may be evaluated. Current styles of supervision are such that it is often very difficult to differentiate between an order, requiring compliance, and a suggestion. When many orders are preceded by such phrases as "Would you . . . ," "Why don't you . . . ," and "If I were you, I'd . . . ," then it takes a very astute and perspicacious subordinate to know what is in the mind of the superior.

A different kind of misunderstanding occurs when a statement intended by the allocator as a directive is taken by the performer to be a delegation. Many allocations may sound like delegations to a naive performer, but, because they occur within the context of an existing set of standard operating procedures, they are in fact intended as directives. In such a situation, the specification of the desired outcome is not a delegation, as would be the case if the communication were taken at face value, but is a directive to institute a specific performance program. Obviously, such misunderstandings can create difficulties for individual allocators and for the organization in general. Just as obviously, the performers may also be adversely affected because of the lack of congruence between the task which they thought was allocated and the task for which they were evaluated.

(2) Criteria Setting: Clearly, one of the most difficult types of decisions confronting evaluators is that of determining the standards to be employed in the appraisal of performance. Koontz and

O'Donnell (1955, pp. 553–555) list and describe several kinds of standards against which performance can be appraised, including physical, cost, capital, revenue, and intangible standards. And where do the standards come from? Here again there are many choices; Haberstroh (1965, p. 1181) describes only some of the most common sources as follows:

> In technical fields, these criteria . . . can frequently be derived from consideration of the state of the art in question. Many criteria pertaining to more global operating results, such as profits, sales, costs, are derived in the same way, by adopting as standard the best performance visible in the appropriate reference class. Other common practices are the use of precedent (doing as well as previously). Other criteria have primarily the function of integrating different facets or departments of an organization. Examples are the use of sales forecasts to keep marketing and production activities in balance, capital budgets to apportion available resources among operating units, production schedules to coordinate functional departments.

J. D. Thompson (1967, pp. 86–93) has attempted to determine what types of evaluative standards are likely to be employed, given differences in the clarity of goals (crystallized vs. ambiguous standards) and differences in knowledge concerning the tasks (complete vs. incomplete knowledge of cause-effect relations). He argues that where standards are crystallized and knowledge is complete, it is appropriate to use efficiency tests which allow assessment of the extent to which perfection is approached in terms of cost per unit of output. Where standards are crystallized but knowledge of cause-effect relations is incomplete, evaluators must usually settle for an instrumental test which determines only the relative effectiveness of the task activity—that is, whether a desired state is achieved at all. Finally, "when standards of desirability are ambiguous or when cause-effect knowledge is believed incomplete, organizations turn to (social) reference groups" (J. D. Thompson, 1967, p. 87), setting their standards in the light of those employed by comparable organizations or looking at the improvement of their own performance over a period of time, using behavior during an earlier period as a standard.

Special problems are confronted in the setting of standards for tasks which are low on predictability. Since the resistance to be overcome is known from performance to performance for predictable tasks, a single uniform standard may be employed across all task performances, but since, by definition, the amount of resistance confronted in performing an unpredictable task is not known from one performance to another, it is impossible for an evaluator to establish a single uniform standard which will be appropriate for use in assessing all performances of the task. When the resistance encountered varies, two possible approaches to setting standards are open to the evaluator. In the first, the evaluator observes many performances of the task against varying known amounts of resistance in order to gain knowledge of the relation between specific degrees of resistance and performance values. The evaluator's aim is eventually to develop a sliding scale such that the standard will vary according to the amount of resistance encountered during a given performance. For example, the success of a fire-fighting crew might be appraised with the use of a sliding scale so that the score assigned takes into account the size and intensity of the blaze encountered. The second approach can be used when knowledge of the level of resistance encountered during a specific performance is not obtainable. In this case, the evaluator observes many instances of task performances against varying degrees of resistance in order to determine the frequency distribution of possible outcomes. This distribution then functions as a standard in appraising a *series* of performances by a given performer, certain ranges of values within the distribution being regarded as acceptable. For example, the death rate of a surgeon performing a certain type of operation may be compared with a distribution of such rates associated with the performance of other surgeons under comparable circumstances. It should be noted that in both cases, the standards employed for the appraisal of outcomes on unpredictable tasks require a considerable fund of knowledge about the outcomes achieved by other performers under comparable circumstances.

In this discussion of unpredictable tasks, we have focused

primarily on the problems associated with the development of standards for appraising outcomes. Because of these problems, evaluators sometimes attempt to employ direct measures of performance properties, comparing the values achieved by performers with a set of uniform standards. This is an appropriate procedure for those properties unaffected by the variability of the resistance encountered, but, as will be recalled, some task properties are so affected. And, as with outcomes, in these instances sliding scales or distributions of performance values achieved under comparable circumstances provide the more appropriate type of standards for assessing the performance values.

(3) Sampling: In defining the sampling component of the evaluation process two types of decisions were identified: selecting the indicators and determining the sample to be taken. We have already considered some of the problems associated with determining the sampling techniques in our discussion of visibility of performances and outcomes. We briefly treat here some problems which may affect the selection of indicators.

The selection of indicators is often a straightforward decision but may also be dangerous for the organization. The dangers involved are similar to those associated with the choice of task properties; that is, just as a performer may neglect important task properties in order to maximize performance values on those properties which are selected to serve as the basis for evaluation, so may efforts be concentrated on maximizing the value of a particular indicator to the neglect of those values the indicator was in fact designed to measure. For example, medical students who know that body temperature of the patient is to be used as an indicator of level of infection might concentrate their energies on bringing down the temperature without concern for controlling the infection itself. The most extreme tactic used by performers to change indicators is the direct manipulation of performance reports, for example, by "devoting considerable effort to reallocating expenses, suppression of information, or outright falsification" (Haberstroh, 1965, p. 1183). Specific instances of the use of such techniques are reported by Berliner (1957) and Dalton (1959).

(4) Appraising: Appraisal of performance requires the evaluator to combine and to apply the other components of the evalua-

tion process so as to arrive at a specific performance evaluation. The amount of discretion in appraising a task performance is necessarily related to the degree to which the other components are elaborated and applicable to the performance in question. There is always some discretion associated with the appraisal of performance. And in those instances where the task properties are not clearly specified, the property values not easily measured, or the standards not clearly defined or easily applied, great discretionary power is involved in appraisal. Thus, task appraisal is more complex to the extent that criteria for task evaluation are vaguely stated and the measurement of task properties is difficult.

Furthermore, not all the samples of a performer's activities or outcomes may in fact be employed in arriving at a performance evaluation. Thus, as Jaques (1956, pp. 37–38) observes, evaluators often do not review carefully all reports on performance reaching their desks: "It was observable that as a superior gained increasing confidence in a subordinate, he turned to reviewing work on the basis of the trend of results, and was not worried by isolated, seemingly bad reports occurring from time to time."

The appraisal component becomes more difficult when it is combined, as is often the case, with the task of communicating the evaluation to the performer. Problems and misunderstandings may be created by faulty or insensitive communication of the evaluation. Negative evaluations, for example, may be made to sound more negative than they in fact are, or they may be so sugar-coated as to appear positive. The manner in which evaluations are communicated to performers may assume greater importance in the eyes of the performer than the actual content of the evaluation.

Chapter 6

Evaluation: Empirical Studies

▲▲

Whereas our next empirical chapter, Chapter Eight, focuses upon the organizational location of specific persons who perform components of the evaluation process, we are here going to discuss some more general characteristics of evaluation processes. We use data from our Five Organizations Study and our studies of professional organizations.

We begin with a discussion of frequency of sampling and of communicated evaluation. Frequency is related to the status of performers and to satisfaction. Competent performers are compared to less competent performers with respect to their perception of the frequency with which they are evaluated and, more specifically, are given negative evaluations. Agreement among the evaluators, using our university faculty sample, is related to the dependence of the evaluator's field of knowledge upon a central body of theory. A central body of theory is expected to be related to increased agreement among evaluators and thus to increased satisfaction of performers.

Visibility of performances and outcomes to evaluators is related to the perceived soundness of their evaluations. Soundness in turn is related to the importance of evaluations to the performer. These relationships are affected by the influence of evaluations upon the distribution of organizational sanctions.

In addition to gaining acceptable evaluations by effort on tasks, performers may also attempt to directly influence the system of evaluation. Such power is related to the satisfaction of performers. After a brief comment on nonperformance bases of evaluation, this chapter concludes with a comparison of two schools, illustrating many of the principles we have discussed.

Frequency of Evaluation

In all our analyses we are concerned with communicated evaluations. When performers learn how they have been evaluated by an influential member of their organization, they can then choose to shape their behavior in order to gain more favorable evaluations. Without such communication, unknown evaluations could produce variation in rewards and punishments without providing clear guidance to performers, who would be left wondering what they did or did not do. Therefore, we emphasize communicated evaluations in the control process.

It was important for our studies that respondents understood we were concerned with communicated evaluations in a broad sense. Otherwise, they would be likely to report only the receipt of formal evaluations, communicated in writing on a periodic basis. To guard against this common misinterpretation, we always introduced questions about the frequency of evaluations received from specific individuals with the explanatory statement:

> Now we want to ask you some questions about how often you receive ratings or evaluations. For example, an evaluator may compliment you on your good work each day or criticize you for mistakes; you may occasionally receive formal written evaluations; an evaluator may simply indicate his judgements of your performance with a smile or a frown; an evaluator may look at how you are

doing and say nothing, yet you may know whether or not he is satisfied.

In general, when you learn in *any* way, directly or indirectly, how well or poorly an evaluator thinks you are doing on a task, you are receiving an evaluation. Please remember that what we mean by evaluations includes much more than formal written evaluations.

We believe that these instructions succeeded in communicating our intended image of communicated evaluations, whether oral or written, verbal or nonverbal.

Only after this explanation did we ask questions like: "How frequently do you learn (each specific evaluator's) evaluation of how well or poorly you are doing on (this task)?" to obtain information on the frequency of each evaluator's communicated evaluations, and: "How frequently does (each specific) evaluator get or receive information about your work on (this task)?" to obtain information on the frequency of sampling. The same seven response categories were used for both questions to measure frequency, as follows: Very Frequently, Frequently, Fairly Often, Occasionally, Seldom, Almost Never and Never.

Frequency of Sampling and Status. We expected, following the work of Jaques (1956), that reported frequency of sampling would be negatively correlated with the organizational status of the respondent. In this study of the Glacier Metal Company in England, Jaques used length of time between reviews by superiors and between reports required of subordinates as an indicator of level of responsibility of the subordinate. He found this measure to be negatively correlated with the status or the grade of the position within the factory. In our Five Organizations study, since our questions were evaluator-specific, we used two measures of frequency of evaluation: the subordinate's report of the highest frequency of sampling by an evaluator of the specific task, and the average frequency of sampling among all evaluators named by a position occupant. Status was measured simply by ordering the positions studied within each organization in terms of their formal rank in the organization's hierarchy. For example, members of the house staff in the hospital were ordered in rank from high to low as follows: chief resident, senior resident, intern or junior resident, and clinical clerk. To our surprise, we found no relation at all between our measures of reported frequency of sampling and position in the organizational hierarchy. We did find variations in frequency of sampling among the positions, as indicated in Table 5, but these differences did not relate to organizational status. Thus, our own findings were not consistent with those reported by Jaques.

Two possible reasons for these differences between our find-

Table 5.

POSITIONAL DIFFERENCES IN FREQUENCY OF SAMPLING,
USING THE MEAN OF THE MEDIAN FREQUENCY
REPORTED BY EACH POSITION OCCUPANT FOR ALL EVALUATORS

Organization	Position	Mean
Hospital	Nurse's Aide	4.0
	Nursing Team Leader	2.6
	Clinical Clerk	2.3
	Intern	2.2
	Senior Resident	2.0
Research Facility	Engineer	2.9
	Draftsman	4.0
	Storekeeper	2.8
	Technical Typist	4.0
Electronics Firm	Assembly Line Worker	3.0
Student Newspaper	Desk Worker	2.8
	Copy Editor	1.8
Football Team	Member of Defensive "Front Eight"	1.6
	Member of Defensive "Back Three"	1.6
	Member of Offensive Line	1.7
	Ball Carrier	1.8

NOTE: Frequency scale uses 1 for Very Frequently, 2 for Frequently, 3 for Fairly Often, 4 for Occasionally, 5 for Seldom, 6 for Almost Never, and 7 for Never.

ings and those reported by Jaques may be advanced. First, Jaques employed absolute measures, for example, the time between supervisory reviews, whereas our own measures were relative. Our respondents may have used their own occupational peers as a reference group in determining how frequent is Very Frequently, and different occupational groups may employ different standards. Second, we employed a task-specific and evaluator-specific measure of sampling frequency, while Jaques used a more general approach measuring the length of periods of review and the time-span of discretion without regard to the type of task performed and without distinguishing between evaluators in terms of their sampling frequency.

Extreme examples of differences between organizational positions with respect to the frequency of sampling are football players and public school teachers. Ninety-one percent of the football players report a median frequency of sampling for all evaluators that is Frequently or Very Frequently. For teachers, the median frequency of sampling was Seldom, combining all four tasks. One teacher on the teacher's evaluation committee said, "If I were to drop dead, the only way they would find out would be by the smell after a few days."

Satisfaction. We found, although this was not a part of our original formulation, that frequency of sampling and frequency of evaluation were each positively related to satisfaction with the evaluation process. Our first data suggesting this relationship between sampling frequency and satisfaction came from our Five Organizations study. We have already described the question used to elicit information on the frequency of sampling. For satisfaction with sampling, we asked: "How satisfied or dissatisfied are you with the way in which decisions are made about what information is to be obtained on how you are doing on your work on (this task)?" The following eight-point scale was used to assess degree of satisfaction or dissatisfaction: Extremely Satisfied, Very Satisfied, Moderately Satisfied, Slightly Satisfied, Slightly Dissatisfied, Moderately Dissatisfied, Very Dissatisfied, and Extremely Dissatisfied. Combining the data from the Five Organizations study for all positions, we found that of the 171 persons for whom one or more evaluators sampled their work Frequently or Very Frequently, 72 percent were Extremely Satisfied or Very Satisfied with the sampling process. For those whose highest frequency of sampling was less than Frequently, only twelve out of thirty, or 40 percent, were Extremely or Very Satisfied. The gamma for this positive relation between frequency of sampling and satisfaction was .57. When we tested the hypothesis separately for each of thirteen positions, combining football players into one group, the results tended to be positive, although the relationship was often weak. Ten of the thirteen positions showed a positive relation between frequency of sampling and satisfaction.

To test the relationship between frequency of communicated evaluations and satisfaction with a large number of cases for a single position, we asked 131 teachers from six schools in a single school district about the frequency of communicated evaluations from principals. Teachers were asked: "How frequently do you learn your principal's evaluation of how well or poorly you are doing on (each task)?" Response categories were in terms of our seven-point frequency scale. To determine degree of satisfaction with the evaluation process, teachers were asked: "You have already been asked how satisfied you are with the way tasks are given, the way standards are set, the way decisions are made about the information needed for evaluating, and the way evaluations are made. In general, considering all these things together, how satisfied are you with the way work is assigned and evaluated for each task?" For this satisfaction question a short scale was used with five response categories: Extremely Satisfied, Very Satisfied, Moderately Satisfied, Slightly Satisfied, and Not At All Satisfied. For each of the four tasks performed by teachers, those who perceived that they were more frequently evaluated by their principal were likely to be more satisfied with the manner in which tasks were assigned and evaluated. The gamma values were .68, .68, .68, and .50 for the tasks of Teaching Subject Matter, Character Development, Maintaining Control, and Record-Keeping, respectively. We found that receiving more frequent evaluations was associated with a more positive view of the evaluation system. This strong relationship for teachers should not be interpreted as a note for very frequent evaluations, but rather as dissatisfaction with infrequent evaluations.

Since the receipt of frequent evaluations was associated with high satisfaction with the assignment and evaluation of tasks, we made an even stronger prediction: that there would be no relationship between frequency of communicated *dissatisfaction* by principals and overall teacher satisfaction with the assignment and evaluation of tasks. If it is indeed desirable to receive more evaluations from the principal, a teacher should be willing to accept more frequent negative evaluations without becoming dissatisfied. To test our prediction, teachers were asked the following question: "How often do you learn in any way, directly or indirectly, that your principal is dissatisfied with how well you are doing on each task or any part of it?" Response categories were as follows: Always, Almost Always, Usually, Fairly Often, Occasionally, Almost Never, and Never. The question used to measure teacher satisfaction with the evaluation process has already been described. Consistent with our expectations, the data revealed no significant relationship between the frequency with which principals were reported to be dissatisfied and overall teacher satisfaction with the evaluation process for three of the four tasks. For the fourth task, Record-Keeping, we did find a statistically significant relationship, but happily it was the most dissatisfied teachers who reported the lowest frequency of negative evaluations by their principal. It appears that it is not the frequency of negative evaluations but the infrequency of any evaluations that produces dissatisfaction among teachers.

When we compared teachers in alternative schools with teachers in public schools, we found that comparisons across positions did not produce the same results as analyses of frequency of evaluation within a single position. Teachers in alternative schools received more evaluations, and they also received more negative evaluations; yet they were more dissatisfied with their allocation and evaluation system than were teachers in the public schools. When the analysis was made within the group of teachers in alternative schools, we had to study evaluations by other teachers since alternative schools usually had no principal. For each of the four tasks, there was a slight, but consistent positive correlation between the frequency of receipt of evaluations from other teachers and the satisfaction of teachers in alternative schools with the allocation and evaluation system. This finding supports the results of analyses done within the public schools.

Negative Evaluations and Competence. We were able to

obtain competence ratings from supervisors for four positions in the Five Organizations study: the football players, assembly line workers, nursing team leaders, and nurse's aides, yielding competence measures for 132 respondents. Fifty-five percent of these performers were rated above average, with the remainder rated average or below average, illustrating the oft-noted tendency for supervisors to give favorable evaluations. We would expect that persons rated as above average in competence would perceive their appraisers as less frequently giving them negative evaluations. We asked the question: "How often when you do (this task) is (your appraiser) dissatisfied with how well you are doing on (this task) or any part of it?" Forty-eight of seventy-two above-average respondents, or 68 percent, perceived their evaluators to be dissatisfied with their work Seldom or more frequently. By comparison, thirty-five of the fifty-nine average or below-average respondents, or 59 percent, viewed their evaluators as dissatisfied Seldom or more frequently. We were thus confronted with an unexpected result. Persons who were regarded as more competent than their fellows by their supervisors were as likely to perceive that they were receiving negative evaluations. Indeed, there was a slight tendency for the more competent workers, compared with their less competent peers, to believe they were receiving more negative evaluations.

Inspection of this relationship among occupants of the four positions suggests that one group, the football players, accounted for the positive relation between competence and receipt of negative evaluations. Football players who were judged the most competent also had the most playing time, and the coaches accordingly spent more of their own time critically evaluating the efforts of these persons who were most likely to represent the team on the field. Less competent players actually had less playing time. The better football players were therefore more frequently evaluated and also perceived themselves to be receiving more negative evaluations than less competent team members. This situation, in which the more competent performers were more likely to carry out the performance activities, was not found among the other three positions examined. When we subtracted the data for the football team, the previously observed positive relationship between competence and the receipt of negative evaluations completely disappeared. Competent and incompetent performers were equally likely to report receiving negative evaluations.

There still remains, however, the intriguing finding of a lack of relationship between competence ratings and frequency of negative evaluations. Perhaps it is accounted for by a tendency on the part of less competent performers to ignore, to overlook, or not to perceive evidence of the dissatisfaction of their superiors. Consistent with this explanation, it may be that workers performing in an average or below-average manner have lower acceptance levels— are satisfied with less favorable evaluations—than do their more competent colleagues. Because their own standards of performance are lower, they may not take account of the dissatisfaction of their superiors.

We have been dealing with communicated evaluations. Obviously, the superior and the subordinate may differ in their perception of the frequency and content of the superior's evaluations. A study of a small sample of hospital personnel in two wards by Seashore (1965), a member of our research group, found that superiors reported communicating evaluations more frequently than subordinates reported receiving them. Similarly, superiors believed they were communicating more negative evaluations than subordinates reported receiving. To test these preliminary results on a larger sample in a different context, J. E. Thompson (1971) compared the perceptions of principals and teachers in six schools with respect to the frequency of evaluation and the frequency of negative evaluation. The data are strongly supportive of Seashore's results. We found, for all four tasks, that principals believed themselves to be communicating evaluations more frequently than was reported by teachers, with gammas ranging from .80 to .83. With respect to negative evaluations, principals reported communicating dissatisfaction far more often than teachers reported their principals to be dissatisfied. For the four tasks, the gammas ranged from .58 to .76. This discrepancy between teachers and principals is clearly important, for we have earlier noted that frequency of evaluation is positively associated with satisfaction with the evaluation process. Principals apparently do not know how infrequently they are perceived as communicating evaluations to their teachers. More generally, superiors should recognize the possibility of discrepant perceptions in

areas as subtle and sensitive as that of the communication of evaluations, and particularly, of negative evaluations to performers.

Agreements Among Evaluators

Our framework indicates that a respondent's satisfaction
with the evaluation process is dependent upon the belief that the
criteria of evaluation are sufficiently clear so that evaluators can
agree in their evaluations. As we shall discuss in detail in Chapter
Nine, perceived disagreements among evaluators are an important
source of problems in an authority system. We studied peer evaluation among university faculty, for we knew we would find diverse
criteria among these evaluators. To determine the amount of agreement for evaluators of the university faculty, we asked the following
type of question: "How much agreement do you think there is
among people in your discipline in their evaluations of (specific
task) by their colleagues?" A five-point scale was employed ranging from Extremely High Agreement to No Agreement At All. Surprisingly, there were no differences between the tasks of research
and teaching in reported amount of agreement among evaluators:
47 percent of the faculty sampled reported Very High or Extremely
High Agreement for teaching, with 48 percent the corresponding
proportion for research. This similarity was unexpected, for most
discussions of evaluations of faculty suggest low reliability in the
evaluation of teaching.

For both teaching and research, perceived high agreement
among evaluators was associated with overall satisfaction with the
evaluation process. Combining the two tasks and dichotomizing both
agreement and satisfaction, we found a gamma of .59 between perceived high agreement among evaluators and high satisfaction with
the evaluation process. Eight-three percent of those who perceived
high evaluator agreement among colleagues were high in satisfaction
with the evaluative process, compared with 56 percent of those who
perceived low agreement among their colleagues.

While we did not find differences between tasks in amount of
perceived agreement among evaluators, we did find differences between disciplinary groupings. In an attempt to explore possible
bases for these differences, we hypothesized that agreement among
evaluators would be more likely when the discipline was perceived

to be based upon a central body of theory. The existence of a central body of theory recognized by all or most members of a discipline should provide the foundation for a common set of evaluative criteria. In order to measure the extent to which particular disciplines were characterized by the existence of such a common theoretical system, we asked respondents: "Some academic fields or disciplines are seen as strongly based on a systematic body of theory which serves as the basis for research hypotheses and dominates teaching and scholarship. Other fields are less reliant on a central body of theory. To what extent does your own field have a central body of theory to guide research, scholarship and teaching?" The five-point scale employed ranged from Extremely Dependent (on a central body of theory) to Not At All Dependent. As expected, perceived agreement among evaluators was positively related to the presence of a central body of theory, reflected by a gamma of .45 for the dichotomized variables. Sixty-four percent of the faculty members who saw their discipline as dominated by a central body of theory perceived high agreement among their evaluators, compared with 40 percent of those who felt their discipline had a low dependence on theory.

Putting the two findings together, we predicted that overall satisfaction with the evaluation process would be positively related to perceived dependence upon theory within a discipline. Since many respondents gave middle-range responses, we trichotomized the responses according to dependence upon theory. We found that high overall satisfaction with the evaluation process was reported by 60 percent of the professors in disciplines perceived to be highly dependent upon theory; 52 percent of those in disciplines with medium dependence upon theory; and 38 percent of those in disciplines with low dependence upon theory. These data support the view that satisfaction with the evaluation process is related to perceived agreement among evaluators, which, for faculty members, is in turn related to perceived dependence of their field of study upon a central body of theory.

Effects of Visibility: A Comparative Study

Influenced by our previous research on evaluations, our colleagues, Meyer and Cohen (1971), examined the evaluation process in various public school settings. They noted that teachers in team situations in open-space settings which broke down the traditional isolation of the self-contained classroom were more oriented toward one another than were teachers in team situations without the elimination of physical barriers. This led us, in turn, to conduct a systematic study of visibility of work and its impact upon the evaluation process. Cohen and Meyer did not attempt to measure directly the visibility or the perceived visibility of the work of the teachers. We, therefore, attempted to develop measures which would permit us to differentiate performers of tasks into those whose work was more visible and those whose work was less visible to others.

In a study conducted by Marram, we collected data from 194 staff nurses employed by hospitals and 244 elementary school teachers. Our intent was to maximize variation in the degree of work visibility by including nurses and teachers working in teams and in nonteam structures. We wished to examine the effect of perceived visibility of task performance on performers' perceptions of the importance of evaluations from a given evaluator and on their perception of the extent to which evaluations of their work were accurate and appropriate—that is, soundly based. Four questions were used to measure visibility of task performance. Each question was both task-specific and evaluator-specific, providing information on the visibility to each evaluator of work performed on each task. The questions were: "On the average, for each task you perform, how frequently do you think (each evaluator) observes aspects of your task performance?" and "On the average, for each task you perform, how frequently do you think (each evaluator) observes the outcome of your performance?" Our seven-point frequency scale provided the response categories for these questions. In addition, we asked: "On the average, for each of these tasks, what proportion of your performance is observed by (each evaluator)?" and "On the average, for each of these tasks, what proportion of the outcomes of your performance is observed by (each evaluator)?" The eight-point proportion scale was employed for these two questions, with the categories Always, Almost Always, Usually, Fairly Often, Occasionally, Seldom, Almost Never, and Never.

We did not know which aspects of work—performances or

outcomes—or which mode of asking the question—emphasizing evaluation frequency or the proportion of work evaluated—would provide the best measures of visibility for our purposes. Since we had no guide from previous research, we asked all four questions. The result of all this effort was humorously simple. The four measures proved to be virtually interchangeable in the sense that there was a high degree of interrelation among them and each was equally strongly associated with the dependent variables that were the focus of our analyses.

We first investigated whether variations in visibility of work were associated with variations in work arrangements, specifically team and nonteam structures. For this analysis, we excluded all nurses and teachers working in "mixed" situations, focusing attention on the eighty-one nurses on nursing teams and the fifty-six teachers working in open-space situations involving primarily team teaching, in contrast with the eighty-nine nurses working in nonteam situations and the one hundred six teachers working in isolated classrooms involving primarily nonteam approaches to teaching. We examined the effect of working situation and teaming on work visibility for three categories of evaluators: superiors (head nurses for nurses, and principals for teachers), peers (other nurses and teachers), and clients (patients and students). Our findings indicated that teaming had little effect on nurses' perceptions of the visibility of their work to any class of evaluators. However, while teaming in open-space situations had little effect on teachers' perception of the visibility of their work to principals, it did have an appreciable positive effect on the visibility of their work to other teachers, and a slight effect on the visibility of their work to students. Comparing teachers in open-space, team situations with those working closed-space, nonteam situations, the visibility of teachers' work both to other teachers and to students was higher for teachers in open-space classrooms for all four tasks.

Team arrangements for nurses appear to have different consequences for work visibility than open-space and teaming arrangements for teachers. This is not surprising when one examines the actual arrangements in each team context. Nursing teams usually consist of a team leader, usually a registered nurse (RN), who supervises the activities of less highly trained workers, including licensed vocational nurses and nurse's aides. Depending on the size of the hospital ward, one or more nursing teams are associated with each ward under the supervision of a head nurse. This type of teaming was introduced in hospitals as a means of maximizing the effectiveness of professionally trained workers—RNs were given responsibility for the care of a group of patients and were allowed to direct the work activities of other less highly trained workers who performed most of the patient care tasks. It is not surprising that this type of team did not increase the visibility of the work of RNs to their head nurses or to other RNs.

By contrast, the creation of teaching teams working in openspace environments does increase the visibility of teachers' work to other teachers. It replaces the traditional one-teacher classroom, where a single teacher assumes all the responsibility for the teaching of a group of students, with a classroom situation in which two or more teachers work cooperatively to teach larger groups of students. The degree of cooperation and interdependence among teachers varies considerably from one team situation to another, but most such situations appear to represent a substantial change in the degree to which the work of a given teacher is visible to other teachers.

An interesting comparison is provided by examining the average level of visibility of work for teachers as compared with nurses (see Table 6). Our data indicate that, in general, nurses perceive their work to be more visible to their superiors and peers than do teachers in either team or nonteam situations. Teaming in openspace classrooms improves the visibility of teachers' work to their peers in part because it brings teachers together in larger classroom situations. Nurses on wards use a common base of operation, called a station, and often cooperate with one another in carrying out specific procedures for patients. Thus, creating teams in such situations has no appreciable effect on the already high visibility of nurses' work to their peers.

Visibility and Soundness of Evaluations. We expected that high visibility of work to an evaluator would increase the likelihood that the performer would believe the evaluator's judgment was soundly based. To measure the dependent variable, we asked: "On the average, for each task you perform, how soundly based are

Table 6.

MEDIAN SCORES FOR THE FREQUENCY OF COMMUNICATED PERFORMANCE EVALUATIONS FOR NURSES IN TEAM AND NONTEAM SITUATIONS AND TEACHERS IN OPEN-SPACE AND CLOSED-SPACE SITUATIONS*

NURSES

Evaluators	Carrying Out Doctor's Orders		Ward Management		Providing Comfort and Support		Record-Keeping		Observation and Assessment	
	Team	Nonteam	Team	Nonteam	Team	Nonteam	Team	Nonteam	Team	Nonteam
Head Nurse	2.2	2.4	2.6	2.9	2.8	2.9	2.4	2.7	2.5	2.6
Other Nurses	2.4	2.5	2.7	2.8	2.7	2.4	2.5	2.6	2.5	2.3
Patients	2.5	3.0	4.0	4.2	2.0	2.3	4.8	4.7	3.2	3.0

TEACHERS

Evaluators	Teaching Subject Matter		Character Development		Maintaining Control		Record-Keeping	
	Open	Closed	Open	Closed	Open	Closed	Open	Closed
Principal	3.9	3.8	3.7	3.7	3.4	3.6	4.2	4.2
Other Teachers	3.4	4.8	3.6	4.3	3.1	4.0	3.9	5.2
Students	2.0	2.4	2.2	2.9	2.0	2.4	3.1	4.1

* Frequency scale uses 1 for Very Frequently, 2 for Frequently, 3 for Fairly Often, 4 for Occasionally, 5 for Seldom, 6 for Almost Never, and 7 for Never.

(each evaluator's) evaluations of your performance?" A five-category scale ranging from Extremely Soundly Based to Not At All Soundly Based was employed. We compared those persons who reported that their evaluators observed more of their work with those who reported that their evaluators saw less of their work, dichotomizing at the median, noting whether visibility affected perceptions of evaluations as soundly based.

For both teachers and nurses, we examined the relationship between visibility of work and soundness of evaluations at three levels: superiors, peers, and clients. Looking first at individual variability in the perception of visibility and soundness, we obtained strikingly powerful and reliable findings. For each task and each measure of visibility, dichotomizing visibility and soundness at each median, and for both teachers and nurses, we found that all the relationships were strongly positive. We also combined the four tasks for teachers and five tasks for nurses and our four measures of visibility to compute mean gammas for teachers and nurses. The relationship for superiors (head nurses and principals) between perceived visibility and soundness was a mean of .70 for nurses and .69 for teachers. The average gamma for peers (other nurses and teachers) was .53 for nurses and .58 for teachers. Finally, for the clients (patients and students), the average gamma was .64 for the nurses and .68 for the teachers. Clearly, individuals, whether nurses or teachers, believed that those superiors, peers, or clients who saw more of their performances or outcomes were better able to judge their work.

Aggregating the data for groups of evaluators, we developed another way of looking at this same relationship between visibility of work and soundness of evaluations. We combined responses for individuals to determine how visible, on the average, work by teachers and nurses was to their superiors, their peers, and their clients. Superiors, peers, and clients were then ranked on this criterion, as well as on the perceived soundness of their evaluations. This analysis indicated that visibility was positively associated with soundness of evaluation in four of the five nursing tasks and in three of the four teaching tasks. The sole exceptions were the nursing task, Providing Comfort and Support, where the head nurses' evaluations were perceived to be the soundest even though this task was least visible to them and, for teachers, the task of Record-Keeping, where the clients were seen to be least sound in the basis of their judgments even though the task was more visible to them than it was to peers or superiors. Except for these two instances, we found that those positions within the organization which observed more of the work of teachers or nurses were judged by performers to make more soundly based evaluations.

Visibility, Soundness, and Importance of Evaluations. We asked both teachers and nurses the following question to determine the importance placed by them on the evaluations they received: "For each task, how important to you is the evaluation of (evaluators)?" Five categories of responses were used, ranging from Extremely Important to Not At All Important. Just as for the analysis of visibility of work and soundness of evaluations, we combined all tasks for superiors, peers, and clients to obtain mean relationships between the soundness of evaluations and the importance of evaluations. Individuals' perceptions of evaluations as soundly based were expected to be positively correlated with the perception of the importance of the evaluator. If an evaluator is thought to have a sound basis for his or her judgments, then there is more reason for the performer to care about them. This does, of course, leave out of consideration the crucial relationship, reported in Chapter Four, between influence on sanctions and perceived importance of evaluations. We refer to this topic later in this section. Examining individual differences, we found that persons who viewed their superiors, peers, or clients as making more soundly based evaluations were more likely to view their evaluations as important. Combining all tasks, the gamma for superiors was .40 for nurses and .48 for teachers; for peers it was .42 and .54 for nurses and teachers respectively; and for clients it was .57 for nurses and .67 for teachers.

In the same way that we related positional differences in visibility of work to positional differences in the soundness of evaluations, so we also aggregated individual responses in order to rank superiors, peers, and clients with respect to the soundness of their evaluations and their perceived importance. For the five nursing tasks the rankings of the three types of evaluators in importance were indeed positively correlated with the perceived soundness of their evaluations. The gammas ranged from .50 to 1.0. For the four teaching tasks the gamma was .50 for each task. Once again the positional analysis reinforced the results of the differences found at the individual level. Just as we previously showed that visibility of work leads to a perception of evaluations as more soundly based, so these results indicated that there is a tendency for evaluations which are more soundly based to be considered more important.

Having found that increased visibility is linked to more soundly based evaluations and that more soundly based evaluations are associated with increased importance of evaluations, we necessarily expected that visibility would be positively related to importance of evaluators. Using individual measures and combining our four measures of visibility for nurses and for teachers, we found similar positive relationships. Combining all tasks, the average gamma for superiors, relating perceived importance and visibility, was .43 for nurses and the same, .43, for teachers; for peers, there was a gamma of .42 for nurses and .46 for teachers; and for clients there was a gamma of .50 for nurses and .34 for teachers. Turning to our positional analysis comparing peers, superiors, and clients, for both teachers and nurses, the results supported the individual analyses. For four out of five nursing tasks and all four teaching tasks there was a positive relationship between visibility and importance. The sole exception was the nursing task, Observation and Assessment, where visibility was highest for other nurses but soundness of peer judgment was considered lowest. Clearly, both individual and positional analyses showed a strong and quite consistent relationship between the visibility and importance of an evaluator.

Examination of the relative size of the gammas for the relationship of visibility to soundness and visibility to importance indicated that visibility of work was more closely related to perceived soundness of the evaluations than it was to perceived importance. This is consistent with our previous analyses showing that influence over sanctions is also related to importance. Using comparisons for peers, superiors, and clients on the four measures of the visibility of the teachers' four tasks and the nurses' five tasks, we compared 108 pairs of gammas relating visibility to soundness of evaluations, on the one hand, and importance on the other. We expected the gammas relating visibility to soundly based judgments would be higher than the gammas relating visibility to importance. This was indeed the case in ninety-six comparisons. Only twelve comparisons failed to support our prediction of a closer relationship of visibility to soundness.

We are now ready to examine how variations in the visibility of work can modify the already demonstrated relationship between evaluators' influence upon sanctions and the perceived importance of their evaluations. For this analysis, we used a different measure of importance, a non-task-specific question which asked performers to indicate the importance to them of the evaluations received from a large number of evaluators. The question: "You may care very much about evaluations from some persons while the evaluations of others, for various reasons, may not be important to you. How important to you are the evaluations of each of the following persons?" For teachers the evaluators to be rated were Superintendent or Assistant Superintendent; Principal or Assistant Principal; Department Chairman or District Supervisor; Individual Teachers; Members of your Teaching Team; The Faculty of your Department; The Faculty of your School; Teachers of the same subject or grade in Other Schools; Volunteer Aides; Parents; and Students. For nurses, the evaluators listed were Director of Nursing Service; Supervisor; Head Nurse; Individual Nurses; Members of your Nursing Team; Doctors; Patients; and Patients' Family. A six-category scale was employed ranging from Extremely Important through Not At All Important and adding Not Applicable to the five-point scale. Later in the interview, following a statement in which we indicated to our respondents the meaning of the phrase "organizational rewards and penalties," we asked two questions about the actual and preferred influence of these evaluators, as follows: "How much influence does each of the persons listed below have on your organizational rewards and penalties?" and "How much influence *should* each of the persons listed below have on your organizational rewards and penalties? Similar response scales were used for these two questions ranging from Extremely Influential through Not At All Influential to Not Applicable.

There was generally a high correlation between influence on sanctions and importance, and between preferred influence on sanctions and importance. Looking at the rankings of the different classes of evaluators on influence, preferred influence, and importance, we found generally high agreement among these three variables for the evaluators of nurses and of teachers. It is the exceptions to this relationship which are interesting, for they seem to indicate the importance of visibility. Unfortunately, we did not have direct measures of the perceived visibility of work for these exceptional cases, yet we are sure from our general knowledge of the situation that the exceptions were all low in visibility. For nurses, the director of the nursing service in the hospital and the supervisor for the floor were far removed from the work situation. These were the only positions which were high in influence on sanctions but were ranked relatively low in importance. This suggests that the low visibility of nurses' work to them, with their probable reliance upon the evaluations of the head nurse, reduced their subjective importance to nurses. For teachers, the only evaluator high in influence who was considered low in importance was the superintendent of schools, who was perceived as relying on the principal for information and was far removed from classroom performance in a position comparable to that of the supervisor of nursing. Visibility seemed to modify, for both nurses and teachers, the generally strong relationship between influence on sanctions and perceived importance of evaluators.

Before turning to a comparison of nurses and teachers with respect to visibility, soundness of evaluation, and the importance of evaluators, we wish to present some findings from our other studies which demonstrate the importance of visibility. In our study of the university faculty, to be reported in greater detail in Chapter Eight, we found sizable differences in the visibility of specific tasks which were associated with major differences in the perception of influence. Colleagues at other universities were rated Extremely or Very Influential by 40 percent of the faculty when research and scholarship was the task, but only 4 percent of the faculty indicated that colleagues at other schools were Extremely or Very Important evaluators of teaching. Clearly, the visibility of published research escapes the usual institutional boundaries and provides information on this task to faculty at other universities. Another interesting example comes from our Five Organizations study in an analysis of persons named as evaluators by football players. The average football player named 1.7 evaluators of his performance who did not influence his rewards and penalties but who were regarded as important. This was a much larger number than was named by any other group in our study. Three-fourths of these noninfluential evaluators were external to the organization of the football team. Playing before thousands of persons obviously provides visible performances which can make outside evaluators important to participants. For example, the high school football coach can be an important evaluator of the college player and can make soundly based evaluations of his play. Visibility of work affects the permeability of organizational boundaries.

Let us now turn our attention to the comparison of nurses and teachers with regard to visibility and resulting differences in their evaluation systems. First, using frequency of observation of performances as a single measure of visibility that is representative of the four measures, we averaged the visibility of performance to superiors, peers, and clients across the five tasks for nurses and the four tasks for teachers. This is a somewhat dangerous method, since it gives each task equal weight, but it is likely to give a reasonable approximation of the visibility of performances to each class of evaluators. Using this method, we found that head nurses were reported as viewing far more of the performances of their subordinates than were principals; and other nurses were reported to see far more of the performances of their colleagues than were teachers, as already noted. The professionally trained evaluators had much greater opportunities to observe the work of nurses than that of teachers. With respect to clients, teachers reported higher visibility of their work to students than nurses reported for patients.

We found exactly the same pattern with respect to the soundness of evaluations. Combining the five tasks for nurses and the four tasks for teachers, the evaluations of head nurses were seen as more soundly based than those of principals, and the evaluations of other nurses were seen as more soundly based than those of other teachers. Similarly, students were seen as making more soundly based evaluations of teachers than were patients of nurses. We recorded the same order, then, in our comparisons of teachers and nurses for both visibility of work and soundness of evaluations.

When we examined the importance of evaluators to nurses

and teachers, the order we found in visibility of work and soundness of evaluations produced very different patterns for nurses and for teachers. For nurses, summarizing across the five tasks, the head nurse, to whom nursing performances were most visible and whose evaluations were perceived to be most soundly based, was considered to be the most important evaluator. Other nurses, ranked second in visibility and soundness, were regarded as being of approximately equal importance with patients, who were ranked lowest on visibility and soundness. Teachers reported a rather different situation. Although principals were regarded as making the most soundly based evaluations, teachers named students—the group to whom their performances were most visible—as the most important class of evaluators. Principals were ranked as second highest in importance. Other teachers, ranking lowest in visibility, were also ranked lowest in soundness and importance of evaluations. The modal situation in the schools we examined was one in which other teachers simply did not have sufficient information available to them to provide a basis for evaluations which would be subjectively important to their peers.

We have already reported that the situation of teachers varies greatly depending on whether they are working in a team or in a nonteam situation. Teachers in teams, compared with teachers working individually in isolated classrooms, were much more likely to report that their work was visible to their colleagues and that their fellow teachers' evaluations were soundly based. They also were much more likely to regard the evaluations of their peers as important. Indeed, working in teams not only increased the importance of peer evaluations, but also increased the teacher's perception of the influence that other teachers' evaluations had on organizational sanctions. Preferred influence was also affected. Teachers who worked in teams were more likely to desire increases in the influence of their peers than were teachers in self-contained classrooms.

It seems clear that teachers described an evaluation system in which, compared with nurses, evaluations were seen as less soundly based. In addition, except for teachers in team situations, the lack of visibility of teachers' work to persons other than their students created problems in evaluation. Although we can only speculate, these difficulties in the evaluation system of teachers may be related to the fact that teachers, compared with nurses, did not want their evaluations to have as much influence upon their rewards and penalties. Only for the task of Teaching Subject Matter did teachers desire a comparable degree of influence of evaluations. Under the usual circumstances of lower visibility, teachers apparently did not trust the evaluation system and, compared with nurses, did not want it to have as much influence upon the distribution of rewards and penalties.

Differences in Power and Instability

We have argued that performers and performer groups vary in their power to affect the structure and operation of the control systems in which they participate. In particular, we expect them to vary in their ability to determine various components of the evaluation systems that regulate their performance of organizational tasks. In general, the greater the ability of performers to determine evaluation system components, the more stable we would expect these systems to be.

Data are available from Magnani's study of 131 teachers in the public school system and have been reanalyzed by Crawford to examine this prediction. In order to measure the power of subordinates to determine various components of their evaluation systems, teachers were asked about two components, criteria-setting and sampling, as these relate to each of the four teaching tasks. For criteria-setting, we asked: "For (each task) how influential are teachers in determining the criteria which the principal uses to judge how well or poorly a teacher is doing in performing (each task) or any part of it?" And we asked a similar question for sampling: "For (each task) how influential are the teachers in determining what information your principal will select or collect for evaluation of performance of (each task)?" System stability was measured by teacher satisfaction with each component and by overall teacher satisfaction with the evaluation system.

The data overwhelmingly supported the view that performers who believed they could directly affect the authority system were much more satisfied with that system. For the four tasks, the gammas between ability to influence the criteria and satisfaction with the criteria were .66 for Teaching Subject Matter; .63 for Character

Development; .64 for Maintaining Control; and .31 for Record-Keeping. This was not unexpected, for we were predicting that performers would be more satisfied with those aspects of the authority system that they helped to determine. What is more interesting is that the gammas were equally high when we related ability to determine the criteria to overall satisfaction with the authority system for each task. The respective gammas were .68, .62, .61, and .49.

The results for the second component of the authority system, sampling, were equally positive. The gammas relating ability to determine the sampling process to satisfaction with sampling were .63, .69, .49, and .63, respectively, for the four teaching tasks. Again, the gammas remained high when we related influence on sampling to overall satisfaction with each task. The gammas were .67, .60, .57, and .71. These data provide strong empirical support for the predicted relationship between the ability to determine components of evaluation systems and the increased stability of those systems

Closer analysis of the distribution of these data indicates that teachers were often satisfied with evaluation systems over which they exercised little influence, but seldom dissatisfied with authority systems over which they exercised considerable influence. In the former situation, they could be satisfied or not, depending on such factors as faith in their principals or shared images of proper work arrangements. But having the ability to determine components of the authority system was a sufficient condition for being satisfied. If performers reported strong influence over system components, they were satisfied with these components and with the evaluation system as a whole. In short, the strong relationship we found was a product of teachers seldom being dissatisfied when they had the power to affect the evaluation system.

Data from this same study analyzed by J. E. Thompson (1971) permit us indirectly to test this same relation between teacher influence upon the components of the evaluation system and instability. Thompson examined influence in terms of the discrepancy between teachers' reports of actual and preferred influence on criteria-setting and sampling for the two tasks of Teaching Subject Matter and Character Development. Preferred influence was measured by questions identical to those just reported for criteria-setting and sampling, except that teachers were asked to report how influential teachers *should* be rather than how influential teachers actually were.

Since virtually all discrepancies between actual and preferred influence were in the direction of teachers wanting more influence, we could use discrepancy scores as indirect measures of ability to influence evaluation components: high discrepancy scores indicated low power. Relating these discrepancy scores to measures of teacher dissatisfaction produced the expected relation. For criteria-setting, the gammas between discrepancies and dissatisfaction were .78 for Teaching Subject Matter and .73 for Character Development. For sampling, the gammas were .79 and .81. Again, these data support the conclusion that lack of power by performers to determine the evaluation system is associated with low satisfaction with the system.

Non-Performance Bases of Evaluation

Our discussion has emphasized the evaluation of task performances, whether by looking at the performances themselves or by examining their outcomes. In order to determine the non-performance bases for evaluation in our Five Organizations study, we asked, "Are there other things aside from the way you perform in general as a (position) that have an important effect upon the organizational rewards and penalties you receive?" Among our 224 respondents sixty-six stated that there were no other influences aside from their performance. We categorized the open-ended responses given by the remaining respondents. Personality and human relations skills were the influences most frequently mentioned; these were cited by eighty-eight respondents as affecting organizational sanctions. Forty-four respondents mentioned "attitude," with football players and team leaders highest on that non-performance basis for evaluation. Age, sex, seniority, appearance, and outside contacts were other categories given occasionally. It is worth noting that race, nationality, or religion were hardly mentioned by our 224 respondents. Only one person mentioned race, a white who believed that blacks were discriminated against.

We can summarize our categorization of the responses to our question concerning non-performance evaluations by noting a strong tendency to base evaluations either upon performances or upon such factors as attitude, personality, and human relations skills, which are closely aligned to the quality of performances of the actors.

We do not mean to imply that the relative emphasis upon the evaluation of performances is present under all circumstances. We studied a Nigerian hospital and a Nigerian factory in 1966–1967, just as the Nigerian Civil War was beginning. Under these exceptional conditions, ethnic status was crucial in both organizations. We have chosen to describe in a separate volume the results of our study in that very different and complex context, but we should note here that, except for the stress upon tribal status, our theory of evaluation and authority was strongly supported by our Nigerian data.

Comparison of Two Schools

Our analytic approach to evaluation has focused on only one or two aspects of a given situation at a time. To conclude this chapter we shall briefly present a comparison of two schools in a single school district which differed dramatically with respect to their evaluation systems. We shall call one school Able, and the other Baker. By comparing these two schools, we can illustrate the interrelationship of several facets of the evaluation system as these variables are joined in the real world. The comparison of these two schools does not avoid problems of context and sample size, but it does provide a glimpse of the interaction of principals and teachers as they are linked by the flow of evaluations.

Teachers in Able School were more aware than teachers in Baker School of the criteria on which their task performances were being evaluated. We asked, "Do you have any idea what criteria (standards) your principal uses to determine how well or poorly you are doing on (each task) or any part of it?" The proportion of teachers in Able School responding "Yes" to this question on each of four teaching tasks was 61 percent for Teaching Subject Matter; 69 percent for Character Development; 76 percent for Maintaining Control; and 69 percent for Record-Keeping. These percentages may seem low; they should therefore be placed in the context of a wider study of six public schools. This study, conducted by Magnani, found substantial ignorance on the part of teachers of the criteria on which they were being evaluated. For Teaching Subject Matter, 53 percent answered "yes" to the question above; for Character Development, 43 percent; for Maintaining Control, 63 percent; and for Record-Keeping, 52 percent. It is apparent that in Able School, the proportion having some knowledge of the criteria was above this level. When we look at Baker School the percentages are markedly different. Only 27 percent of the teachers reported some knowledge of the criteria used for evaluating Teaching Subject Matter; 38 percent for Character Development; 47 percent for Maintaining Control; and 33 percent for Record-Keeping. In Baker School we observed a lower than average level of knowledge of criteria, knowledge which is essential if sanctions based upon evaluations are to influence the performance of task activities.

We have already reported that more frequent communication of evaluations is associated with teacher satisfaction. In response to the question, "How frequently do you learn your principal's evaluation of how well or poorly you are doing on (each task)?" we observed wide discrepancies between the two schools. Teachers in Able School reported receiving evaluations more often than teachers in Baker School. The proportion from Able School answering Very Frequently or Frequently to this question was 84 percent for Teaching Subject Matter, Character Development, and Maintaining Control; and 53 percent for Record Keeping. For Baker School the proportion reporting Very Frequent or Frequent receipt of evaluations was 22 percent for Teaching Subject Matter; 46 percent for Character Development; 22 percent for Maintaining Control; and 13 percent for Record Keeping. The frequency of communicated evaluations was thus much higher in Able School than in Baker School.

We would also expect teachers to regard those situations as more satisfactory in which they were able to participate in setting the criteria for their evaluation. The proportion of teachers in Able School responding that teachers were Extremely Influential or Very Influential in determining criteria was 45 percent for Teaching Subject Matter; 27 percent for Character Development; 36 percent for Maintaining Control; and 27 percent for Record-Keeping. These percentages may seem low, but in Baker School only 5 percent of the teachers saw themselves as Extremely or Very Influential in affecting criteria for Teaching Subject Matter; none for Character Development; 10 percent for Maintaining Control; and 5 percent for Record-Keeping. Similarly, the proportion of teachers in Able School reporting that teachers were Extremely or Very Influential in determining the sample of information used for evaluation was 50 percent for Teaching Subject Matter; 41 percent for Character Development; 50 percent for Maintaining Control; and 33 percent for Record-Keeping. The corresponding percentages for Baker School were approximately 5 percent for each of the four tasks. Clearly, teachers in Able School, compared with teachers in Baker School, perceived themselves as being much more influential in determining crucial aspects of the evaluation process. These findings support the results reported earlier in this chapter which showed that power to affect the evaluation system led to satisfaction.

These differences in knowledge of criteria, frequency of communicating evaluation, and influence on the evaluation process should produce major differences in teacher satisfaction. They did. We asked, "You have already been asked how satisfied you are with the way tasks are given, the standards are set, the way decisions are made about the information needed for evaluating, and the way evaluations are made. In general, considering all these things together, how satisfied are you with the way work is assigned and evaluated for (each task)?" Teachers from Able School were considerably more satisfied than were those from Baker School. The proportion in Able School saying that they were Very or Extremely Satisfied was 92 percent for Teaching Subject Matter, Character Development, and Maintaining Control; and 84 percent for Record-Keeping. The corresponding percentages from Baker School were 13 percent for Teaching Subject Matter and Character Development, and 18 percent for Maintaining Control and Record-Keeping. Similarly, we found that teachers in Able School were less likely to express dissatisfaction and to suggest changes than were teachers in Baker School.

Turning our attention to the responses of the two principals at these schools, we found that the principal at Able School reported evaluating his teachers frequently, communicating his evaluations frequently, and frequently indicating his dissatisfaction to them. He perceived that organizational rewards and penalties were extremely important to teachers and that evaluations were very influential in determining the distribution of rewards and penalties in his school. In contrast, the principal of Baker School reported that he evaluated his teachers fairly often, communicated his evaluations only occasionally, and indicated his dissatisfaction to teachers only occasionally. He saw organizational rewards and penalties as moderately important to teachers, and evaluations as only moderately influential in affecting the distribution of rewards of penalties in his school. When asked what changes he would suggest in the evaluation system for teachers in his school, the Able principal indicated a desire for greater teacher involvement and identified self-evaluation as the ultimate goal. In contrast, the principal at Baker School had no suggestions for modifying the evaluation process.

In this section we have focused on information gathered in two schools which exhibit sizable and consistent differences on numerous aspects of the evaluation process. The disparities between the schools are evident both from the data on teachers and from the reports of their principals. The consistency of our findings suggests that the various aspects of the evaluation process which we have examined separately do, in fact, constitute an interrelated set of variables, so that it is appropriate to speak of an organization's *system* of evaluation.

Chapter 7

Authority in
Formal Organizations

▲▲

Our analyses in the two preceding theoretical chapters enable us to develop a model of authority in a systematic fashion. We have previously decided that this model will emphasize authority stemming from authorization rather than from endorsement. We have also stressed the importance of the evaluation process in effecting control over the performance of organizational tasks. Our task now is to combine our notions of authorization, control, and evaluation to form a single model of authority relations. The model is meant to be particularly applicable to the study of control systems in formal organizations, but we do not believe that it is limited to these settings.

Model

So far, authorization has been only vaguely defined as normative regulation of the power-wielder from above. We need a more precise formulation of this concept. Also, we have been inclined to talk of evaluation as if it were a somewhat impersonal, disembodied process. This defect must also be remedied. Both deficiencies may be addressed by positing four types of organizational positions. The positions are differentiated by the nature of the tasks performed and by the extent to which position occupants exercise control over organizational sanctions. Participants in one position, C, have been allocated certain organizational tasks, for example, processing and transforming materials, treating clients, selling products, or controlling the work of their subordinates, D. Participants in the third position, B, have been allocated the task of evaluating the task performance of participants in position C. (It should be noted that an evaluation of task performance may be viewed as a goal, and, as for any goal, to be operative, it must be allocated to some participants in the form of a task.) Participants in the fourth position, A, have been allocated the task of authorizing the control attempts of B. It is their task to support and regulate B's attempts to control C. Authorization by A is viewed as a form of evaluation: participants in the A position are allocated the task of evaluating the evaluators.

The model focuses primarily on the control relations linking B and C. More precisely, we attempt to determine who exercises what type of control over C as C performs a given organizational task. Other relations—for example, attempts by C to control D, and attempts by A to evaluate B's control attempts over C—are included only as they impinge on the B to C relation. The model is applicable to virtually any organizational position or participant, and it is usually possible to examine a given organizational position from the perspective of more than one analytical position. For example, principals in elementary schools may be treated for some purposes as B's, attempting control over teachers (C's), under the authorization of superintendents (A's). Students over whom teachers attempt to exercise control would be analyzed as D's. Alternatively, principals may be treated as C's, attempting control over teachers (D's), but controlled by superintendents (B's), the superintendent's control attempts being authorized by members of the Board of Education (A's).

Authority in formal organizations is to be defined in terms

of attempts by one set of participants (B) to control the performance of organizational tasks by another set of participants (C),
the control attempts consisting of evaluations which affect the distribution to C of organizational sanctions. Further, participants engaged in control attempts (B) are themselves regulated in their
exercise of power by yet a third set of participants (A), the regulation consisting of evaluations which affect the distribution of organizational sanctions to B. The establishment of a pattern in which
some control others but are themselves subjected to control is fundamental to the model. Two levels of control are described: one set
of participants is viewed as authorizing a second set to control a
third set. Control is exerted *by* those authorized, and control is
exerted *over* those authorized.

The types of control attempts may also be further explicated.
Since our conception of control emphasizes the central role played
by evaluations, our identification of types of control attempts is
based on our analysis of the components of the evaluation process.
Paralleling our discussion of this process in Chapter Five, we identify four types of control attempts or control tasks: the attempt to
allocate a task to a participant; the attempt to set the criteria by
which a task performance is to be evaluated; the attempt to determine the sample which is to be drawn of task performances or the
results associated with them; and the attempt to appraise a task performance. From the perspective of the evaluation process, these
four types of control tasks identify the basic components of organizational control systems.

When authorized, the four types of control tasks constitute
four distinguishable authority rights. It should be emphasized, moreover, that this classification is not only a product of our analytical
framework. These four types of control tasks are often distinguished
by the organizational participants themselves, and each may be
assigned to and performed by different participants in the organization. For example, in an industrial firm, a superintendent may allocate tasks to workers, engineers may set the criteria for acceptable
tolerance limits, a foreman may select the sample of work to be
evaluated, and inspectors may perform the task of appraising.

Clearly, the control agent who appraises C's task performance and assigns an evaluation to it which influences the organiza-

tional sanctions C receives is an organizational evaluator for C. However, others may also be regarded as part of the organizational system evaluating C without being in a position to appraise C's task performance directly. They are part of the evaluation system to the extent that they have some voice in determining the tasks on which C receives performance evaluations, what portion of C's work is considered in arriving at an evaluation, or the criteria to be used in evaluating C's performance. Hence, persons allocating tasks to C, sampling C's task performances, and establishing the criteria by which such tasks are to be evaluated are viewed as a part of the evaluation system for C since they can directly or indirectly influence performance evaluations of C. Each of these components is involved in every evaluation, and the exercise of each may have a significant impact on the resulting evaluation.

This brings us to an important point. We began by distinguishing between the several components of the evaluation process and by recognizing that the individual components could be assigned to particular agents as control tasks. But the control tasks thus distinguished are not independent of one another. They are a part of a larger sequence of activities—the evaluation process. The attempts by individual control agents to control the task performances of C by exercising a particular component of the evaluation process are expected to be interrelated in specific ways. To capture this notion of interdependence, agents exercising the four types of control tasks are viewed as together constituting a control system. In other words, if we are to understand how task performances are controlled in many of today's complex organizations, we must be prepared to examine authority systems as opposed to simply authority relations.

Scope. Before further elaborating our model of authority, we wish to state more explicitly the characteristics of organizations within which it is expected to apply. Although the model is believed to be widely applicable, it does not apply to all formal organizations. Five scope conditions are proposed. The model of authority is limited to formal organizations in which: (1) the distribution of organizational sanctions to participants is dependent on evaluations made of participants; (2) evaluators who influence the distribution of organizational sanctions attempt to base their evaluations on the performance of organizational tasks by participants; (3) evaluators who influence the distribution of organizational sanctions to participants are themselves evaluated on their performance of the control task; (4) the set of participants attempting to control the evaluator is different from the set of participants whom the evaluator is attempting to control; (5) participants consider important those organizational sanctions whose distribution is dependent on evaluations of their performances.

The first condition excludes organizations in which organizational sanctions are absent or are distributed independently of evaluations made of participants. Examples of such organizations have already been described in Chapter Three. The second condition excludes organizations in which, although sanctions may be distributed on the basis of evaluations, no attempt is made by organizational evaluators to base their evaluations even partly on the performance of organizational tasks by participants. Thus, this condition excludes organizations in which evaluations are based entirely on the status characteristics of participants or on other bases unrelated to the performance of organizational tasks. The third condition indicates that our attention is focused on authority rather than on power systems. Those who are empowered to distribute organizational sanctions must be regulated as they exercise this power. The fourth condition excludes authority systems in which the regulation occurs exclusively by endorsement since we wish to develop a model that focuses on authorized power.

The first four scope conditions are not unduly restrictive in that they appear to exclude very few organizations or parts of organizations, at least in industrial societies.

Motivational Basis. Inasmuch as our theory locates certain inconsistencies and deficiencies in the evaluation process which affect the performance evaluations received by participants (C), it is important that these participants not be indifferent to these evaluations. If performance evaluations were of no consequence to C, C could hardly be expected to be concerned about inadequacies in the way evaluations of performances were made. The theory can be applied only to organizations whose participants place some value on the performance evaluations made of them. Hence, we added our fifth scope condition. Like the four previous scope conditions, this condition is viewed as not very restrictive. We do not require that C place a "high" value on the sanctions received that are based on evaluations, only that C consider those sanctions important. The degree of importance attached to sanctions is presumed to fluctuate greatly between and within organizations, but we rarely expect to encounter organizations whose participants place no importance on the sanctions received that are influenced by organizational evaluators.

Further, it should be noted that we place a restriction on the theory by attempting to specify one basis on which participants come to value their evaluations. By the first two scope conditions, the distribution of organizational sanctions is affected by the evaluations made of the task performances of participants. An authority system may be viewed as a device by which the organization attempts to determine for participants whose evaluations are to be taken into account. To the extent that organizational rewards and penalties are valued, performance evaluations linked to them will also be valued. We would expect, therefore, that in an organizational context, most participants will value their performance evaluations because at least some of the attendant sanctions are important to them. Also, in situations in which evaluations are perceived to be regularly linked to sanctions, we would expect that over a period of time the evaluations themselves would become valued. That is, evaluations may come to be valued symbols, themselves sources of gratification or deprivation.

Authorized Power

We can now formulate more precisely our model of authority. We will say by definition that B has power over C with respect to C's performance of a given organizational task to the extent that B's control attempts help to determine the organizational sanctions received by C. This power is authorized to the extent that: (1) B's organizational evaluators, A, if aware that B was attempting to exercise control over C with respect to a given task, would *not* negatively evaluate B for making the attempt; and (2) the organizational evaluators of *C* and of all other participants whose compliance is necessary to support *B*'s attempt to control *C*'s performance of the task would, if aware of noncompliance, negatively evaluate those not complying.

We will also say by definition that any *B* who is authorized by *A* to exercise a given type of attempt to control *C*'s performance of a task holds an authority right over *C* with respect to that task. Four kinds of authority rights are identified: the right to allocate a task; the right to set criteria by which the task will be evaluated; the right to select the sample of work to be evaluated; and the right to appraise the work by comparing the sampled work with the criteria in order to arrive at a performance evaluation.

Power is viewed as one actor's attempt to control the performances of another by means of evaluations linked to sanctions. Power is not defined in terms of the success of the control attempt, but in terms of one actor's ability and willingness to sanction another. Further, the definition is restricted both as to the types of sanctions employed and the kinds of performances over which control is attempted: we are concerned only with power backed by organizational sanctions and we focus only on attempts to control the performance of organizational tasks.

Two criteria are employed to specify the concept of authorization. The first criterion focuses on the normative regulation of *B,* the power-wielder, by *B*'s own organizational evaluators, *A*. It specifies that if *B* is to have an authority right to attempt a given type of control over *C*, then *B*'s organizational evaluators must not prohibit *B* from making the control attempt. It is not required, however, that *A* positively evaluate *B*'s attempt to control *C*, only that *A* not negatively evaluate *B*'s control attempt. The absence of a negative evaluation is construed as covering a broader range of behaviors than is the presence of a positive evaluation. That is, *A* may permit *B* to engage in certain control attempts which *A* does not positively approve.

The second criterion focuses on the normative support provided for *B*'s control attempt. Such support is especially problematic when *B* does not hold all the authority rights but must depend on the cooperation of others to help carry out the control attempt. By the second criterion of authorization, others whose compliance is necessary to support B's control attempt are required to comply by their own organizational evaluators. For example, an inspector on an assembly line may be authorized to determine the sample necessary for making a performance evaluation but not be authorized to allocate the task, set the criteria, or appraise the performance. In such a case, the inspector's control attempt will be meaningless unless the other participants in the evaluation process support his control attempt by carrying out their assignments. In sum, authorization of each of the various types of control attempts involves—in addition to a consideration of the relations among a particular control agent, B, the object of control, C, and the authorizer of the relation, A— consideration of the relations among the various types of B's and the extent to which their control attempts are authorized and coordinated.

Organizational evaluators (A) normatively regulate the power relationship between B and C by granting or refusing to grant authorization to B to exercise specified types of control attempts. It would be possible to analyze the control attempts exercised by A over B in terms of the several components of the evaluation process (does A allocate to B the task of controlling C; does A sample B's performance, etc.), but we shall not attempt to do so in the present analysis. It is B's power over C which is the focus of our present work and it is this relation which is described most fully in terms of the evaluation components exercised.

Our conception of authorized power allows for the possibility of some ignorance on the part of organizational evaluators of the actions of those under their control; the phrase "if aware of" is a part of both defining criteria. This caveat expresses our recognition that not every control attempt and not every response to a control attempt is under surveillance. In those cases where a given performance is unobserved by relevant evaluators, the criteria of authorization may still be applied in a hypothetical fashion. Such hypothetical applications are not only a useful tool for the analyst investigating authority relations; we believe that they describe the actual behavior of many members of existing systems. Subordinate members of authority systems often attempt to anticipate the reactions of their superiors and adjust their own behavior accordingly. Such predictions constitute a part of the stable set of expectations important to the functioning of any organization. C views as authorized a control attempt by B which is unknown to A but which, if known, would be supported by A.

Our general definition allows for the possibility of varying degrees of authorization and conflicts in authorization. B's authorization would be regarded as incomplete if, for example, B were subject to negative evaluations by some, but not all, evaluators for engaging in a given control attempt or if some of the evaluators permitted, while others prohibited, noncompliance with the control attempt. Hence, one way in which to examine degrees of authorization is in terms of the configurations of permissive, prescriptive, and proscriptive actions of organizational evaluators.

There still remains a degree of vagueness in our model of authority. In particular, the second criterion of authorization, applicable to the case where B does not exercise all components of the evaluation process, stipulates only that "all other participants whose compliance is necessary to support B's attempt to control C's performance of the task" would be negatively evaluated by their organizational evaluators for failure to carry out the appropriate control attempts. Which other participants are expected to supplement B's control over C varies according to the type of authority right exercised by B.

Thus, to take a specific case, we will say, by definition, that B has the right to allocate a given task to C to the extent that: (1) B's organizational evaluators, A, if aware that B was attempting to allocate a given task to C, would not negatively evaluate B for making the attempt; and (2.1) the criteria-setter would be negatively evaluated by the organizational evaluator for failing to set criteria for the task B has allocated; (2.2) the sampler would be negatively evaluated by the organizational evaluator for failing to establish sampling procedures for examining C's work on the task B has allocated; and (2.3) the appraiser would be negatively evaluated by the organizational evaluator for failing to compare the sampled work with the criteria to arrive at a performance evaluation of C for the task B has allocated. Similar specificity can be provided for the other three rights, the second criterion being appropriately modified to cover all rights not exercised by the *B* under investigation.

The foregoing definition of an authority right underlines the point that we are dealing with a system of relationships. It emphasizes one aspect of this system by indicating for each right the manner in which power and authorization relations link a number of persons or positions to constitute a control system. These relations are summarized in Figure 2, which exhibits the links involved in the right to allocate.

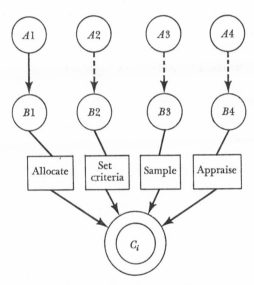

FIGURE 2. The right to allocate.

The type of control that *B* attempts to exercise over *C* is indicated by the box attached to the arrow. The solid arrow linking *A*1 and *B*1 means that *B*1 would not be negatively evaluated by *A* for attempting to exercise the right; and the dotted arrows linking *A*2 and *B*2, *A*3, and *B*3, *A*4 and *B*4 mean that some *B*'s would be negatively evaluated by an *A* for not supporting *B*1's allocation attempt, that is, for failing to exercise their respective components of the evaluation process. Other rights could be diagrammed in a similar fashion with the dotted and solid arrows linking the various A's and B's modified appropriately. In a complete system then, each B would (1) not be negatively evaluated by the organizational evaluator for attempting to exercise the right; and (2) would be negatively evaluated by the organizational evaluator for not attempting to exercise the right. Thus, to the extent that the control system is authorized, what from C's standpoint are rights exercised by B become, from B's standpoint, duties to be performed. This appears to us to capture the essence of the concept of normatively regulated power.

Our definitions focus exclusively on the links between those exercising control tasks and those authorizing the performance of these tasks. The description of these links is crucial to our conception of authority as authorized power. However, there is another aspect of the control system which is neglected by these definitions but which is implicit in our model of the evaluation process. If we reexamine Figure 1, it is clear that certain structural relations among those exercising the various components of the evaluation process are implied. For simplicity, we may conceive of these relations as a number of communication links among the right-holders, although in many cases they undoubtedly are power relations which are themselves subject to authorization.

Let us construct a minimal description of the communication links involved in a control system in which each component is exercised by a different actor. The allocator would need to inform the sampler that a given task has been given to C so that the sampler will be aware of the types of tasks on which an evaluation of C's performance is to be based. If the task is a new one for which no criteria of evaluation exist, the allocator would also need to inform the criteria-setter of the nature of the task so that the criteria-setter can determine the properties, weights, and standards to be employed. The criteria-setter, in turn, must communicate information on the task properties selected to the sampler so that he can determine the nature of the sample to be drawn. The criteria-setter must also inform the appraiser of the weights used in combining properties and the standards to be employed in appraising performance. Finally, the sampler, or someone acting under the sampler's direction, must communicate to the appraiser the observed values on the selected properties contained in the sample. The appraiser may or may not communicate the performance evaluation directly to C. However, the evaluation will be taken into account when decisions are made as to how sanctions are to be distributed to C. This description is summarized in Figure 3, an amplification of Figure 1.

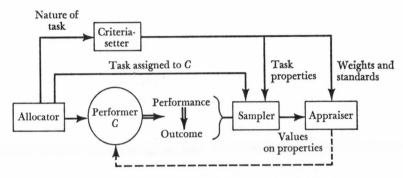

FIGURE 3.   Communication links among right-holders.

When we consider the authorization links together with the communication links among right-holders, the full complexity of organizational control systems becomes apparent. We do not assume that all attempts to exercise power in organizations are authorized attempts. This is a matter to be empirically determined. Nor do we insist that all the communication links suggested by our rational model of the evaluation process will be observed in functioning organizations. The nature of these links and the type of information communicated must be determined by research. The system described is unusually complex because of our assumption that each of the rights is exercised by a separate actor. One major way in which control systems are simplified in operation is to allow a single participant to exercise more than one authority right.

Differentiation or the lack of it may increase or reduce the number of actors involved in the control process, but it does not alter the basic components of the system. Our model holds that allocation, criteria-setting, sampling, and appraising are present in all evaluation systems. Several actors may cooperate together in carrying out one component or one actor may carry out two or more components, but these components must be exercised if the task performances of organizational participants are to be evaluated.

Authority System

We have defined authority as authorized power and have identified four types of authority rights. We have also described some of the interconnections which exist among the right-holders and their authorizers, but we have been careful not to define precisely the concept of authority system. We now define this concept, as well as consider appropriate definitions for other necessary concepts, such as authority structures and formal authority.

The designation of boundaries to constitute an authority system as a unit of analysis is somewhat arbitrary. One could, by analyzing one position at a time, specify the authority system of an entire organization across all tasks performed by participants in the organization, or one could limit the analysis to some relevant subset of positions and tasks. Our own approach is conditioned by our theoretical interest in problems arising in the evaluation process and responses to those problems.

We define an authority system as a set of relationships in which all power regularly exercised over and by a performer (C) relevant to the evaluation of C's performance of a given organizational task is authorized. Some important characteristics of this definition should be noted. First, this is a person-centric model of authority systems; the authority system is identified as it impinges on a given organizational participant. Further, the system is task-specific in that it refers to the system of rights exercised over and by C with respect to C's performance of a given organizational task. Also, only those rights which are regularly exercised are considered to be a part of the system. The notion of regularity is admittedly vague, for a right exercised as infrequently as once a year may clearly be included. The decisive criterion would seem to be the expectations of the recipient; the regular is the expected. Our intent, of course, is to focus attention on the operant system of authorized power as opposed to the system as officially constituted.

To identify an authority system, we begin with a participant, C, and with one of the organizational tasks which is considered in the evaluation of C's performance by organizational evaluators. The choice of task greatly affects the size of the unit defined as the authority system, for the size of the system is determined by the generality of the performance to be evaluated. If one were to focus on the authority system associated with a very general task and its evaluation—for example, the yearly formal evaluation made of a nurse's aide—the system would perforce include almost all rights exercised over and by that aide in the course of the year. At the other extreme, if one chose the evaluation associated with the task of performing a specified kind of block by a football lineman, the resulting system would be limited perhaps to a single case of allocation, criteria-setting, sampling, and appraising, all performed by the line coach. Having selected the task, we then identify all participants who exercise authority rights over C with respect to that task. This process involves identification of those B's exercising control attempts of a specified type, as well as a determination of whether B is authorized to perform the control task. In a formal organization we wish to determine the specific set of authority rights distributed over positions and exercised by position occupants. In addition, certain of C's relationships with subordinates (D) are also included in the authority system. In particular, we include rights C exercises over others when the performance of those others affects C's performance of the specified task and, hence, affects evaluations made of C's performance. The inclusion of certain of C's subordinates is in recognition of the existence of interdependence in complex organizations. For our purposes, interdependence is present when more than one participant contributes to a common outcome which is used as the basis of evaluation. Thus, the authority system not only includes all rights exercised by B over C with respect to the task for which C is being evaluated, but also includes authority rights exercised by C over those with whom C is interdependent.

Positional Authority

As we have seen, our model of authority systems is person-centric, and it is conceivable that each of several occupants of a given organizational position might describe an authority system unique to each occupant. While this is possible, we do not believe it likely. One of the purposes of formal organizations is to specify relationships in such a manner that the situation of one occupant is comparable to that of another in the same position. In addition to examining individual participants and their relevant authority systems, authority can be analyzed as associated with positions.

Let us consider first the case of a number of participants occupying the same organizational position. For present purposes, we may view a position as a location within an organization whose occupants share a common organizational title and are members of the same organizational context. Examples of organizational positions are quarterback of a university football team and nurse's aide on the pediatrics ward of a hospital. We will say that authority rights exercised over a position are *structural* to the extent that a given right-holder exercises identical rights over the occupants of this position. For example, we may find that a team leader regularly exercises the right to allocate tasks to a group of aides in the pediatrics ward of a hospital, while the head nurse regularly exercises the right to determine the sample of their work to be drawn in arriving at an evaluation. These two rights would then be regarded as structural. We believe that the amount of structure exhibited by authority rights is an important variable for participants in a given organizational system. A participant entering a situation where authority rights are highly structured is in a very different environment from a participant in a situation where there is little or no order in the location of authority rights. It should be noted that structure is regarded as a variable, not simply as being present or absent, and that a given situation may be characterized by the degree to which one or more authority rights are structured.

The concept of structure moves us closer to the analysis of rights associated with positions rather than persons, but it does not take us all the way. For rights to be truly positional, they must be formalized as well as structural. The concept of structure focuses on the extent to which a given superior treats subordinates in a uniform fashion, that is, as occupants of a common position. However, it does not concern itself with comparability among right-holders or with what might happen if a given superior were replaced. To cover these situations, we will say that authority rights exercised by a given position are *formalized* to the extent that its occupants exercise identical rights over the occupants of another position. For example, we may find that all team leaders in the medical ward regularly exercise the right to allocate certain tasks to their aides. As with the concept of structure, formalization is viewed as a variable and we may expect to find greater and lesser degrees of formalization associated with the exercise of authority rights by a given position.

To illustrate the differences between authority rights that are structural and those that are formalized, let us consider the case of an assembly bench worker in the electronics firm. If the supervisor of the assembly line treats all members of the work group in like manner, exercising the same kinds of authority rights over each for the various tasks they perform, then these authority relations are structural. If our assembly bench worker is transferred to another work group and discovers that the new supervisor behaves quite similarly to the former one, exercising the same rights over the worker and all peers, we say that these authority relations are not only structural but also formalized in that they remain constant for different occupants of the superior position.

We may speculate that authority by endorsement is likely to be highly structured, C granting legitimation to B's power in part because B wields it fairly and equitably. We would also expect authority by authorization to be highly structured, the A's seeing to it that B accords subordinates equal treatment. In fact, many organizations establish an appeals system by which C can complain directly to A of alleged unfair treatment by B. On the other hand, authority by endorsement is less likely to be formalized than authority by authorization. One of the important objectives of the hierarchical structure with its tiers of offices would seem to be to gain some control over the rights exercised by office incumbents. It is in the interests of the organization to see to it that authority rights exercised by persons in the same position are comparable. This formalization simplifies the evaluation of those engaged in performing control tasks and also rationalizes succession processes as occupants move into and out of offices.

To summarize, we have further developed in this chapter our conception of authority as authorized power and have employed the components of the evaluation process in order to differentiate four types of authority rights. Because these rights are seen to be aspects of a larger process, we have specified the types of coordination links among right-holders which allow the separate right-holders to function as part of a control system. Finally, we have defined the concept of authority system, and specified criteria for determining the extent to which particular authority systems are structural and formalized.

Chapter 8

Authority: Empirical Studies

▲▲

Most of the data in the first portions of this chapter are drawn from the Five Organizations study, in which we gathered detailed information on the four authority rights identified by our conception of evaluation. We report on our operationalization of these rights, on the number of right-holders for the several positions examined, and on the propriety of these rights, and we develop a measure of the degree to which the rights are consensual. The chapter concludes with a description of some of the major findings in a study of the exercise of authority in a university faculty.

Operationalizing Authority Rights

We have identified four key authority rights within the context of an organization: allocation, criteria-setting, sampling, and appraisal. We now indicate the manner in which these rights were operationalized in our field studies.

As previously described, prior to interviewing participants about their authority systems, the research team identified one or more specific tasks performed by these participants. Participants occupying similar positions within each type of organization were asked about the same task. All questions relating to the control system surrounding the participant, C, were task-specific questions. That is, we did not inquire about evaluation and authority rights in some general or diffuse sense, but focused attention on rights exercised with respect to a particular task performed by a particular participant, C_i.

Our most detailed analysis of authority systems was conducted in connection with the Five Organizations study. In this investigation, we explored such matters as the number of persons exercising one or more of the specific evaluation components over C, the extent to which each of the control attempts was authorized, and the propriety of these attempts as viewed by C. Later studies sacrificed some of this detail in order to focus on other factors affecting the evaluation process.

As discussed in Chapter Seven, our concept of authority rights contains two separable components: power, the willingness and ability of actors to manipulate sanctions in attempting to control others, and authorization, the support and regulation of control attempts by others superior to the power-wielder. In attempting to operationalize these concepts, both power and authorization may each be viewed as subsuming two components. Power may be subdivided into two parts: the exercise of a specific control attempt, and the promise of negative sanctions for noncompliance to the attempt. And authorization may be specified by two criteria, the first relating to attempts by others to regulate B, the power-wielder; the second, to attempts by others to support B's control attempts. This second aspect of authorization was not fully operationalized in the Five Organizations study, except in relation to criteria-setting. Indeed, this aspect of our model of the authority system was developed after the completion of the Five Organizations study. In particular, our conception of a control system involving interdependent actors, in contrast to our formulation of individual control attempts, was not fully developed during the period when we were collecting detailed data on authority systems. As a result, we do not have any data which reflect the interdependence of rights indicated in our final formulation.

We proceed now to report those measures which we did use in the Five Organizations study in order to determine the distribution of authority rights. We will discuss measures for each right in turn, employing the following labeling conventions. Persons or position occupants who were named by the respondent C_i as task allocators are hereafter labeled Ba_i. The "B" refers to any person named by C as attempting to exercise any type of control over him. The "a" indicates that the control attempt is that of allocation. In a similar manner we use "e" (for evaluation), "c", and "s" to indicate attempts to exercise appraising, criteria-setting, and sampling controls, respectively. In all cases the subscript "i" refers to a particular individual. For example, more than one particular allocator, Ba_i, may assign tasks to C_i, a particular performer.

Allocating. Allocating a task to C sets the goal for C's work and informs C that he or she is subject to evaluation on the basis of the performance of that task. In order to determine who allocated the task to C_i, each respondent was first asked: "Which people decide you should do (this task) or any part of it or decide when (or for whom or how) you should do it?" An alternative form asked of respondents who had difficulty in understanding the question was: "Is there anyone who requires you to do (this task) or any part of (this task) or requires you to do some part of it in a particular way?" Pretest versions of this question had simply asked, "Which people decide you should do (this task)?" This form of the question was discarded because too many respondents indicated that no one decided what they were to do, that it was simply their job to carry out certain tasks. Often, particular tasks are associated with a position in an organization, and many respondents did not know who was responsible for establishing the existing division of labor. This problem was largely resolved when we added phrases like "who decides when, or for whom, or how" C_i was to perform the task.

These questions tap the first aspect of power: Who is attempting to exercise a specified type of control over C_i? But having the power to exercise a given control attempt means more than

Evaluation and the Exercise of Authority

merely attempting to exercise that control. It also means that there exists the probability of negative sanctions for C_1 in the case of failure to comply with the control attempt. Thus we need to inquire whether C_i's noncompliance to Ba_i's allocation would be negatively evaluated by an organizational evaluator. If the same person who allocates a task to C_1 is also named by C_1 as an appraiser, then there is no need to inquire further. That is, if Jones assigns tasks to Smith and also evaluates Smith's performance on those tasks, then clearly Jones has the potential of providing negative evaluations—linked to organizational sanctions—to Smith. We determined whether C_i's allocator was also named as an appraiser in our question on appraising, to be discussed below. However, if a given allocator, Ba_i, was not also named as an appraiser, we asked C_1: "I notice that although (Ba_i) gives you this task, he doesn't evaluate you on it. Would any of your evaluators, (Be_i) disapprove if you didn't do (this task) for (Ba_i)?" By this method we determined whether any appraiser, Be_i, who controlled organizational sanctions was expected to punish noncompliance with Ba_i's allocation.

The two questions just described provide information only on the power structure—information on who is attempting to exercise one type of control over C_1 and on whether noncompliance to the control attempt results in negative evaluations linked to organizational sanctions. To determine whether such power is authorized we must also learn whether there is normative regulation—both containment and support—of such control attempts within the organization. Having identified which organizational participants were designated as allocators, we asked the following question to determine whether the Ba_i's named by C_1 were viewed as subject to regulation by the organizational hierarchy: "If $(Ba_i$'s) superiors knew (Ba_i) was giving you (this task) or any part of it, would they disapprove?" An answer of "No" to this question was taken as evidence that Ba_i's superiors would not take negative action against Ba_i for Ba_i's allocation to C_1. It is important to note that we have not assumed that higher-level superiors in the organization endorse, or support, or even have knowledge of all specific actions taken by lower-level supervisors. This assumption would be unrealistic. Rather, we assume that there is in most organizations a general disposition to approve of those actions which fall within the domain of authority of a participant in the organization, and that the way to determine the boundaries of that domain is to inquire as to whether attempts to exercise a given type of control attempt (in this case, allocation), if known to superiors, would not be approved.

As we have said, we did not operationalize the second criterion of authorization in the Five Organizations study. Had we done so, we would obviously have attempted to learn C_i's opinion on whether the criteria-setter, the sampler, and the appraiser, if different from the allocator, would have been subject to negative evaluations from their own superiors for failing to set criteria for, sample, and appraise the task performances or outcomes in question.

To summarize, for the Five Organizations study, an individual, Ba_1, was said to possess the authority right to allocate tasks to C_1 if: (1) Ba_1 was described by C_1 as attempting to allocate a specified task to C_1; (2) C_1 was subject to negative evaluation for noncompliance to the task allocation; and (3) Ba_1 was reported as not being subject to negative evaluation by A_1 for attempting to allocate the task to C_1.

Now that the general rationale of our approach has been described and illustrated for the case of allocation, the operationalization of the other three authority rights can be more briefly described.

Appraising. The second right to be discussed is the right to appraise how well a task that has been allocated to C_1 has been performed. In asking questions of respondents, we referred to this control attempt as "evaluating"; but for our theoretical discussion, the term *appraising* is used in order to distinguish this component from the general process of evaluation.

We were interested in identifying only those appraisers whose judgements had some influence on the distribution of organizational rewards. Further, we did not want to limit our attention to only those individuals who conducted relatively infrequent, formal evaluations; we wished to include those who carried out more frequent, informal evaluations as well. To clarify our purpose to respondents, we prefaced our question with the following explanation: "There may be many people who evaluate or judge how well or poorly you're doing on (this task). Some may make a judgement about your work every time you perform (the task) while others only occasionally do so. Although many people may make these evaluations, perhaps not all of them help to determine or influence your organizational rewards and penalties (such as promotions, salary, recommendations, days on or off, choice of shift)." Then we asked, "Whose evaluations of how well or poorly you are doing on (this task) or any part of it help to determine or influence your organizational rewards and penalties?" This question addressed the first criterion of power: Who is attempting to exercise this type of control? The second criterion was unnecessary for this particular right, since it does not make sense to speak of noncompliance to an appraisal attempt. A C_1 is unlikely to be in a position to prevent a Be_1 from appraising his work.

We turn then to the criteria for authorization. In order to determine whether the particular individuals named by C_1 as appraisers were viewed as being regulated in their control attempts by others in the organizational hierarchy, we asked the respondent the following question for each appraiser (Be_1) named: "If (Be_1's) superiors knew Be_1's) evaluations of your work on (this task) were influencing your organizational rewards and penalties, would they disapprove?" As before, we did not operationalize the second aspect of authorization relating to the compliance of other participants— the allocator, the criteria-setter, and the sampler—in C's control system.

Thus only two criteria were operationalized to determine who held the authority right to appraise C_1's task performance. An individual, Be_1, was regarded as possessing the right of appraising if described by C_1, as (1) influencing C_1's organizational rewards and penalties by evaluating C_1's task performance and (2) as not being subject to negative evaluations from A_1 for carrying out these evaluations.

Criteria-Setting. The question we asked to determine which participants were attempting to set criteria for the evaluation of the task performed by C_1 was: "In order to evaluate how well or poorly a person does a task, standards must be set to define what is satisfactory or unsatisfactory work, even though these standards may be vague. A standard, then, is the level which is set to distinguish good work from poor work. Who sets the standards for judging how well or poorly you are doing on (this task) or any part of it?" It should be noted that we focused only on the setting of standards as the most important and most apparent aspect of criteria-setting. We did not attempt to inquire about selecting task properties and determining their relative weights. As for appraising, it did not seem reasonable to consider noncompliance by C_1 to the attempt to set criteria, and it was thus unnecessary to operationalize this aspect of the power to set criteria.

The first criterion for authorization was operationalized in the usual manner. We asked: "If $(Bc_1$'s) superiors knew (Bc_1) was setting standards for judging your work on this task, would any of them disapprove?"

Now we come to the single occasion when we attempted to operationalize part of the second criterion for authorization. We did not establish whether the allocator or the sampler, if different from the criteria-setter, would be subject to negative evaluations from their superiors for failure to allocate the task or sample the performance of C_1. But we did ask C_1 the following question if the criteria-setter named was someone other than an appraiser: "If the standards set by (Bc_1) were *not* used by (Be_1) in evaluating you, would any of $(Be_1$'s) superiors disapprove?" It seemed to us particularly important to ask this question since all other right-holders are likely to come into direct contact with C_1 in exercising their control attempts. Allocators, appraisers, and samplers usually relate directly to C_1 in attempting to control C_1's performance. The criteria-setter is likely to be more distant; standards often are developed for an entire class of task performances. Therefore, for Bc_1 to have an authority right over C_1, it is essential that Be_1 use Bc_1's criteria in evaluating C_1's performance.

Collecting these measures, we see that an individual, Bc_1, was regarded as possessing the right to set criteria for the evaluation of C_1's task performance if Bc_1 was described by C_1 as (1) setting standards for judging work on the task performed by C_1 that (2) were employed by C_1's appraiser, and (3) whose activities as criteria-setter were not expected to be negatively evaluated by A_1.

Sampling. To determine who attempted to control C_1 by

deciding what information to collect in order to evaluate C_i's task performance, we asked C_i: "An evaluator must have some information (idea) about how you are doing on your work in order to evaluate it. Does (Be_i) himself decide what information will be obtained on how you are doing on your work on (this task)? Does anyone else make this decision (about what information will be obtained on how you are doing your work)?" We expected that the person who appraised C_i's performance would often also be the one who decided what information to collect on which to base the evaluation. But we also inquired about those situations in which persons other than the appraiser would determine the nature of the sample.

It seemed to us possible that C_i could try to refuse to comply with the attempt to gather information relating to his or her task performance. Performers can conceal portions of their work or attempt to claim someone else's products as the result of their own performance. Hence, to tap the second aspect of the power to sample, we asked C_i: "If you didn't permit the information specified by (Bs_i) to be obtained, would any of the evaluators (Be_i) you've mentioned disapprove?"

The first criterion of authorization was operationalized as usual: "If any of $(Bs_i$'s) evaluators knew (Bs_i) was deciding what information was to be obtained, would any of them disapprove?"

No attempt was made to fulfill the second criterion of authorization by determining whether C_i's allocator, criteria-setter, or appraiser would be negatively evaluated for failing to act in support of Bs_i's attempt to determine the sample to be taken of C_i's performance.

Thus, an individual, Bs_i, was said to possess the right to determine the sample to be used for the evaluation of C_i's task performance if Bs_i was described by C_i as (1) determining the nature of the information to be obtained for use in evaluating C_i's task performance; (2) C_i was subject to negative evaluation for noncompliance with efforts to obtain the information, and (3) Bs_i was reported as not being subject to negative evaluation for determining the nature of the information to be obtained.

We have described the manner in which we operationalized the four types of control attempts and their authorization. We made no attempt in our research to develop measures of endorsement. Also, we did not attempt directly to measure validity since, by definition, control attempts that are authorized are valid. It only remains for us to describe briefly the manner in which we examined the propriety of the authority rights exercised. Quite simply, we asked respondents, after they had told us of someone who exercised power over them, whether in their opinion this person *should* have the right to exercise that control attempt. Specifically, for allocation, we asked C_i for each Ba_i named: "Do you think (Ba_i) *should* have the right to give you (this task)? For appraisal: "Do you think (Be_i) *should* have the right to influence your organizational rewards and penalties by his or her evaluations of your work on (this task)?" For criteria-setting: "Do you think (Bc_i) *should* have the right to set standards for judging how well or poorly you are doing on (this task)?" And for sampling: "Do you think (Bs_i) *should* have the right to decide what information is to be obtained?" We did not attempt to determine the composition of the ideal authority system from the point of view of the respondent, but rather attempted to ascertain the respondent's reaction to those named as actually engaged in control attempts over performances.

This completes our presentation of the operationalization of the four authority rights. We have attempted to make clear where our operationalization was more limited than our theoretical formulation; and we have attempted to suggest the manner in which the operational definitions could be extended so as to be made more consistent with the more recent theoretical developments. We now describe some of the empirical findings based on the Five Organizations study and on our later research.

Analysis of Authority Rights

Positional Differences. One measure of interest is the number of individuals or occupants of positions who exercise one or more of the four control attempts. Some persons exercise only one of these control attempts while others may exercise several. An individual who is both an allocator and an appraiser is counted only once by this measure, whereas two different individuals, one an allocator and the other an appraiser, are counted as two exercisers. The number of different individuals who exercise some type of control is one indication of the complexity of the control system as it impinges upon the performer. The mean number of exercisers of authority rights by position is reported in the right-hand column of Table 7.

The first and most important thing to note from the data summarized in the right-hand column of Table 7 is that all position incumbents reported that more than one superior exercised control over them. Even occupants of positions engaged in relatively routine tasks in relatively simple and clearly defined structures—for example, storekeepers in the research organization and assembly line workers in the electronics firm—reported that an average of three or more individuals participated in their control systems. Across the entire sample of 224 respondents in sixteen positions, the average number of exercisers reported by each performer was 4.5. This finding suggests that discussions or measures of organizational authority systems which imply that there is a single superior exercising control over a set of subordinates represent a considerable simplification of these systems.

Further, cursory inspection of this part of Table 7 reveals sizable variations among positions in the number of exercisers. Nursing team leaders, for example, reported more than twice as many individuals engaged in control attempts as were reported by football team members. In general, there seemed to be slight tendency for the largest number of exercisers to be associated with positions near the middle of the organizational hierarchy rather than with positions relatively higher or lower in the hierarchy, although the limited number of hierarchies means the data can only weakly support this relationship. There was also a tendency for persons occupying professional positions in professional organizations—the hospital and the research organization—to report, on the average, a larger number of exercisers than other respondents did.

Also, as might be expected, positions varied in the number of persons reported as exercising each type of control attempt. The first four columns of Table 7 report information on the average number of persons attempting to exercise each of the four types of control. There is a slight tendency for performers to name a larger

Table 7.

Mean Number of Exercisers
by Type of Control Attempt and Position

	Allocators	Appraisers	Criteria-Setters	Samplers	All Types
Hospital					
Nurse's Aide	3.6	3.5	2.2	2.4	5.4
Nursing Team Leader	4.7	3.2	4.0	2.5	6.7
Clinical Clerk	4.0	3.9	4.2	3.7	6.2
Intern	3.6	4.6	4.3	4.1	6.0
Senior Resident	2.7	3.7	3.2	3.6	5.5
Research Facility					
Engineer	2.1	3.4	1.9	1.7	4.3
Draftsman	3.3	5.3	3.3	4.3	6.0
Storekeeper	2.8	2.2	3.0	2.2	3.8
Technical Typist	3.5	2.7	1.7	1.0	5.4
Electronics Firm					
Assembly Line Worker	2.2	2.8	2.1	2.4	3.5
Student Newspaper					
Desk Worker	2.5	1.9	1.5	1.4	3.1
Copy Editor	2.4	1.7	2.1	1.5	3.8
Football Team					
Member of Defensive "Front Eight"	1.7	2.2	2.3	2.2	3.2
Member of Defensive "Back Three"	1.6	1.4	2.0	1.6	2.6
Member of Offensive Line	2.2	2.3	2.1	1.9	3.0
Ball Carrier	2.5	2.5	2.1	2.0	4.5
All Positions					
Mean	2.8	3.0	2.7	2.5	4.5
Total Exercisers	636	674	613	553	

number of allocators and appraisers than criteria-setters and samplers. Analysis within responses from a single position supports the tendency indicated by differences in the means for all positions. Of sixty-four comparisons of the means, forty-two comparisons show the number of allocators or appraisers as higher than the number of criteria-setters or samplers, with eighteen reversals and four ties. This difference in the number of exercisers may reflect a genuine tendency among the positions examined for criteria-setting and sampling to be concentrated among a smaller set of actors than allocating and appraising are. It is also partially explained by the fact that performers reported having less knowledge of who set criteria and made sampling decisions as compared with knowledge of who allocated and appraised their work. For seven out of nine positions for which data are available, the proportion of "Don't know" responses was higher for criteria-setting and sampling than for allocating or appraising. A criteria-setter may establish work standards for a whole class of tasks of the type being carried out by performers but may have no direct contact with them. Similarly, the sampler may determine the basis for inspecting the work for a large number of tasks without communicating directly to particular performers.

Another comparison focuses on the manner in which the various rights cluster. For example, are persons named as allocators also likely to be named as appraisers or as criteria-setters? What proportion of exercisers is named as exercising all four of the rights? Data relating to these questions can be reported for two positions: nursing team leaders in the hospital and assembly line workers in the electronics firm. These positions were selected for illustrative purposes because the data are based on a relatively large number of respondents—twenty-nine team leaders naming a total of 195 exercisers and twenty-five bench workers naming a total of eighty-six exercisers—and because the two positions differ greatly in complexity of structure.

A comparison of these two positions shows a much higher proportion of exercisers who engaged in all four types of control attempts for bench workers than for team leaders—38 percent as compared with 19 percent. This is one indicator of the greater simplicity of the control system impinging on the assembly line workers in contrast to nurses. Bench workers were likely to name their bench supervisor and their line leader, and often the assistant supervisor, as exercising all four types of control. Some team leaders reported their nursing supervisors, head nurses, and assistant head nurses as exercising all four types of control, but this was much less common. Nurses were more likely to see their superiors as specializing in some subset of control attempts rather than exercising all types of control. A very high proportion of exercisers (24 percent) were described by team leaders as allocating tasks to them but as engaging in no other type of control attempt. As might be expected, the persons most often mentioned as only allocators were physicians and members of the house staff, residents and interns. By comparison, only 3 percent of exercisers were named by bench workers as persons who specialized in allocation. Team leaders and bench workers were about equally likely to name a position as specializing in setting criteria—11 and 7 percent respectively. The nurses named the nursing office as setting criteria and the bench workers named either the division head or the quality control department. The bench workers were more likely than the nurses to report appraisers exercising no other right—10 percent compared with 1 percent. The appraisers were usually inspectors.

Authorization and Propriety. Being named as an exerciser, the performer's noncompliance being subject to negative evaluation, and support and regulation of the exerciser by other evaluators were the three criteria used to indicate the existence of an authority right in the Five Organizations study. We also determined whether a person reported to be exercising a particular type of control attempt was viewed as properly doing so. Data relating to these measures are reported in Table 8.

Perhaps the most notable information contained in Table 8 with respect to authorization is the extremely low reported levels of unauthorized attempts to exercise control. The proportion of respondents indicating either that their own noncompliance would not result in negative evaluations or that their exerciser's control attempt would be subject to negative evaluations is 2 percent or less for three of the four types of control attempts. These statistics are based on approximately 550 to 650 control links, depending on the type of control attempt, reported by the 224 respondents. The only type of control marked by appreciably higher levels of unauthorized exercise is criteria-setting, and we can only speculate upon the reasons. It is important to recall that to determine compliance with criteria-setting, we asked about the compliance of Be_1, C_i's appraisers, to the

Table 8.

AUTHORIZATION AND PROPRIETY OF EXERCISERS
BY TYPE OF CONTROL ATTEMPT
FIVE ORGANIZATIONS STUDY

	AUTHORIZATION		PROPRIETY	
	Proportion of exercisers for whom C_i's compliance was not required	*Proportion of exercisers whose A_i's would disapprove*	*Proportion of exercisers, authorized and unauthorized, whose control attempts were not viewed as proper*	*Proportion of right-holders whose control attempts were not viewed as proper*
Allocators	.02	.01	.05	.05
Appraisers	*	.01	.04	.04
Criteria-Setters	.06**	.04	.04	.03
Samplers	.004	.02	.03	.02

* Not determined because it is not possible for C_1 not to comply with the receipt of a performance evaluation.
** Question asked about the compliance of Be_1 rather than C_1.

standards set by Bc_1, rather than about the compliance of C_1, the performer. This might possibly account for some of the difference in response to this question, but it does not explain the greater tendency for respondents to report that criteria-setters they named were more likely to be negatively evaluated by A_1 for their control attempt. Perhaps criteria-setters are more likely to have their control attempts questioned because they are more distant from performers, although samplers, also more distant than allocators and appraisers, are not as high as criteria-setters in the proportion of unauthorized exercisers.

Before leaving the topic of authorization, we feel compelled once again to emphasize the very low levels of unauthorized exercise found in all the organizational positions. For example, the largest proportion of unauthorized behavior reported by any set of position occupants for any single type of control attempt was .14. Desk workers on the student newspaper reported that 14 percent of those attempting to set criteria for their work were unauthorized to do so. Further, examining each position for each of the four types of control attempts, unauthorized exercisers were not widespread in that 58 percent of the positions reported no unauthorized exercisers of each type of control attempt. Such findings led us to collect less detailed data on authorization in subsequent studies and to concentrate our attention on other aspects of control systems.

Given the low levels of unauthorized control attempts indicated in Table 8, we do not present detailed data on differences among positions. The student newspaper and the hospital were clearly the top two organizations in the proportion of unauthorized exercisers. Since the student newspaper did not have complex control systems, as noted in Table 7, this indicates a relatively high level of unauthorized exercisers. In Chapter Ten we will report additional data on the bases for these problems in the student newspaper.

With regard to propriety, in Table 8 we see in comparing columns three and four with columns one and two that, in general, with the exception of criteria-setting, respondents were more likely to perceive control attempts to be improper than to be unauthorized. Yet the proportion of improper control attempts, like unauthorized ones, was low. Respondents were less likely to consider control attempts by right-holders improper than to consider control attempts by unauthorized exercisers improper. The greater propriety of control by right-holders was present for all four rights. The comparison of column four with column three understates the strength of the relationship, partly by rounding of these small proportions to the nearest percent, but especially because the differences between these columns are produced only by the small proportion of exercisers who are unauthorized and consequently not right-holders. Our respondents did indeed show a tendency to accept the system of authorized power.

Again, it does not seem profitable, given the low level of impropriety, to report in detail about each position. Instead, we will comment briefly on the nine positions revealing relatively high levels of impropriety. These positions were: senior residents, clinical clerks, interns, and nurse's aides in the hospital; engineers and technical typists in the research organization; copy editors and desk workers at the student newspaper; and offensive linemen on the football team.

Considering positions within the hospital first, senior residents reported that 17 percent of their exercisers were improperly engaged in control attempts, clinical clerks, 18 percent, and interns, 9 percent. For all three positions, the most frequent improper exercisers were other members of the house staff—other residents, interns, and clerks. Apparently there was some difficulty in relating to peers or near-peers in the hospital context. The next most frequent improper exercisers for house staff were the medical consultants. Some of these physicians apparently were viewed as inappropriately attempting to offer more than advice. For nurse's aides, the most frequently named improper exercisers were physicians, followed closely by house staff. Aides seemingly resented receiving orders and evaluations from physicians, preferring to be controlled by members of the nursing hierarchy. Nursing team leaders reported a very high number of allocators among physicians and house staff, but the nurses did not tend to regard these control attempts as improper.

Within the research organization, engineers regarded 13 percent of their exercisers as improperly exercising control. Most frequently named were the heads of related departments, for example, the head of the design division. Technical typists reported that 17 percent of those attempting to control their performances were doing so improperly. Almost without exception those named were the authors of the papers being typed. Technical typists clearly wanted authors to go through the proper channels and preferred to receive orders and evaluations from the coordinator of their typing pool.

Desk workers and copy editors on the student newspaper reported 10 and 11 percent, respectively, of their exercisers to be improperly engaged in control attempts. Positions named as improperly exercising control included the staff editor, the news editor, and the night editor. Since all these positions would ordinarily be expected to exercise some control over desk workers and copy editors, we may speculate that these reports reflect personality clashes, judgements that the occupant of the position was incompetent, or more general lack of consensus concerning the authority system.

Finally, and somewhat surprisingly, members of the offensive line on the football team regarded 9 percent of their exercisers as engaging in improper control attempts. Positions named as improperly attempting control were the spread player coach and the back coach. Offensive linemen apparently resented the control attempts of these coaches even though their activities were highly interdependent with those of players legitimately controlled by these coaches. They appeared to regard two coaches, the head coach and their own assistant coach, as sufficient. Virtually none of the other positions on the football team reported any impropriety.

In addition to these specific and sometimes idiosyncratic bases of impropriety, we found a more general source of perceived impropriety. We asked our interviewers to probe for reasons whenever respondents labeled any authorized link as improper. A qualitative analysis of these unstructured responses suggested the hypothesis that impropriety is often a product of inappropriate role distance between the controller and the performer. It appeared that if the right-holders were far removed from the performer, they were more likely to be viewed as unaware of the problems faced by the subordinate and as not making proper allowances in regulating performances. On the other hand, if the controllers were close to the performer, they were more likely to be viewed as lacking objectivity or as inclined to interfere unduly with performances.

This hypothesis that inappropriate role distance led to perceived impropriety was pursued in a separate small study under the direction of K. U. Barchas (1966). This study was based on a sample of ten nurses and ten nurse's aides drawn from a hospital different from the one in the Five Organizations study. We asked these nurses and aides about only two of the four rights: Who appraised their work and who set the criteria on which evaluations were based? The twenty respondents reported a total of fifty-nine appraisal links and forty-four criteria-setting links. We asked respondents about the propriety of each of these links and to give a reason for their judgement, whether it was judged proper or improper.

Appropriate role distance was not the most frequent explanation given by nurses to explain why they judged appraising and criteria-setting links to be proper. The largest number of respondents referred to the responsibility or accountability of right-holders and the corresponding necessity of having control rights. Nevertheless, of the fifty-two proper appraisal links, appropriate role distance was mentioned for eighteen, or 35 percent; thirteen exercisers were reported to be "close enough" to appraise performance properly, and five exercisers were reported as "far enough removed" to allow for proper appraisal. Only four of the forty-one criteria-setting links were viewed as proper because of appropriate role distance.

Consistent with the findings of our larger study, impropriety was a rare phenomenon: only seven of the fifty-nine appraisal links and three of the forty-four criteria-setting links were labeled improper. Remarkably, six of the seven appraisal links were labeled improper because of problems with role distance; for four of the six links, the appraiser was regarded as being "too far removed" for proper evaluation, and for two of the six, as "too close." Two of the three improper criteria-setting links were viewed as having controllers too far removed from the work for which they were establishing standards. In short, in eight of the ten cases of perceived impropriety, respondents gave reasons directly related to role distance. Further, for seven of these eight cases, role distance was the only explanation offered by the respondent to justify reactions to the exerciser. Although based on a very small study, these findings suggest that inappropriate role distance may play an important part in accounting for the perceived impropriety of control attempts.

Measure of Structural Authority Rights. As noted in Chapter Seven, most of our analysis is focused on authority systems—authority links defined by the respondent. These links may vary considerably from person to person even for those occupying the same position and working in the same organizational location. For example, two team leaders in the pediatrics department working on the day shift may not name the same persons as allocators. Each may interact with different physicians, members of the house staff, and nurses and may interact in different ways with the same persons. Even if their situations were objectively identical, team leaders might perceive them differently. Nevertheless, the team leaders occupy the same position in an organizational structure, and we would expect them, in general, to be subject to the same form of control system. By definition, authority rights exercised over a position are structural to the extent that a given right-holder exercises identical rights over the occupants of this position.

To operationalize this view of structure, we measured the amount of consensus among persons occupying the same position in an organizational context concerning the rights exercised over them by others. We searched the literature in vain for an appropriate measure of consensus, and were forced to develop our own.

Up to this point, our analysis has largely been based on all occupants of the sixteen positions in the Five Organizations study. However, for the analysis of consensus we need to move the level of analysis down to the level of specific work groups located in specific organizational contexts. For example, the nurse's aides in our sample were employed in five contexts within the hospital: two wards within the department of internal medicine, one ward within the department of pediatrics, and two wards within surgery. Within these contexts, nurse's aides were further differentiated by shift. Thus, for example, we examined the amount of consensus among nurse's aides working on the day shift of one ward within the pediatrics department. Using similar criteria, forty-four distinguishable work groups were identified for the sixteen positions.

In order to permit cross-group comparisons for each of the positions it was necessary to develop broader categories of right-holders. Thus, for example, while the football team had specialized coaches who were named as right-holders by individual respondents, the positions we used to measure the degree of structure in the authority rights were: head coach, the respondent's own particular coach, other defensive coaches, other offensive coaches, the freshman coach, and other team members. We asked members of the diverse positions studied to help us produce these condensed lists of positions in a manner that would not distort the information received.

We now describe the measure of consensus used in this analysis. Assume, for example, that there are five nurse's aides in a work group. Each of these five respondents is asked to report who is exercising each component of the evaluation process for the specified task. Then, for each exerciser named, we determine whether he or she is authorized to engage in that control attempt. This defines our set of right-holders for each of the authority systems for each respondent. In order to determine consensus we decided that an authority link would be declared *structural* when a majority—more than half —of the respondents reported the particular right to be exercised by the same position occupant. This criterion for consensus may appear to be low, but in our experience sociologists tend to exaggerate the amount of consensus existing in the perceptual world of actors. It is, in fact, a demanding criterion: the majority of subordinates must agree that the occupant of a particular position does indeed have a right and is regularly exercising it for a given task. Also, by using a majority as the criterion, no more than one authority structure can be found for a particular right over a given position for a specific task.

Returning to our example, then, we first determine the proportion of nurse's aides in the work group who report a given position as exercising a specific right—say, team leaders named as allocators. If half or more of the nurse's aides attribute this right to this position occupant, then we say that this right is structurally present. If fewer than half of the nurse's aides attribute this right to the team leader, then we say that this right is not structurally present. The same procedure is performed for occupants of other positions named by one or more nurse's aides as exercising a specific right, such as the head nurse, the nursing supervisor, interns, and physicians.

Having established which links between positions are structural and which are not, we can then compute two measures relating to consensus, one for individual respondents and one for each group. First, we can measure the extent to which the responses of each nurse's aide are in accord with the majority of the aide's peers. To do this, for each aide, we simply divide the number of correct assignments of the structural authority right by the sum of correct assignments plus errors of omission plus errors of commission. In effect, we reduce the score of each aide for each time that the occupant of a position is given an authority right that is not granted by the majority of the aides in the work group, and we also reduce the score for each time that the aide fails to grant an authority right to the occupant that has been granted that right by a majority of the aides in the work group. This calculation provides a proportion which represents the extent to which each aide has reproduced the consensual authority structure. The mean of these proportions for all respondents in the work group provides a single score that represents the degree of consensus within the group concerning the distribution of a given authority right across right-holders. Note that this measure gives equal weight to respondents, not to responses. The calculation of these measures is illustrated in Table 9, which is based on five respondents reporting whether occupants of eight positions hold a given right.

A set of studies carried out by one of our co-workers, Charles Brody, revealed that there was a slight tendency for group consensus scores to vary inversely by group size. One method used to test the relationship between size of work group and amount of consensus combined the data for all organizational positions in the Five Organizations study and yet controlled for position. Within each organizational context, and for each position, we labeled the largest work group found "large" and the smallest work group "small." Combining results across all positions, consensus scores on allocation for small groups was .76 compared with .71 for large groups; for appraisal, .84 for small groups and .76 for large; for criteria-setting, .69 for small groups and .61 for large; and for sampling, .79 for small groups and .65 for large. Similar results were obtained when each work group in the sample was paired with another within the same position, allowing the groups to vary only in size. These paired comparisons, which controlled for organizational position and context, supported the view that consensus was somewhat lower for larger work groups, although for criteria-setting no such tendency was apparent.

It is not appropriate to present here detailed consensus scores for forty-four work groups on four types of control attempts. We do, in Table 10, present some illustrative data from three positions—interns, nurse's aides, and assembly line workers—operating in twelve work groups. Comparisons of the consensus scores for interns shows a higher level of consensus for allocation among surgical interns and relatively low levels of consensus for allocation among interns in pediatrics and internal medicine. Surgical interns were likely to agree that their allocations came primarily from residents, the surgical faculty, and chief of service, while medical and pediatric interns reported that they also received allocations from medical consultants, attending physicians, and nurses. This pattern of allocation is consistent with that reported by Coser (1958) who describes the

Table 9.

ILLUSTRATION OF THE CALCULATION OF CONSENSUAL MEASURES OF AUTHORITY

Positions of Right-Holders	*Respondents* 1	2	3	4	5	*Proportion reporting that position occupant holds given right*
A	X	X	X	X	X	1.00
B		*X*		*X*		0.40
C	X	O	X	O	X	0.60
D	X	X	X	X	O	0.80
E		*X*				0.20
F	*X*					0.20
G	*X*					0.20
H	*X*					0.20
Extent of respondent's agreement with authority structure (individual consensus score)	3/6	2/5	3/3	2/4	2/3	
	.50	.40	1.0	.50	.67	

Group consensus score
$$= \sum_i \left(\frac{\text{Agreements with majority of respondents}}{\text{Agreements} + \text{Disagreements}} \right) \Big/ (n)$$

Group consensus score
$$= \frac{.50 + .40 + 1.0 + .50 + .67}{5} = .61$$

Key:

X = Respondent states that an occupant of the position has a specific authority right and the majority of respondents agree.

X = Respondent states that an occupant of the position has a specific authority right but the majority of respondents do not agree (error of commission).

O = Majority of respondents report that the occupant of a position has a specific authority right but the respondent does not agree (error of omission).

Table 10.

CONSENSUS SCORES ON AUTHORITY RIGHTS
FOR SELECTED WORK GROUPS

INTERNS

	Pediatrics	Internal Medicine	Surgery
Allocators	.38	.59	.71
Appraisers	.90	.83	.62
Criteria-setters	.80	.81	.46
Samplers	.90	.59	.60
	n = 5	n = 7	n = 9

NURSE'S AIDES

	Pediatrics		Internal Medicine		Surgery	
	Day	Night	Day	Night	Day	Night
Allocators	.78	.91	.75	1.00	.87	1.00
Appraisers	.69	.76	.64	1.00	1.00	1.00
Criteria-setters	.49	.62	.77	1.00	.41	.61
Samplers	.33	.43	.89	—	.67	.56
	n = 6	4	n = 3	2	n = 2	3

ASSEMBLY LINE WORKERS

	Bench W	Bench Y	Bench Z
Allocators	1.00	1.00	.69
Appraisers	.95	.86	.82
Criteria-setters	.74	.33	.59
Samplers	.74	.86	.70
	n = 7	n = 7	n = 7

"pine tree" type of organization prevalent in surgery in contrast to the "oak tree" authority structure found in internal medicine. Yet it does not explain the lower consensus among surgical interns on the other three rights.

Comparisons for nurse's aides revealed the relatively higher consensus scores reported by aides on the night shift compared with the day shift for all three wards. Although these scores may be somewhat affected by group size, our observations also indicate that night staffing structures tend to be simpler and less problematic than day staffing patterns.

Assembly line workers tended to produce higher consensus scores than those found in the hospital, at least for allocation and appraising. Reduced scores and variability for criteria-setting were produced by disagreements among workers concerning the authority of the line supervisory structure as compared with the staff group of inspectors and quality control personnel.

We earlier stated that respondents in the Five Organizations study appeared to have more knowledge of allocation and appraisal than they did of criteria-setting or sampling. This condition is again revealed by the consensus measures. Combining data for the entire sample of positions, consensus concerning who held the right to allocate tasks and appraise performances was slightly higher than consensus concerning who set the criteria or made the sampling decisions. The mean consensus score across all positions was .75 for allocation; .79 for appraisal; .71 for criteria-setting; and .70 for sampling.

Authority in a University Faculty

Having learned from our previous studies that most exercised power within formal organizations is both authorized and proper, and having established that the four components of evaluation are sometimes separated and assigned as authority rights to occupants of different positions, we turned our attention to other matters in our study of a university faculty, conducted in association with Hind (1968). A major limitation of the Five Organizations study was that only one task was studied for each position. We wished in the university study to test our assumption that authority systems may vary depending on the task carried out by the performer. Because we wished to examine the control system associated with more than one task, we decided to focus on a more generalized right—the right to make evaluations which have some influence on the distribution of organizational sanctions—rather than distinguishing between the four components of evaluation. We also attempted to move beyond the mere determination of who held the right to evaluate in order to examine variations among evaluators in perceived influence on organizational sanctions. Similarly, we did not simply determine the propriety or impropriety of each evaluator for each task, but we attempted to ascertain the amount of influence performers would prefer that a given evaluator have on sanctions for a specified task.

These are among the matters to be discussed in this section, but we shall also report other findings of interest from this study which relate to the operation of an evaluation system in a complex professional organization.

Influence of Evaluations. Data were collected by Hind in a major large private university. The sample consisted of 100 faculty members randomly selected but stratified so as to provide approximately equal numbers of assistant, associate, and full professors. Faculty members were asked to describe the control system to which they were subject in the performance of four types of tasks. We defined these tasks for respondents and then proceeded to attempt to make clear our concept of organizational evaluator in the following manner:

> For the purposes of this study, I would like to concentrate on some of the activities you may perform as a faculty member, and I would like to group them together into the following categories: (1) classroom teaching; (2) research and scholarship; (3) university service, including committee service, administrative work, advising, and other noninstructional student contacts; (4) external service, including consulting, service to professional organizations, membership on government boards, etc. It is partly on the way in which faculty members carry out some or all of these activities that they are judged by persons who have some influence, either direct or indirect, over university rewards. I have in mind here such tangible rewards as promotion, salary increases, research support, office and clerical support, and the like. Of course, I recognize the importance of intangible rewards for one's efforts, but in this study it is necessary to limit concern to those factors determining tangible rewards.

For each of the four tasks, respondents were asked the following questions: "How much influence does the evaluation of your (specific task) have in determining your university rewards?" and "How much influence do you think the evaluation of your (specific task) *should* have on your university rewards?" Response alternatives provided were on the five-point scale: Extremely Influential, Very Influential, Moderately Influential, Slightly Influential, and Not At All Influential.

The last two tasks, university service and external service, were perceived by faculty as having little influence upon the distribution of university rewards. Evaluations of university service were perceived as Very or Extremely Influential by only 8 percent of the sample, and external service by only 3 percent. Since there was no strong desire expressed by faculty to increase the influence of these tasks upon university sanctions, we can appropriately focus our analysis on the remaining two tasks: classroom teaching, and research and scholarship. These are generally viewed as the principal tasks of a university faculty member and were viewed by our sample of respondents as having the most influence on their university rewards.

Comparing the tasks of research and teaching, the responses of our sample supported the view that research or scholarship in a major university is more influential than teaching in affecting university rewards. Twenty percent of the faculty viewed evaluations of teaching as Very or Extremely Influential compared with 78 percent who viewed research as Very or Extremely Influential. While most faculty members recognized that evaluations of their research were more influential than evaluations of their teaching, they expressed the desire to reduce the disparity between the influence of research and that of their other major task, teaching. When asked how much influence they believed teaching should have on their rewards, 51 percent felt that teaching should be Very or Extremely Influential, a marked increase over their perception of the existing situation. The parallel question for research revealed that 67 percent of the respondents felt that research and scholarship should be Extremely or Very Influential. Thus, although the percentage of faculty who felt that teaching should be at least Very Influential was more than double the number who reported it currently had that degree of influence, the decline in the desired influence of research was not so great as to make teaching and research equal in preferred influence. Apparently, the faculty members wished to reduce the disparity between the effect of evaluations of teaching and research on their university rewards but not change the existing rank order in which research was viewed as the more influential task.

Respondents were asked to report their degree of satisfaction with the way in which each of their specific tasks was evaluated and also were asked to state how satisfied they were, in general, with the evaluation system to which they were subject. Specific questions were: "In general, how satisfied are you with the way in which your (specific task) is evaluated?" "Now I would like to ask your judgement about the way in which your overall work as a faculty member is evaluated by people having some influence over your university rewards. In general, then, how satisfied are you with the way your total activities as a member of the faculty are judged?" The five-point scale was used, response categories varying from Extremely Satisfied to Not At All Satisfied. These data also reveal the greater role played by research evaluations as compared with teaching evaluations. Dichotomizing both satisfaction scales at the medians, the relationship between overall satisfaction with the evaluation process and satisfaction with the evaluation of research was higher, expressed by a gamma of .90, than the relationship between overall satisfaction and satisfaction with the evaluation of teaching, expressed by a gamma of .59. We are dealing here with a part-whole relationship in which research was clearly a larger part of the whole than teaching.

In order to investigate the relation between the evaluation system and the expenditure of effort on tasks by performers, we asked respondents the following question: "Here is a schedule showing activities we have been talking about, plus a few others. I would like to get your best estimate of the way in which you divide the time you devote to the activities listed. Would you tell me about what percent of the time you devote to these functions is spent on each one of them? The total, of course, should add to 100 percent." We then asked: "Now would you let me know, if it were simply a matter of your own preference, how you *would like* to divide your time among these same functions?" In connection with the first question, respondents were given a list of the following functions, with spaces for estimating proportion of time spent on each: undergraduate classroom teaching, graduate classroom teaching, other undergraduate teaching, other graduate teaching, research and scholarship, university service, and external service. For the second question, respondents were asked to indicate their preferences beside their responses to the first question. There was no column heading on the response form for these items on preferences so that respondents could not have anticipated the question on preference while responding to the question on actual time spent.

Comparing responses to the questions on actual allocation of effort with the questions on preferred allocation of effort, 40 percent of the respondents indicated that they wanted to spend more time on research than they were currently doing, and only 16 percent wanted to reduce the time allocated to research. In contrast, for every category of teaching, whether in or out of the classroom, undergraduate or graduate, more faculty of every rank and in every disciplinary group indicated they wanted to reduce the time spent on teaching than indicated they wanted to increase the time spent on teaching. Although the direction of all of these findings with respect to teaching was consistent, some of the differences were slight. These results were consistent with our expectation that efforts of organizational participants would be directed toward those aspects of work which had most influence on the distribution of organizational sanctions.

Given correlational data, of course, we have no way of examining causality in this relation nor do we wish to argue that the relation between research and university sanctions is the only basis for explaining why faculty should want to spend more time on research. We believe that some faculty members find research attractive for less extrinsic reasons. Nevertheless, we believe that organizational participants, including professors, desire to achieve some balance between the time or effort spent on various tasks and the rewards associated with those tasks. If this is the case, then balance could also be achieved by increasing the influence of teaching on university rewards. And, as already suggested, faculty desired such a change: 53 percent of the faculty wanted to increase the influence of teaching on university rewards, whereas only 2 percent wanted the influence of teaching to be decreased. Apparently, professors do not want to get out of teaching, although, given their preference, they would spend more time in research; and they would like to see the reward structure of the university more accurately reflect the teaching that they do.

Another way of examining the relation between expenditure of effort and the receipt of university rewards is to ask whether the perceived amount of influence on rewards of a task is related to the time spent on the task. Among professors who saw teaching as Moderately, Very, or Extremely Influential, 65 percent were above the median in time spent on undergraduate teaching and 77 percent were above the median in time spent on graduate teaching. By contrast, for those who viewed teaching as only Slightly or Not At All Influential, only 43 percent were above the median for undergraduate teaching and 47 percent were above the median for graduate teaching. Similarly, for research, those who saw research as highly influential in the university's evaluation process were more likely to be above the median in time spent on research, compared with those who saw research as less influential, the respective proportions being 63 percent and 40 percent. These data are persuasive in support of our hypothesized relationship since they demonstrate that the same persons who perceive either teaching or research to be more rewarded by the university are likely to spend more time on that activity.

Influence of Evaluators. Up to this point, we have been discussing the influence that evaluations of two tasks, teaching and research, had upon university rewards. We now turn our attention to the evaluators of each of these tasks. We were particularly interested to learn whether the specific persons or groups named as organizational evaluators and the amount of relative influence attributed to these evaluators varied as a function of the type of task performed.

Data for this analysis came from responses to the following questions, which were asked for each task examined. "Here is a list of people who are potential evaluators of your (specific task). Would you tell me which of them, or others not on the list who might come to mind, make evaluations of your (specific task) which might influence university rewards? (1) students, (2) department head, (3) department colleagues, (4) faculty members in other departments, (5) members of your discipline in other universities, (6) persons having a say in government or foundation grants, (7) other outsiders (please name), (8) dean of the school and his staff, (9) appointment and promotion committee (faculty committee advisory to the Dean), (10) other faculty committees, (11) provost and his staff, (12) president, (13) trustees. Among those who evaluate your (specific task) and influence university rewards, I would like to know which ones are the most influential. How influential are (specific evaluators') evaluations of your (specific task)?" The previous five-point influence scale was again used for this question. Table 11 reports these data on perceived influence of evaluators for the two principal tasks, with the evaluators grouped together where only a few in related categories were named by respondents.

The first point to make about these companion tables is that faculty members did indeed perceive different sets of evaluators as having influence on one task but not on another. Differing authority systems were associated with the task of teaching and the task of research in this university. Further, more positions appear to be involved in the evaluation of research than in the evaluation of teaching. Combining the number of different sets of evaluators named by each faculty member gave a total of 232, or mean of 2.3 classes of evaluators, for teaching compared with a total of 329, or mean of 3.3 classes of evaluators, for research.

It is also clear from these data and further analysis that faculty members looked to their own colleagues, including their department head, for influential evaluations in a pattern that is believed to be appropriate for professionals operating in bureaucracies. For both teaching and research, the number of collegial evaluators within the university or at other institutions was more than three times as large as the number of university administrators named as organizational evaluators. University administrators were not only named less often but were perceived as lower in influence than professional colleagues. For example, from Table 11, we see that the dean and his staff were named as Very or Extremely Influential for teaching by 10 percent of the sampled faculty, as compared with 20 percent reporting this level of influence for their colleagues, exclusive of the department head. Similarly 22 percent reported high influence for the dean's evaluation of research, whereas 61 percent reported a similar level of influence for departmental colleagues. In general, the department head, departmental colleagues, and students were perceived as more

Table 11.

Perceived Influence of Evaluators, for Teaching and Research

TEACHING INFLUENCE

	Position	Extremely	Very	Moderately	Slightly	Not at All	Not Named
1.	Students	6	13	17	22	5	37
2.	Department head	17	18	12	5	4	44
3.	Department colleagues	4	15	27	8	6	41
4.	Other faculty	0	1	4	11	1	83
5.–7.	Outsiders	0	4	4	6	1	85
8.	Dean and staff	3	7	2	9	2	78
9.	A and P committee	2	1	0	3	0	94
10.	Other committees	0	0	0	0	0	100
11.–13.	Provost, president, trustees	1	2	1	1	0	95

RESEARCH INFLUENCE

	Position	Extremely	Very	Moderately	Slightly	Not at All	Not Named
1.	Students	0	0	1	2	2	94
2.	Department head	34	27	5	2	2	30
3.	Department colleagues	33	28	12	5	3	18
4.	Other faculty	0	2	9	6	2	81
5.	Colleagues at other institutions	15	25	22	6	2	30
6.	Grantmakers	4	4	3	8	0	80
7.	Other outsiders	3	2	1	2	1	91
8.	Dean and staff	7	15	7	5	1	65
9.	A and P committee	7	4	1	4	1	83
10.	Other committees	0	0	0	0	0	100
11.	Provost and staff	1	5	6	1	1	86
12.–13.	President, trustees	0	2	1	2	1	95

N = 100 or percent for each row.

highly influential evaluators of teaching than was the dean, while for research the dean ranked behind the department head, departmental colleagues, and colleagues at other institutions. Other university administrators were perceived as even less influential than the dean. This relatively low level of perceived influence of university administrators compared with colleagues and students probably results from the combination of a belief that administrators lack knowledge of appropriate evaluative criteria and of the low visibility of faculty performances to administrators.

We can see the impact of visibility of performance by noting that students were seen as more influential evaluators of teaching than was any administrative group. Students were most often named by faculty as evaluators of teaching although they were lower than department heads, and approximately equal to departmental colleagues, in the reported influence of their evaluations. Even this relatively strong picture of student influence in the evaluation of teaching actually understates students' effect on this process. Teaching is most visible to students. Therefore, students are the primary source upon which other evaluators rely in arriving at evaluations of teaching effectiveness. When asked the sources of information used by department heads and colleagues when evaluating teaching, 81 percent of the faculty reported that students were the primary source of information for department heads, and 93 percent reported that students were the primary source of information for colleagues. It is important to note, however, that being in a position to observe performances does not alone provide a basis for sound evaluations. Faculty agreed that students were the primary source of information for evaluation of teaching but disagreed about the quality of that source; comments volunteered by over half of our respondents revealed an even split between those who regarded students as a reliable source of information and those who regarded student opinions as worthless or misleading.

The importance of visibility in the evaluation process can also be seen in the participation of colleagues from outside the university. Faculty respondents perceived their colleagues at other institutions as important evaluators: 68 percent of the faculty sample named colleagues at other institutions as influential evaluators of research, and 40 percent regarded these distant colleagues as Very or

Extremely Influential. But whereas research, through publications and conference presentations, was visible to those qualified evaluators, teaching was much less so. Only 15 percent of the faculty named any outsiders as evaluators of teaching, and only 4 percent saw teaching evaluations by outsiders as Very or Extremely Influential.

More generally, it is clear from Table 11 that organizational evaluators, those who influence the distribution of organizational rewards, need not be members of the organization in question. For the two tasks combined, 19 percent of all evaluators named were located outside the formal boundaries of the organization whose rewards were at stake. This permeability of the organizational boundaries was most clear for research, as we have noted. It is not surprising, therefore, that, in general and within each rank, younger faculty were more concerned with the evaluation of research and less concerned with the evaluation of teaching than were older faculty. The younger faculty, who aspired to mobility and sought to attract offers which would allow them either to leave or to improve their position in their home institution, were appropriately emphasizing the task for which the organizational boundaries were most permeable.

The influence of persons outside the organization is also revealed by the impact of those controlling research grant funds. Overall for our sample, the impact of these external sources of funds was not very high, only 8 percent of the faculty viewing them as Extremely or Very Influential evaluators of research. In a related analysis, however, we were able to show that the perceived influence of grantmakers varied with the amount of money received from external sources. We categorized departments into three groups: departments receiving less than $1000 of grant funds per faculty member per year, departments receiving between $1000 and $10,000, and departments receiving more than $10,000 per faculty member per year. In departments receiving low amounts of grant funds, only 8 percent of the faculty assigned any influence to these sources and none saw them as Very or Extremely Influential. In departments with medium funding, 20 percent of the faculty saw grantmakers as having some influence, with 8 percent viewing them as Very or Extremely Influential. And in departments receiving the highest amount of external funding, 31 percent of the faculty saw evaluations by grantmakers as having some influence, with 17 percent reporting them to be Very or Extremely Influential. Thus, although the proportion of faculty who perceived the sources of grant funds as high in influence on university rewards was never particularly high, the amount of funds received by a department from outside grantmakers was directly related to their perceived influence.

Summarizing the major findings of our research on the university faculty, we found that in this professional organization, professional colleagues were perceived to have far more influence on organizational rewards compared with administrative superiors. Also, evaluations of research—by all evaluators combined—had far more influence on university rewards than did evaluations of teaching. Since the faculty expended considerable effort on teaching, many wanted a better balance between effort and rewards. For teaching, students were influential evaluators, since teaching performances were most visible to them. For research, colleagues in other institutions were regarded as influential evaluators since the visibility of published research made the boundaries of the university permeable with respect to this task. In Chapter Six we noted that greater dependence on theory in a discipline was associated with more perceived agreement among evaluators, and more agreement among evaluators was positively related to satisfaction with the evaluation system. This finding appears to be an important basis for the professional emphasis on collegial evaluations, that is, evaluations based on a shared body of knowledge. Finally, the number, types, and influence of organizational evaluators were found to vary according to the nature of the task being performed. Control systems in complex organizations are often task-specific; hence, it is not uncommon for organizational participants to be subject to more than one control system.

Chapter 9

Incompatibility and Instability of Authority Systems

▲▲▲

Having completed the presentation of our conception of authority and authority systems, we can move on to an important aspect of our theory. We believe that incompatibility of authority systems is a sufficient condition for system instability. Our theory is formulated at the structural level in the sense that both the independent and dependent variables refer to characteristics of authority systems. However, underlying the theory are some social psychological assumptions concerning individual motivation and behavior which must also be described. These assumptions will first be discussed, and then the central concepts of incompatibility and instability will be presented.

Acceptance Level for a Performance Evaluation

Given that participants attach some importance to the evaluations made of their performance by evaluators who influence the distribution of organizational sanctions, we make the important assumption that the participants will attempt to maintain—that is, both achieve in the present and ensure for the future—evaluations of their performance at a level which is acceptable to them. The minimal level of a performance evaluation which is satisfactory to the participant being evaluated (C), is, by definition, the participant's acceptance level for that evaluation.

The concept of acceptance level is closely related to the notion of level of aspiration, which psychologists have defined in terms of the degree of difficulty of the goal toward which the person is striving (Lewin and others, 1944; Siegel and Fouraker, 1960). Acceptance level is perhaps slightly more precise than level of aspiration because our emphasis is on the *minimal* level satisfactory to the individual in contrast to the more diffuse *desired* level. It should also be noted that acceptance level is concerned with performance evaluation for a specified task. Therefore, acceptance level is more specific than concepts which focus on the degree of acceptability of numerous facets of a social relationship as that relationship is evaluated by one of its participants. For example, the concept of acceptance level differs in degree of specificity from Thibaut and Kelley's (1959, p. 21) concept of comparison level, which is defined as a standard by which participants assess the costs and rewards, hence the overall attractiveness, of a given social relationship as compared with other potential relationships. Our concept is very similar to the notion of criteria of satisfaction proposed by March and Simon (1958, p. 182), although again our task-specific focus is somewhat more explicitly stated. One of the few instances that has come to our attention in which a concept similar to acceptance level has been applied to a specific performance evaluation is a study by Howard and Berkowitz (1958). These authors employ the concept of desired performance level to refer to the level of aspiration held by a subject for certain task evaluations, and the study is designed to show how deviations of received evaluations from this level influence the perceptions of evaluators.

It is important to note that acceptance level pertains only to the criteria employed by C to evaluate the acceptability of the performance evaluation received. Satisfaction with other aspects of the job situation is excluded from attention, as is satisfaction with the operation of the authority system. Indeed, the latter—degree of satisfaction with the authority system—is one of the indicators used to measure instability, the dependent variable.

We are not concerned with attempting to specify the determinants of C's acceptance level. We believe, with March and Simon (1958, pp. 182–183), that acceptance level will generally follow the same principles which help to account for aspiration level. As they note: "The most important proposition is that, over time, the aspiration level tends to adjust to the level of achievement. That is to say, the level of satisfactory performance is likely to be very close to the actually achieved level of recent performance." They also point out certain qualifications to this generalization; namely, that the adjustment of criteria (acceptance level) is a relatively slow process, that the level tends not to remain absolutely constant, but to increase slowly with time, and that "individuals adjust their criteria to the achieved levels of other individuals with whom they compare themselves, and to the levels that are established as norms by relevant reference groups" (March and Simon, 1958, p. 183). We may also speculate that acceptance level is affected not only by past performances and by reference groups but by more basic personality factors such as need-achievement motivation. (See McClelland and others, 1953). Given such determinants, it follows that participants performing the same tasks may have differing acceptance levels; a given participant may be satisfied with a rating of "fair," while another is satisfied only when a rating of "excellent" is attained.

Organizational evaluators (B) will attempt to influence the acceptance levels of performers. Standards established by criteria-setters to distinguish unsatisfactory from satisfactory work are clearly attempts to influence C to set the acceptance level at or somewhat above the point below which work is defined as unsatisfactory by organizational evaluators. However, although we would ordinarily expect to find a high correlation, there is no necessary relation between the standards which C uses to arrive at an acceptance level and the standards which are set by C's criteria-setter for evaluating C's performance. The level of evaluation which is satisfactory to C need not be the same level which satisfies B. A given C

may expect performance evaluations on a given task which are higher than those which B expects for C, while another C may be satisfied with low evaluations even though B is dissatisfied with the level of performance. The term *acceptance level* is therefore to be distinguished from the concept of standard, and will apply only to the minimal level of performance evaluation satisfactory to C, the performer of the task and the recipient of the evaluation.

In our definition of acceptance level, we specify that C will not only attempt to achieve a given level of evaluation in the present but will also attempt to ensure that level for the future. The reference to future evaluations serves as a reminder that we are dealing with recurrent tasks and continuing performance evaluations. Hence, it is possible that while an isolated performance evaluation might be above C's acceptance level, the trend or direction of evaluations might be such as to cause C to be dissatisfied with the evaluations received.

The twin assumptions—that C places some value on performance evaluations received and that C establishes an acceptance level for these evaluations—together provide the motivational basis for our study of the results of incompatibility. Because the participant cares about performance evaluations, and has developed a basis for determining their acceptability, evaluations which are below the acceptance level (or threaten to become so) are regarded as unsatisfactory by the participant and will motivate some sort of corrective action designed to raise evaluations to the acceptance level or above. This conclusion would seem to be a special case of the more general social psychological postulate that frustration in an individual's realization of goals within a given framework will motivate search behavior.

The fact is, however, that we shall not be concerned with any and all factors which cause a participant to be dissatisfied with performance evaluations, but only with a subset of these factors. This subset is defined by the concept to which we now turn: incompatibility.

Incompatibility

We have assumed that C will attempt to maintain evaluations of performance at least as high as his or her acceptance level.

An authority system is incompatible with C's motivation to maintain a desired level of evaluation if it functions in such a manner that C is prevented by the system from maintaining evaluations of performance at or above C's acceptance level. If a particular aspect of an authority system acts to prevent C from maintaining evaluations of performances of the specified task at or above C's acceptance level, then by definition, an incompatibility is said to exist within the system. [An authority system will be said to be incompatible to the extent that it contains such incompatibilities.] Thus, the two components of incompatibility are: the receipt by C of evaluations below the acceptance level; and the perception that it is the authority system that prevents attainment by C of evaluations at or above the acceptance level.

It is important to emphasize that incompatibility is a property of the authority system, not a characteristic of the person who is the object of the control attempt. Incompatibility refers to the existence of certain problems in the authority system which are present and would affect any occupant of the C position who had the same or higher acceptance level for evaluations received.

Obviously, there are factors besides system incompatibility which may cause the participant to fail in the attempt to maintain evaluations of performances at the acceptance level. Chief among these is the degree of task competence possessed by the participant. While this and other factors leading to unsatisfactory evaluations may be of practical significance, they are irrelevant to our definition of incompatibility.

Types of Incompatibility

One way to get a firmer grasp on the concept of incompatability is to ask: What are the necessary requirements of a compatible authority system from the perspective of the performer who is being controlled? In the simplest case, C would receive an unambiguous allocation which did not conflict with other allocations received for the same or other tasks. C would have available the necessary resources and facilities—including appropriate authority rights over other participants—for carrying out the task. C's activities would affect the values of the relevant properties for performances and outcomes on which C would be evaluated. The sample taken of C's work would provide valid information as to the values actually achieved. Finally, the standards for evaluation of the task would be set appropriately so that C could expect to receive evaluations at the acceptance level by adjusting the level of effort.

This oversimplified review of the requirements of a compatible authority system suggests that there are several different ways in which an authority system can be incompatible. To identify these ways, we distinguish four types of incompatibility: contradictory evaluations; uncontrollable evaluations; unpredictable evaluations; and unattainable evaluations. Each type and a number of subtypes will be considered in turn.

Type I: Contradictory Evaluations. An authority system is incompatible if it places C in a situation in which the receipt of one performance evaluation at or above C's acceptance level necessarily entails the receipt of another performance evaluation below acceptance level. The receipt of contradictory evaluations that influence sanctions means that the participant is both rewarded and punished for the same behavior.

CASE A: CONFLICTING CRITERIA. (1) Conflicting Standards. The standards employed for assessing task performance may conflict in such a manner that the performer who receives acceptable evaluations according to one set of standards necessarily receives evaluations below acceptance level according to the other set of standards. Such a problem is most apt to occur when the authority system is somewhat differentiated, with more than one actor either setting or employing the criteria.

For example, an intern in the hospital we studied reported: "A patient may have an immunological problem which has to do with a particular organ system. Immunology may disagree with the consultants specializing in the organ system, and I'll be criticized by one for following the advice of the other." As this example suggests, the participant who receives allocations and evaluations from rightholders who represent different specialty groups is particularly likely to be subject to these problems.

Another frequently occurring instance of conflicting criteria in the medical center concerned the issue of how many tests were to be ordered by the house staff for patients under their care. Some attending physicians favorably evaluated the house staff for conducting a minimal number of carefully selected laboratory tests on patients because this provided evidence of good judgement and kept down the cost of care to the patient. Others would unfavorably evaluate minimal testing because they believed that the primary goal of the center was the training of physicians, and that the house staff learned more from each patient when extensive laboratory tests were conducted.

Students of organizations will recognize that we are attempting in these examples to state more cautiously and specifically the "unity of command" administrative principle which asserts that it is undesirable to place a member of an organization in a position where he or she receives orders from more than one superior. This principle has been enunciated by Gulick (1937, p. 9), among others:

> In building a structure of coordination, it is often tempting to set up more than one boss for a man who is doing work which has more than one relationship. Even as great a philosopher of management as Taylor fell into this error in setting up separate foremen to deal with machinery, with materials, with speed, etc., each with the power of giving orders directly to the individual worker. The rigid adherence to the principle of unity of command may have its absurdities; these are, however, unimportant in comparison with the certainty of confusion, inefficiency, and irresponsibility which arises from the violation of the principle.

However, as Simon (1957), notes in his critique of scientific management, such a principle appears to ignore the important contributions which specialized expertise can make to improving the quality of decisions and work performance. He suggests as more defensible the narrower prescription that: "In case two authoritative commands conflict, there should be a single determinant person whom the subordinate is expected to obey; and the sanctions of authority should be applied against the subordinate only to enforce his obedience to that one person" (1957, p. 25). This statement is more consistent with our own view since it does not attempt to proscribe or condemn all conflicts which may occur among right-holders but rather focuses on those cases in which performers are made to suffer for the defects of the authority structure.

(2) Conflicting Properties. A classic example of conflicting properties often occurs between the properties of speed and accuracy. A technical typist may be negatively evaluated for not typing fast enough; yet, if he or she were to type faster, evaluations below acceptance level would be received for committing too many errors. Another example of this incompatibility was reported by a clinical clerk in the hospital, who complained that his evaluator wanted his written comments on the work-up of a patient to "be concise, but to contain all the necessary information." At his level of train- ing and experience, the medical student perceived these require- ments as incompatible. Obviously, this type of incompatibility may occur both with a single evaluator and when properties used by two evaluators conflict.

CASE B: CONFLICTING SAMPLES. As we noted in our earlier discussion of sampling, one of the most important decisions made by the sampler is whether or not to collect information on the perfor- mance, the outcome, or both. When both information sources are used by samplers, Type IB incompatibility can result from a con- flict between the evaluation based upon an outcome and the evalua- tion based upon the performance leading to that outcome. That is, C may be subjected to contradictions between the kind of perfor- mance that is allowed and the kind of outcome that is expected.

For example, a member of the front eight on the defensive unit of the football team reported: "The coach says I should be more aggressive in tackling. But when I'm more aggressive, I'm more likely to mess up tackles and get low evaluations." By one interpre- tation of this statement, the player can either be aggressive and more frequently fail to achieve the outcome of a tackled opponent, or be less aggressive and be more successful in achieving the desired out- come. Either way the player receives evaluations below acceptance level.

A very similar type of contradiction frequently occurs when C is allocated a task by directive, but appraised on the basis of a sample of final outcomes. The evaluator may expect a performer to achieve results that are impossible to achieve by following the allocated performance program. Thus, a participant who received allocations by directive is more likely to be subjected to an incompatibility of this type if performance evaluations are based on outcome values rather than on performance values.

CASE C: CONFLICTING ALLOCATIONS. The first two cases of Type I incompatibility arise in connection with the evaluation of a given task. The third case focuses on the problems which may develop for C when other tasks are allocated to C which conflict with C's performance of the task under analysis.

The tasks may compete for scarce resources, such as time, thereby permitting adequate performance on one of the tasks, but not on both. Problems of this type are illustrated by the following examples. A senior technical typist reported: "All the manuscripts are 'due tomorrow.' The other day I had to drop the other manuscripts to finish a publication, and I had to rush the publication with the result that it was sloppy. The time factor is the main problem, but I am blamed for poor work." An engineer in the research facility reported: "One physicist gave me a job to do. Then another physicist came in with a rush job which I worked on. As a result, the first physicist's job just sits and he, not knowing about the rush job, gets mad at me." And a copy editor reported: "I'm rewriting a story, and someone wants you to type something or run an errand. These things interrupt your train of thought, and your performance in rewriting is impaired. This results in a low rating from the night editor."

Because our construct of the authority system is specific to a given task, conflicting allocations can give rise to incompatibility which occurs across system boundaries. In this respect, Type IC incompatibility is unique among the incompatibilities identified by the theory. This incompatibility is said to exist within the authority system only if it results in evaluations below acceptance level on the task isolated for analysis.

In summary, C is subjected to an incompatibility of Type I to the extent that the evaluations of C's performance conflict in such a way that achievement of one evaluation at least equal to acceptance level necessarily means that C cannot avoid evoking another evaluation of his or her performance below acceptance level. This contradiction can arise between evaluations received from a single evaluator or from several evaluators and may be due to conflicting standards being employed, conflicting samples being drawn, or conflicting allocations being received.

Type II: Uncontrollable Evaluations. An authority system is incompatible if it places C in a situation in which evaluations below C's acceptance level are received for performances or outcomes C does not control.

Type II incompatibility occurs when C lacks control over the values which are attributed to C's performance or outcome so that C obtains evaluations below acceptance level. In ideal circumstances, the values associated with C's performance and outcome would be a regular function of the quality of C's own performance, but this may not be the case for several reasons.

CASE A: COORDINATION FAILURE IN CONTROL SYSTEM. The most obvious and simple instance of incompatibility of this type occurs when an unsatisfactory performance or outcome is noted, and the evaluation is incorrectly assigned to a participant whose performance in no way contributed to the outcome—that is, a C who neither performed the task nor had control over those who did. A bench worker in the electronics firm reported an instance of coordination failure as follows: "Each girl has her own identification stamp or tag. If the wrong tag or stamp gets on a component, they think it's your work and you get blamed for someone else's mistakes." And an intern related the following example: "Dr. Doe's patient got a wrong dosage. Although the other intern wrote the order, Dr. Doe and the attending physician gave me a low evaluation."

It would appear that problems of this type are more likely to occur in complex authority systems. Incorrect attribution of a performance evaluation to a performer is highly unlikely when a single actor holds all or most of the authority rights—especially when a single B allocates the task to C and samples and appraises the performance. But when control tasks are distributed among several actors, coordination problems among them are likely to generate errors in identifying which workers were given which allocations.

CASE B: INTERDEPENDENCE OF PERFORMERS. Just as coordination failures among evaluators may result in incompatibility, so specialization among performers may lead to confusion and errors when they are evaluated for their contribution to an outcome. Performer interdependence is present, by definition, when more than one participant contributes to a task outcome which is used as the basis for evaluation. Such interdependence is very common in formal organizations. As Gulick has asserted: "Work division is the foundation of organization; indeed, it is the reason for organization" (1937, p. 3). With many different workers contributing to a common product, the control task of assessing and sanctioning individual contributions becomes very difficult.

The problem, of course, is that outcomes produced interdependently may be only irregularly related to any given participant's performance. Participants who are evaluated on the basis of such outcomes may, therefore, lose control of their evaluations. Since there are many different bases for specialization or work division, there are many ways in which Type IIB incompatibilities may occur. A few examples will have to suffice.

A competent decision-maker may be prevented from maintaining evaluations at the acceptance level because of incompetent implementation of his or her decisions by others. For example, a senior mechanical engineer in the research center complained that he was often blamed for errors in his designs that were the fault of the drafting group. Conversely, a participant who implements another's faulty decision may incorrectly be blamed for an unsatisfactory outcome. An instance of this was reported by another engineer in the research center: "A physicist designed and tested a prototype. I was told to follow this design in my own work. But the physicist's design was poor, causing my design to be unsatisfactory, with the result that I received a low evaluation."

When two or more performers carry out implementation activities which contribute to a common outcome, there is also the possibility of incompatibility. For example, a football lineman reported: "Sometimes the ball carrier will run into me when I have opened up a big hole, and then it looks as if I didn't take out my man." But interdependence can cut both ways, as a ball carrier reminds us: "If the hole isn't opened in the line, I can't get through with the ball, and the outcome is not good because blockers didn't do their job." A copy editor reported receiving unacceptably low evaluations from the night editor because: "Someone writes a pretty crummy story to start with. I'm supposed to rewrite it, and there really isn't enough in it to do anything with." And a woman working on printed circuits in the electronics plant: "I only loaded the circuit board, and someone else was supposed to touch it up. They messed up on their part, and then I got blamed."

Of course, interdependence does not necessarily produce incompatibility. If C has sufficient authority rights to control the contributions of others with whom C is interdependent, C can establish a regular relation between the performance and the evaluations received. In addition, when the performance of others contributing to the common outcome is of such quality that C is not prevented from maintaining acceptable evaluations, then there is no incompatibility. When these others perform in a constant and satisfactory manner, then the only reason for unsatisfactory outcomes would be C's own performance, and C's evaluations would be a function of C's performance.

CASE C: ACTIVE TASKS. We have defined an active task as one which is relatively low in clarity, predictability, and efficacy, and we have suggested that active tasks pose special problems for the evaluation of task performance. Active tasks complicate the inference procedures linking performance and outcome values with performance characteristics. By contrast, evaluation of inert tasks is relatively straightforward since both performance and outcome values are a direct function of the quantity and quality of the performer's task activities.

Many types of workers are confronted by at least some active tasks. Persons higher in the organizational hierarchy are particularly likely to confront such tasks since they are expected to deal with the internal structure of relations in the organization—always somewhat unpredictable—as well as with the environment of the organization, which is a major source of uncertainty for most organizations. (See Emery and Trist, 1965; Terreberry, 1968; J. Thompson, 1967.) But, as we have previously argued, professionals are probably the largest class of workers confronted by a high proportion of active tasks. At any rate, we can learn something about the evaluation problems posed by active tasks and responses to those problems by focusing on professional workers.

The nature of the task performed, in particular, the professional's inability to control the outcome of a given task, has no doubt contributed to the emphasis placed by professional groups on performance. Hughes (1958, p. 95) has noted: "One of the differences between lay and professional thinking concerning mistakes is that to the layman the technique of the occupation should be pure instrument, pure means to an end, while to the people who practice it, every occupation tends to become an art." In other words, the means for accomplishing an end become ends in themselves; emphasis is shifted from the outcome (end), which cannot be fully controlled, to the performance (means), which can more nearly be controlled. Hughes himself suggests that emphasis on performance helps professionals protect themselves against the "great unavoidable risks" which accompany this type of work (Hughes, 1958, p. 97).

The outcome of a competent performance need not be success and often is failure—a thesis well expressed in the classic aside of the surgeon: "Brilliant operation. Too bad the patient died!" As another example, an intern reported that upon completing a competent treatment of a burn, he had instructed the patient to keep his arm up. The patient's failure to do so defeated the purpose of the treatment. As a consequence, the intern was criticized by his evaluators when they saw the unsatisfactory condition of the wound. The attempt to evaluate active tasks by their outcomes may produce incompatibility, since the evaluation may be predominantly a function of the resistance rather than the quality of the performance. For this reason, individuals assigned active tasks are frequently evaluated by sampling their performances rather than outcomes of their performances. Thus, the surgeon may be evaluated not on the basis of the outcome—the patient died—but on the skill with which the required activities were performed—assessments leading to the rating "brilliant."

But there are problems associated with the evaluation of performance. We have already noted the limitations imposed on the direct observation of performance: psychological resistance on the part of the performer, work-group norms protecting performers from "undue interference," the impossibility of observing certain types of performance, and the financial and psychological costs of routine surveillance. Some of these problems may be overcome if indirect measures of performance are employed. Thus, Freidson and Rhea (1963) point to the use of medical records for the evaluation of physicians. Evaluation of physician performance is not typically based on a direct inspection of ongoing task performances but on attempts to reconstruct the performance after the fact.

The variable and uncertain nature of the resistance encountered affects performance as well as outcome values, but direct or indirect performance evaluations are better suited than outcome evaluations to take the actual nature and amount of resistance into account. By doing so, incompatibility can be avoided.

Even if the nature and degree of resistance encountered by a given task performance is unknown, evaluators may still have some knowledge of the distribution of resistance over a number of performances, permitting them to take a probabilistic approach to the evaluation of outcomes of active tasks. Hughes (1958) has noted that professional groups tend to take a statistical view of professional errors of judgement. In a similar manner, businesses distinguish between those risks where the distribution of outcomes is known, such as in the actuarial tables of life insurance companies, and those where no distribution of outcomes is known. The former, as Smelser (1963, p. 87) notes, become "manageable through aggregation. Uncertainty is managed by pooling the individual into an aggregation with known average characteristics," whereas the latter remain completely unpredictable. In short, when the distribution of resistance across a series of tasks is known, this knowledge permits evaluators to compare the proportion of successful outcomes for one performer with those of other performers under like circumstances. Thus, the death rate for all premature babies provides a valid measure of the performance of a pediatrics unit, but only if the sample and comparison group do not differ in the assignment of difficult cases.

In summary, for active tasks, the probability of incompatibility increases to the extent that evaluations are based on outcomes rather than on performances, unless either the actual amount of resistance encountered is considered or aggregating over tasks permits probabilistic approaches to evaluation.

As should be apparent, Type II incompatibility covers a

rather wide and diverse set of problems which may beset the evaluation process. These problems, while diverse, have a common theme: C's lack of control over the values attained on performances or outcomes owing to circumstances beyond C's control. This general theme has been voiced by writers in administrative science who have stated as one of their administrative principles that "responsibility should not exceed control." Thus, Urwick (1943, p. 46) quotes F. W. Taylor to the effect that "authority and responsibility must correspond" and goes on to spell out this principle as follows: "To hold a group or individual accountable for activities of any kind without assigning to him or them the necessary authority to discharge that responsibility is manifestly both unsatisfactory and inequitable. It is of great importance to smooth working that at all levels authority and responsibility should be coterminous and coequal." And Koontz and O'Donnell (1955, pp. 277–294) warn of the same problem, first labeling it "exacting responsibility without delegating authority," and later as "the Principle of Parity of Authority and Responsibility." In our own work we have tried to go beyond the assertion of this principle to examine some of the more frequent ways in which it is violated so as to cause performers to receive evaluations below their acceptance level.

Type III: Unpredictable Evaluations. An authority system is incompatible if it places C in a situation in which C receives evaluations below the acceptance level because C is unable to predict accurately the relationship between attributes of C's performance and the level of rating contained in the performance evaluation.

In order for performers to believe that they are able to improve their evaluations by altering their performances, they must be aware of what level of performance is associated with what level of performance evaluation. Type III incompatibility occurs when performers are unable to prevent their evaluations from falling below their acceptance levels because they are unable to predict the level of evaluations they will receive from the quality of their performance.

CASE A: MISUNDERSTANDINGS OF ALLOCATIONS. Sometimes C is not aware that a task has been allocated to him or her. The allocator may have forgotten to communicate with C, or the allocation may be stated in an ambiguous fashion. The ambiguity may involve whether an allocation has in fact been given (for example, was the communication an order or only a suggestion?), or it may concern the type of allocation (for example, was the allocation a directive or a delegation?). When allocations are unclear, for whatever reason, C may be confronted with evaluations that were not anticipated and thus may be subject to an incompatibility.

CASE B: MISUNDERSTANDINGS OF CRITERIA. C's failure to understand the criteria by which C's performance is to be evaluated may result from a lack of specificity in the criteria themselves or from failures on the part of the evaluators to communicate clearly the criteria they plan to use. We have already noted that organizational goals may be vague and diffuse and have suggested the close relation which exists between goals and evaluation criteria. J. Thompson (1967, pp. 83–98) has considered what kinds of evaluative standards organizations may appropriately employ when their goals are "crystallized" or when their goals are ambiguous. The assignment of diffuse goals to C by way of vague allocations or the establishment of vague quality criteria provides C with no specific guidelines to shape behavior. Vaguely defined goals often make the evaluation process arbitrary and *post hoc* at every step, with the result that performers are unable to relate their performances to the evaluations received. (We have already noted that some attempts to solve this problem have the effect of leading evaluators to emphasize the concrete—the measurable and communicable—goal components at the expense of the less quantifiable components, resulting eventually in a displacement of goals.) On the other hand, goals and evaluation criteria may be quite clear and specific, but not be communicated to performers. In either case, performers lack sufficient information on the criteria used in the evaluation of their performance to make rational adjustments in their performance in order to achieve acceptable evaluations.

For example, a desk worker on the newspaper staff reported: "I didn't know what they were judging me on. I was only told that we had to get the work done. They didn't mention any standards to follow. They would give me information for a story and say, 'Write it,' without telling me how it should be done, how long it should be, along what theme, etc." And a bench worker in the electronics firm said that she did not get a raise when it was due, and did not know until then that her work had been unsatisfactory, or afterward, why it had been so judged. She commented: "I want to do better, but I don't know what's wrong."

Occupants of a position who act upon false information about the criteria used in their evaluations provide an extreme instance of this type of incompatibility. For example, university faculty may be told and may act on the belief that community service, teaching, and research are all taken into account in the evaluations made of them, when, in practice, community service is not considered at all. All those conditions which impede communication between the participants and the evaluators tend to increase the probability of this type of incompatibility.

Those being evaluated need not, of course, know all the details of the evaluation process in order to avoid Type III incompatibility. It is sufficient that they know enough about the basis upon which evaluations are made to be able to make the adjustments in their behavior necessary to produce acceptable evaluations.

CASE C: NONREPRESENTATIVE SAMPLES. Type III incompatibility also can occur as a consequence of unreliable sampling of the participant's performance. To the extent that the sample taken is nonrepresentative, the subsequent evaluations cannot be predicted accurately by C from knowledge of the criteria to be employed and C's own assessment of his or her performance. As a consequence, C may be unable to make the adjustments in performance necessary to maintain evaluations at the acceptance level. In contrast to Type II incompatibility where unsatisfactory evaluations are based, invalidly, upon outcomes uncontrolled by participants, Type IIIC incompatibility occurs when, although participants are in control of their performances or the outcomes associated with those performances, the sample taken of the work is so unreliable that they are prevented from maintaining their evaluations at acceptance level.

Type IV: Unattainable Evaluations. An authority system is incompatible if it places C in a situation in which the standards used to evaluate C are so high that C cannot achieve evaluations at the acceptance level.

Although the evaluations participants receive may be a function of their performance, and this function may be known to them, participants may still be unable to achieve evaluations at their acceptance level because, no matter how much effort is expended, they cannot produce performances of the necessary quality. We do not insist that all participants must be satisfied with the standards that are used for their evaluation. Some performers may believe the standards employed to be too rigorous or demanding compared with other work situations with which they are familiar. But such dissatisfaction does not of itself cause an incompatibility. Incompatibility of Type IV occurs only if standards are set at such a level that it is impossible for participants, given the circumstances under which their performance occurs, to attain evaluations at their acceptance level.

CASE A: INAPPROPRIATELY HIGH STANDARDS. The problem of inappropriately high standards sometimes occurs when a participant is new to a job but is expected to perform at the same level as more experienced participants. This sort of problem was reported by a worker on the assembly bench in the electronics firm: "The line leader evaluated me too low on an instrument which I hadn't worked on for a long time. They like us to be able to switch instruments, and I wasn't doing a bad job, considering how long I'd been on the other instrument." Also, this type of problem is more likely to occur for tasks which are newly developed or so rarely performed that criteria-setters do not know what level of performance can reasonably be expected. In addition, Type IVA incompatibility appears to be common in highly competitive situations in which superiors seek perfection in performance.

CASE B: ACTIVE TASKS. Active tasks not only pose problems of lack of control for participants (Type IIC incompatibility), they also create difficulties in the setting of criteria for evaluation. When the resistance to the task performance varies, the evaluator needs either knowledge of the relation between specific degrees of resistance and a specific outcome, which may be hard to attain, or knowledge of the frequency distribution of outcomes generated by past performances of the task under comparable conditions. In the latter case, the development of standards for evaluating outcomes of active tasks requires a larger sample of outcomes than is necessary for evaluating outcomes of inert tasks.

Because the standards employed in the evaluation of active

tasks are problematic, and because professional workers are often confronted by active tasks, professionals attempt to gain control over the setting of standards that will govern their performance. Professional associations may be viewed as coalitions of practitioners who organize in part to establish and maintain control over the criteria to be used in the evaluation of professional performances. Specifically, professionals attempt to exclude clients—who are deeply affected by professional performance and quick to evaluate a practitioner on the basis of a single outcome (their own case) but lack the qualifications to do so—and administrators—who also lack professional qualifications and seek to impose inappropriate criteria of professional performance—from the evaluation process. In this manner, professionals attempt to prevent both clients and administrators from setting unattainable standards for their work.

Hughes (1958, p. 93) has noted that attempts by occupational groups to gain control over standards is widespread: "Who has the right to say what a mistake or a failure is? The findings on this point are fairly clear; a colleague-group (the people who consider themselves subject to the same work risks) will stubbornly defend its own right to define mistakes, and to say in a given case whether one has been made." But although all or most occupation groups may make this claim, some are more successful than others in having it recognized as legitimate by others, and none have been more successful in this regard than have the professionals. The relative success of professionals is not just a product of equity, but of organizational skill and power. In shifting emphasis from outcomes to performances, professionals seek to avoid the problem of unattainable standards which often accompanies the performance of active tasks.

CASE C: LACK OF FACILITIES. "Facilities" may refer to physical equipment, such as tools or machines, or to organizational prerogatives, such as authority rights. Regardless of effort expended, organizational participants without the necessary facilities may not be able to achieve evaluations at or above their acceptance level. For example, workers at the electronics plant reported that they were required to maintain production levels on machines which were too old to perform at maximum efficiency. And members of the house staff reported low evaluations resulting from incomplete work-ups of patients because the hospital laboratory was incapable of performing most tests submitted after 10 P.M.

Facilities may also refer to authority rights. If participants are evaluated on their ability to control the performance of others, they must have sufficient power and authorization to achieve control. If participants lack important rights, or if authorization is incomplete, they may find it impossible to achieve the degree of control necessary to maintain evaluations at acceptance level. For example, a department chairman in a university may be expected by the dean to support good teaching, but may lack important rights over the department faculty. Several members of the house staff reported that nurses were asked to implement their decisions but because they were "more responsible to their nursing leaders than to physicians," doctors' orders were sometimes not followed. Thus, for participants who are evaluated for their control over another, the less their authority, the greater is the probability of Type IVC incompatibility.

Like Type II incompatibility, Type IVC incompatibility may be viewed as an attempt to specify the managerial principle that "authority and responsibility must correspond."

A Related Formulation. At approximately the same time that our concept of incompatibility was being developed, a somewhat related formulation was proposed by Kahn and his colleagues (Kahn and others, 1964). The two approaches differ in specificity, Kahn's work dealing with a given participant's entire occupational role whereas our approach focuses on a single task for each participant. Further, Kahn addresses himself to a greater variety of sources of problems for participants whereas we limit our approach to those problems caused by the operation of the control system as mediated by the flow of task evaluations. The two approaches are similar in that they attempt to locate work-related problems which impinge on persons located in positions in formal organizations. Kahn distinguishes two broad types of problems: role conflict and role ambiguity (Kahn and others, 1964, pp. 18–26). Five subtypes of role conflict are recognized:

(1) *Intra-sender conflict,* which occurs when the different prescriptions or proscriptions from a single member of the

role set are mutually contradictory or conflicting. This subtype of role conflict is similar to our own Type IA incompatibility: contradictory evaluations, conflicting criteria.

(2) *Inter-sender conflict*, "when pressures from one role sender oppose pressures from one or more other senders" (1964, p. 20). Again, this subtype is similar to Type IA incompatibility except that we do not distinguish between instances where one evaluator is involved and those where more than one is involved.

(3) *Inter-role conflict*, which occurs when "the role pressures associated with membership in one organization are in conflict with pressures stemming from membership in other groups" (1964, p. 20). This type of conflict is not considered in our formulation since we restrict attention to intraorganizational control attempts.

(4) *Person-role conflict*, a type of conflict generated by a combination of "sent role pressures and internal forces," such as the conflict "which may exist between the needs and values of a person and the demands of his role set" (1964, p. 20). This type of conflict is also excluded from consideration in our formulation.

(5) *Role overload*, a consequence of the participant being subjected to a number of role demands from various members of his role set, each of which is appropriate and legitimate, but which together are impossible to accomplish. This problem is captured in our formulation as an instance of Type IC incompatibility: contradictory evaluations, conflicting allocations.

Kahn and his associates (1964, pp. 22, 25) describe role ambiguity as follows: "Each member of an organization must have certain kinds of information at his disposal if he is to perform his job adequately. Communication processes and the distribution of information are matters of concern in every organization and are closely linked to criteria of organizational effectiveness. The availability of role-related information also may have profound implications for personal adjustment . . . Role ambiguity is conceived as the degree to which required information is available to a given organizational position."

Kahn does not develop specific subtypes of role ambiguity

corresponding to his treatment of role conflict, but does suggest several "important areas of ambiguity" in organizational roles.

First, lack of clarity concerning responsibilities: Kahn argues that often people "simply do not know what they are 'supposed' to do." The expectations others hold for their behavior may be vague and inconsistent. This subtype clearly corresponds with our Type IIIA: unpredictable evaluations, misunderstandings of allocations.

Second, lack of information about performance evaluations: Kahn asserts: "Doubts about how others evaluate us, about how satisfied they are with our performances are frequent sources of anxiety. A meaningful and satisfying self-identity rests in part on clear and consistent feedback from those around us. Such feedback is also important if one is to anticipate accurately the rewards and punishments he might receive from his associates" (1964, p. 25). In a very real sense, Kahn here states what is from our point of view not a specific type of incompatibility, but the basic premise underlying our whole approach. He argues, in effect, that performance evaluations are important to people not only because they help form and bolster self-conceptions but because they are directly linked to organizational sanctions.

Third, lack of information: Kahn notes that role ambiguity may be caused by a lack of the information required for role performance anywhere in the organization, by its presence in some but not in other parts of the organizations, and, occasionally by its being present in C's role set but withheld by superiors or subordinates. Since the notion of "information required for role performance" is a rather vague and general one, it relates to a number of our types of incompatibility, but probably most closely to Type III: unpredictable evaluations.

Finally, in their discussions of both role conflict and role ambiguity, Kahn and his associates distinguish between objective and subjective versions of each. Objective conflict or ambiguity represents "a condition in the environment"; subjective conflict or ambiguity is "a state of the person" (1964, p. 22). This is a necessary and useful distinction which these authors are able to operationalize by obtaining data on conflict and ambiguity both from members of the role set (objective) and from the focal participant, the victim of the conflict and ambiguity (subjective). The same theoretical distinction applies to our own formulation, but we have attempted to operationalize only the latter. We focus on subjective perceptions of incompatibility because we believe that they will allow us to make more accurate predictions of our dependent variable, instability. We operate on the W. I. Thomas premise that, "If men define situations as real, they are real in their consequences."

General Determinants of Incompatibility. One might assume that the types and amount of incompatibility are randomly distributed throughout authority systems in formal organizations so that participants would be equally likely to be subject to a given type or amount of incompatibility irrespective of what position they occupy. Such a view, however, would certainly be inconsistent with our overall perspective on formal authority systems. Rather, it appears that certain general factors which characterize authority systems may help to account for variations in the amount and type of incompatibility present in a given system. Among the general factors which we would expect to exert some effect are: the nature of the tasks performed, the complexity of the authority system, the degree of interdependence among participants, the relative frequency of evaluation, and the age of the system.

We have previously described the manner in which *active tasks* create special problems for evaluation systems. While it is by no means the case that all performers of active tasks are automatically subject to incompatibilities, we would expect that the higher the proportion of active tasks confronting system participants, the more likely it is that incompatibilities will be present.

Our conception of an authority system provides us with a simple and direct measure of the *complexity* of that system. Complexity refers to the number of persons (B's) who exercise at least one authority right over the participant (C) engaged in the performance of a given task. The larger the number of right-holders, the more complex the authority system. We would expect systems characterized by a relatively high degree of complexity to be especially prone to Type 1 incompatibility—contradictory evaluations—and to Type IIA incompatibility—uncontrollable evaluations due to coordination failures in the control system.

The larger the number of persons whose work affects in

some manner the task outcomes which are the basis on which *C*
is evaluated, the greater the amount of *interdependence* to which *C*
is subject. It will come as no surprise that participants characterized
by a high degree of interdependence are viewed as more likely to be
subject to incompatibilities of Type IIB: uncontrollable evaluations
due to interdependence of performers. Participants in this situation
might also experience a higher degree of Type IVC incompatibility
—unattainable evaluations due to a lack of facilities, in particular,
an absence of sufficient authority rights to control the task contributions of others to the common outcome.

The effects of *frequency of communicated evaluation* on
incompatibility appear ambiguous. On the one hand, if any incompatibilities are present so that *C*'s evaluations are below acceptance
level, then a higher frequency of communicating these evaluations
will increase the occurrence of incompatibility. On the other hand,
frequency may alleviate incompatibility in that the more often a
problem occurs, the more likely it is to receive attention and be resolved. Nevertheless, we can speculate that infrequent evaluations
will be related to the occurrence of Type III incompatibilities: unpredictable evaluations. This type of incompatibility is particularly
likely to occur given the absence of information as to what is
expected (misunderstanding of allocation), the level of performance
required (misunderstanding of criteria), or the basis which performances are or should be sampled on (nonrepresentative sampling).
The argument is that the receipt of an evaluation provides important
information to *C*, not simply about the performance, but about the
authority system in which *C* is operating. If evaluations are communicated infrequently, then Type III incompatibility is more
likely to be present.

An important condition affecting the amount of incompatibility in an authority system is the *newness* of that system. Stinchcombe (1965, pp. 148–149) describes some of the reasons for the
"liability of newness," most of which can be expected to increase
the amount of incompatibility present in the system:

> As a general rule, a higher proportion of new
> organizations fail than old. This is particularly true of
> new organizational forms.

The process of inventing new roles, the determination of their mutual relations and of structuring the field of rewards and sanctions so as to get maximum performance, have high costs in time, worry, conflict, and temporary inefficiency. For some time until roles are defined, people who need to know things are left to one side of communication channels. John thinks George is doing what George thinks John is doing. Bottlenecks which experience will smooth out create situations that can only be solved with a perpetual psychology of crisis.

The designers of organizations and, especially, new forms of organizations, are not infallibly prescient and so cannot foresee all the contingencies that the creation of new relationships will produce. All organizations experience a period of "shake-down"—some longer, some shorter—and a part of that shake-down operation concerns itself with the removal of at least the most blatant incompatibilities.

These four factors are variables which characterize the authority system. They are not exhaustive, but they are representative of systematic variables affecting the degree and types of incompatibility.

Instability

Incompatibility is one characteristic by which the state of an authority system may be described. An authority system may also be described in terms of its stability or instability. By definition, as we have noted, an authority system is unstable to the extent that it contains internal pressures for change. The pressures are internal in the sense that they are generated by the operation of the authority system itself rather than coming from some source external to the authority system. An unstable state is a potentially explosive one; unstable systems are in tension and, as such, are highly susceptible to change. Actual changes may or may not occur, depending on a variety of factors, but the potential for change is present in an unstable authority system. Stable authority systems do not contain internal pressures for change and, therefore, will change only as a result of externally generated pressures, for example, changes in technology or inconsistencies in the status structure of the organization and of the society.

A central proposition of our theory is that incompatibility is a sufficient condition for instability of authority systems. We do not argue that compatible systems—systems lacking incompatibilities—will be stable, because there are many other factors which may produce system instability. But we do argue that incompatibility, although not a necessary condition, is a sufficient condition for instability.

We have assumed that, in an authority system in which participants value the evaluations of their performance by organizational evaluators, participants will attempt to maintain these evaluations at or above acceptance level. In the preceding section, we have identified ways in which the authority system can be incompatible with this effort. Participants so thwarted by their authority systems are expected to be under tension. Such an expectation is borne out both by the social psychological literature (see, for example, Deutsch and Solomon, 1959; Harvey, Kelley, and Shapiro, 1957; Jones, Gergen, and Davis, 1962) as well as by Kahn's organizational studies (Kahn and others, 1964, pp. 66, 85). Further, such participants can be expected to engage in a variety of more or less adaptive coping responses in seeking resolution of the incompatibility. Some of these coping responses are more likely to result in actual changes in the authority system than are others, but each is considered as indicative of the presence of instability.

Attempts to Resolve Incompatibility

As briefly described in Chapter Three, a participant C might attempt to resolve the incompatibility of the authority system in three general ways. First, and most simply, C may leave the system, either by moving to another position within the same organization or by leaving the organization altogether. The probability of this response is affected by the availability and relative desirability of known alternatives to the present situation (see March and Simon, 1958, pp. 83–111; Thibaut and Kelley, 1959, pp. 21–24 et passim.) It is also affected by the extent to which C perceives that the authority system might be changed in such a manner as to resolve the incompatibilities.

Second, C may resolve the incompatibility to which he or

she is subject by lowering the acceptance level to that which can be attained in the authority system as it is presently constituted. Such an action means that C decides to be satisfied with less "return" for participation in the system than C previously was willing to accept. We argued earlier that acceptance level is different from the concept *level of aspiration,* but perhaps the former often follows the same principles as the latter. Research has shown that a given subject's level of aspiration is influenced by general cultural values (for example, pressures toward "self-improvement" in Western culture), by the specific standards of the membership or groups to which conduct is referred, and, most importantly, by past performances. Thus, as Deutsch (1954, p. 208) notes: "A main factor which determines the subjective probability of future success and failure is the past experience of the individual in regard to his ability to reach certain objectives. If the individual has had considerable experience with a given activity, he will know pretty well what level he can expect to reach or not to reach." The same factor no doubt affects whether a participant will lower the acceptance level. Repeated failures in the past may lead to a lowering of acceptance level, although present responses to the situation assuredly are affected by the attitudes of others confronting the same situation.

The decisions by C to leave the system or to lower acceptance level are two kinds of responses which may be made to resolve incompatibility. However, we do not expect either to be common. Recall that, by definition, incompatibility exists when the receipt of evaluations below acceptance level occurs in conjunction with the perception that the problem lies in the authority system, not in the performance of the participant. In such situations, the resolution of tensions associated with unacceptable evaluation is particularly likely to take the form of reactions to the authority system itself. The first two types of responses to incompatibility—withdrawal from and adaptation to the authority system—act to conserve the system without altering its present configuration.

Our interest centers upon the third set of alternatives for resolving incompatibility. Here we consider reactions which result in the creation of pressures for change in the existing authority system. The following reactions are taken as evidence for the existence of instability:

1. *Dissatisfaction* with some specific component of the authority system or with the authority system as a whole. This indicator is viewed as highly general for the level of tension experienced by C and, hence, present in the system. It should characterize not only those participants who attempt to change the system but also those who intend to leave the system and those who subsequently resolve incompatibility by lowering their acceptance level.

2. The *communication of dissatisfaction* with the system to others in the organization. The communication of dissatisfaction to others, whether subordinates, peers, or superiors, is distinguished from being dissatisfied and indicating this dissatisfaction to a member of our research team. The former is viewed as a direct attempt to change the system, whereas the condition of being dissatisfied is viewed primarily as an indicator of tension in the system.

3. *Suggesting changes* in the system to others in the organization as a consequence of dissatisfaction with the system. Here we have an even more specific attempt to change the system than merely communicating dissatisfaction to others concerning it. Presumably, in order to make suggestions for changes in the system, C needs to diagnose the defects in the present system and to formulate an alternative arrangement. Positive suggestions for change are hence more specific and direct attempts to change the existing system than either being dissatisfied or expressing one's dissatisfaction to others.

4. *Noncompliance* with the exercise of an authority right as a consequence of dissatisfaction with the system. Some types of noncompliance are unintentional, and others, such as occur when conflicting allocations are received, are unavoidable. We have attempted to eliminate these categories by focusing on those acts of noncompliance which occur because the participant is dissatisfied with the system. To refuse to comply out of dissatisfaction with present authority arrangements is, in effect, to notify others that the present system is intolerable. The behavior to which we refer here is closer to "nonconformity" than to other forms of deviance, as Merton uses this term. Merton (1957, pp. 360–361) notes that the noncomformist "challenges the legitimacy of the norms and expectations he rejects" and hence is more likely to "announce his dissent" rather than "try to hide his departures from the prevailing norms of the group." Further, by deviating from the existing system, "the

nonconformist aims to change the norms of the group, to supplant what he takes to be morally illegitimate norms with norms having an alternative moral basis." This type of noncompliance to a control attempt can be the strongest possible form of communication to others that the authority system is unsatisfactory.

Indeed, such noncompliance may, in its effect on others in the authority system, go well beyond the communication of C's discontent with the system as it is presently constituted. C's noncompliance may serve to spread the locus of incompatibility from C's position to other related positions. For example, given interdependence, one participant's decision to noncomply may affect the outcomes of another participant, subjecting the latter to an incompatibility. Also, to the extent that a given evaluator B is being evaluated on the basis of ability to control a performer C, C's noncompliance to B's control attempt may place B's own evaluations in jeopardy. That is, if C resorts to noncompliance in an attempt to resolve incompatibility, C's superiors may be placed in an incompatible position to the extent that C's noncompliance causes them to receive evaluations below their acceptance levels. These superiors can be expected to be more hospitable to negotiations aimed at reorganizing the authority system.

In summary, while a number of possible reactions on the part of participants can occur if subjected to incompatibility, some of these reactions appear to leave the existing system intact while others seek to change it. The former include decisions to leave the system or to lower acceptance levels to those which can be attained in the system as presently constituted. The latter reactions are those which are indicative of pressures for change in the existing authority system. This set of instability responses is the focus of attention in the present study. These responses include dissatisfaction with some components of the authority system or with the system as a whole; expression of dissatisfaction with the system to others in the organization; suggestions to others in the organization that the system be changed as a result of dissatisfaction with the system; and noncompliance with the exercise of any authority right as a consequence of dissatisfaction with the system. We assume that this set is sufficiently varied so that if a system is unstable, the instability is indicated by the regular occurrence of at least one of these responses.

The interrelation of these responses is complex. If instability is indicated by one response, the probability of its being indicated by another may be changed. For example, a participant subjected to incompatibility who makes suggestions for the alteration of the system may be less likely to resort to noncompliance as a vehicle for effecting change in the system. Yet the participant who expresses dissatisfaction with the system may be more likely at the same time to suggest changes in the system or, alternatively, to resort to noncompliance to call attention to the problem. In general, we expect that the greater the incompatibility or the greater the number of types of incompatibility experienced, the greater the probability that each of the various instability responses will occur.

Central Hypotheses

Seven specific hypotheses have been derived from the basic incompatibity-instability proposition. Given all that has been said, these predictions should be self-explanatory.

Presence of Instability. (1) An incompatible authority system is more likely to be unstable than a compatible system. (2) An authority system which contains more incompatibilities is more likely to be unstable than a system which contains fewer incompatibilities. (3) An authority system with more frequent incompatibility is more likely to be unstable than a system with less frequent incompatibility.

Degree of Instability. (4) An incompatibile authority system is likely to be more unstable than a compatible system. (5) An authority system which contains more incompatibilities is likely to be more unstable than a system which contains fewer incompatibilities. (6) An authority system with more frequent incompatibility is likely to be more unstable than a system with less frequent incompatibility.

Cost of Incompatibility and Degree of Instability. The final general hypothesis relating incompatibility and instability requires a word of explanation. The degree to which an authority system is incompatible for a given participant can be expressed in terms of the cost incurred by that participant as a consequence of incompatibility. It follows directly from our theory that the more frequently incompatibilities occur within the system and the more important to the participant are the evaluations forced below acceptance level, the greater is the cost of incompatibility to the participant. Thus, cost of incompatibility is viewed as a product of two variables: frequency of evaluations below acceptance level and importance of evaluations below acceptance level. Hence, our seventh hypothesis:

(7) An authority system with more costly incompatibility is more likely to be unstable than a system with less costly incompatibility. Or alternatively: The more costly an incompatibility in an authority system is, the more that incompatibility is associated with instability.

Factors Affecting Instability

We do not systematically identify additional factors which account for the amount and type of instability generated by a given type or amount of incompatibility. Nevertheless, we can identify several likely candidates which might find their place in such a systematic list.

Institutionalized Transience. We have already noted that high levels of incompatibility may be associated with high turnover rates in positions, since one response to incompatibility is to leave the system. Now, however, we focus on a different phenomenon. Some occupants of organizational positions are routinely defined as temporary; transience is institutionalized as a part of the job definition. Such positions are often found in training institutions where trainees are routinely moved from one position to another as a means of increasing their range of experience. Also, the creation of temporary work teams assigned to specific projects with a definite termination date, is increasingly characteristic of various industrial and scientific organizations.

Participants defined as transient or those who are members of temporary systems are expected to be less likely than nontransient participants or those in permanent systems to react strongly to a given amount of incompatibility (Miles, 1964). One basis for this prediction is the belief that participants in such circumstances are more likely to "grin and bear it," knowing that their torment is temporary. Coser (1962) has provided a graphic description of the types of problems, many of which are incompatibilities in our terms, which beset the nurse-intern relations in the general hospital. She then goes on to suggest how the transience of the intern reduces the expression of instability in the situation (1962, p. 28):

> The turnover of interns is institutionalized, and is a safety valve against violent disruption in nurse-intern relations. By the time tensions with the nurse accumulate, the intern is on the verge of leaving the ward. His expectation of departure helps cool his anger. 'Thank God I'm getting the hell out of here soon,' or 'I won't be sorry when I won't have to see *her* again'—such reflections ease present discomforts. The nurse also rejoices in advance to 'see these boys go'; and, as the next group of interns comes in, she might say—as one of the head nurses actually did say a few days after the arrival of two new interns—'We have some very nice doctors here now; they're human beings, not children, like those who were here before.' By the time a new head of steam has built up, these interns will be almost ready to leave.

Instability responses to incompatibilities in these situations are dampened not only by expectations of release from the system in the near future but also because participants have very little stake in the system. Why should participants struggle to reform and improve a structure only to leave before the benefits of their efforts are seen? Instability responses take effort and are often unpleasant actions in which to engage. There are costs associated with expressing instability, and participants who will not receive appropriate rewards for their efforts are less likely to pay these costs than others who have something to gain by modifying the system.

Trainee or Student Status. Numerous accounts of student socialization (for example, Becker and others, 1961; Mechanic, 1962b; Olesen and Whittaker, 1968) give ample evidence that students are frequently subjected to all four types of incompatibilities. Contradictory evaluations are often forthcoming from faculty members who make little or no effort to coordinate their demands or reconcile conflicting criteria. Uncontrollable evaluations frequently occur since students are often dependent on others for satisfactory outcomes but lack control rights over them. Unpredictable evaluations are very common since both allocations and criteria are frequently vague and diffuse, providing students with little guidance in their performances. And unattainable evaluations occur because students frequently lack necessary facilities for carrying out assigned tasks and because standards are set impossibly high.

In spite of the high incidence of incompatibility, students are expected to be less likely to exhibit instability behavior than nonstudents subjected to comparable levels of incompatibility. The transience of occupancy in the student role is a part of the explanation, but only a part. Low rates of instability are also expected from students or trainees because of the special significance which is attributed to performance evaluations. Evaluations take on a different meaning when individuals occupy a role which acknowledges their unfinished preparation, as opposed to one which presumes full competence on the part of the incumbent. Thus, one aspect of the student role is "acknowledged incompetence" in the performance of allocated tasks, and the evaluation of performance is viewed as one of the major training mechanisms. Kendall (1963), for example, reports that house staff officers in general hospitals are very anxious to be in situations where they receive frequent evaluations. She notes that "Most house officers welcome having their work closely supervised by accomplished physicians, for without this they cannot readily increase their knowledge or improve their skills" (1963, p. 200).

Finally, students are expected to react with less instability to a given amount of incompatibility because there is a less clear relation between performance evaluations and immediate organizational sanctions than for regular position incumbents. Students, because they are defined less than fully competent, are less likely to be held strictly accountable for their mistakes or to be sanctioned for errors. Also, students often place less emphasis on obtaining the immediate rewards offered by the system than on doing sufficiently well in the system to be able to move into desirable positions in other organizations (Shepard, 1954, p. 459).

This is not to argue that participants in student roles do not place any value on their performance evaluations and, hence, fall outside the scope of our theory. It is rather to argue that students apply a somewhat different calculus in linking evaluations with sanctions, that they place less emphasis on particular performance evaluations and as a consequence are less likely to react to incompatibilities with instability behavior.

Composition Effects. Do participants in an organization react only to their own problems or are they likely to react to problems afflicting their colleagues occupying the same organizational position? This is the type of question which may be addressed by compositional analysis (Blau, 1960; Davis, Spaeth, and Huson, 1961). The general argument, as stated by Blau (1957, p. 64) is that "if ego's *X* affects not only ego's *Y* but also alter's *Y,*" a compositional effect is observed. Our expectation is that there will be a relationship between incompatibilities in the authority systems of other occupants of the same position and the instability of the system of a given participant in that position. Specifically, the greater the extent of incompatibility experienced by other occupants of the organizational position held by *C,* the more likely it is that *C*'s authority system will be unstable, even though *C* personally experiences no incompatibility.

Positional Problems. Compositional effects occur because of *C*'s reaction to the incompatibilities in the authority systems of colleagues who occupy the same position as *C,* even though *C* is not subject to these incompatibilities. A different kind of situation occurs when *C* notes that his or her peers are subject to problems similar to those experienced by *C,* and, for this reason, is more likely to exhibit instability.

This latter type of situation should be quite common in formal organizations where a number of persons occupy the same position. Because the structure of relations is formalized, the types of problems affecting one occupant of an organizational position are likely to be inflicted upon other occupants. It should be noted, however, that while we can speak of formalized or positional problems—

factors associated with the authority system which create difficulties in the evaluation process—it is not possible, given our formulation, to speak of formalized incompatibility. For a given type of incompatibility to be formalized, it would need to be present in the authority system of every occupant of that position. However, as we have emphasized, incompatibility is defined in terms of problems which thwart attainment of evaluations at or above a participant's acceptance level, and participants are expected to differ to some degree in setting their acceptance levels. Some will be satisfied only with ratings of "excellent" while others are satisfied with ratings of "satisfactory." Positional problems which frustrate participants with relatively high acceptance levels may go unnoticed by participants with lower acceptance levels.

In spite of the difficulties created by varying acceptance levels, it is still possible to characterize positions, and not simply particular occupants, in terms of their level of incompatibility. To the extent that problems are positional, participants with similar acceptance levels should all experience incompatibility. Moreover, since participants who are prevented from attaining evaluations at a given acceptance level are necessarily prevented from attaining evaluations at any higher acceptance level, the response patterns of participants subject to positional problems should "scale" in the manner described by Stouffer, Guttman, and others (1950). That is, if for a given position, positional problems were arranged in order according to the level at which they prevent attainment, we would expect that all occupants experiencing incompatibility from those problems which prevent attainment at a high level of acceptance should also experience incompatibility from those problems which prevent attainment at lower levels of acceptance. Using this reasoning, we may obtain some information on the extent to which problems producing incompatibilities are positional in nature.

Also, we would expect that, the more incompatibility is a result of positional problems, the more likely the authority systems of occupants of the position will be unstable. We make this prediction for several reasons, some of which are related to compositional effects. First, we believe that positional problems are more likely to be perceived; shared experiences are more likely to be discussed with the result that the source of trouble within the system will be pinpointed. This further suggests that reactions to positional problems are more likely to be focused rather than diffuse or vague. Second, individuals who for some particular reason are not subject to an incompatibility which affects others in their position are more likely to feel threatened to the extent that the problem is positional. For, if the problem is general to the position, then the situation of the unthreatened participant is exceptional, and the circumstances making it so may be subject to change (for example, an evaluator who makes allowances for the problem may be replaced by another who does not). Third, we expect reactions to positional problems to be more likely because there is strength in numbers. Individual participants affected by nonpositional problems are more likely to seek to adjust themselves to the incompatibility rather than make a fuss. But problems perceived as general are more likely to evoke an active response as participants collectively seek redress of their grievances.

The four factors just considered—institutionalized transience, student status, compositional effects, and positional problems—are all expected to help account for the *amount* of instability associated with a given amount of incompatibility. The fifth and final factor to be discussed—status in the hierarchy—is expected to help explain the *type* of instability which occurs in authority systems.

Status in Hierarchy. As we have explained, our analytical model for authority systems is constructed around a particular occupant of an organizational position. The model is applicable to the analysis of virtually any position within the hierarchy, for example, from nurses' aide to chief resident. Up to this point, we have not attempted to make differential predictions depending on where the position is located in the hierarchical structure of the organization. Organizational positions, however, clearly differ in terms of power, scope of responsibility, security of tenure, and status prerogatives, and it would be curious indeed if such factors had no effect on the way in which incumbents attempted to resolve incompatibilities. We make the quite straightforward prediction that occupants of positions higher in the status and power hierarchy are more likely than lower participants to engage in instability *acts* calculated to resolve incompatibilities. That is, rather than merely being dissatisfied, higher status respondents should be more likely to act on the basis of their dissatisfaction: to express their dissatisfaction to other participants, to make suggestions for change, and to noncomply with control attempts as a way of indicating their dissatisfaction with the system.

Summary

We have introduced so many variables and advanced so many arguments in this chapter that the reader may have lost sight of the general theoretical model. We will therefore attempt to provide a summary of the argument, emphasizing the most general predictions and showing how some of the more detailed arguments relate to the larger conception. This overview will be aided by reference to Figure 4.

The analysis begins with the isolation of an authority system which we define as all authority rights regularly exercised over and by C relevant to the evaluation of C's performance of a given organizational task. To fall within the scope of our theory, C must place some value on the evaluations of his performance made by organizational evaluators. The minimal level of a performance evaluation which is satisfactory to C is, by definition, C's acceptance level for that evaluation. Allowances are made in our formulation for the fact that different occupants of the same organizational position may establish differing levels of acceptance.

Authority systems may be characterized as compatible or incompatible. By definition, an authority system is incompatible if it functions in such a manner that C is prevented by the system from maintaining evaluations of performance at or above C's acceptance level. There are various ways in which authority systems can be incompatible, and we have distinguished four types of incompatibility: contradictory evaluations, uncontrollable evaluations, unpredictable evaluations, and unattainable evaluations. An authority system is defined as incompatible if it contains one or more of these types of problems; and the more problems it contains, the more incompatible it is. While our theory does not purport to identify systematically all factors which contribute to the likelihood of an incompatibility being

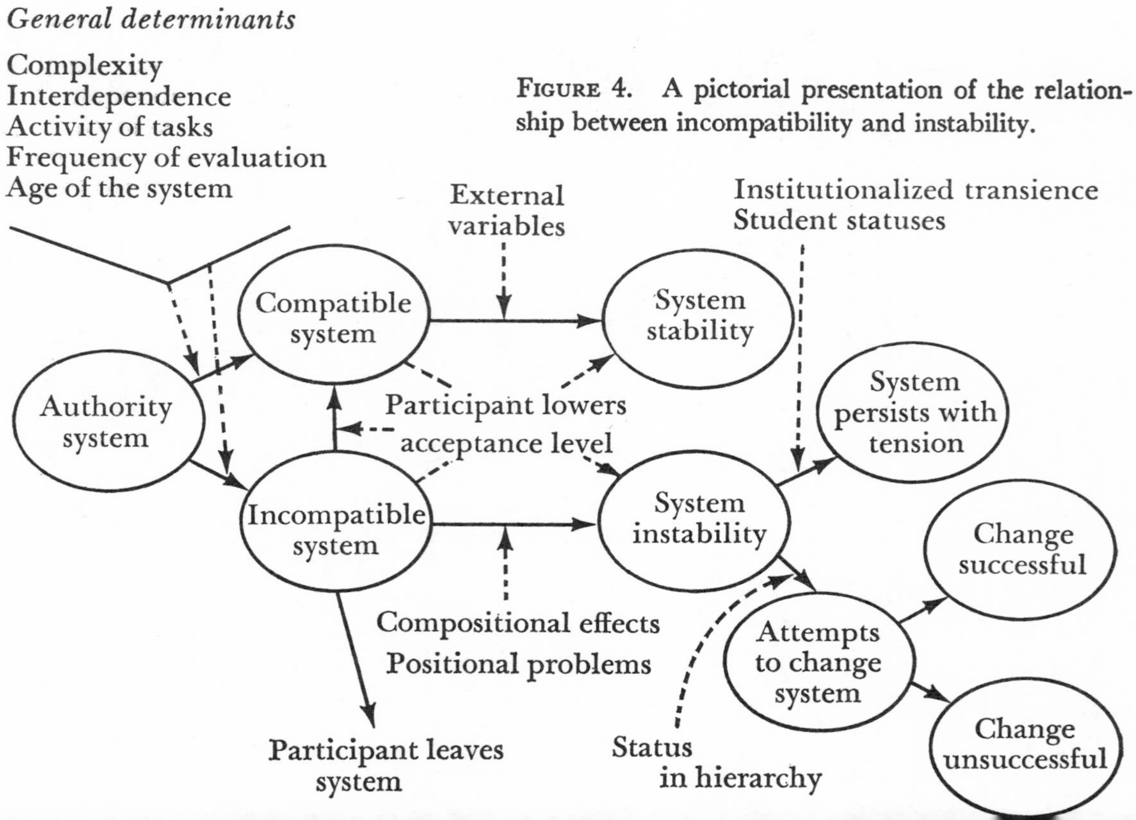

General determinants

Complexity
Interdependence
Activity of tasks
Frequency of evaluation
Age of the system

FIGURE 4. A pictorial presentation of the relationship between incompatibility and instability.

Institutionalized transience
Student statuses

External
variables

Compositional effects
Positional problems

Status
in hierarchy

Participant lowers
acceptance level

Participant leaves
system

Authority
system

Compatible
system

Incompatible
system

System
stability

System
instability

System
persists with
tension

Attempts
to change
system

Change
successful

Change
unsuccessful

present, we would expect the following to be important: the complexity of the authority system, the degree of interdependence among performers, the extent to which the tasks performed are active in nature, the frequency of evaluation, and the age of the system.

Compatible authority systems are more likely to be stable than incompatible systems, although the stability of an authority system will also be affected by various external factors—factors other than the presence of incompatibility. Incompatible authority systems are expected to be unstable, that is, to contain pressures for change. However, two possible responses to incompatibility—leaving the system and lowering of acceptance level—do not involve pressures for change in that the former removes the participant from the system and the latter moves the system directly into a compatible state. The lowering of acceptance level means that evaluations which were formerly viewed as unacceptable are now perceived to be acceptable, with the result that an incompatible system becomes a compatible one.

The amount of instability present in the system is expected to be a function of the amount of incompatibility present as well as the cost of the evaluations below acceptance level. In addition, both compositional effects and the extent to which the problems are viewed as positional are expected to affect the strength of the instability reaction to a given amount of incompatibility.

Given the presence of instability in an authority system, whether those subject to this condition actively attempt to alter the system or respond in a more passive fashion appears to be affected by certain special features of C's position. Thus, certain positions are defined as temporary in nature, and we would expect occupants of these positions to be more likely to suffer in silence. Also, the relative status of the position in the hierarchy is expected to affect the nature of the occupant's response to incompatibilities: those in positions higher in the hierarchy are expected to respond more actively to any problems confronting them.

All attempts to resolve incompatible authority systems will not meet with success. In some cases, efforts to alter the existing system of authority will result in no changes at all. In other situations, efforts to change incompatible systems may succeed only in substituting one type of incompatibility for another. But we do expect some efforts to resolve incompatibilities to be successful. We have not yet attempted to determine the conditions under which attempts to resolve incompatibilities will be more or less successful. This remains an important area of indeterminacy in our theoretical efforts.

Chapter 10

Incompatibility and Instability: Empirical Studies

▲▲

The Five Organizations study was designed specifically to test the proposition that incompatibility leads to instability. In this chapter, we will present an overview of the results of that test.

First, the basic measures of incompatibilty and instability are described. These measures are then employed to test our proposition for each position as well as for the sample as a whole. Variables which influence the likelihood that incompatibility and instability will occur are also examined. Finally, we evaluate alternative explanations for the basic findings presented.

Measuring Incompatibility

An incompatibility can appear only when an evaluation is below the acceptance level of the person being evaluated. Early in the interview we attempted to communicate this concept of acceptance level to respondents with the following explanation: "I'm now going to ask you how often *you* are dissatisfied when you learn what your rating or evaluation is. Some people are dissatisfied whenever their evaluator is dissatisfied. Others are dissatisfied when their evaluators are fairly satisfied, for they want to be told their work is exceptional. Still others are satisfied with a low rating because they expected to do poorly on a particular job, perhaps because it was difficult. When you learn what (the appraiser's) rating or evaluation is on (this task) or any part of it, how often is the rating or evaluation *low enough to make you dissatisfied?*"

The phrase, "low enough to make you dissatisfied," was used throughout the interview to refer to an evaluation below the respondent's acceptance level. Our pretests and subsequent field experience demonstrated that, despite some initial difficulty, this idea was successfully communicated. Indeed, many respondents spontaneously used the phrase in their answers to various later questions. Interviewers were careful to emphasize that "dissatisfied" in this phrase referred to the level of the evaluation received, not with how it was made or who made it.

The general model of the questions used to identify the presence and frequency of instances of incompatibility was as follows: A description of a particular kind of incompatibility was given and the respondent, C, was asked if he or she had ever experienced this type of problem when performing the focal task. If C answered affirmatively, the next question asked was: "How often does this happen to you on (this task)?" Each respondent was handed a card containing the following scale: Always, Almost Always, Usually, Fairly Often, Occasionally, Seldom, Almost Never, and Never. Reports that an incompatibility occurred Almost Never or Never were not considered to indicate sufficient frequency to represent the presence of incompatibility. An evaluation problem which was reported as occurring Almost Never was taken as a statement by the respondent that the evaluation problem was confronted rarely if ever. As one respondent succinctly stated: "I never say 'never'." All respondents reporting the presence of an incompatibility Seldom or more frequently were asked: "When this happens, which evaluators are giving you evaluations low enough to make you dissatisfied?" as well as: "Can you give me examples?" If the examples supplied were irrelevant, that is, judged by the interviewer not to be an instance of incompatibility, the interviewer repeated the original question describing the incompatibility and then proceeded to ask the related questions again.

One set of criteria, a fairly loose set, was used to determine whether any incompatibility, regardless of type, was present in C's authority system. Under these criteria an incompatibility was said to be present if C reported its occurrence more frequently than Almost Never, gave an illustration which indicated that C understood the meaning of incompatibility, and described a problem which adversely affected the performance evaluations C received from authorized evaluators of the focal task. For analysis of the presence or frequency of any specific incompatibility, the criterion for relevance was more strict, requiring that the majority of C's examples be coded as relevant to that specific incompatibility. In every case, the coding of relevance was done by at least two of the researchers.

We may now report the nine incompatibility questions organized in terms of the four different types of incompatibilities which they measure. The order in which the incompatibility questions were asked was determined arbitrarily, except that the first question on inappropriately high standards was chosen to provide an easy introduction to a set of difficult concepts. For some incompatibility questions, slightly different phrasings of the question were available to interviewers if respondents failed to understand the first version. In some cases, prearranged examples were developed to aid in comprehension. As was the case with our operationalization of the authority rights, there were some small discrepancies between our theoretical description of the various types and subcategories of incompatibility and our measurement of these concepts. Theoretical work to improve our understanding of the various forms of incompatibility continued beyond the instrument preparation and data collection stages. We shall note these discrepancies as we describe the questions.

Type I: Contradictory Evaluations. Type I incompatibilities occur when an authority system places C in a situation in which the receipt of one performance evaluation at or above C's acceptance level necessarily entails the receipt of another performance evaluation below acceptance level. Three questions were used to measure Type I incompatibility:

> *Conflicting Standards.* Sometimes when you are evaluated by more than one person, the way they evaluate you may make it impossible for you to obtain evaluations which satisfy you from all of them. In other words, doing work for which you receive an evaluation which satisfies you from one evaluator may cause you to receive from another evaluator an evaluation low enough to make you dissatisfied. Does this ever happen to you on (this task) or any part of it?

Alternative version; used if necessary to improve *C*'s understanding:

> Does it ever happen on (this task) or any part of it that if you do work which receives a rating or evaluation which satisfies you from one evaluator, the rating or evaluation you receive from another will therefore be low enough to make you dissatisfied?

> *Conflicting Properties.* Sometimes one person may evaluate different aspects (or parts) of your work in such a way that it is impossible for you to receive evaluations from him which satisfy you on all aspects (or parts) of your work. In other words, doing work which receives an evaluation from him which satisfies you on one aspect (or part) may cause you to receive an evaluation from him on another aspect (or part) low enough to make you dissatisfied. Does this ever happen to you on (this task) or any part of it?

Example, if needed:

> Well, for example, a Little League Baseball coach may find that a parent of one of the boys on his team wants him both to win the championship and to give every kid, regardless of ability, equal playing time. Many Little League coaches have discovered, to their sorrow, that it is impossible to satisfy a parent on both of these aspects.

Conflicting Allocations. A person may have a number of different tasks to perform. Some of these tasks may interfere with each other in such a way that he cannot do well on all of them, and as a result, he may not be able to avoid being given some evaluations which are low enough to make him dissatisfied. Do you ever have other tasks which interfere with you (doing this task) or any part of it so that sometimes you cannot avoid being given a rating of evaluation on (this task) low enough to make you dissatisfied?

No question was asked to tap the problem of conflicting samples.

Type II: Uncontrollable Evaluations. Type II incompatibilities occur when the performer is placed in a situation in which evaluations are received below acceptance level for performances or outcomes that are beyond the performer's control. Two questions were used to measure Type II incompatibility. The first indicates an incompatibility resulting from incorrectly attributing the performance of another person to the person being evaluated. The second question identifies incorrect evaluations that result from active tasks, where the outcome does not provide an appropriate basis for judging the quality of the performance.

Incorrect Attribution. Sometimes people are evaluated on work which they had nothing to do with. Does this ever happen to you on (this task) or any part of it so that you receive a rating or evaluation low enough to make you dissatisfied?

Active Tasks. There may be other things which affect the outcome or end-result of (this task) or any part of it besides how well you do your work. For example, a fisherman may be fishing very well, but the fish are just not biting that day. If one judges him on the number of fish caught, one mistakenly concludes that he did not fish well. Do you ever find that even though you have done a good job on (this task) the outcome or end-result is not good, and therefore you receive a rating or evaluation low enough to make you dissatisfied?

A third subtype of Type II incompatibility, performer inter-dependence, was not measured separately here since it is closely related to an aspect of Type IV incompatibility and is covered there under lack of facilities.

Type III: Unpredictable Evaluations. An authority system produces Type III incompatibility when participants are unable to predict the relationship between attributes of their performance and the level of rating contained in the performance evaluation. The performers lack information about the properties, weights, or standards for evaluating their work, and that lack of information is the cause of their receiving evaluations below acceptance level. One question was used to measure Type III incompatibility:

> *Misunderstandings of Criteria.* Do you ever find that because you have insufficient or incorrect information about how you are evaluated on (this task) or any part of it, you therefore do work which receives a rating or evaluation low enough to make you dissatisfied?

Alternative version, used if necessary to improve C's understanding:

> Do you ever have insufficient or incorrect information on the way you are evaluated on (this task) or any part of it which leads you to work in such a way that you receive a rating or evaluation on (this task) low enough to make you dissatisfied?

For Type III incompatibility only one question was used as an indicator of its presence or frequency. Other subtypes discussed in Chapter Nine—misunderstandings of allocations and incompatibilities arising from nonrepresentative sampling—were, unfortunately, not fully appeciated by us until most of the interviewing had been completed.

Type IV: Unattainable Evaluations. Type IV incompatibility arises when an authority system places participants in a situation in which the standards used to evaluate them are so high that they cannot achieve evaluations at their acceptance level. Three questions were used to identify Type IV incompatibility. The first directly articulates the definition of the type:

> *Inappropriately High Standards.* Do you ever find that for (this task) or any part of it standards are being used which are much too high, so that you receive a rating or evaluation low enough to make you dissatisfied?

The second question tapping Type IV incompatibility indicates that standards are unattainable because of dependence on the work of others whose performances are unsatisfactory and over whom the performer lacks sufficient authority rights. A combination of questions was used to identify this type of incompatibility. First, respondents were asked about others with whom they were interdependent:

> Often the way one person does his work affects how well or poorly another person is able to do his work. Are there any groups or individuals who work with you on any part of (this task) whose work affects how well or poorly you do and, therefore, affects the evaluations made of your work?

If the respondent replied affirmatively, he or she was asked to name those others. Then, for each person indicated, the respondent was asked:

> How often do you find that you are performing well, but because (name of person or group mentioned) is not doing a good enough job, you receive evaluations on (this task) low enough to make you dissatisfied?

For those persons or groups named whose work Seldom or more frequently caused the performer to receive evaluations below the acceptance level, the respondent was asked:

> *Lack of Facilities.* You have told me that (name of person or groups) work in such a way that you sometimes receive a rating or evaluation on (this task) low enough to make you feel dissatisfied. Does this ever hap-

pen because you do not have enough control over the
way their work is assigned or evaluated?

It is possible to argue that this question focusing on insufficient rights, could justifiably be regarded as Type II incompatibility, for the performer is being blamed as a result of the poor
work of others. Some of the examples given by respondents did fit
Type II incompatibility, but most of the examples given in response
to this question indicated that the task of controlling these other performers was indeed assigned to the respondent, and the lack of sufficient authority rights produced a situation in which the standards
were unattainable.

The third question assigned to Type IV contained elements
of Type I incompatibility in instances of evaluations taking place
too soon.

> *Evaluated Too Soon.* On (this task) or any part
> of it, are you ever evaluated before you finish, and, there-
> fore, given an evaluation or a rating low enough to make
> you dissatisfied, although if your evaluator were to wait
> until you completed the task, he would give you an
> evaluation which would satisfy you?

Type I incompatibilities were found occasionally in responses
to this question. The first of these instances was a situation in which
contradictory evaluations were based upon an outcome and the
performance leading to that outcome. If the evaluator had waited
for the outcome, then the earlier negative evaluation of the performance would have been reversed. A second instance of Type I incompatibility was the presence of conflicting tasks which delayed
the accomplishment of the focal task, thereby producing an evaluation below the acceptance level when the evaluator evaluated too
soon. Yet neither of these was typically indicated by the examples
given by performers in response to this question. Most of the examples indicated that evaluators simply used criteria which were too
demanding to allow the respondent sufficient time to achieve the
necessary quality of performance for an acceptable evaluation.

Having completed our brief discussion of the nine questions

used to determine incompatibility, we now develop our summary measures of incompatibility.

Summary Measures of Incompatibility. The presence of an incompatibility was indicated by answering "Yes" to one of the nine incompatibility questions, giving a relevant example by the loose criteria, and indicating that the problem described occurred more frequently than Almost Never. From these basic data, we developed three summary measures of incompatibility. The first measure was simply based on the reported presence or absence of incompatibility. The report of incompatibility in an authority system does not take into account the frequency of incompatibility or the number of different incompatibilities reported. It is an all-or-nothing measure.

The second measure of incompatibility counted the number of incompatibilities which fulfilled our strict relevance criteria. Among all respondents for whom specific incompatibilities were present, the median number of different incompatibilities was determined. By splitting at that median, we produced a trichotomy of three or more different incompatibilities, one or two different incompatibilities, or no incompatibilities.

The third measure of incompatibility was based on the reported frequency of incompatibility. The development of this measure required some assumptions and indirect measures. Our technique was simply to use two different models for determining the frequency of incompatibility and then to limit further analyses to those persons for whom the two models gave similar ratings.

Our first submeasure for the frequency of incompatibility summed responses for the nine questions in the following manner: Seldom was scored as 1; Occasionally as 2; Fairly Often as 3; and Usually, Almost Always, or Always were all scored as 4. The last three categories were given an equal score to prevent too much weight being given to an incompatibility which occurred very often. Then the total scores on this new measure were trichotomized into "high" frequency, for scores greater than 7, "medium" for scores from 7 to 4, and "low" for totals from 3 to 1. A fourth and lowest group contained those persons reporting no incompatibilities.

Because of the obvious difficulties of adding across questions and the arbitrary assigning of weights to terms like Occasionally, we developed a second submeasure: the highest frequency reported for any specific incompatibility among those which met the strict relevance criteria. The maximum frequencies were collapsed into four categories: Fairly Often or higher; Occasionally; Seldom; and no incompatibilities reported. This measure avoided additivity assumptions but did not use some important information, such as the reported frequency of the other specific incompatibilities.

Our cautious compromise did not rely completely on either submeasure for estimating the frequency with which respondents reported the occurrence of incompatibility within their authority system. Instead, we limited our use of the frequency measure to those respondents who were grouped similarly by both submeasures. The two submeasures both provided four groupings. Of the 224 respondents, 168 gave us complete agreement between the two submeasures. Therefore, in our subsequent tests of hypotheses, the empirical statements using frequency of incompatibility are limited to the 168 authority systems for which the two submeasures agree.

We have, therefore, created three summary measures of incompatibility: presence or absence of one or more incompatibilities, number of different incompatibilities, and the frequency with which incompatibilities occurred when performers were evaluated for their work. With these summary measures, we can now examine factors which affect the distribution of incompatibility.

Distribution of Incompatibility

Incompatibility by Position. If incompatibilities were mainly a product of personal or interpersonal factors rather than a statement of a situational problem, we would expect incompatibilities to spread approximately evenly across different positions and organizations. The data in Table 12 show that incompatibility is to a large extent a function of organization and position, and hence is not primarily a reflection of personal or interpersonal problems. The distribution of incompatibility by type across the sixteen positions in five organizations ranged from complete absence of a specific incompatibility for storekeepers to 95 percent of the Front Eight on the

Table 12.

Distribution of Incompatibilities by Type in Sixteen Positions

	At least one specific incompatibility Percent	Type I (contradictory) Percent	Type II (uncontrollable) Percent	Type III (unpredictable) Percent	Type IV (unattainable) Percent	N[a]
Nurse's Aide	44	33	23	8	24	22–25
Nursing Team Leader	76	50	50	10	44	24–29
Clerk	78	86	11	12	56	7–9
Intern and Junior Resident	81	62	32	10	52	19–21
Senior Resident	70	44	40	0	44	9–10
Engineer	71	67	20	0	57	5–7
Draftsman	50	50	25	0	50	4–6
Storekeeper	0	0	0	0	0	4–5
Technical Typist	50	67	25	0	50	3–4
Assembly Line Worker	24	4	16	4	8	24–25
Desk Worker	53	50	30	29	20	10–15
Copy Editor	50	17	36	8	21	12–14
Member of Front Eight	95	90	42	15	45	19–20
Member of Back Three	60	20	60	0	20	5
Offensive Lineman	67	46	69	20	7	13–15
Ball Carrier	62	40	58	17	23	10–13
All Positions	61	39	35	10	32	200–223

[a] Position N varies slightly across incompatibility types because of variations in the number of codeable responses.

football team reporting the presence of specific incompatibility. Busching (1969) presents and discusses the distribution of each of the nine incompatibility responses among the organizations and positions. His detailed data reinforce the conclusion that there was enormous variability in reports of incompatibility among positions and organizations.

If we were to play the game of considering our five organizations as random samples, which they are not, we could reject the null hypothesis that these samples came from the same population. The null hypothesis would be rejected for the presence of any incompatibility; rejected for Types I, II, and IV; and even rejected, despite the low frequencies, for six of the nine individual incompatibility questions. The distribution of incompatibility was patterned, not distributed by chance, and was related to characteristics of the specific organizations and positions we studied.

We can also eliminate the possibility that the respondents were merely reporting the general level of incompatibility, and not really differentiating the various types of incompatibility. Were this the case, positions relatively high on one type of incompatibility would be relatively high on the other types. However, ranking the fifteen positions reporting some incompatibility on each type, we see that the association among the rank orders for the four types was only moderate. Kendall's Coefficient of Concordance (W) expresses the degree of association among rank orders (1948). W was .38 on a scale from 0 (nonagreement) to 1.0 (perfect agreement), and the null hypothesis of no relationship among the four types could not be rejected. The differences among positions in reports of incompatibility did reflect differences in the likelihood of the occurrence of each type of incompatibility.

Incompatibilities and Incompetence. The concept of incompatibility, we are arguing, focuses upon problems of authority systems, not upon the personal qualities of the participant. Logically, there need be no relationship between incompatibility and the individual's competence to perform his organizational tasks. Happily, we also found no empirical relationship.

It took considerable effort for us to obtain from supervisors ratings of competence for the persons we interviewed. To overcome their resistance, we asked the supervisors whether each worker was Far Above Average, Moderately Above Average, Slightly Above Average, About Average, Slightly Below Average, Moderately Below Average, or Far Below Average. These vague terms, plus no pressure from us to check the tendency for supervisors to report most persons as above the average, enabled us to obtain ratings of 132 respondents.

When we related the reported presence of incompatibility to the competence ratings by supervisors of the 132 respondents, there was no relationship between the respondents' competence and the probability that they would report an incompatibility in their authority systems. Combining respondents across organizations into four competence groups of approximately equal numbers, we find that the probability of reporting an incompatibility was .62 for the most competent group, .67 for the second group, .61 for the third group, and .63 for those rated least competent. The gamma expressing the relationship between competence and reporting an incompatibility was .005, almost exactly zero.

In Chapter Six, we showed that competence bore little relationship to receiving negative evaluations. Now we have presented data indicating that incompatibility is a problem of an authority system, unaffected by the competence or incompetence of its victim.

Influences upon Incompatibility

We investigated the contribution of four variables to the amount of incompatibility: the complexity of the authority system, interdependence, frequency of evaluation, and length of time in the organizational position. We hypothesized that complexity and interdependence would increase incompatibility, that longer time in a position would reduce it, and we made no prediction on the effect of evaluation frequency.

Complexity of the authority system was measured by counting the number of distinct persons who exercised one or more authority rights over the performer. The total for these four components constituted the measure of complexity, with the number of superiors ranging from 1 to 20.

Interdependence was measured by counting the number of

persons mentioned as affecting, by the quality of their work, the level of the performer's evaluations. The data were obtained from responses to the second question described under Type IV incompatibility. Interdependence using this measure varied from 0 to 15.

Frequency of communicated evaluation was difficult to operationalize because of our emphasis upon evaluations by specific appraisers. We had no data on the total frequency of communicated evaluation. Instead, we used an imperfect measure, the median frequency of communicated evaluation for all the appraisers of each performer. For each appraiser, the respondent used a seven-point scale, ranging from Very Frequently to Never, to answer the question, "How frequently do you learn (each specific evaluator's) evaluation of how well or poorly you are doing on (this task) or any part of it?" The median of these responses constituted our measure of the frequency of communicated evaluation. Unfortunately, we did not know whether a person who was evaluated Very Frequently by one appraiser and Seldom by another, for example, was evaluated more or less frequently than a respondent who was evaluated Fairly Often by each of three appraisers. Our measure defined these two reports as equivalent. The lack of a single question on the total frequency of communicated evaluation for a respondent necessarily makes suspect our analysis of the impact of frequency of communicated evaluation upon incompatibility.

Length of time refers to the period of time participants had occupied their present position. Responses to a direct question about the length of time that respondents had occupied their position were scored as follows: 1 for less than six weeks; 2 for six weeks to three months; 3 for three months to six months; 4 for six months to one year; 5 for one to two years; 6 for two to four years; 7 for four to eight years; 8 for eight to sixteen years; and 9 for more than sixteen years.

Table 13 presents the distribution of these four variables for respondents in all positions studied except storekeeper since no incompatibility by the strict criterion was reported for that position. The positions are ranked in this table on the basis of their mean responses. We used five different methods to test the impact of these structural variables upon incompatibility. The advantages and disadvantages of each technique are described in Busching (1969).

Table 13.

MEAN SCORE AND RANK ORDER OF FIFTEEN POSITIONS ON FOUR STRUCTURAL VARIABLES

Position	Complexity		Interdependence		Evaluation Frequency		Time in Position	
	Mean	Rank	Mean	Rank	Mean	Rank	Mean	Rank
Nurse's Aide	5.3	(4)	2.0	(9)	2.9	(5)	7.4	(3)
Nursing Team Leader	6.3	(1)	5.2	(2)	3.4	(8)	6.0	(6)
Clinical Clerk	4.0	(7)	3.7	(5)	4.3	(14)	4.3	(13)
Intern	5.9	(3)	4.5	(3)	3.2	(7)	4.8	(12)
Senior Resident	4.4	(6)	5.4	(1)	3.8	(11)	5.3	(11)
Engineer	4.5	(5)	3.3	(6)	4.1	(13)	7.1	(4)
Draftsman	6.0	(2)	4.0	(4)	3.5	(9)	7.5	(2)
Technical Typist	2.5	(15)	2.1	(8)	3.0	(6)	6.5	(5)
Assembly Line Worker	3.4	(9)	0.5	(15)	3.6	(10)	8.1	(1)
Desk Worker	3.1	(11)	1.1	(13)	4.0	(12)	4.0	(15)
Copy Editor	3.7	(8)	1.0	(14)	4.5	(15)	4.2	(14)
Member of Front Eight	3.1	(10)	1.9	(10.5)	2.7	(2)	5.4	(10)
Member of Back Three	2.6	(14)	2.4	(7)	1.8	(1)	5.8	(8)
Offensive Lineman	3.0	(12.5)	1.8	(12)	2.8	(4)	5.5	(9)
Ball Carrier	3.0	(12.5)	1.9	(10.5)	2.76	(3)	5.85	(7)

First we examined the association between rank order on one of the structural variables, such as complexity, and each indicator of incompatibility. Second, we dichotomized respondents into those above and below the median for the five organizations on each structural variable, relating the result to incompatibility. Third, we controlled for positional effects by dichotomizing respondents on each structural variable according to the median for their own position, and then examined the association with the incompatibility measures. Because the variance within positions was often small, this third method had serious deficiencies. A fourth test simply counted the number of positions within which internal analysis by the third method gave a positive or negative result. For example, we found that when complexity was divided at the position medians, its association with incompatibility was weak. However, of the eleven positions examined on this variable, nine showed a positive relationship between incompatibility and complexity. This fourth measure, then, examined the consistency of the relationship across positions. A fifth method interrelated the four structural variables in order to see their joint effect on incompatibility, as well as to test the relationship of each to incompatibility when the other structural variables were controlled. These varied operations each told us something different about the relationship of the structural variables to incompatibility.

We do not present our findings in detail, but merely summarize our results. Interdependence was the structural variable most strongly associated with incompatibility. Complexity also had a positive effect on incompatibility. Frequency of communicated evaluations appeared to have a very slight positive effect on incompatibility, except in simple organizational structures where its effect was negative. Time in position appeared to reduce incompatibility for simple authority systems but had little effect on systems with high complexity and high interdependence. In summary, positions characterized by the highest incompatibility were likely to exhibit high interdependence, high complexity, and somewhat higher turnover of position occupants.

Consensus. Because we found that consensus as to the nature of the authority system was slightly higher in simple structures than in complex structures, and that high complexity of authority systems was associated with a high probability of incompatibilities, we predicted that consensus among participants as to the nature of their authority system would be negatively correlated with the presence of incompatibilities. The data supported this hypothesis, although the relationship was not very strong. Among 187 performers for whom we had data on both consensus and incompatibility, the gamma was −.20 when both variables were dichotomized. We then checked to see whether this relationship between consensus scores for individual participants and incompatibility could be a product of the level of group consensus. We divided the 187 cases into ninety-three participants who were in work groups where the level of consensus concerning the authority system was high, and ninety-four performers in work groups exhibiting low consensus. The negative relationship between consensus and incompatibility was slightly strengthened by controlling for group consensus. In high consensus groups the gamma became −.21, and in low consensus groups it became −.34. The relationship between consensus among participants as to the nature of their authority systems and the presence of incompatibility was consistently in the predicted negative direction. This supported the finding that complexity leads to incompatibility.

Active Tasks and Incompatibilities. We hypothesized that active tasks would be associated with incompatibilities. Since only one task was used for each position in the Five Organizations study, positional factors influencing the likelihood of incompatibilities could not be controlled. Thus we could make only an imperfect test of this hypothesis. But a preliminary inspection of the distribution of incompatibilities by position was at least encouraging.

The clearest test of the relationship was found in the comparison of the nurse's aides and the nursing team leaders. From our observations in the hospital, nursing team leaders engaged in many more active tasks than did nurses aides. Both were often carrying out orders, but the degree of unpredictability which necessarily was built into the tasks of the team leaders was usually lacking for the nurses aides. We therefore expected nursing team leaders to exhibit more incompatibilities, and they did: 76 percent of the nursing team leaders reported at least one incompatibility, compared with only

44 percent of the nurse's aides. If we are willing to ignore the many problems introduced as we move from one organization to another, other data also support the proposition that active tasks are associated with incompatibilities. The clinical clerks, interns, and senior residents each had a high proportion of performers reporting incompatibilities, ranging from 70 percent to 81 percent. The data for engineers also showed a high proportion reporting incompatibilities. The only other group for whom 60 percent or more reported incompatibilities were the football players, who face relatively unpredictable opponents. The two groups lowest in incompatibilities were storekeepers and assembly line workers, both performing less active tasks. The only negative data among the sixteen positions were produced by the defensive linemen on the football team. In summary, incompatibilities did tend to be associated with what we considered to be the more active tasks.

We can now discuss our measures of the instability of authority systems. We present the questions used to determine the presence of each index of instability, as well as our methods of categorizing responses to those questions. Then, we develop summary measures of instability that can be used to test the proposition that incompatibility leads to instability.

Measuring System Instability

The instability measures can be divided into four groups: dissatisfaction with some component of the authority system; general dissatisfaction; acts which indicate the instability of the authority system; and combinations of dissatisfaction and instability acts.

Absolute and Relative Dissatisfaction. When respondents answered one of our satisfaction questions, they could choose any one of eight possible responses: Extremely Satisfied, Very Satisfied, Moderately Satisfied, Slightly Satisfied, Slightly Dissatisfied, Moderately Dissatisfied, Very Dissatisfied, or Extremely Dissatisfied.

Throughout this study, people who said they were Extremely Satisfied or Very Satisfied were considered satisfied. Using similar reasoning, everybody responding as Slightly Satisfied or less satisfied was considered Dissatisfied. The problematic response was Moderately Satisfied. We used Moderately Satisfied as a swing category, sometimes combining it with those who were satisfied and sometimes with those who were dissatisfied. The criterion used was very simple. The Moderately Satisfied persons were lumped together with the smaller of the two groups for their position, whether satisfied or dissatisfied.

This technique may be made clearer by noting that persons who reported themselves Slightly Satisfied or less satisfied are hereafter called absolutely dissatisfied, while relatively dissatisfied refers to the possible combination of the Moderately Satisfied with these categories. Relative dissatisfaction refers to the response pattern for the occupants of a position. If most people were satisfied, then it makes sense to say that those who were only Moderately Satisfied were relatively dissatisfied. If few people were satisfied, the Moderately Satisfied were combined with the satisfied.

Right-Specific Dissatisfactions. We asked all respondents about their satisfaction with the exercise of each of four authority rights. The specific questions were:

> For allocation: "How satisfied or dissatisfied are you with the way (this task) is given to you, or with the ways decisions are made as to when you should do it?"
> For appraisal: "How satisfied or dissatisfied are you with the *way* evaluations are made of how well or poorly you do your work on (this task)?"
> For criteria-setting: "How satisfied or dissatisfied are you with the *way* the standards are set for judging how well or poorly you do your work on (this task)?"
> For sampling: "How satisfied or dissatisfied are you with the way in which decisions are made about what information is to be obtained about how you are doing on your work with (this task)?"

In the questions for appraisal and criteria-setting we believed it necessary to emphasize the word *way* so that the respondent would separate the manner in which evaluations were made from the level off evaluations received. Performers might receive negative evaluations and be dissatisfied with those evaluations without necessarily being dissatisfied with the system which produced those evaluations.

These questions on right-specific dissatisfaction were asked at the end of four separate portions of the questionnaire, after the questions relating to authority rights for each of the four components. This separation in time provided four separate opportunities for us to note the dissatisfaction of a respondent.

General Dissatisfaction. Each question on right-specific dissatisfaction covered only one component of the total authority system. We also needed a measure of general satisfaction or dissatisfaction. We asked two questions to tap the level of general satisfaction. The first was asked prior to the incompatibility questions:

> *General Dissatisfaction (I).* I have already asked you how satisfied you are with the way (this task) is given, the way standards are set, the way decisions are made about the information needed for evaluating, and the way evaluations are made. In general, considering all these things together, both for you and for others who work with you, how satisfied or dissatisfied are you with this way of organizing for doing (this task)?

Then, after the series of questions on incompatibilities, we asked the second question:

> I am now going to ask you some questions about how you feel about the way work on (this task) is assigned and evaluated, both for you and for others who work with you. You have already told me who does what on (this task); that is, the way (this task) is assigned and the way people are evaluated, including the way decisions are made about the information needed to evaluate their work, and the way standards are set. For the remaining questions, I will refer to these things as *the way this task is assigned and evaluated*. We will continue to talk about only (this task) and this work group.

> *General Dissatisfaction (II).* In general, how satisfied or dissatisfied are you with the way (this task) is assigned and evaluated?

There were three reasons for our asking twice about general satisfaction. First, the level of overall satisfaction was sufficiently important for us to seek a greater degree of reliability through the use of widely separated responses. Second, by asking the question twice, we could see whether merely asking questions about incompatibilities produced a "trail of fire." Would people, led by our probing to examine the way in which evaluations were made, suddenly come to understand deficiencies of the system and thereby reduce their satisfaction with it? Third, if incompatibility led to dissatisfaction, we could be more certain of this relationship if we had a measure of satisfaction before, as well as after, the reports of incompatibility. We would not then be dealing only with reduction of dissonance.

We were pleased to learn that there was no tendency for the level of general satisfaction later in the interview to be either higher or lower than the level of general satisfaction on the earlier question. In addition, for almost all respondents the answers to these two questions were identical or within one scale position of each other. We could use this high correlation between responses to provide a slightly more reliable indicator of general satisfaction. The answers to the two questions were averaged for each respondent. Then the scores were classified into four categories of general dissatisfaction with the authority system: Dissatisfied, Relatively Dissatisfied, Relatively Satisfied, and Satisfied.

Summary Measures of Dissatisfaction. Two summary measures of instability were developed from general dissatisfaction. The first was the presence or absence of general dissatisfaction, in which all respondents who were either Dissatisfied or Relatively Dissatisfied were coded as exhibiting general dissatisfaction with the authority system. The second measure expressed the degree of general dissatisfaction, using the four categories of dissatisfaction ranging from dissatisfied through the two relative categories to the group that was satisfied.

Three summary measures of instability were developed from dissatisfaction with the four components of authority. The first was whether relative dissatisfaction with any component was present. The second measure was whether dissatisfaction with any component using only absolute criteria was present. The third measure counted

the number of system components with which the participant was
relatively dissatisfied.

Instability Acts. In addition to measures of respondent satisfaction and dissatisfaction, we also attempted to measure attempts
by performers to alter their authority system. We distinguished between those attempts which individual performers made to change
their system and collective attempts to change the system in which
performers acted in concert to express dissatisfaction, suggest changes,
or engage in noncompliance.

Individual acts indicating instability were tapped by the
following questions:

> Are you ever dissatisfied enough with the way
> (this task) or any part of it is assigned and evaluated
> that . . .
> *Communicate Dissatisfaction.* . . . you tell others
> in your work group or elsewhere in the organization that
> you are dissatisfied?
> *Suggest Change.* . . . you suggest a change to
> others in your work group or elsewhere in the organiza-
> tion?
> *Noncompliance with Allocations.* . . . you don't
> do some of your assignments on (this task) or you decide
> to delay before doing them?
> *Noncompliance with Sampling.* . . . you don't
> allow information to be obtained on how you are doing
> on some part of (this task)?

Early field experience revealed that if respondents had not
reported engaging in an individual act of a given type, then they
were not only unlikely to report engaging in its collective version, but
also they were likely to be offended by the question designed to
detect the presence of the collective version of the act. Therefore,
each of the following questions was asked only if its individual
version had received a positive response:

> Are you and others whom you work ever dissatis-
> fied enough with the way (this task) or any part of it is
> assigned or evaluated so that . . .

Communicate Dissatisfaction. . . . you get together and together decide to express dissatisfaction?

Suggest Change. . . . you get together and together decide to suggest that a change be made?

Noncompliance with Allocations. . . . you get together and together decide not to do some of your assignments on (this task) or to delay doing some of them?

Noncompliance with Sampling. . . . you get together and together decide not to allow information to be obtained on how you are doing on some part of (this task)?

For each of these questions on instability acts, if respondents gave an affirmative reply, they were asked how frequently they performed the act. Answers were selected from the scale: Very Frequently, Frequently, Fairly Often, Occasionally, Seldom, Almost Never, Never.

An instability act was coded as present if, on any of these individual or collective questions, the respondent reported engaging in the act more frequently than Almost Never; gave a relevant example indicating that the act did occur within the authority system being analyzed for the focal task and was based upon dissatisfaction with that authority system; *and* did not report *both* that he or she was no longer engaged in the act *and* that a change correcting the situation either had been made or was pending.

In addition, we coded instability as present, even if the respondent reported that he or she was no longer engaged in the act, as long as a change correcting the situation neither had been made nor was pending. The fact that the performer was no longer engaged in the instability act, perhaps after repeated failure, appeared to us to indicate continuing pressure for change in the authority system. On the other hand, we did not code as instability those acts which had produced changes in the system. If we had not made that decision, then those high status persons whose suggestions, criticisms, or noncompliance often led to changes in the system would erroneously be viewed as frequently attacking the system. The responsiveness of the system is a source of its stability.

Summary Measures of Instability Acts. From these basic

data, we developed three measures. The first was the presence of any instability act. The second was the number of types of instability acts. There were four types of acts: communication of dissatisfaction, suggestion of changes, noncompliance with allocations, and noncompliance with sampling. The second summary measure merely counted how many of these types were present and expressed the results in three categories: two or more types, one type, and no instability acts.

The third summary measure, the relative frequency of instability acts, provided a particularly sensitive measure of the intensity of instability. It necessitated, however, controlling for the differences among organizational positions in the frequency of such instability acts. For example, nursing team leaders engaged in instability acts more frequently than did nurse's aides. Since we wished to control for such positional factors in testing the relationship between incompatibility and instability, we needed a measure which would take into account such interpositional differences. We therefore developed a measure which defined for each respondent his or her relative frequency of instability behavior compared with other occupants of the same position.

This third summary measure of instability acts was determined as follows: For all occupants of a given position who had been coded as engaging in a given instability act, the median frequency of engaging in this act was determined. Those frequencies equal to the median frequency were given a score of 2; those higher in frequency than the median frequency were given a score of 3; and those lower than the median, but more frequent than Almost Never, were scored 1. Those respondents who had no coded instability acts were given a score of zero. For each respondent, these scores were added across all eight questions. All respondents whose total score was zero were characterized as zero on this variable. The median score of the remaining respondents was then determined. Those scoring above the median were classified as high; those below the median were categorized as low. Each respondent then was classified as having a zero frequency of instability acts, or a high or low frequency if any instability acts were reported, and this tripartite division reflected a comparison of the respondent's instability acts with those of other persons in the same position.

Summary Measures Combining Dissatisfaction with Instability Acts. Up to this point, our measures have been based on either dissatisfaction or instability acts, but not both. The remaining three summary measures attempt to summarize across all indices of instability, including both dissatisfaction and instability acts. They, therefore, provide the most general test of our hypothesis.

The first measure simply recorded for each respondent the presence of an instability act or relative dissatisfaction. Either an instability act or relative dissatisfaction with a component of the authority system or with the system as a whole was taken to indicate the presence of instability. The second measure of instability noted the presence of an instability act or dissatisfaction by absolute criteria with any system component or with the authority system as a whole. The difference between the two measures is the use of relative dissatisfaction for the first measure and absolute dissatisfaction for the second.

Our third measure of instability combined instability acts and relative dissatisfaction in order to determine the relative degree of instability for the authority systems of different respondents. Since there were four components of the authority system for which dissatisfaction could be expressed and four types of instability acts, this measure simply counted the number of types of instability acts and occurrences of relative dissatisfaction with the components of the authority system. The categories were four or more, three, two, one, and zero occurrences of relative dissatisfaction or instability acts.

Effects of Instability Behavior

The reports on instability acts, prior to determining whether a change had been made in the system, provided us with an imperfect and indirect method of determining the likelihood that instability behavior produces desired changes in the authority system. Some instability behavior was reported by 125 (56 percent) of the persons in our sample. These persons also reported on the correction or noncorrection of various problems. We gave each of these 125 persons equal weight in deriving a measure of the proportion of behaviors which were successful in producing correction of problems. We did this by giving each person a total score of 1.0 to be divided between successful and unsuccessful instability behavior. For example, a person who engaged in three separate instances of instability behavior and was successful in one of them was given a success score of .33. The mean probability of success for instability behaviors, using this technique for our sample, was .16. Five out of six instability attempts did not result in a resolution which was successful from the standpoint of the actor. We can only speculate on whether this tentative statistic is likely to be an underestimate or an overestimate of the true proportion in the complex universe of formal organizations. But the general magnitude of this figure does serve as a guide to thought about the nature of instability in authority systems.

We hypothesized that higher status persons would be more likely to suggest changes than would persons lower in the organization. That is, if they did engage in instability acts, they would be more likely to take direct steps to change the system by suggesting alternatives because they had prestige, power, and influence to invest in these attempts. To test this hypothesis we needed to find an organization which contained a sufficiently large number of persons of both high and low status who engaged in instability behavior. It was imperative that these people be members of the same organization. Only the data for nursing team leaders and nurse's aides provided a sufficient number of persons exhibiting instability acts for even a preliminary test of this hypothesis. The results were clear, although they must necessarily be viewed with the caution appropriate to a single test on a small population.

Of the nineteen team leaders reporting instability acts, thirteen expressed dissatisfaction, and fourteen suggested changes; these two forms of instability behavior were thus approximately equal. With respect to noncompliance, only three of the team leaders engaged in noncompliant behavior. Of the ten nurse's aides engaging in instability behavior, eight expressed dissatisfaction, four reported noncompliance, and only two suggested changes. It does appear that if instability behavior is initiated, higher status persons are more likely to suggest changes than are lower status persons.

Incompatibility and Instability

We now report tests of our hypothesis that incompatibility leads to instability. Different summary measures of incompatibility were related to varied summary measures of instability. A more detailed presentation and discussion of these tests is contained in Laing (1967). First, we compared compatible authority systems and incompatible authority systems with respect to instability; those who reported any incompatibility present were contrasted with those for whom it was absent for all nine incompatibility questions. We related the presence or absence of incompatibility to each of the six measures of the presence of instability (Table 14) and the five measures of the degree of instability (Table 15). Our second group

Table 14.

RELATION OF PRESENCE OF INCOMPATIBILITY TO SIX MEASURES
OF THE PRESENCE OF INSTABILITY

Measure of Presence of Instability	*Gamma*	*Proportion of Incompatible Systems Showing Instability*	*Proportion of Compatible Systems Showing Instability*	*How Many of 16 Positions Support the Hypothesis?*
Relative Dissatisfaction with Any Component	+.70	.86	.51	14 (all but senior residents and desk workers)
Absolute Dissatisfaction with Any Component	+.67	.73	.35	Insufficient data
General Dissatisfaction	+.47	.52	.28	12 (all but senior residents, draftsmen, copy editors, and clinical clerks)
Any Instability Act	+.58	.59	.28	14 (all but engineers and storekeepers)
Any Instability Act or Relative Dissatisfaction	+.78	.92	.58	13 (all but senior residents, desk workers, and engineers)
Any Instability Act or Absolute Dissatisfaction	+.54	.71	.42	15 (all but copy editors)

Table 15.

RELATION OF PRESENCE OF INCOMPATIBILITY TO FIVE MEASURES
OF THE DEGREE OF INSTABILITY

Measure of Degree of Instability	Gamma	Proportion of Incompatible Systems Showing High Instability	Proportion of Compatible Systems Showing High Instability	How Many of 16 Positions Support the Hypothesis?
Number of Components with which Relatively Dissatisfied	+.51	.47	.27	13 (all but senior residents, desk workers, and clinical clerks)
Degree of General Dissatisfaction	+.38	.14	.09	13 (all but senior residents, copy editors, and draftsmen)
Number of Types of Instability Acts	+.59	.30	.06	15 (all but storekeepers)
Relative Frequency of Instability Acts	+.57	.32	.09	15 (all but storekeepers)
Number of Types of Instability Acts and Components with which Relatively Dissatisfied	+.57	.28	.09	15 (all but senior residents)

of results counted for each respondent the number of incompatibilities reported. Those reporting no incompatibilities were compared on instability with those reporting one or two incompatibilities, and these groups were compared with those reporting three or more incompatibilities. With this second measure of incompatibility, we then used our measures of the presence (Table 16) and degree (Table 17) of instability in order again to test the association between incompatibility and instability. Our third and final set of tests used the frequency of incompatibility, combining maximum frequency for any one incompatibility with frequencies added across various reported incompatibilities. The reader will recall that for these tests we used data only for persons for whom these two measures of the frequency of incompatibility gave similar rankings. We contrasted persons whose frequency of incompatibility was high, medium, low, and zero with respect to the presence (Table 18) and degree (Table 19) of instability associated with each level of incompatibility.

Our varied measures of incompatibility and instability had some inadequacies. By using multiple approaches to testing their relationship, we hoped to present convincing evidence of its existence. We predicted in every case a positive gamma as a measure of the relation between incompatibility and instability. In addition, we planned to look at the size of gamma to see the extent to which we

Table 16.

RELATION OF NUMBER OF INCOMPATIBILITIES TO SIX MEASURES
OF THE PRESENCE OF INSTABILITY

Measure of Presence of Instability	Gamma	Probability of Instability for Systems with Three or More Incompati- bilities	Probability of Instability for Compatible Systems	Do Nurses, Interns, and Front Eight Support the Hypothesis?
Relative Dissatisfaction with any Component	+.52	.86	.57	All support
Absolute Dissatisfaction with any Component	+.46	.71	.41	Insufficient data
General Dissatisfaction	+.25	.53	.35	All but interns
Any Instability Act	+.45	.64	.30	All but front eight
Any Instability Act or Relative Dissatisfaction	+.59	.89	.63	All support
Any Instability Act or Absolute Dissatisfaction	+.39	.74	.47	All but front eight

Table 17.

RELATION OF NUMBER OF INCOMPATIBILITIES TO FIVE MEASURES
OF THE DEGREE OF INSTABILITY

Measure of Degree of Instability	*Gamma*	*Proportion of Systems with Three Or More Incompati- bilities Showing High Instability*	*Proportion of Compatible Systems Showing High Instability*	*Do Nurses, Interns, and Front Eight Support the Hypothesis?*
Number of Components with which Relatively Dissatisfied	+.36	.54	.30	All support
Degree of General Dissatisfaction	+.19	.14	.14	All support
Number of Types of Instability Acts	+.42	.31	.08	All but front eight
Relative Frequency of Instability Acts	+.42	.35	.10	All but front eight
Number of Types of Instability Acts and Components with which Relatively Dissatisfied	+.40	.31	.13	All support

were improving our predictions of instability of authority systems as a result of knowledge of the incompatibility of those systems.

The gamma calculated for all cases might be an artifact of differences among the varied positions and organizations which we studied. Accordingly, we have also computed gamma separately for each of the sixteen organizational positions studied and summarized the nature of these results.

We contrasted in Table 14 those authority systems where one or more incompatibilities were reported with those where par-

Table 18.

RELATION OF FREQUENCY OF INCOMPATIBILITY TO SIX MEASURES
OF THE PRESENCE OF INSTABILITY

Measure of Presence of Instability	Gamma	Probability of Instability for High Incompatibility	Probability of Instability for Low Incompatibility	Do Nurses, Interns, and Front Eight Support the Hypothesis?
Relative Dissatisfaction with any Component	+.58	.88	.57	All support
Absolute Dissatisfaction with any Component	+.59	.78	.41	Insufficient data
General Dissatisfaction	+.31	.67	.35	All but interns
Any Instability Act	+.51	.75	.30	All support
Any Instability Act or Relative Dissatisfaction	+.61	.96	.63	All support
Any Instability Act or Absolute Dissatisfaction	+.47	.83	.47	All support

ticipants reported no incompatibilities. For our 224 respondents, we found that every gamma was positive; the proportionate reduction in error ranged from 47 percent to 78 percent.

For all three measures of dissatisfaction as indices of instability, the data strongly supported the hypothesis. Of the sixteen organizational positions studied, only the senior residents consistently failed to support the hypothesis. The gamma for the relation between incompatibility and dissatisfaction was highly positive, ranging from .47 to .70.

We also predicted that instability acts would be more likely in systems reporting at least one incompatibility than in compatible

Table 19.

RELATION OF FREQUENCY OF INCOMPATIBILITY TO FIVE MEASURES
OF THE DEGREE OF INSTABILITY

Measure of Degree of Instability	Gamma	Proportion of Systems with High Frequency of Incompatibility Showing High Instability	Proportion of Compatible Systems Showing High Instability	Do Nurses, Interns, and Front Eight Support the Hypothesis?
Number of Components with which Relatively Dissatisfied	+.43	.62	.30	All support
Degree of General Dissatisfaction	+.24	.21	.14	All but interns
Number of Types of Instability Acts	+.49	.42	.08	All support
Relative Frequency of Instability Acts	+.47	.42	.10	All support
Number of Types of Instability Acts and Components with which Relatively Dissatisfied	+.46	.38	.13	All support

authority systems. For the 224 respondents, the probability of instability acts given the presence of incompatibility was .59, as opposed to .28 for compatible systems. The results within each organizational position also supported this prediction. Fourteen of the sixteen positions produced positive gammas in their tests of the relationship, one had no instability acts and, therefore, produced a gamma of zero, and the sole negative result was produced by the engineers.

We now turn to two measures of instability which combined instability acts and dissatisfaction. The data again showed a strong positive relationship between the presence of incompatibility and the combined instability measures, with gammas of .78 and .54.

To summarize the impact of the presence of one or more incompatibilities, each of the six measures of the presence of instability persistently and strongly supported the hypothesis. The knowledge that an authority system was compatible or incompatible enabled us, on the average, to reduce error in the prediction of system instability by substantial proportions. In general, the tests of the hypothesis within the sixteen organizational positions also provided support. The few negative cases were instructive. As we will discuss later, both senior residents and workers on the student newspaper fell only marginally within the scope of our theory.

Having discussed the material in Table 14, we can more briefly discuss and summarize the remaining five tables relating various measures of incompatibility to measures of the instability of authority systems. Table 15 is similar in form to Table 14, but Tables 16 through 19 do not report tests of the hypothesis within each of the sixteen positions. For the last four tables, we used summary measures of incompatibility which divided respondents into three groups on the basis of the number of incompatibilities and four groups for analysis of the frequency of incompatibility. These multiple divisions made it extremely difficult to do tests within the small sample of persons in each position.

To devise a within-position test, we therefore limited ourselves to three positions which had at least twenty occupants, an adequate proportion of respondents in each of the columns and rows, and were diverse in context and task. Using these criteria, the three positions of nursing team leader, intern or junior resident, and the front eight on the defensive unit of the football team provided data for our within-positions tests. The failure of the hypothesis for any one of these three positions is recorded in the right-hand column of Tables 16 through 19.

Incompatibility is associated with instability. This bald statement is supported by the results of all six tables. Every gamma is positive and they indicate a strong relationship and, therefore, a sizable proportional reduction in error. No single indicator of either incompatibility or instability could be taken as a sufficiently reliable or valid measure on its own, but the cumulative and mutually supportive positive associations provide considerable empirical support for the proposition that incompatibility leads to instability. The consistency of these tables is very encouraging, taking into account the problems of measurement and sampling.

Other empirical data not contained in these six tables lend further support to the relationship between incompatibility and instability. No one of our nine incompatibility questions is sufficiently broad to stand for the total concept of incompatibility. Yet each of the nine incompatibility questions is indeed, as predicted, positively associated with each of the summary measures of instability for our 224 cases. In the same fashion, we can use each of the instability questions as a measure which represents part of the concept of instability. Each of these partial measures is itself positively associated with every one of the summary measures of incompatibility for the combined sample of 224 cases. Therefore, we can be relatively sure that our relationships between summary measures are not the product of statistical mumbo-jumbo.

Another more stringent criterion for looking at the relationship between incompatibility and instability is to ask whether each of our associations is monotonic. In a monotonic relationship the probability of instability increases as we advance each level in the number of incompatibilities or frequency of incompatibility. Similarly, as instability, by whatever measure, increases, the data should reveal greater incompatibility for each successive rise in instability. Thus, a monotonic relationship between a measure of incompatibility and a measure of instability indicates no ties or reversals of direction as we move toward higher and higher levels of incompatibility and instability.

Despite the strictness of this criterion, most of our relationships are monotonic. Eliminating the associations in Table 14, where only presence or absence are recorded for both variables, we have twenty-seven pairs of measures to examine. Of these, twenty are monotonic, a surprisingly high level of order in the data.

Variables Affecting the Relationship

Cost of Incompatibility. Let us now turn our attention to the negative cases, those positions not providing general support for our proposition. Tables 14 and 15 test the proposition for each of the sixteen positions. If we examine the failures for these hypotheses, there is a concentration of negative cases among senior residents, desk workers, copy editors, and storekeepers. The errors for storekeepers are probably based upon the extremely limited sample, for we had only one storekeeper who expressed any incompatibility, and his responses alone determined whether we had a positive or negative relationship. For the senior residents, desk workers, and copy editors, we found a very instructive set of negative findings. What each of those positions has in common is a relative lack of importance of the rewards and penalties available to the organization.

Senior residents, for example, who did not support our proposition in six out of eleven tests, are in their last year of training at the hospital. They are going to leave it and are relatively independent of the hospital and the evaluations of their teacher-physicians. They expressed to us in their interviews a sense of independence and a feeling that their status as senior residents did not fully express the fact that within a few short months they would be applying their knowledge as independent medical practioners. Even if evaluations were improperly assigned to senior residents, even if they reported incompatibilities, the impact upon their life chances or even on immediate rewards and penalties of the hospital, was minimal. Accordingly, it seems likely that senior residents only marginally fall within the scope of our theory.

This leads to consideration of the cost of incompatibility, where cost is conceived in terms of the participant's personal goals. We now examine the relationship between the cost of incompatibility and the occurrence of instability.

As we noted in Chapter One, the choice of the student newspaper and the football team as settings for our empirical studies was in part dictated by their character as voluntary associations. Participants were not being paid on the basis of their performance. Readers well informed about college football may doubt the last statement, believing that football scholarships are dependent on performance, but at the university we studied, the only requirement for a scholarship was that the student try out for the team. He need not make the team nor were there differentials in financial benefits between the star and the bench-warmer.

Among the many differences between these two organizations were the permanence of the set of evaluators, and the perceived importance of the evaluations, rewards and penalties. Among football players, evaluations were carried out by coaches and assistant coaches who were full-time employees of the university. Among members of the student newspaper, evaluations were conducted by other students elected or selected for temporary periods of service.

Let us now turn our attention to the impact of the importance of evaluations to the participant upon the relationship between incompatibility and instability. Because we became interested in this issue late in our series of empirical studies, the following question was asked only of respondents on the football team and the student newspaper: "How important to you are the evaluations you received from your performance on (this task)?" The data were dichotomized for all football team and newspaper staff respondents into two categories: Very Important or Extremely Important and Moderately Important or less important. Unfortunately, there was no way to avoid sorting most of the football players into the higher category, and most of the newspaper staff into the lower category. Forty-eight of the football players saw their evaluations as high in importance and only five saw them as low, while the newspaper staff reversed this pattern, with eight reporting their evaluations as highly important and twenty-one seeing them as low in importance.

It was, therefore, not possible to test the relationship while controlling both for organizational context and importance of evaluations. Our findings must, therefore, remain ambiguous as to whether the *real* independent variable is the cost of incompatibility or some other variable which is associated with the differences between the two organizations. Thus, when we present measures of association, we do so for all respondents and for the participants in the more heavily represented organization in each category of importance of evaluations.

In every comparison, Table 20 shows that the correlation between incompatibility and instability was higher where the performance evaluations were seen as more important. Where performance evaluations mattered more, then incompatibility was more likely to lead to instability.

In summary, when the incompatibility of an authority system

Table 20.

PROBABILITY OF INSTABILITY AND THE COST OF INCOMPATIBILITY

| Measure of Instability | IMPORTANCE OF PERFORMANCE EVALUATIONS | | | |
| | HIGH *Incompatibility* | | LOW *Incompatibility* | |
	Present	Absent	Present	Absent
Presence of Any Instability Act	.47	.09	.32	.27
	Gamma = +.80 (Football Team only: +.77)		Gamma = +.14 (Newspaper Staff only: +.45)	
Presence of General Dissatisfaction	.49	.18	.80	.54
	Gamma = +.80 (Football Team only: +.77)		Gamma = +.54 (Newspaper Staff only: +.58)	
Presence of Any Instability or Absolute Dissatisfaction	.60	.18	.80	.73
	Gamma = +.74 (Football Team only: +.84)		Gamma = +.20 (Newspaper Staff only: +.18)	
Number of Authority Systems	[45]	[11]	[15]	[11]

was more costly, then participants in that system were more likely to evidence instability. Our interpretation is that participants who do not view their evaluations as very important can afford to attack the system with relative abandon. On the other hand, when evaluations are important to the participant, he is more likely to refrain from attacking the system unless it begins to force him to receive unacceptable evaluations. If incompatibility does occur, the participant who places much worth on the evaluations of his performance has strong motivation to attempt a correction of deficiencies in the authority system, unlike the participant to whom the evaluations are relatively unimportant. In short, our empirical analysis for these two organizations indicates that participants who valued the evaluations of performances were much more sensitive to incompatibility than were participants for whom evaluations were of less importance.

By each of three measures of instability, incompatibility was a more effective predictor of instability when performance evaluations within the system were relatively important to the participant. The generally weak relationships between incompatibility and instability, when evaluations were relatively unimportant to the participant, suggests the value of delimiting the scope of the theory to those authority systems in which participants value organizational sanctions influenced by evaluations of performances. We see our findings on participants who regard performance evaluations as more important (the football team), and participants who saw their evaluations as less important (the student newspaper staff) as explaining to some degree the failures of our predictions for the positions of senior resident, copy editor, and desk worker.

Positional Incompatibility. The various incompatibilities reported by respondents in our studies can be considered positional if they are general for a position, rather than a result of personal experiences, present only for some occupants of a position. Thus, if a given phenomenon is positional, each occupant who entered that position will be exposed to it. Accordingly, if we have a positional problem which is a source of incompatibility for a given position, we shall expect all occupants in that position to be exposed to that problem.

Problems vary in the level of attainment that they prevent. For example, a problem may prevent the attainment of very high evaluations and yet allow any evaluation up to that high value. If an occupant of the position does not have a very high acceptance level, no incompatibility will be present for that occupant. Since occupants have different acceptance levels, problems which produce incompatibilities for some may not produce them for others.

Thus, the extent to which positional problems produce incompatibility varies both with the level of attainment prevented by the problems and the different acceptance levels of the occupants. The latter, the acceptance level, should be the only factor which produces differences in incompatibility among occupants exposed to a positional problem. Therefore, if positional sources of incompatibility were arranged in order according to the level at which they prevented attainment, we would expect that all occupants who experienced incompatibility from those sources which prevented attainment at a high level would also experience incompatibility from those which prevented attainment at a low level. Empirically, when asked questions which identify the different types of incompatibilities, the response pattern of all the respondents exposed to positional sources of incompatibility should form a Guttman scale (Stouffer, Guttman and others, 1950; Torgerson, 1958). We shall use this expected pattern to measure positional incompatibility. To the extent that we discover a scale in Guttman's sense, we shall infer that the incompatibilities are positional.

The coefficient of reproducibility developed by Guttman provides our measure of agreement. High reproducibility indicates high scale agreement, and, by inference, positional incompatibility. We are not concerned with the absolute value of this measure. We would expect some agreement on the types of incompatibility from the way in which these types were operationalized. Furthermore, Festinger (1947) and Green (1954) have shown that the coefficients of reproducibility for small numbers of categories are likely to be artifically high. We repeat, therefore, that this measure is not being used as an absolute measure but only to determine differences among groups on the extent to which there is positional incompatibility.

We can test the validity of this measure of positional incompatibility by comparing coefficients of reproducibility across successively narrowing categories of respondents. As we reduce the boundaries of categories from organizations to positions, and to work units within positions, we would expect that agreement on positional incompatibilities would increase. We found that this was true; of thirty-one reductions in the boundaries of groups, twenty-one showed an increase in the amount of agreement.

We hypothesized that positional incompatibilities would increase the relationship between incompatibility and instability. When we ranked positions by the degree to which incompatibilities were positional, and compared that rank order with the ranking of the degree of association between incompatibility and instability, we found a gamma of .45 for instability acts only, and a gamma of .63 when we combined instability acts and relative dissatisfaction. Positions in which incompatibilities were positional showed a higher association between incompatibility and instability.

Alternatively, we separated those positions which were high in positional incompatibility from those whose incompatibilities were less positional. Again, all the relationships were in the predicted direction. Those systems characterized by positional incompatibility showed a higher association between incompatibility and instability than those with a low level of positional incompatibility. Using presence or absence of incompatibility and any instability act or relative dissatisfaction as the dependent measure, the gamma for positions high in positional incompatibility was .82 compared with .53 for those low in positional incompatibility. Using other measures of instability, we found the same pattern. For example, in the case of general dissatisfaction the gamma increased from .39 to .49 as we moved to positions higher in positional incompatibility, and for any instability act the gamma increased from .50 to .71 going from low to high positional incompatibility.

We found a complex relationship between the level of positional incompatibility and the measures of instability. When positional incompatibility was high, dissatisfaction decreased, but instability acts increased. These data indicated two reactions to positional incompatibility, one which reduced one measure of instability and another which increased instability as measured by a second variable. The attitudinal indicator, dissatisfaction, was lower; the behavioral indicator, instability acts, was higher.

The higher level of satisfaction associated with positional incompatibility, would seem to indicate a favorable response to the degree to which various aspects of the authority system are shared. Evidently, the perceived equity and regularity of similar treatment of position occupants act to increase satisfaction for the participants.

The increase in instability acts against the system that is associated with the level of positional incompatibility may result from focusing the locus of problems in the evaluation process. Since shared experiences are more likely to be articulated and expressed, positional incompatibility is more likely to be perceived and defined as a result of specific aspects of the authority system. A clearly perceived problem is more likely to stimulate direct action. According to this argument, positional incompatibility, where sources have been pinpointed, should lead to more specific acts against the authority system, rather than to diffuse indicators of dissatisfaction.

This same sharpening or focusing was disclosed when we checked on the tendency for participants not experiencing incompatibility to join those who did experience it in reacting against the system—a form of contagion. Greater amounts of incompatibility increased this contagion. Detailed analysis showed, however, that a higher level of positional incompatibility reduced this contagion. We found that the increased association between incompatibility and instability where positional incompatibility was high was primarily produced by a reduction in the dissatisfaction of compatible respondents. Compatible respondents were less likely to join incompatible respondents in reacting against incompatibility when the problem was positional. If fear of similar inequity is a factor which elicits instability in situations exhibiting contagion, our data indicated that this threat was reduced when the incompatibility was positional. Positional incompatibility is more likely to be considered predictably patterned and less likely to spread capriciously; as a result, it was less likely to produce instability behavior from compatible respondents.

We have shown that the relationship between incompatibility and instability was markedly increased when we found an incompatibility was positional. For the skeptical reader, we are pleased to note that we found the level of positional incompatibility was independent of the amount of incompatibility, with a gamma of .03 expressing the lack of relationship. Positional incompatibility, as predicted, made more salient the need to strike at the authority system which was preventing the attainment of acceptable evaluations.

Time in Position. Earlier in this chapter, we reported that longer occupancy of position was associated with a lower frequency of incompatibilities, at least for simple authority systems. Our approach also led us to predict a positive relationship between time in position and the relationship between incompatibility and instability. The same reasons which led us to predict that incompatibility would decrease as time increased also led us to predict that the relationship between incompatibility and instability would be stronger as time increased. Short occupancy of, or high transiency in, a position allows each individual to adjust to his temporary incompatibility without reacting against the authority system, and this should be reflected in a reduced relationship between incompatibility and instability. On the other hand, increased time in a position gives participants an opportunity to pinpoint the sources of incompatibility within the authority system and to react against them. When we ranked the sixteen positions according to the mean period of occupancy and also ranked the positions on the degree of association between incompatibility and instability acts or relative dissatisfaction as our measure of instability, the gamma was .44. As predicted, longer occupancy of position was associated with a stronger relationship between incompatibility and instability.

Other attempts to measure the impact of time in position upon this relationship, combining across all positions for the 224 respondents, produced generally supportive results. The only exception occurred when we used only instability acts as our measure of instability. For that measure, transiency increased the relationship between incompatibility and instability; but all the other summary measures showed the expected positive impact of time in position.

Closer inspection of our data showed that the increased relationship between incompatibility and instability produced by a longer period in a position came from a reduction of the instability of those who were not subjected to incompatibility, rather than from an increase in the percentage of incompatible respondents who exhibited instability. Gamma, our measure of relationship, will increase as the number of incompatible respondents not exhibiting instability decreases, or as the number of compatible respondents evidencing instability decreases. For each of three measures, increased time in position produced a marked reduction in the proportion of those without incompatibilities who exhibited instability, reductions ranging from 11 per cent for any instability act to 20 per cent for general dissatisfaction, to 16 per cent for any act or relative dissatisfaction.

It appears, therefore, that time not only reduced incompatibility, but tended to reduce other sources of instability outside the authority system. Thus, among systems characterized by long occupancy of position and in which incompatibility existed, incompatibility was likely to be one of the few remaining sources of instability. In conclusion, our data suggested that time increased awareness of the problems produced by incompatibility, decreased tolerance for incompatibility, and also decreased the number of other problems affecting the system. For these varied reasons, but particularly because of the last, time also increased the association between incompatibility and instability.

Impropriety of Authority Systems Related to Incompatibility. We noted in Chapter Eight that impropriety tends to be perceived when unauthorized power is exercised. Most authorized exercise of power is perceived as proper. But let us reflect on the possible use of perceived impropriety for an authorized linkage as an indicator of instability. Each respondent who reports that an authorized link should not exist is essentially expressing a desire for change in the authority system. We therefore can relate the data on impropriety to the presence of an incompatibility in the authority system, the number of incompatibilities present, and the frequency of incompatibility for our respondent. However, the number of improprieties for authorized systems is so small that we can do no detailed analysis.

Combining the data for our 224 respondents, we find a slight tendency for impropriety to be more likely in incompatible than in compatible authority systems. The gamma is .21. Similarly, as the number of incompatibilities rises, the likelihood (although low in all cases) of an improper authority link in the system tends to increase slightly. The gamma is again low and positive, .13. Finally, using the frequency of incompatibility for each respondent as our independent measure, we again find a slight positive relationship with impropriety in the authority system, a gamma of .18. Although the data are limited and all interpretations are suspect, we find by internal analysis that the most positive relationship comes with the presence of three or more incompatibilities or of a high frequency of incompatibility. There is little or no difference in the probability of impropriety when the number of incompatibilities increases from zero to one or two, or when the frequency of incompatibility goes from zero to low to medium.

In summary, each of the three hypotheses predicting the presence of some impropriety as a function of the incompatibility of the authority system has received some report from the data. However, the probability of impropriety appears to increase markedly only when the degree of incompatibility present increases to extreme levels. The relationships in the data are sufficiently weak to suggest that other factors are likely to be more important in predicting the impropriety of authority systems.

Alternative Explanations

Relationship Not an Artifact of Interviews. A skeptical reader might propose an alternative explanation for our findings. It could be argued that the empirical support for the relationship between incompatibility and instability was an artifact of the manner in which the data were obtained. The argument would be that, since all data used in testing the hypotheses derived from structured interviews, we never had independent observations of incompatibility and instability. Since respondents were likely to attempt to achieve consistency in their answers, as a response to the social aspects of the interview situation as well as to such social-psychological processes as the reduction of cognitive dissonance, their responses were more a product of their attempts to achieve balance than of their attempts to report organizational phenomena.

Since such difficulties are inherent in any research which uses each interview of a respondent as a case for examining the relationship between two variables, we attempted to provide means for controlling the effects of such processes. The questions used to detect the presence of incompatibility were sufficiently complex, respondents who reported incompatibility were asked for so much corroborating detail, and the responses were so closely examined for internal consistency and relevance, that we believe it would have taken determined effort by particularly intelligent and articulate respondents in order to fabricate incompatibilities. We can therefore assume that the independent variable, incompatibility, is unlikely to be a produuct of a balancing procedure. The alternative explanation of our skeptical reader would accordingly state that respondents would attempt to report evidence of instability if they had already reported incompatibility, thereby lending artificial support to our hypotheses.

This alternative explanation cannot predict the relationship already demonstrated between incompatibility and dissatisfaction with respect to each of the four components of the authority system, since the questions used to detect right-specific dissatisfaction preceded the incompatibility questions. Our skeptic is then reduced to noting that the questions used to determine whether or not respondents engaged in instability acts could still be explained by this balance process. The questions about instability acts were asked after the incompatibility questions. We cannot provide direct empirical data to refute this specific charge, but we can test a hypothesis whose form is similar to this alternative explanation. The reader will recall that we asked respondents two questions about their general satisfaction with the authority system. The first question preceded the incompatibility questions in order to avoid the "trail of fire", and the second came immediately after the incompatibility questions: Our skeptic's alternative explanation would predict that the relationship between incompatibility and the second measurement of general dissatisfaction would be higher than the relationship between incompatibility and the first measure of general dissatisfaction. Contrary to this alternative explanation, we found that the relationship between incompatibility and general dissatisfaction was stronger when general dissatisfaction was indicated by the early question (gamma was .33) than when we used the second question (gamma was .25).

To summarize, internal analysis of the response patterns showed no evidence for believing that the relationship between incompatibility and instability was purely a product of "response set" or an attempt to present a balanced image to the interviewer.

Instability Not Simply Product of Receiving Low Evaluations. We have stated that an authority system is incompatible to the extent that it prevents focal participants from maintaining evaluations of their performance at an acceptable level. By this definition, an authority system is incompatible only if it satisfies two conditions:

Participants receive evaluations of their performance which are unacceptably low, and the system is the cause of this unacceptably low level of evaluation. Note that an incompatible authority system *forces* participants to receive unacceptably lower evaluations from their organizational evaluators. Our skeptical reader might wonder whether the mere receipt of unsatisfactory evaluations could be the cause of instability, and whether the entire conceptual apparatus we labored to produce could have merely brought forth a mouse. This would be the case were the concept of incompatibility to add nothing to our ability to predict the instability of authority systems.

It would be more parsimonious for our skeptic to state that the mere receipt of unacceptable evaluations is a sufficient condition for system instability. The skeptic could present as the alternative hypothesis the view that authority systems in which the focal participant receives unacceptable evaluations are higher in instability than those systems in which the participant receives only acceptable evaluations. Obviously, since we have found a positive relationship between incompatibility and instability, and the receipt of unacceptable evaluations is a necessary condition for the presence of incompatibility, we also would predict a positive relationship between the receipt of unacceptable evaluations and the presence of system instability. Our task now is to test the relative strength of that relationship between low evaluations and instability compared with the strength of the relationship between incompatibility and instability.

To measure how often the respondent received unacceptable evaluations required an operationalization of the concept of acceptance level. Respondents were asked how often each of their appraisers were dissatisfied with their performance of the given organizational task. They were then given the following introduction to the concept of acceptance level: "I'm now going to ask you how often *you* are dissatisfied when you learn what your rating or evaluation is. Some people are dissatisfied whenever their evaluator is dissatisfied. Others are dissatisfied when their evaluator is fairly satisfied, for they want to be told their work is exceptional. Still others are satisfied with a low rating because they expect to do poorly on a particular job, perhaps because it is difficult." Immediately after this introduction, the respondent was asked for each of his appraisers: "When you learn what (the appaiser's) rating or evaluation of you is (on this task) or any part of it, how often is the rating or evaluation *low enough to make you dissatisfied?*"

In a manner similar to that used to measure the presence of incompatibility, unacceptable evaluations were coded as present in these data if the respondent reported that evaluations by one or more organizational evaluators were unacceptably low Seldom or more frequently. Otherwise, we coded unacceptable evaluations as absent. Since few measurement assumptions were necessary, the measurement of the presence or absence of unacceptable evaluations was comparable to the equally simple characterization of authority systems as incompatible or compatible.

Examination of the data gave strong support to the view that the concept of incompatibility added considerably to our ability to predict instability. Using our eleven summary measures of instability, there were no exceptions to the statement that incompatibility was more highly related to instability than was the receipt of unacceptable evaluations. For all eleven measures of instability, the positive correlation or gamma between unacceptable evaluations and instability was markedly increased when incompatibility was substituted as the independent variable. The average gamma rose from .38 to .58. We can, therefore, reject the notion that the receipt of unacceptable evaluations, rather than the presence of system incompatibility, was the basis for our ability to predict instability acts or dissatisfaction.

Pictorial Presentation

Our theoretical approach to the impact of incompatibility is illustrated in Figure 5. The organizations we studied are not a random sample of any known population, and the proportions in our figure are to be viewed only as representative of an order of magnitude. The proportions are means of various measures, and it would be inappropriate to detail the ways they were computed, for that would invest the results with too much importance. But we can use these proportions to sketch in an overall view of relationships.

A larger proportion of authority systems are incompatible than are compatible. Various structural or task characteristics affect

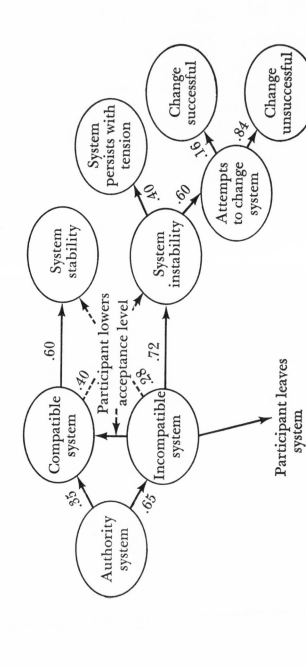

FIGURE 5. A pictorial presentation of the relationship between incompatibility and instability, with estimated proportions.

the likelihood that an authority system will be incompatible. The compatible systems sometimes show instability, and the incompatible systems often are stable. But the clear tendency is for incompatible systems to be unstable. Because we studied current participants, we have no data on leaving the authority system as a response to incompatibility. Compositional effects, such as contagion, and the level of positional incompatibility affect the strength of the relationship between incompatibility and instability.

When system instability is present, it may be expressed only in dissatisfaction or tension concerning the existing system or in attempts to change the system. Persons in higher status positions are more likely to seek change directly. Most attempts to change the authority system, thereby removing the source of incompatibility, are unsuccessful, but some succeed.

Thus incompatibilities are seen to produce strong pressures upon authority systems. Incompatibilities produce tension and action, with a corresponding tendency toward the resolution of evaluation problems produced by the authority structure. But a sufficient number of incompatibilities persist so that they are likely to be a major source of strain in authority systems.

Chapter 11

Theory of Evaluation
and Authority

▲▲

In this last chapter, we do not intend to summarize completely the theoretical and empirical work of previous chapters. Rather, after ten years of work, with numerous errors, false starts, and some successes, we can begin to develop a more systematic theory of evaluation and authority. The theory, a set of logically interrelated principles, does not yet allow deduction of all our empirical findings or of all the assertions in our theoretical chapters. It does, however, permit sufficient deduction to encourage us in our belief that this work is moving in a useful and promising direction, toward the development of the kind of social theory that is often discussed but seldom realized.

It is reasonable to ask why we did not present this theory in the first chapter as the basis for our theoretical and empirical work. The reason is historical. It is only after considerable empirical research and many theoretical revisions that we have begun to understand many of the implications of this approach to the study of evaluation and authority. We now perceive closer links among the varied studies we have completed than we expected when we planned them. Although the theory did not guide our early studies, it is increasingly evident that the conceptual apparatus we subsequently developed can lead to an interrelated and valid set of propositions. The provisional theory we present omits some of the empirical and theoretical work in earlier chapters, for much of this material cannot yet be related to our propositions and deductions. This chapter is oriented toward the future, with the hope that it will stimulate better integration of empirical research and theory in the study of organizations.

The form of this presentation is taken from Emerson (1972), but it differs from his in style and in reliance upon our own empirical studies. Emerson states well our goal:

> Formal theory construction is not taken as an end in itself . . . , even though it might be a worthy end. At this stage of theory in progress, I have chosen to emphasize relatively broad substantive coverage at the expense of logical or mathematical rigor. Thus, in presenting "derivations," I will identify the previous assertions upon which they depend, but I provide no elaborate logical "proofs." If the general flow of the reasoning is clear, I will be content for the moment.

In the theory, eighteen propositions are stated as principles from which other statements are deduced. Propositions, accordingly, do not logically depend on other principles. Theorems and corollaries are principles which are deduced from previous statements. Thus, all theorems and corollaries are products of a deductive process, although, in the spirit of the quotation above, no logical proofs are given. We suggest after each theorem the statements from which the theorem might follow. The source of each corollary is indicated by its label to be the immediately preceding proposition or theorem.

We use numeric labels to distinguish theoretical statements and to indicate their status—whether proposition, theorem, or corollary. Propositions and theorems are labeled with whole numbers, and proposition labels are given in boldface. Corollaries are indicated by decimal numbers. For example, statement **1** is a proposition, 1.2 is its second corollary, 4 is a theorem, and 4.1 is the first corollary to theorem 4.

Each of the propositions, theorems, and corollaries is stated in one of two basic forms. The first statement predicts that one variable, Y, increases with increases in another variable, X. Predictions of this first type are stated in the form: "The more the X, then the more the Y." The second statement not only predicts that Y increases as X increases, but also adds that the strength of this relation increases as a third variable, Z, increases. The basic form used in stating the second type is: "To the extent that Z is higher, the more the X, then the more the Y."

We intend the statements to predict empirical tendencies, not deterministic certainties. As in all scientific theory, we assume for simplicity in stating each principle that variables other than those identified in the principle are either constant or randomly distributed. Even if all other things were equal, lack of certainty in the predicted relations would result from errors in measuring variables or from the inherently probabilistic nature of underlying social and psychological processes. In fact, we think that the theory could be restated in the forms: "The more the X, then the more likely that Y is high," and "To the extent that Z is higher, the greater is the likelihood that as X increases, Y increases."

To simplify the deductions and to facilitate communication, we state all principles in simple, nonprobabilistic forms. We do not distinguish between necessary and sufficient conditions, nor do we predict relations that are more complex than the simple monotonic forms described above.

Even with these simplifications and omitting much of the detail contained in earlier chapters, the theory is nevertheless complex. It is an attempt to begin developing a formal theory. It is not a true exercise in formal logic. We shall be satisfied if the reader obtains from this chapter an intuitive sense of the interweaving of our principles and a feeling for their broad substantive coverage.

Empirical evidence from our studies supports many of the principles. After presenting each set of principles, we briefly summarize the evidence and provide a reference to chapters containing fuller presentation of the data. Readers should be cautious in interpreting the support given to these principles by our previous research. Our tests were often indirect, and more direct tests were sometimes based on small numbers of respondents or few organizational contexts. This summary of the major results is no substitute for a careful reading of previous chapters presenting empirical findings. Having given this warning, we also wish to point out that, to the extent that the principles are interrelated, empirical support for one hypothesis also provides support for associated hypotheses. Seeking to develop and test a set of interrelated principles, we care more about the pattern of support for these principles than about the strength of evidence for any single hypothesis.

The theory is organized into eleven sets of statements. After each set, we present related empirical results. The first set contains the scope conditions, and the next ten sets present the definitions, propositions, theorems, and corollaries that form the theory. The sets are:

    I.   Scope Conditions
   II.   Sanctions and Evaluations
   III.   Evaluations and Effort
   IV.   Evaluations and Control
   V.   Soundly Based Evaluations
   VI.   Visibility of Work
   VII.   Propriety of Authority Systems
   VIII.   Task Conceptions and Work Arrangements
   IX.   Impropriety, Incompatibility, and Instability
   X.   Other Sources of Instability
   XI.   Propriety and Control Tasks

Set I: Scope Conditions

To fall within the scope of the theory, organizational arrangements must satisfy several conditions. The organization must distribute sanctions (rewards and penalties) on the basis of evaluations of participants. These evaluations must be based on performances of organizational tasks. The evaluators must themselves be subject to evaluation for their performance of control tasks by participants other than those they are attempting to control. Finally, participants must care about the organizational rewards and penalties whose distribution is influenced by evaluations. Participants' concern about those sanctions makes evaluations important to them and provides a basis for controlling their performances.

These scope conditions need not apply to entire organizations; they can characterize specific arrangements within organizations. For example, an organization that determines salaries exclusively on the basis of seniority is outside the scope of the theory with regard to salary-related behavior. If, however, that same organization distributes promotions, vacations, thick rugs, or pleasant assignments on the basis of evaluations of performance, and if these sanctions are valued by participants, then all behavior related to these sanctions and evaluations falls within the scope of the predictions. The scope of the theory is sufficiently broad to apply to most organizational arrangements.

Scope Condition 1. The distribution of organizational sanctions to participants depends on evaluations made of participants.

Scope Condition 2. Evaluators who influence the distribution of organizational sanctions attempt to base their evaluations on the performance of organizational tasks by participants.

Scope Condition 3. Evaluators who influence the distribution of organizational sanctions to participants are themselves evaluated on their performance of the control task.

Scope Condition 4. The set of participants attempting to control the evaluator differs from the set of participants whom the evaluator is attempting to control.

Scope Condition 5. Participants consider important those organizational sanctions whose distribution depends on evaluations of their performances.

While it would be inappropriate to treat these scope conditions in the same manner as the other assertions of the theory, we can comment on their connection with the empirical studies. Conditions 1 and 2 guided our selection of organizations, and Condition 2 underlies our task-specific approach to the study of control systems. Evidence that superiors were themselves subject to evaluation for the performance of their control tasks was collected only in the Five Organizations study. Data for the sixteen positions studied revealed so few unauthorized control attempts that it did not seem profitable to continue testing for authorization in subsequent research (Chapter Eight). Condition 4 simply allows the theory to focus on regulation of the power-wielder from above (authorized power) rather than from below (endorsed power). The motivational basis for the theory is provided by Condition 5, which asserts that participants place importance on sanctions distributed by the organization. While there are other possible reasons why participants attribute importance to evaluations, we emphasize the important role of organizational rewards and penalties in providing a basis for organizational control. Although there was considerable variation in the degree of importance attributed to sanctions that depend on evaluations, all the organizations we studied contained participants who placed some importance on organizational sanctions.

Set II: Sanctions and Evaluations

The principles included in Set II establish the linkages between sanctions, evaluations, and the motivation of participants. It is asserted that participants will place more importance on those evaluations that influence more important sanctions or have more influence on sanctions. These linkages are expected to apply not only to evaluations but also to evaluators and tasks. Thus, the theory attempts to explain why participants in organizations care more about certain evaluations, evaluators, and tasks. An organization helps participants to decide which of many evaluations to attend to by its use of rewards and penalties.

> *Definition.* Evaluations are *central* to the extent that they are believed by performers to influence the distribution of those organizational sanctions performers consider more important.

Evaluation and the Exercise of Authority

Performers consider more important . . .
1 evaluations that are more central.
  1.1 evaluators whose evaluations are more central.
  1.2 tasks whose evaluations are more central.

Definition. Evaluations are *influential* to the extent that they are believed by performers to have a greater effect on the distribution of organizational sanctions.

Performers consider more important . . .
2 evaluations that are more influential.
  2.1 evaluators whose evaluations are more influential.
  2.2 tasks whose evaluations are more influential.

Most of the data relating influence on sanctions to perceived importance is derived from the Five Organizations study, reported in Chapter Four. Data for football players and student newspaper workers showed a positive relation between the importance placed by participants on sanctions controlled by the organization and the importance they placed on evaluations of their performances. Data from all sixteen positions in this study were used to test the relation between perception of the evaluator's influence on organizational sanctions and the evaluator's importance to the participant. Again, the results were strongly supportive. This finding was replicated in Marram's study of teachers and nurses (Chapter Six). Additional support for these associations came from Turner's study of diocesan clergy. As reported in Chapter Four, assistant pastors were more likely to perceive as important those evaluators who had more influence on the distribution of organizational sanctions. Further, this relation was stronger for older than for younger assistant pastors, suggesting that the strength of the sanctions as a basis for controlling participants increased with time.

Statements 1.2 and 2.2 apply to tasks. We could not test these assertions using data from the Five Organizations study since only one task was studied for each position. Later studies all examined more than one task per position; in all these studies—of public school teachers, alternative school teachers, nurses, pastors, and faculty—the data provided strong supportive evidence for these corollaries (Chapters Four, Six, and Eight). Since older assistant pastors showed a stronger relationship between influence and importance of evaluators, older assistant pastors were more likely than younger assistant pastors to place high importance on tasks regarded as important by their organizational superiors (Chapter Four).

The connection between influence on organizational sanctions and importance attributed to a task or an evaluator by a performer was not perfect. Factors other than influence on sanctions also can determine importance. Each performer may have internal standards that reflect previous experiences or relations outside this organizational context. This applies especially to participants who subscribe to standards supported by control systems different from those operating in the present situation. For example, professional workers may have internalized standards from previous socialization settings or work experiences. Participants in professional positions in the Five Organizations study were somewhat more likely than nonprofessionals to attribute importance to evaluators who had little or no influence over organizational sanctions (Chapter Four). Nevertheless, professional participants were not sufficiently different in this regard to constitute an exception to the set of principles.

Set III: Evaluations and Effort

The previous principles assert that each participant places importance on evaluations, tasks, and evaluators to the extent that they influence sanctions. But given that evaluations are important, what can participants do to affect them? If evaluations reflect the performer's level and direction of effort, then, by exerting effort, performers can affect the level of their evaluations. By "level and direction of effort" we refer to such matters as how long, how hard, and in which direction the performer works. By "level of evaluation" we refer to the score given a performer by an organizational evaluator on a scale which permits interpretation of higher or lower quality as assessed by some standard.

Assuming that effort by performers does affect their evaluations in this manner, Set III principles assert that their efforts will be directed toward affecting those evaluations, pleasing those evaluators, and performing those tasks that are perceived to be more central and influential.

> *Definition.* Performers believe that *effort affects evaluations* to the extent that they perceive that the direction and level of their effort on a task positively relate to the level of evaluations they receive.

To the extent that performers believe that effort affects evaluations, they exert more effort to affect evaluations . . .

    3   they consider more important.
       3.1   given by evaluators they consider more important.
       3.2   of tasks they consider more important.
    4   that are more central (from 1 and 3).
       4.1   given by evaluators whose evaluations are more central.
       4.2   of tasks whose evaluations are more central.
    5   that are more influential (from 2 and 3).
       5.1   given by evaluators whose evaluations are more influential.
       5.2   of tasks whose evaluations are more influential.

Our only data relating directly to the effect of evaluations on effort came from the study of a university faculty. Hind asked faculty both how they divided their time among tasks and how they would prefer to spend their time. The data supported statements 3.2 and 5.2: faculty both spent more time on those tasks perceived as more influential and more important, and preferred to do so (Chapter Eight). We believe, however, that considerable indirect support for this set of principles is provided by each of our studies.

Set IV: Evaluations and Control

The next principles begin by restating the major assertions of Set III from the standpoint of the evaluator, but in so doing reveal an interesting aspect of control systems. Just as performers attempt to affect evaluations by the level and direction of their effort, so evaluators attempt to use their evaluations to regulate the performers' effort. Fate control—control over sanctions—becomes behavior control when sanctions are made contingent on effort. Here we have an apparent paradox of control systems: participants more in control of their evaluations, in the sense that they can affect evaluations by exerting effort, are more controlled by the evaluation system.

Statement 10 and its two corollaries introduce another factor affecting the importance of evaluations. In addition to importance resulting from influence on sanctions, performers will place more importance on those evaluations that can be affected by their efforts. Evaluations which do not depend on performers' activities are less salient to them. Participants emphasize those aspects of the world that can be affected by their activities. Hence, they attribute more importance to evaluations they can affect.

> *Definition. Control* over performers by evaluations
> of their performances on a task denotes the extent to
> which evaluations affect the direction and level of effort
> by performers on a task.

To the extent that performers believe that effort affects evaluations . . .

  6 performers are more controlled by evaluations.

  6.1 performers are more controlled by evaluators.

  6.2 on certain tasks, performers are more controlled on those tasks.

To the extent that performers believe that effort affects evaluations, they are more controlled . . .

  7 by evaluations they consider more important.

  7.1 by evaluators they consider more important.

  7.2 on tasks whose evaluations they consider more important.

  8 by more central evaluations (from 1 and 7).

  8.1 by evaluators whose evaluations are more central.

  8.2 on tasks whose evaluations are more central.

  9 by more influential evaluations (from 2 and 7).

  9.1 by evaluators whose evaluations are more influential.

  9.2 on tasks whose evaluations are more influential.

To the extent that performers believe that effort affects evaluations . . .

    10   they consider evaluations more important.

      10.1   they consider evaluators more important.

      10.2   on certain tasks, they consider those tasks more
      important.

While we did not operationalize the concept of control, the
findings summarized under Sets II and III clearly provide a great
deal of indirect support for these assertions.

For Statement 10, although our faculty study did provide
information on the relation between influence on sanctions and the
level of effort, we have no direct evidence bearing on the relationship
between importance placed on evaluations and the belief that effort
affects those evaluations. But indirect support is provided by data
related to the next set of principles.

Set V: Soundly Based Evaluations

If effort affects evaluations, greater control can be exercised
over performers through evaluations. This relation can be strengthened if evaluations are based on criteria that performers judge to be
appropriate. In judging criteria, performers may use standards that
conflict with the evaluator's criteria. The performers' standards can
be acquired, for example, from previous training or experience or
can be derived from persons outside the specified authority system.
When performers' standards are congruent with the criteria used by
evaluators, however, control is reinforced because performers attach
additional importance to evaluations. We will say that performers
consider evaluations soundly based to the extent that they believe
not only that evaluations are affected by their effort, but also that
performances they consider better receive higher evaluations. If
performers believe evaluations are more soundly based, they attach
greater importance to evaluations, are more controlled by evaluations, and are motivated to produce work of higher quality as
defined both by their standards and by the criteria used by evaluators.

Definition. A participant considers evaluations *soundly based* to the extent that he or she believes that (a) the quality of performances or outcomes as judged by the participant is affected by the performer's effort, and (b) performances or outcomes considered better by the participant receive higher evaluations.

11   Performers believe that effort affects evaluations to the extent that they consider evaluations soundly based (from definition of *soundly based*).

Performers are more controlled . . .

12   by evaluations they consider more soundly based (from 6 and 11).

12.1   by evaluators whose evaluations they consider more soundly based.

12.2   on tasks whose evaluations they consider more soundly based.

Performers consider more important . . .

13   evaluations they consider more soundly based (from 10 and 11).

13.1   evaluators whose evaluations they consider more soundly based.

13.2   tasks whose evaluations they consider more soundly based.

Our study with Marram of teachers and nurses provides data relating performers' beliefs concerning the soundness of evaluations by various types of evaluators—superiors, peers, and clients—and the perceived importance of these evaluators. Analyses based both on positions and on individuals showed a positive association between perceived importance and soundness of evaluations (Chapter Six). These findings also lend indirect support to the principles in Set IV.

Set VI: Visibility of Work

Although many factors may be expected to affect the relation between effort, quality of work, and level of evaluation, one of the most significant factors is the visibility of performances and outcomes. The more visible the work, the more objective is the basis for evaluations. We expect visibility to contribute to the soundness and importance of evaluations and to the control of performers.

> *Definition.* Work is *visible* to the extent that evaluators are able to observe relevant aspects of task performances or of the outcomes produced by those performances.

To the extent that participants believe that evaluations are based on more visible performances or outcomes . . .

14 participants consider evaluations more soundly based.
15 performers are more controlled by evaluations (from 12 and 14).
   15.1 performers are more controlled by evaluators.
   15.2 on certain tasks, performers are more controlled on those tasks.
16 performers consider evaluations more important (from 13 and 14).
   16.1 performers consider evaluators more important.
   16.2 on certain tasks, performers consider those tasks more important.

The relation between visibility of performances and outcomes and performers' belief in the soundness of evaluations was strongly positive in the study of nurses and teachers carried out with Marram. This relation holds in comparisons among various classes of evaluators and for various nursing and teaching tasks (Chapter Six). An interesting sidelight of this same study was the differing impact of teaming on visibility. For teachers in public schools, the use of teaching teams and open-space school rooms greatly increased the visibility of performances to peers and superiors. Teams among nurses in hospitals did not have a similar effect.

The same study examined the relation between visibility of work to evaluators and the importance placed upon evaluators by performers. Occupants of positions like director of nursing and superintendent of schools were regarded as very influential on sanctions but perceived as less important evaluators, presumably because performers believed that these evaluators were too far removed from the work place to observe performances. In this manner visibility tended to modify the generally strong relation between influence on sanctions and importance.

This study of teachers and nurses also examined within each group of evaluators the relation between visibility and importance of evaluators. As expected, this relation was positive, but not as strong as the relation linking visibility to soundness of evaluations (Chapter Six).

Set VII: Propriety of Authority Systems

We use the concept of propriety to describe the extent to which a participant approves the normative order supporting the existing authority arrangements. This overall assessment is based on many considerations. Is the system fair? Are the participant's efforts accurately reflected in the evaluations received? Can the participant obtain desired rewards through efforts on organizational tasks? Clearly, many of these questions simply raise the issue of whether participants believe that their evaluations are soundly based.

In our theoretical discussions throughout this volume, we have taken care to separate the idea of propriety, the participants' willing approval of authority norms, from the idea of validity, the participants' recognition of the existence of the authority norms. While these ideas are analytically distinct, we expect them to be empirically related. We believe that power relationships in which the participants' behavior is regulated by norms are more likely to be approved by participants than are power relationships in which there is no normative regulation. Authority systems vary greatly in propriety. But focusing just on the distinction between authority systems and unauthorized systems of power, we expect authority systems to be regarded as more proper than unauthorized systems of power.

We also expect propriety to be affected by the extent to which participants perceive their authority system to be usual or customary or widely applicable to persons in the same or similar positions. Specific arrangements in which participants are regularly

involved come to seem natural, even inevitable. What is customary
or expected tends to become what is accepted or expected, now in a
normative sense. Participants evaluate their situation by comparing
it with others of whom they have knowledge. The more similar the
authority systems in which comparable actors are involved, the more
likely that participants will regard their own systems as proper.

> *Definitions.* An *authority system* is the set of rela-
> tionships of authorized power regularly exercised over
> and by a performer *C* that is relevant to the evaluation
> of *C*'s performance of an organizational task.
>   *B*'s power over *C* with respect to a given task is
> *authorized* to the extent that: (a) *B*'s evaluators, if aware
> that *B* was attempting to exercise control over *C*, would
> not evaluate *B* negatively for making the attempt, and
> (b) the evaluators of *C* and of all other participants whose
> compliance is necessary to support *B*'s attempt to control
> *C*'s performance, if aware of noncompliance, would
> evaluate negatively those not complying.
>   An authority system is considered *proper* to the
> extent that participants approve of the system, believing
> it appropriate.

17 Performers consider authority systems more proper if
    they consider evaluations of their performances more
    soundly based.

> *Definitions.* Authority systems are *structural* to the
> extent that an occupant of a position *B* exercises the same
> authorized power over each of several occupants of a
> counterposition *C*.
>   Authority systems are *formalized* to the extent that
> each of several occupants of a position *B* exercises the
> same authorized power over the occupants of a counter-
> position *C*.

Performers consider authority systems more proper . . .

18 than systems of unauthorized power.
19 to the extent that they believe that those systems are

widely applicable across occupants of positions or
through time.

19.1 to the extent that those systems are more structural.

19.2 to the extent that those systems are more formalized.

19.3 if those systems have persisted for a longer period
of time.

19.4 if the performers have been in those systems for a
longer period of time.

Strong empirical support for Statement 17 is contained in
our several studies of teachers and nurses conducted with Magnani,
Marram, McCauley, and Thompson. Teachers and nurses who
perceived that their evaluators' judgments were soundly based were
more likely to believe that these evaluators *should* have the authority
rights they exercised (Chapter Six).

Data from our Five Organizations study on authorization
and propriety supported Statement 18 that authority systems are
more likely to be proper than are unauthorized systems of power
(Chapter Eight). The evidence is not as strong as we would wish
because we found relatively few unauthorized systems among the
positions studied.

We have almost no evidence regarding Statement 19. Indirect
support for Statement 19.4 is provided by our analysis of positional
incompatibility and by the finding that persons who have been in
an authority system for a longer period of time are slightly less
likely to report incompatibilities (Chapter Ten).

Set VIII: Task Conceptions and Work Arrangements

Organizations allocate tasks to performers and evaluate the
quality of their work, but whether performers can achieve good
performances and outcomes depends on the match between the
nature of the work to be performed and the arrangements for carrying out that work. Differences among tasks are analyzed in terms of
the extent to which participants believe they can predict the nature
and amount of resistance to be encountered in performing a task.

The more that participants believe it is not possible to predict in advance the resistance to be overcome, the more active the task. It should be noted that our approach to differences among tasks focuses on the subjective beliefs of participants rather than on the objective characteristics of the tasks themselves. We attempt to determine beliefs about task characteristics held by occupants of relevant organizational positions, and we refer to these collective beliefs as task conceptions.

Participants working on more active tasks will want to be given sufficient autonomy to respond to the uncertain and changing situations confronting them. For active tasks, performers resist arbitrary constraints on their behavior. By contrast, inert tasks— tasks regarded as posing relatively predictable amounts and types of resistance—can be performed effectively by following standardized procedures. Such tasks also can be subdivided more readily among performers, promoting efficiency without threatening effectiveness. Such is not the case for active tasks; to subdivide them among a set of performers is to endanger effectiveness and create costly and complex interdependence among workers.

> *Definitions. Task conceptions* refer to participants' beliefs concerning the characteristics of their tasks.
>
> A task is considered *inert* to the extent that participants believe that the resistance to carrying out task activities is predictable from performance to performance.
>
> A task is considered *active* to the extent that participants believe that the resistance to carrying out task activities is unpredictable from performance to performance.

20 To the extent that performers believe that their tasks are active, they consider evaluations of their performances more soundly based if they are given more autonomy.

To the extent that performers believe that their tasks are active, they consider authority systems more proper if . . .

21 they are given more autonomy (from 17 and 20).

21.1 there are fewer rules controlling their task activities.

21.2 there is less minute specialization of personnel.

21.3 decision-making is less centralized.

Data concerning task conceptions and work arrangements were gathered from teachers in public and alternative schools and from nurses. As described in Chapter Four, our studies provided strong empirical support for the association between conceptions of tasks as active and the establishment of work arrangements delegating autonomy to performers. Active tasks were operationalized as tasks low on predictability, clarity, and efficacy, but these three dimensions were so closely interrelated that we were unable to separate their effects. Task conceptions were related not only to existing but also to preferred work arrangements; participants with active tasks were more likely both to have and to prefer autonomy in selecting task activities. Data on performer preferences provided support for Statement 21, which associates the delegation of active tasks with perceived propriety of the authority system.

Set IX: Impropriety, Incompatibility, Instability

Participants who regard their authority system as improper for whatever reason are more likely to be dissatisfied with the system and to take action to change it. Motivations and efforts to change existing authority systems are regarded as indicators of the more general concept, system instability.

Instability refers to the presence of internal pressures for change. Major indicators of this state are participants' dissatisfaction with a specific component of the authority system or with the authority system as a whole, communication of dissatisfaction with the authority system to others in the organization, suggestion of changes in the authority system to others in the organization, or noncompliance with the exercise of an authority right as a consequence of dissatisfaction with the authority system.

Since participants' belief that their evaluations are soundly based is an important factor affecting the propriety of the system, any condition that seriously interferes with the receipt of soundly based evaluations is an important source of instability. In our work we have identified a number of problems or inadequacies, termed incompatibilities, that can beset an evaluation system. These incompatibilities may upset the link between performers' efforts and quality of performances or outcomes, and they may interfere with the connection between quality of work and level of evaluation. In Principle 26 four types of incompatibilities are identified: contradictory evaluations, uncontrollable evaluations, unpredictable evaluations, and unattainable evaluations. Their common characteristic is that they act to prevent performers from maintaining performance evaluations at a level acceptable to them. Performers in incompatible authority systems who receive evaluations below their acceptance levels are unable to attain acceptable evaluations by altering their performances. The source of the unacceptable evaluations is in the authority system, not in the performer. Consequently, the performer's effort does not affect evaluations, and, hence, evaluations are not considered soundly based.

Principle 29 deals with a group of factors that make incompatibility more likely and therefore increase the probability of instability. Unlike most of our principles, which predict a relatively direct link between variables, this principle describes a more indirect set of connections. Whereas incompatibility is expected to be directly linked to instability, for example, interdependence does not lead directly to incompatibility, although we believe that more interdependent systems are more likely to contain incompatibilities. Also, the diverse properties contained in this principle, though potentially related to each other, cannot easily be linked to the rest of the theory. Therefore, they are expressed as a single, composite proposition instead of a number of principles each requiring its own development.

The next set of principles (30, 31, 32) begins by analyzing the impact of increased cost of incompatibility. If evaluations below acceptance level are more important, then the relation of incompatibility to instability should be all the stronger. Performers will struggle against a system which gives them important evaluations that are unacceptable to them.

> *Definition.* An authority system is *unstable* to the
> extent that it contains internal pressures for change.

Authority systems are more unstable to the extent that . . .

22 performers consider them less proper.

23 performers consider evaluations of their performances less soundly based (from **17** and **22**).

Definitions. Acceptance level is the minimum level of a performance evaluation that is satisfactory to the performer.

An authority system exhibits *incompatibility* to the extent that it prevents performers from maintaining evaluations of their performances at or above their acceptance level.

24 Performers consider evaluations of their performances less soundly based to the extent that they are in more incompatible authority systems (from 11 and the definition of *incompatibility*).

25 Performers consider authority systems less proper to the extent that they are in more incompatible authority systems (from **17** and **24**).

Authority systems are more unstable to the extent that . . .

26 they are more incompatible (from 23 and 24).

26.1 performers are placed in a situation in which the receipt of one performance evaluation at or above acceptance level necessarily entails receiving another evaluation below acceptance level. (Type I incompatibility—contradictory evaluations.)

26.2 performers receive evaluations below acceptance level for performances or outcomes they do not control. (Type II incompatibility—uncontrollable evaluations.)

26.3 performers receive evaluations below acceptance level because they are unable to predict accurately the relationship between attributes of their performances and the level of evaluations they receive. (Type III incompatibility—unpredictable evaluations.)

26.4 the standards used to evaluate performers are so high that they cannot achieve evaluations at or above acceptance level. (Type IV incompatibility—unattainable evaluations.)

Performers in more incompatible authority systems . . .

27   are less controlled by evaluations (from 12 and 24).

28   consider evaluations less important (from 13 and 24).

Definitions. Authority systems are more *complex* if more participants exercise authority over the performer.

Authority systems are *interdependent* to the extent that other participants contribute to outcomes that are used as a basis for evaluating the performer.

29   Authority systems are more incompatible if any of the following is true:

they are more complex.

they are more interdependent.

evaluations are very infrequently communicated to performers.

performances and outcomes are very infrequently sampled.

the criteria for evaluation are not communicated to performers.

evaluators do not share a set of criteria.

The strength of the relationship between incompatibility and instability in authority systems is greater if the evaluations below acceptance level are . . .

30   considered more important by performers.

31   more central (from 1 and 30).

32   more influential (from 2 and 30).

Unlike some of our other sets of principles where empirical evidence is at best sparse or indirect, principles 26.1 to 26.4, relating incompatibility of authority systems to system instability, are overwhelmingly supported by our research. The Five Organizations study was designed to test these principles, and most of Chapter Ten is devoted to describing the empirical evidence. The association between incompatibility and instability was examined using a variety of indicators. The principles were tested combining respondents from all five organizations and within each of sixteen positions. Virtually all measures and tests provided strong support for the principles.

Evidence that incompatibility was a characteristic of the

authority system rather than of the participant can be cited. The amount and type of incompatibility varied greatly across organizations and positions. Further, the presence or amount of incompatibility reported was independent of the performer's competence. Systems with considerable incompatibility were more likely to be described as improper. Finally, instability was more strongly associated with system incompatibility than with the mere receipt of low evaluations (Chapter Ten).

Evidence relating to Principle 29 is reported in Chapter Ten. Authority systems characterized by high interdependence and high complexity were likely to exhibit more incompatibility. Frequency of communicated evaluations did not have a clear relation to incompatibility in the Five Organizations study. But, as reported in Thompson's study of public school teachers and McCauley's study of teachers in public and alternative schools, infrequent communication of evaluations or infrequent sampling did result in a breakdown of organizational control. Teachers did not know the criteria by which they were being evaluated, nor did they get sufficient feedback concerning their performances to be able to consider their evaluations soundly based (Chapter Six).

Hind's study, reported in Chapter Six, noted the importance of agreement among evaluators. Those fields believed by university faculty to be more dependent on a central body of theory were higher in perceived agreement among evaluators, with corresponding higher satisfaction with the evaluation system. When evaluators disagree on the basis for evaluation, performers have more difficulty in attaining their personal goals through evaluations of their performances.

Set X: Other Sources of Instability

Principles 33 to 35.4 predict instability on a number of bases previously discussed. All are deduced from previous statements. The last principles in this set, beginning with 36, rest on a different assumption—namely, that performers prefer systems in which the importance of evaluations on various tasks reflects the effort performers devote to those tasks, whether because of internalized work standards or others' demands. Authority systems are more stable if performers receive more important evaluations for those tasks on which they expend greater effort.

To the extent that performers believe that their tasks are active, authority systems are more unstable if . . .

33 performers are given less autonomy (from 21 and 22).
   33.1 there are more rules controlling task activities by performers.
   33.2 there is more minute specialization of personnel.
   33.3 decision-making is more centralized.

Authority systems are more stable . . .

34 than systems of unauthorized power (from 18 and 22).
35 to the extent that performers believe that those systems are widely applicable across occupants of positions or through time (from 19 and 22).
   35.1 to the extent that those systems are more structural.
   35.2 to the extent that those systems are more formalized.
   35.3 if those systems have persisted for a longer period of time.
   35.4 if the performers have been in those systems for a longer period of time.

Authority systems are more unstable to the extent that performers exert more effort on tasks whose evaluations . . .

36 they consider less important.
37 are less central (from 1 and 36).
38 are less influential (from 2 and 36).

The study of university faculty in Chapter Eight provided strong support for 38, documenting the attempt by faculty to balance effort and the importance of evaluations. Hind found that more effort was devoted to tasks that were more influential and that dissatisfaction increased when the influence of evaluations of a task did not match the expenditure of time on that activity.

Set XI: Propriety and Control Tasks

The final set of principles differs from all previous ones in that it deals with the performance of a control task by an organizational evaluator. All earlier principles apply without modification to evaluators who are organizational participants engaged in performing tasks for which they are subject to evaluation by their superiors. We do not propose to restate the foregoing principles by substituting the term *evaluator* for *performer*. But we would like to emphasize the special nature of a *control task*—the task of affecting, by means of evaluations, the direction and level of effort by performers. We have alluded to this special nature already in discussing Set IV principles. In order to obtain control over performers through evaluations made of their performances, evaluators need to allow performers to obtain control over the evaluations they receive. This two-way process is mutually supporting.

Statement 39 asserts that evaluators will regard the authority system that regulates their exercise of control tasks as more proper if they have more control over performers. This statement is not intended to imply that evaluators, innately power hungry, are satisfied only with systems that provide them with unlimited power. Rather, control over performers is the mechanism by which evaluators pursue their assigned goals. If evaluators are themselves evaluated and sanctioned for their goal attainment, they can be expected to seek and utilize control opportunities provided by the system.

The statements in this set assert that an evaluator obtains control over a performer by doing those things that make evaluations more soundly based from the perspective of both performer and evaluator.

Most of these principles would seem to benefit both the controller and the controlled: each has a surer hold on his own fate. Evaluators and performers are locked together in mutual interest. One may question whether all their behavior is mutually advantageous; but it does seem plausible to conclude that in a well-designed and well-functioning evaluation system, the interests of both evaluators and performers may be served by quality performances on the part of the performers. But all evaluation systems in formal organizations are not well-designed, nor do they function perfectly.

The linkages between performer and evaluator are remarkably symmetric. Only three propositions need be added to the preceding principles to derive the principles applying to control tasks.

> *Definition.* A *control task* assigns to an evaluator the task of affecting, by means of evaluations, the direction and level of effort by performers.

Evaluators consider authority systems for control tasks more proper to the extent that . . .

39   evaluators have more control over performers.

40   evaluators consider their evaluations of performances or outcomes more soundly based.

41   performers believe that effort affects evaluations (from 6 and 39).

42   performers consider evaluations more soundly based. (from 12 and 39).

43   performers believe that evaluations are based on more visible performances or outcomes (from 15 and 39).

44   authority systems are less incompatible for performers (from 27 and 39).

45   evaluators believe that their evaluations are based on more visible performances or outcomes (from 14 and and 40).

46   evaluators have more control over performers for those control tasks for which evaluators receive evaluations they consider more important.

To the extent that performers believe that effort affects evaluations, evaluators consider authority systems for control tasks more proper if . . .

47   performers consider evaluations more important (from 7 and 39).

48   their evaluations of performers are more central (from 8 and 39).

49   their evaluations of performers are more influential (from 9 and 39).

50   performers consider evaluations more important on those tasks for whose control evaluators receive evaluations they consider more important (from 7 and 46).

Definition. A task is *delegated* if a performer is given sufficient autonomy to make nontrivial decisions concerning the path to the allocated goal. By contrast, a *directive* instructs a performer to carry out a prescribed set of activities toward the allocated goal.

To the extent that evaluators believe that tasks they are controlling are more active, they consider authority systems for those tasks more proper if . . .

   51   the tasks are delegated to performers (from 20 and 42).
      51.1   allocators prescribe fewer rules to performers.
      51.2   there is less minute specialization of personnel.
      51.3   decision-making is less centralized.

All our empirical studies were oriented toward performers rather than evaluators. Consequently, our data cannot be used to test the principles in this set. But we believe that these principles, closely integrated into our theory, supplement the early statements in explaining much behavior in organizations.

Final Word

Every theory must be selective, but we are well aware that phenomena important to the operation of organizations are not included in the theory. For example, the theory pays little attention to the impact on the authority system of social and political processes occurring outside that system. Important processes within the specified system also are ignored by the theory. For example, we reported in Chapter Six that performers who considered evaluations important were motivated to affect the design and operation of the authority system. Authority systems in schools were found to be more stable when teachers were more able to affect the components of the system by which their perforance was evaluated. The theory does not predict whether performers' abilities to affect the design or operation of the authority system will be used to make evaluations more soundly based or merely to ensure that only consistently high evaluations are received. Indeed, to what extent does the interweaving of the fates of participants in complex authority systems produce tendencies toward shared work standards? Such indeterminacy is additional testimony that this provisional theory requires considerable refinement and further development.

But we want to conclude on a different note. The principles stated in this theory emphasize the importance of evaluation processes. Performers and evaluators have their behavior shaped by evaluations made of them by others. Much that is right and much that is wrong in current organizations can be explained in terms of evaluation processes. The obstensible goals of organizations—their public goals—often are not built into the evaluation system. This lack results in goal displacement. We believe that evaluation is a fundamental process in all human interaction and specifically in the operation of authority systems in organizations. Accordingly, we must apply and extend knowledge of evaluation if we are to control the organizations that so often control us.

Bibliography

▲▲

ABEGGLEN, J. C. *The Japanese Factory*. New York: Free Press, 1958.

ANDERSON, B., BERGER, J., COHEN, B. P., AND ZELDITCH, M., JR. "Status Classes in Organizations." *Administrative Science Quarterly,* Sept. 1966, *11,* 264–283.

ANDERSON, R. "Incompatibility and Instability: Measurement and Empirical Investigations." Unpublished report for the Evaluation and Authority Research Team. Stanford, Calif.: Department of Sociology, Stanford University, 1966.

ARENDT, H. *The Origins of Totalitarianism.* (2nd ed.) New York: World, Meridian Books, 1958.

ARGYLE, M., GARDNER, G., and CIOFFI, F. "Supervisory Methods Related to Productivity, Absenteeism, and Labour Turnover." *Human Relations,* Feb. 1958, *11,* 23–40.

BALES, R. F. "Some Uniformities of Behavior in Small Social Systems." In G. E. Swanson, T. M. Newcomb, and E. L. Hartley (Eds.), *Readings in Social Psychology.* (rev. ed.) New York: Holt, Rinehart, and Winston, 1952.

BALES, R. F. "The Equilibrium Problem in Small Groups." In T. Parsons, R. F. Bales, and E. A. Shils (Eds.), *Working Papers in the Theory of Action.* New York: Free Press, 1953.

359

BALES, R. F., and SLATER, P. E. "Role Differentiation in Small Decision-Making Groups." In T. Parsons and R. F. Bales (Eds.), *Family, Socialization and Interaction Process*. New York: Free Press, 1955.

BARCHAS, K. U. "Authority, Role Distance, and Legitimacy." Unpublished report for the Evaluation and Authority Research Team. Stanford, Calif.: Department of Sociology, Stanford University, 1966.

BARCHAS, P. R. "Active Tasks and Problems of Evaluation." Unpublished report for the Evaluation and Authority Research Team. Stanford, Calif.: Department of Sociology, Stanford University, 1966.

BARITZ, L. *The Servants of Power. A History of the Use of Social Science in American Industry*. Middletown, Conn.: Wesleyan University Press, 1960.

BARNARD, C. I. *The Functions of the Executive*. Cambridge, Mass.: Harvard University Press, 1938.

BARNARD, C. I. "Functions and Pathologies of Status Systems in Formal Organizations." In W. F. Whyte (Ed.), *Industry and Society*. New York: McGraw-Hill, 1946.

BECKER, H. S., GEER, B., HUGHES, E. C., and STRAUSS, A. *Boys in White: Student Culture in a Medical School*. Chicago: University of Chicago Press, 1961.

BEER, S. *Cybernetics and Management*. New York: Wiley, 1959.

BENDIX, R. *Work and Authority in Industry*. New York: Wiley, 1956.

BENDIX, R., and FISHER, L. H. "The Perspectives of Elton Mayo." *Review of Economics and Statistics*, 1949, *31*, 312–319.

BENNIS, W. G., BERKOWITZ, N., AFFINITO, M., and MALONE, M. "Authority, Power, and the Ability to Influence." *Human Relations*, May 1958, *11*, 143–155.

BERGER, J., COHEN, B. P., and ZELDITCH, M., JR. "Status Characteristics and Expectation States." In J. Berger, M. Zelditch, Jr., and B. Anderson (Eds.), *Sociological Theories in Progress*, Vol. 1. Boston: Houghton Mifflin, 1966.

BERGER, J., ZELDITCH, M., JR., and ANDERSON, B. (Eds.) *Sociological Theories in Progress*. 2 vols. Boston: Houghton Mifflin, 1966, 1972.

BERLINER, J. S. *Factory and Manager in the U.S.S.R.* Cambridge, Mass.: Harvard University Press, 1957.

BETHEL, L. L., ATWATER, F. S., SMITH, G. H. E., and STACKMAN, H. A., JR.

Essentials of Industrial Management. New York: McGraw-Hill, 1954.

BIDWELL, C. E. "The School as a Formal Organization." In J. G. March (Ed.), *Handbook of Organizations.* Chicago: Rand McNally, 1965.

BIERSTEDT, R. "An Analysis of Social Power." *American Sociological Review,* Dec. 1950, *15,* 730–738.

BIERSTEDT, R. "The Problem of Authority." In M. Berger, T. Abel, and C. H. Page (Eds.), *Freedom and Control in Modern Society.* New York: Van Nostrand, 1954.

BLAU, P. M. *The Dynamics of Bureaucracy.* Chicago: University of Chicago Press, 1955.

BLAU, P. M. "Formal Organizations: Dimensions of Analysis." *American Journal of Sociology,* July 1957, *63,* 58–69.

BLAU, P. M. "Structural Effects." *American Sociological Review,* Apr. 1960, *25,* 178–193.

BLAU, P. M. *Exchange and Power in Social Life.* New York: Wiley, 1964.

BLAU, P. M., and SCHOENHERR, R. A. *The Structure of Organizations.* New York: Basic Books, 1971.

BLAU, P. M., and SCOTT, W. R. *Formal Organizations.* San Francisco: Chandler, 1962.

BOWERS, D. G., and SEASHORE, S. E. "Predicting Organizational Effectiveness with a Four-Factor Theory of Leadership." *Administrative Science Quarterly,* Sept. 1966, *11,* 238–263.

BRYLD, W. F. *Evaluation and Authority in a Pre-Service Teacher Training Program.* Unpublished Ph.D. dissertation. School of Education, Stanford University, 1973.

BUCHER, R. "Social Process and Power in a Medical School." In M. N. Zald (Ed.), *Power in Organizations.* Nashville, Tenn.: Vanderbilt University Press, 1970.

BUCKLEY, W. (Ed.) *Modern Systems Research for the Behavioral Scientist.* Chicago: Aldine, 1968.

BURNS, T. R. *The Theoretical Analysis of Organizational Systems, Participant Satisfaction and System Stability: A Comparison of Two Theoretical Strategies.* Unpublished Ph.D. dissertation. Department of Sociology, Stanford University, 1969.

BUSCHING, B. C. *Problems of Evaluation in Five Formal Organizations.* Unpublished Ph.D. dissertation. Department of Sociology, Stanford University, 1969.

CAMILLERI, S. F., and BERGER, J. "Decision-Making and Social Influence: A Model and an Experimental Test." *Sociometry,* Dec. 1967, *30,* 365–378.

CAPLOW, T. *Principles of Organization.* New York: Harcourt Brace Jovanovich, 1964.

CARTWRIGHT, D. (Ed.) *Studies in Social Power.* Ann Arbor, Mich.: Institute for Social Research, University of Michigan, 1959.

CARTWRIGHT, D. "Influence, Leadership, Control." In J. G. March (Ed.), *Handbook of Organizations.* Chicago: Rand McNally, 1965.

CLARK, B. R. "Faculty Organization and Authority." In T. F. Lunsford (Ed.), *The Study of Academic Administration.* Boulder, Colo.: Western Interstate Commission for Higher Education, 1963.

CLARK, P., and WILSON, J. Q. "Incentive Systems." *Administrative Science Quarterly,* Sept. 1961, *6,* 129–166.

CLOWARD, R. A. "Social Control in the Prison." In R. A. Cloward and others, *Theoretical Studies in Social Organization of the Prison.* Pamphlet 15. New York: Social Science Research Council, 1960.

COHEN, A. K. *Deviance and Control.* Englewood Cliffs, N.J.: Prentice-Hall, 1966.

COLLINS, O. "Ethnic Behavior in Industry: Sponsorship and Rejection in a New England Factory." *American Journal of Sociology,* Jan. 1946, *51,* 293–298.

COSER, R. L. "Authority and Decision-Making in a Hospital: A Comparative Analysis." *American Sociological Review,* Feb. 1958, *23,* 56–73.

COSER, R. L. *Life in the Ward.* East Lansing, Mich.: Michigan State University Press, 1962.

COSTNER, H. A. "Criteria for Measures of Association." *American Sociological Review,* June 1965, *30,* 341–353.

CROZIER, M. *The Bureaucratic Phenomenon.* Chicago: University of Chicago Press, 1964.

CYERT, R. M., and MARCH, J. G. *A Behavioral Theory of the Firm.* Englewood Cliffs, N.J.: Prentice-Hall, 1963.

DAHL, R. A. "The Concept of Power." *Behavioral Science,* 1957, 2, 201–215.

DALTON, G. W., BARNES, L. B., and ZALEZNIK, A. *The Distribution of Authority in Formal Organizations.* Cambridge, Mass.: Division of Research, Harvard Business School, 1968.

DALTON, M. *Men Who Manage.* New York: Wiley, 1959.

DAVIS, J. A., SPAETH, J. L., and HUSON, C. "A Technique for Analyzing the Effects of Group Composition." *American Sociological Review*, Apr. 1961, *26*, 215–225.

DAVIS, K. *Human Society*. New York: Macmillan, 1948.

DAY, R. C., and HAMBLIN, R. L. "Some Effects of Close and Punitive Styles of Supervision." *American Journal of Sociology*, Mar. 1964, *69*, 499–510.

DENNISON, G. *The Lives of Children*. New York: Random House, 1969.

DEUTSCH, M. "Field Theory in Social Psychology." In G. Lindzey (Ed.), *Handbook of Social Psychology*, vol. 1. Reading, Mass.: Addison-Wesley, 1954.

DEUTSCH, M., and SOLOMON, L. "Reactions to Evaluations by Others as Influenced by Self-Evaluations." *Sociometry*, June 1959, *20*, 93–112.

DORNBUSCH, S. M. "The Military Academy as an Assimilating Institution." *Social Forces*, May 1955, *33*, 316–321.

EMERSON, R. M. "Power-Dependence Relations." *American Sociological Review*, Feb. 1962, *27*, 31–41.

EMERSON, R. M. "Exchange Theory, Part I: A Psychological Basis for Social Exchange." In J. Berger, M. Zelditch, Jr., and B. Anderson (Eds.), *Sociological Theories in Progress*, vol. 2. Boston: Houghton Mifflin, 1972.

EMERY, F. E., and TRIST, E. L. "The Causal Texture of Organizational Environments." *Human Relations*, Feb. 1965, *18*, 21–31.

ENDO, R. "Active Tasks and Errors in Evaluation." Unpublished report for the Evaluation and Authority Research Team. Stanford, Calif.: Department of Sociology, Stanford University, 1966.

ETZIONI, A. *A Comparative Analysis of Complex Organizations*. New York: Free Press, 1961.

ETZIONI, A. *Modern Organizations*. Englewood Cliffs, N.J.: Prentice-Hall, 1964.

ETZIONI, A. "Dual Leadership in Complex Organizations." *American Sociological Review*, Oct. 1965, *30*, 688–698.

EVAN, W. M., and ZELDITCH, M., JR. "A Laboratory Experiment on Bureaucratic Authority." *American Sociological Review*, Dec. 1961, *26*, 883–893.

FESTINGER, L. "The Treatment of Qualitative Data by Scale Analysis." *Psychological Bulletin*, Mar. 1947, *44*, 149–161.

FREIDSON, E. "Client Control and Medical Practice." *American Journal of Sociology*, Jan. 1960, *65*, 374–382.

FREIDSON, E. "Review Essay: Health Factories, the New Industrial Sociology." *Social Problems,* Spring 1967, *14,* 493–500.

FREIDSON, E. *Profession of Medicine.* New York: Dodd, Mead, 1970.

FREIDSON, E., and RHEA, B. "Processes of Control in a Company of Equals." *Social Problems,* Fall 1963, *11,* 119–131.

FRENCH, J. R. P., JR., and RAVEN, B. "The Bases of Social Power." In D. Cartwright (Ed.), *Studies in Social Power.* Ann Arbor, Mich.: University of Michigan Press, 1959.

FRENCH, J. R. P., JR., and SNYDER, R. "Leadership and Interpersonal Power." In D. Cartwright (Ed.), *Studies in Social Power.* Ann Arbor, Mich.: University of Michigan Press, 1959.

GALBRAITH, J. K. *The New Industrial State.* Boston: Houghton Mifflin, 1967.

GINGER, A. F. (Ed.) *The Relevant Lawyers.* New York: Simon and Schuster, 1972.

GOFFMAN, E. *The Presentation of Self in Everyday Life.* Garden City, N.Y.: Doubleday, 1959.

GOFFMAN, E. *Asylums.* Garden City, N.Y.: Doubleday, 1961.

GOODMAN, L. A., and KRUSKAL, W. H. "Measures of Association for Cross Classifications." *Journal of the American Statistical Association,* Dec. 1954, *49,* 732–764.

GOODMAN, P. *Compulsory Mis-Education.* New York: Horizon Press, 1965.

GOSS, M. E. W. "Influence and Authority Among Physicians in an Out-Patient Clinic." *American Sociological Review,* Feb. 1961, *26,* 39–50.

GOULDNER, A. W. *Patterns of Industrial Bureaucracy.* New York: Free Press, 1954.

GOULDNER, A. W. "Cosmopolitans and Locals." *Administrative Science Quarterly,* Dec. 1957, March 1958; *2;* 281–306, 444–480.

GOULDNER, A. W. "Organizational Analysis." In R. K. Merton, L. Broom, and L. S. Cottrell, Jr. (Eds.), *Sociology Today.* New York: Basic Books, 1959.

GREEN, B. F., JR. "Attitude Measurement." In G. Lindsey (Ed.), *Handbook of Social Psychology.* Reading, Mass.: Addison Wesley, 1954.

GROSS, E. "Universities as Organizations: A Research Approach." *American Sociological Review,* Aug. 1968, *33,* 518–544.

GROSS, E., and GRAMBSCH, P. V. *University Goals and Academic Power.* Washington, D.C.: American Council on Education, 1968.

GROSS, N., MASON, W. S., and MC EACHERN, A. W. *Explorations in Role Analysis.* New York: Wiley, 1958.

GULICK, L. "Notes on the Theory of Organizations." In L. Gullick and L. Urwick (Eds.), *Papers on the Science of Administration.* New York: Institute of Public Administration, Columbia University, 1937.

HABERSTROH, C. J. "Organization Design and Systems Analysis." In J. G. March (Ed.), *Handbook of Organizations.* Chicago: Rand McNally, 1965.

HAGE, J., and AIKEN, M. "Routine Technology, Social Structure, and Organizational Goals." *Administrative Science Quarterly,* Sept. 1969, *14,* 366–376.

HALL, R. H. "Intraorganizational Structural Variation: Application of the Bureaucratic Model." *Administrative Science Quarterly,* Dec. 1962, *7,* 295–308.

HALL, R. H. "Some Organizational Considerations in the Professional-Organizational Relationship." *Administrative Science Quarterly,* Dec. 1967, *12,* 461–478.

HALL, R. H. *Organizations: Structure and Process.* Englewood Cliffs, N.J.: Prentice-Hall, 1972.

HALPIN, A. W. *The Leadership Behavior of School Superintendents.* Columbus: Ohio State University Press, 1956.

HARRISON, P. M. *Authority and Power in the Free Church Tradition.* Princeton, N.J.: Princeton University Press, 1959.

HARTMANN, H. *Authority and Organization in German Management.* Princeton, N.J.: Princeton University Press, 1959.

HARVEY, O., KELLEY, H. H., and SHAPIRO, H. M. "Reactions to Unfavorable Evaluations of the Self Made by Other Persons." *Journal of Personality,* 1957, *25,* 394–411.

HEINECKE, C., and BALES, R. F. "Developmental Trends in the Structure of Small Groups." *Sociometry,* Mar. 1953, *16,* 7–38.

HICKSON, D. J., PUGH, D. S., and PHEYSEY, D. C. "Operations Technology and Organization Structure—an Empirical Reappraisal." *Adminstrative Science Quarterly,* Sept. 1969, *14,* 378–397.

HILL, W. W., and FRENCH, W. L. "Perceptions of the Power of Department Chairmen by Professors." *Administrative Science Quarterly,* Mar. 1967, *11,* 548–574.

HIND, R. R. *Evaluation and Authority in a University Faculty.* Unpublished Ph.D. dissertation. School of Education, Stanford University, 1968.

HIND, R. R. "Analysis of a Faculty: Professionalism, Evaluation and the Authority Structure." In J. V. Baldridge (Ed.), *Academic Governance*. Berkeley, Calif.: McCutchan, 1971.

HIND, R. R., DORNBUSCH, S. M., and SCOTT, W. R. "A Theory of Evaluation Applied to a University Faculty." *Sociology of Education*, Winter 1974, *47*, 114–128.

HOLT, J. *How Children Fail*. New York: Pitman, 1964.

HOMANS, G. C. *Social Behavior: Its Elementary Forms*. New York: Harcourt Brace Jovanovich, 1961.

HOWARD, R. C., and BERKOWITZ, L. "Reactions to the Evaluators of One's Performance." *Journal of Personality*, 1958, *26*, 495–507.

HUGHES, E. C. "Race Relations in Industry." In W. F. White (Ed.), *Industry and Society*. New York: McGraw-Hill, 1949.

HUGHES, E. C. *Men and Their Work*. New York: Free Press, 1958.

HURWITZ, J. I., ZANDER, A. F., and HYMOVITCH, B. "Some Effects of Power on the Relations Among Group Members." In D. Cartwright and A. Zander (Eds.), *Group Dynamics*. Evanston, Ill.: Row, Peterson, 1953.

JACKSON, P. W. *Life in the Classrooms*. New York: Holt, Rinehart, and Winston, 1968.

JANDA, K. F. "Toward the Explication of the Concept of Leadership in Terms of the Concept of Power." *Human Relations*, Nov. 1960, *13*, 345–363.

JANOWITZ, M. "Changing Patterns of Organizational Authority: The Military Establishment." *Administrative Science Quarterly*, Mar. 1959a, *3*, 473–493.

JANOWITZ, M. *Sociology and the Military Establishment*. New York: Russell Sage Foundation, 1959b.

JAQUES, E. *Measurement of Responsibility*. Cambridge, Mass.: Harvard University Press, 1956.

JONES, E. E., GERGEN, K. J., and DAVIS, K. E. "Some Determinants of Reaction to Being Approved or Disapproved as a Person." *Psychological Monographs*, 1962, whole no. 521.

KAHN, R. L., and KATZ, D. "Leadership Practices in Relation to Productivity and Morale." In D. Cartwright and A. Zander (Eds.), *Group Dynamics*. Evanston, Ill.: Row, Peterson, 1953.

KAHN, R. L., WOLFE, D. M., QUINN, R. P., SNOEK, J. D., and ROSENTHAL, R. A. *Organizational Stress: Studies in Role Conflict and Ambiguity*. New York: Wiley, 1964.

KAST, F. E., and ROSENZWEIG, J. E. *Organization and Management: A Systems Approach*. New York: McGraw-Hill, 1970.

KATZ, D., MACCOBY, N., GURIN, G., and FLOOR, L. A. *Productivity,*

Supervision, and Morale Among Railroad Workers. Ann Arbor, Mich.: Institute for Social Research, University of Michigan, 1951.

KATZ, D., MACCOBY, N., and MORSE, N. C. *Productivity, Supervision and Morale in an Office Situation.* Ann Arbor, Mich.: Institute for Social Research, University of Michigan, 1950.

KAUFMAN, H. *The Forest Ranger: A Study in Administrative Behavior.* Baltimore: Johns Hopkins Press, 1960.

KENDALL, M. G. *Rank Correlation Methods.* London: Griffin, 1948.

KENDALL, P. L. "The Learning Environments of Hospitals." In E. Freidson (Ed.), *The Hospital in Modern Society.* New York: Free Press, 1963.

KERR, C., and FISHER, L. H. "Plant Sociology: The Elite and the Aborigines." In M. Komarovsky (Ed.), *Common Frontiers of the Social Sciences.* New York: Free Press, 1957.

KOONTZ, H., and O'DONNELL, C. *Principles of Management.* New York: McGraw-Hill, 1955.

KORNHAUSER, W. *Scientists in Industry: Conflict and Accommodation.* Berkeley: University of California Press, 1962.

LAING, J. D. *Organizational Evaluation and Authority: A Test of Theory.* Unpublished Ph.D. dissertation. Department of Political Science, Stanford University, 1967.

LAZARSFELD, P. F., and MENZEL, H. "On the Relation Between Individual and Collective Properties." In A. Etzioni (Ed.), *Complex Organizations.* New York: Holt, Rinehart, and Winston, 1961.

LEAVITT, H. J. "Unhuman Organizations." *Harvard Business Review,* July–Aug. 1962, *40,* 90–98.

LEVINGER, G. "The Development of Perceptions and Behavior in Newly Formed Social Power Relationships." In D. Cartwright (Ed.), *Studies in Social Power.* Ann Arbor, Mich.: Institute for Social Research, University of Michigan, 1959.

LEWIN, K., DEMBO, T., FESTINGER, L., and SEARS, P. "Level of Aspiration." In J. McV. Hunt (Ed.), *Personality and the Behavior Disorders.* New York: Ronald Press, 1944.

LIKERT, R. *New Patterns of Management.* New York: McGraw-Hill, 1961.

LIKERT, R. *The Human Organization: Its Management and Values.* New York: McGraw-Hill, 1967.

LIPPITT, R., POLANSKY, N., and ROSEN, S. "The Dynamics of Power." *Human Relations,* Feb. 1952, *5,* 37–64.

LIPSET, S. M., TROW, M. A., and COLEMAN, J. S. *Union Democracy*. New York: Free Press, 1956.

LITTERER, J. A. *Organizations: Structure and Behavior*. New York: Wiley, 1963.

LITTERER, J. A. *The Analysis of Organizations*. New York: Wiley, 1965.

LITWAK, E. "Models of Bureaucracy Which Permit Conflict." *American Journal of Sociology*, Sept. 1961, *67*, 177–184.

MC CAULEY, B. L. *Evaluation and Authority in Radical Alternative Schools and Public Schools*. Unpublished Ph.D. dissertation. School of Education, Stanford University, 1971.

MC CAULEY, B. L., DORNBUSCH, S. M., and SCOTT, W. R. *Evaluation and Authority in Alternative Schools and Public Schools*. Technical Report 23. Stanford, Calif.: Stanford Center for Research and Development in Teaching, 1972.

MC CLEERY, R. H. *Policy Change in Prison Management*. Lansing, Mich.: Governmental Research Bureau, Michigan State University, 1957.

MC CLEERY, R. H. "The Governmental Process and Informal Social Control." In D. R. Cressey (Ed.), *The Prison: Studies in Institutional Organization and Change*. New York: Holt, Rinehart, and Winston, 1961.

MC CLELLAND, D. C., ATKINSON, J. W., CLARK, R. W., and LOWELL, E. L. *The Achievement Motive*. New York: Appleton-Century-Crofts, 1953.

MAGNANI, L. L. *Task Conception and the Property of Autonomy*. Unpublished Ph.D. dissertation. Department of Sociology, Stanford University, 1970.

MANNHEIM, K. *Man and Society in an Age of Reconstruction*. New York: Harcourt Brace Jovanovich, 1950.

MARCH, J. G. (Ed.) *Handbook of Organizations*. Chicago: Rand McNally, 1965.

MARCH, J. G., and SIMON, H. A. *Organizations*. New York: Wiley, 1958.

MARRAM, G. D. *Visibility of Work and the Evaluation Process: Evaluation and Authority for Nurses in Hospitals and Teachers in Open and Closed Schools*. Unpublished Ph.D. dissertation. School of Education, Stanford University, 1971.

MARSH, R. M., and MANNARI, H. "Lifetime Commitment in Japan: Roles, Norms and Values." *American Journal of Sociology*, Mar. 1971, *67*, 795–812.

MEAD, G. H. *Mind, Self and Society*. Chicago: University of Chicago Press, 1934.

MECHANIC, D. "Sources of Power of Lower Participants in Complex Organizations." *Administrative Science Quarterly*, Dec. 1962a, 7, 349–362.

MECHANIC, D. *Students Under Stress: A Study in the Social Psychology of Adaptation*. New York: Free Press, 1962b.

MERTON, R. K. *Social Theory and Social Structure*. (rev. ed.) New York: Free Press, 1957.

MEYER, J., and COHEN, E., with BRUNETTI, F., MOLNAR, S., and LUEDERS-SALMON, E. *The Impact of the Open-Space School upon Teacher Influence and Autonomy: The Effects on an Organizational Innovation*. Technical Report 21. Stanford, Calif.: Stanford Center for Research and Development in Teaching, 1971.

MICHELS, R. *Political Parties*. New York: Free Press, 1949.

MILES, M. B. "On Temporary Systems." In M. B. Miles (Ed.), *Innovations in Education*. New York: Bureau of Publications, Teachers College, Columbia University, 1964.

MIYAMOTO, S. F., and DORNBUSCH, S. M. "A Test of Interactionist Hypotheses in Self-Conception." *American Journal of Sociology*, Mar. 1956, 61, 399–403.

MOUZELIS, M. P. *Organization and Bureaucracy*. Chicago: Aldine, 1967.

NADEL, S. F. *The Theory of Social Structure*. New York: Free Press, 1957.

OLESEN, V. L., and WHITTAKER, E. W. *The Silent Dialogue: A Study in the Social Psychology of Professional Socialization*. San Francisco: Jossey-Bass, 1968.

PARSONS, T. *The Social System*. New York: Free Press, 1951.

PARSONS, T. *Structure and Process in Modern Societies*. New York: Free Press, 1960.

PARSONS, T. "On the Concept of Political Power." *Proceedings of the American Philosophical Society*, 1963, 107, 232–262.

PEABODY, R. L. *Organizational Authority*. Chicago: Aldine-Atherton, 1964.

PELZ, D. C. "Influence: A Key to Effective Leadership in the First-Line Supervisor." *Personnel*, 1952, 29, 209–217.

PENNINGS, J. "Measures of Organizational Structure: A Methodological Note." *American Journal of Sociology*. Nov. 1973, 79, 686–704.

PERROW, C. "The Analysis of Goals in Complex Organizations." *American Sociological Review*, 1961, 26, 854–866.

PERROW, C. "Hospitals: Technology, Structure, and Goals." In J. G. March (Ed.), *Handbook of Organizations*. Chicago: Rand McNally, 1965.

PERROW, C. "A Framework for the Comparative Analysis of Organizations." *American Sociological Review*, Apr. 1967, *32*, 194–208.

PERROW, C. *Organizational Analysis: A Sociological View*. Belmont, Calif.: Wadsworth, 1970.

PERROW, C. *Complex Organizations—a Critical Essay*. Glenview, Ill.: Scott Foresman, 1972.

PERRUCCI, R., and GERSTL, J. E. *Profession Without Community: Engineers in American Society*. New York: Random House, 1969.

PIVEN, F. F., and CLOWARD, R. A. *Regulating the Poor: Functions of Public Welfare*. New York: Random House, 1972.

PUGH, D. S., HICKSON, D. J., HININGS, C. R., and TURNER, C. "Dimensions of Organization Structure." *Administrative Science Quarterly*, June 1968, *13*, 65–91.

RAVEN, B. H., and FRENCH, J. R. P., JR. "Legitimate Power, Coercive Power, and Observability in Social Influence." *Sociometry*, June 1958, *21*, 83–97.

REEDER, L. G., DONOHUE, G. A., and BIBLARZ, A. "Conceptions of Self and Others." *American Journal of Sociology*, Sept. 1960, *66*, 153–159.

RIDGEWAY, V. F. "Dysfunctional Consequences of Performance Measurements." *Administrative Science Quarterly*, Sept. 1956, *1*, 240–247.

ROETHLISBERGER, F. J., and DICKSON, W. J. *Management and the Worker*. Cambridge, Mass: Harvard University Press, 1939.

RUBENSTEIN, A. H. "Setting Criteria for R&D." *Harvard Business Review*, Jan.-Feb. 1957, *35*, 95–104.

SCHOPLER, J. "Social Power." In L. Berkowitz (Ed.), *Advances in Experimental Social Psychology*, vol. 2. New York: Academic Press, 1965.

SCOTT, W. R. "Theory of Organizations." In E. L. Faris (Ed.), *Handbook of Modern Sociology*. Chicago: Rand McNally, 1964.

SCOTT, W. R. "Reactions to Supervision in a Heteronomous Professional Organization." *Administrative Science Quarterly*, June 1965, *10*, 65–81.

SCOTT, W. R. "Professionals in Bureaucracies—Areas of Conflict." In H. M. Vollmer and D. L. Mills (Eds.), *Professionalization*. Englewood Cliffs, N.J.: Prentice-Hall, 1966.

SCOTT, W. R. "Professional Employees in a Bureaucratic Structure: Social Work." In A. Etzioni (Ed.), *The Semi-Professions and Their Organization*. New York: Free Press, 1969.

SCOTT, W. R. "Professionals in Hospitals: Technology and the Organization of Work." In B. S. Georgopoulos (Ed.), *Organization Research on Health Institutions.* Ann Arbor, Mich.: Institute for Social Research, University of Michigan, 1972.

SCOTT, W. R., DORNBUSCH, S. M., BUSCHING, B. C., and LAING, J. D. "Organizational Evaluation and Authority." *Administrative Science Quarterly,* June 1967, *12,* 93–117.

SCOTT, W. R., DORNBUSCH, S. M., EVASHWICK, C. J., MAGNANI, L., and SAGATUN, I. *Task Conceptions and Work Arrangements.* Research Memorandum 97. Stanford, Calif.: Stanford Center for Research and Development in Teaching, 1972.

SEASHORE, M. J. "Comparative Perceptions of Evaluation Processes." Unpublished report for the Evaluation and Authority Research Team. Stanford, Calif.: Department of Sociology, Stanford University, 1965.

SECORD, P. F., and BACKMAN, C. W. *Social Psychology.* New York: McGraw-Hill, 1964.

SELZNICK, P. "An Approach to a Theory of Bureaucracy." *American Sociological Review,* Feb. 1943, *8,* 47–54.

SELZNICK, P. "Foundations of the Theory of Organization." *American Sociological Review,* Feb. 1948, *13,* 25–35.

SELZNICK, P. *TVA and the Grass Roots.* Berkeley: University of California Press, 1949.

SELZNICK, P. *Leadership in Administration.* Evanston, Ill.: Row, Peterson, 1957.

SHARTLE, C. L. "Studies in Naval Leadership." In H. Guetzkow (Ed.), *Groups, Leadership and Men.* Pittsburgh: Carnegie Press, 1951.

SHEPARD, H. A. "The Value System of a University Research Group." *American Sociological Review,* Aug. 1954, *19,* 456–462.

SHERIF, M., and SHERIF, C. W. *Groups in Harmony and Tension.* New York: Harper and Row, 1953.

SIEGEL, S., and FOURAKER, L. E. *Bargaining and Group Decision-Making: Experiments in Bilateral Monopoly.* New York: McGraw-Hill, 1960.

SILBERMAN, C. E. *Crisis in the Classroom: The Remaking of American Education.* New York: Random House, 1970.

SIMON, H. A. "Comments on the Theory of Organizations." *American Political Science Review,* Dec. 1952, *46,* 1130–1139.

SIMON, H. A. *Administrative Behavior.* (2nd ed.) New York: Macmillan, 1957.

SIMON, H. A. "On the Concept of Organizational Goal." *Administrative Science Quarterly,* June 1964, *9,* 1–22,

SLATER, P. E. "Role Differentiation in Small Groups." *American Sociological Review,* June 1955, *20,* 300–310.

SMELSER, N. *Collective Behavior.* New York: Free Press, 1963.

STINCHCOMBE, A. L. "Social Structure and Organizations." In J. G. March (Ed.), *Handbook of Organizations.* Chicago: Rand McNally, 1965.

STOGDILL, R. M., and COONS, A. E. (Eds.) *Leader Behavior: Its Description and Measurement.* Columbus: Bureau of Business Research, Ohio State University Press, 1957.

STOUFFER, S. A., GUTTMAN, L., SUCHMAN, E. A., LAZARSFELD, P. F., STAR, S. A., and CLAUSEN, J. C. *Studies in Social Psychology in World War II.* Vol. 4: *Measurement and Prediction.* Princeton, N.J.: Princeton University Press, 1950.

SULLIVAN, H. S. *Conceptions of Modern Psychiatry.* Washington, D.C.: William Alanson White Psychiatric Foundation, 1947.

TANNENBAUM, A. S. *Control in Organizations.* New York: McGraw-Hill, 1968.

TERREBERRY, S. "The Evolution of Organizational Environments." *Administrative Science Quarterly,* Mar. 1968, *12,* 590–613.

THIBAUT, J. W., and KELLEY, H. H. *The Social Psychology of Groups.* New York: Wiley, 1959.

THOMPSON, J. D. "Authority and Power in 'Identical' Organizations." *American Journal of Sociology,* Nov. 1956, *62,* 290–301.

THOMPSON, J. D. *Organizations in Action.* New York: McGraw-Hill, 1967.

THOMPSON, J. E. *Evaluation and Authority in Elementary Schools: A Comparison of Teachers and Administrators.* Unpublished Ph.D. dissertation. School of Education, Stanford University, 1971.

THOMPSON, V. A. *Modern Organization.* New York: Knopf, 1961.

TORGERSON, W. S. *Theory and Methods of Scaling.* New York. Wiley, 1958.

TURNER, D. E. *Some Effects of Bureaucracy upon Professionals Who Work in a Complex Organization: Authority and Evaluation in the Roman Catholic Church.* Unpublished Ph.D. dissertation. Department of Political Science, Stanford University, 1971.

UDY, S. H., JR. " 'Bureaucracy' and 'Rationality' in Weber's Organization Theory: An Empirical Study." *American Sociological Review,* Dec. 1959a, *24,* 791–795.

UDY, S. H., JR. *Organization of Work.* New Haven, Conn.: HRAF Press, 1959b.

UDY, S. H., JR. "Technical and Institutional Factors in Production

Organization." *American Journal of Sociology,* Nov. 1961, *67,* 247–254.

UDY, S. H., JR. *Work in Traditional and Modern Society.* Englewood Cliffs, N.J.: Prentice-Hall, 1970.

URWICK, L. T. *The Elements of Administration.* New York: Harper and Row, 1943.

VANCE, S. *Industrial Administration.* New York: McGraw-Hill, 1959.

VERBA, S. *Small Groups and Political Behavior.* Princeton, N.J.: Princeton University Press, 1961.

WAGER, L. W. "Leadership Style, Hierarchical Influence, and Supervisory Role Obligations." *Administrative Science Quarterly,* Mar. 1965, *9,* 391–420.

WEBER, M. *Max Weber: Essays in Sociology.* H. H. Gerth and C. W. Mills (Eds. and Trans.). New York: Oxford University Press, 1946.

WEBER, M. *The Theory of Social and Economic Organization.* A. M. Henderson and T. Parsons (Trans.), T: Parsons (Ed.). New York: Free Press, 1947.

WHEELER, S. "The Structure of Formally Organized Socialization Settings." In O. G. Brim, Jr., and S. Wheeler (Eds.), *Socialization After Childhood.* New York: Wiley, 1966.

WHITE, R., and LIPPITT, R. *Autocracy and Democracy.* New York: Harper and Row, 1960.

WHYTE, W. F. *Street Corner Society.* (rev. ed.) Chicago: University of Chicago Press, 1955.

WHYTE, W. F., and others. *Money and Motivation.* New York: Harper and Row, 1955.

WOLIN, S. *Politics and Vision.* Boston: Little, Brown, 1960.

WOODWARD, J. *Management and Technology.* London: H.M.S.O., 1958.

WOODWARD, J. *Industrial Organization: Theory and Practice.* London: Oxford University Press, 1965.

WOODWARD, J. *Industrial Organization: Behaviour and Control.* London: Oxford University Press, 1970a.

WOODWARD, J. "Technology, Material Control, and Organizational Behavior." In A. R. Negandhi and J. P. Schwitter (Eds.), *Organizational Behavior Models.* Kent, Ohio: Comparative Administration Research Institute of the Bureau of Economic and Business Research, 1970b.

ZELDITCH, M., JR., BERGER, J., and COHEN, B. P. "Stability of Organizational Status Structures." In J. Berger, M. Zelditch, Jr., and B. Anderson (Eds.), *Sociological Theories in Progress,* vol. 1. Boston: Houghton Mifflin, 1966.

Index

▲▲

Name Index

ABEGGLEN, J. C., 93
ARENDT, H., 93
ARGYLE, M., 152

BALES, R. F., 35, 47, 48
BARCHAS, K. U., 225
BARITZ, L., 50
BECKER, H. S., 274
BEER, S., 144
BENDIX, R., 50, 94
BENNIS, W. G., 34
BERGER, J., 2, 47, 98
BERKOWITZ, L., 244
BERLINER, J. S., 148, 161
BETHEL, L. L., 135
BIBLARZ, A., 97
BIDWELL, C. E., 90
BIERSTED, R., 60
BLAU, P. M., 32, 35, 44, 46, 47, 51, 52, 54, 55, 62, 92, 96, 148, 276
BOWERS, D. G., 52
BRODY, C., 229
BUCHER, R., 54
BUCKLEY, W., 144
BUSCHING, B. C., 294, 296

CAMILLERI, S. F., 2
CAPLOW, T., 49, 58
CARTWRIGHT, D., 31
CLARK, B. R., 54, 65
CLOWARD, R. A., 24, 54
COHEN, B. P., 2, 39, 47, 98
COHEN, E. G., 155, 173, 174
COLEMAN, J. C., 27
COLLINS, O., 98

COONS, A. E., 52
COSER, R. L., 229, 274
COSTNER, H. A., 28
CROZIER, M., 98
CYERT, R. M., 70

DAHL, R. A., 31, 32, 44
DALTON, M., 53, 88, 98, 148, 152, 161
DAVIS, J. A., 268, 276
DAY, R. C., 152
DENNISON, G., 24
DEUTSCH, M., 268
DICKSON, W. J., 42, 43, 44, 88
DONOHUE, G. A., 97
DORNBUSCH, S. M., 2, 12, 25, 77, 83, 97, 113

EMERSON, R. M., 31, 32, 33, 57, 58, 333
EMERY, F. E., 254
ETZIONI, A., 10, 48, 54, 92
EVAN, W. M., 44, 54, 60

FESTINGER, L., 321
FISHER, L. H., 51
FOURAKER, L., 244
FREIDSON, E., 54, 85, 86, 150, 151, 155, 256
FRENCH, J. R. P., JR., 32, 40, 44, 54, 60

GALBRAITH, J. K., 70
GERGEN, K. J., 260
GERSTL, J. E., 122
GINGER, A. F., 24
GOFFMAN, E., 53, 83

374

GOODMAN, L. A., 24, 27
GOSS, M. E. W., 54, 69
GOULDNER, A. W., 40, 41, 50, 52, 66, 150, 152
GRAMBSCH, P. V., 54
GREEN, B. F., JR., 321
GROSS, E., 54
GROSS, N., 34
GULICK, L., 83, 249, 253
GUTTMAN, L., 277, 321

HABERSTROH, C. J., 145, 159, 161
HALL, R. H., 11
HALPIN, A. W., 54
HAMBLIN, R., 152
HARRISON, P. M., 50
HARTMANN, H., 50
HARVEY, O., 268
HEINECKE, C., 47
HICKSON, D. J., 77
HILL, W. W., 54
HIND, R. R., 12, 13, 25, 340, 353, 354
HOLT, J., 24
HOMANS, G. C., 35, 45, 46
HUGHES, E. C., 85, 98, 255, 256, 261
HURWITZ, J. I., 97
HUSON, C., 276
HYMOVITCH, B., 97

JACKSON, P. W., 24
JANOWITZ, M., 54
JAQUES, E., 153, 162, 165, 166, 167
JONES, E. E., 268

KAHN, R. L., 54, 152, 262, 263, 264, 268
KAST, F. E., 144
KATZ, D., 54, 152
KAUFMAN, H., 54, 151
KELLEY, H. H., 31, 32, 33, 48, 57, 58, 78, 92, 244, 268
KENDALL, M. G., 294
KENDALL, P. L., 275
KERR, C., 51
KOONTZ, H., 136, 151, 158, 257
KORNHAUSER, W., 54
KRUSKAL, W. H., 27

LAING, J. D., 309
LEAVITT, H. J., 85

LEWIN, K., 244
LIKERT, R., 52, 54
LIPPITT, R., 32, 34
LIPSET, S. M., 27
LITTERER, J. A., 43, 136

MC CAULEY, B. L., 25, 108, 347, 353
MC CLEERY, R. H., 54
MC CLELLAND, D. C., 245
MC EACHERN, A. W., 34
MAGNANI, L. L., 15, 108, 113, 115, 185, 347
MANNARI, H., 93
MANNHEIM, K., 30
MARCH, J. G., 70, 73, 147, 244, 245, 268
MARRAM, G. D., 21, 22, 25, 108, 110, 111, 155, 338, 343, 344, 347
MARSH, R. M., 93
MASON, W. S., 34
MEAD, G. H., 97
MECHANIC, D., 37, 274
MERTON, R. K., 149, 152, 270
MEYER, J., 155, 173, 174
MICHELS, R., 69
MILES, M. B., 274
MIYAMOTO, S. F., 97

NADEL, S. F., 58

O'DONNELL, C., 136, 151, 159, 257
OLESEN, J. L., 274

PARSONS, T., 58, 59, 66
PEABODY, R. L., 50
PELZ, D. C., 52
PENNINGS, J., 56
PERROW, C., 51, 54, 70, 77, 78, 83, 86, 87
PERRUCCI, R., 122
PIVEN, F. F., 24
POLANSKY, N., 32, 34
PUGH, D. S., 55

RAVEN, B. H., 32, 40, 44, 60
REEDER, L. G., 97
RHEA, B., 54, 151, 155, 256
RIDGEWAY, V. F., 147
ROETHLISBERGER, F. J., 42, 43, 44, 88
ROSEN, S., 32, 34
ROSENZWEIG, J. E., 144

RUBENSTEIN, A. H., 147

SCHOENHERR, R., 55
SCHOPLER, J., 31
SCOTT, W. R., 2, 11, 12, 25, 46, 51, 54,
    77, 78, 86, 87, 90, 113
SEASHORE, M. J., 52, 171
SEASHORE, S. E., 52
SELZNICK, P., 51, 66, 70, 88
SHAPIRO, H. M., 268
SHARTLE, C. L., 54
SHEPARD, H. A., 276
SHERIF, C. W., 35
SHERIF, M., 35
SIEGEL, S., 244
SILBERMAN, C. E., 24
SIMON, H. A., 40, 66, 70, 71, 73, 88,
    147, 244, 245, 249, 268
SLATER, P. E., 35, 48
SMELSER, N., 256
SOLOMON, L., 268
SPAETH, J. L., 276
STINCHCOMBE, A. L., 266
STOGDILL, R. M., 52
STOUFFER, S. A., 277, 321

TANNENBAUM, A. S., 53
TAYLOR, F. W., 257
TERREBERRY, S., 255
THIBAUT, J. W., 31, 32, 33, 48, 57, 58,
    78, 92, 244, 268

THOMAS, W. I., 265
THOMPSON, J. D., 77, 81, 83, 88, 159,
    254, 258
THOMPSON, J. E., 19, 25, 171, 186,
    347, 353
THOMPSON, V. A., 51, 53, 97
TORGERSON, W. S., 321
TRIST, E. L., 254
TROW, M. A., 27
TURNER, D. E., 14, 15, 25, 125, 127,
    338

UDY, S. H., 77, 98
URWICK, L. T., 257

VANCE, S., 135, 142
VERBA, S., 40, 47

WAGER, L. W., 52
WEBER, M., 31, 32, 37, 38, 39, 49, 50,
    59, 61
WHEELER, S., 83
WHITTAKER, E. W., 274
WHYTE, W. F., 48, 64
WILSON, J. Q., 65
WOLIN, S., 51
WOODWARD, J., 77, 87

ZANDER, A., 97
ZELDITCH, M., JR., 2, 44, 47, 54, 60, 98

Subject Index

A

Acceptance level, 243-247, 284-285,
    328
    and aspiration level, 244, 269
    defined, 246, 351
    lowering of, 268-269
Administrative principles
    authority and responsibility, 257,
        262
    unity of command, 249-250
Administrators. See Evaluators
Agreement
    on authority rights, 226-233, 298-
        299

on evaluation frequency, 171
    among evaluators, 172-173, 353
    on task importance, 130-131
    See also Consensus
Allocating, 69-76, 136-137, 158, 200-
    202, 211-213, 221-226
    conflicts in, 251, 287
    exercises, 217-221
    misunderstanding of, 257-258
    noncompliance to, 270-271, 304-
        305
Appraising, 142-143, 161-162, 213-
    214, 221-226
    discretion in, 162
    exercisers, 217-221

Aspiration level and acceptance level, 244, 269

Authority
  as authorized power, 17, 40-42, 58-64, 192-204, 209-217, 221-226, 346
  complexity of systems of, 156, 252, 265, 295-298, 352-353
  dimensions of, 38-45
  as endorsed power, 40-42, 58-64, 207, 217
  formal, 42-45, 49-64
  in formal organizations, 49-56, 58, 63-64, 192-208
  incompatibility of, 243-331
  informal, 42-45, 53-54
  in informal groups, 45-49, 57-58, 63-64
  instability of systems of, 90-91, 243-331
  as legitimate power, 37, 56-59, 192-204
  model of, 192-204
  positional, 43-44, 205-207, 226-233
  propriety of, 17, 38-42, 87-91, 114-116, 221-226, 346-347
  rights of, 194-204, 206-207, 209-242, 346-347, 354
  as structural element, 55-56
  systems of, 195, 199-206, 346-347
  task-specific, 2, 9, 204-205, 210, 232-242
  theory of, 332-358
  validity of, 38-42, 217
Authorized power. *See* Authority
Autonomy, 107-116, 348-349

B

Bureaucratization
  in archdiocese, 125-133
  and tasks, 82-87

C

Centralization, 82-85, 354, 356-357
Change
  in authority systems, 307
  pressures for, 91, 267

suggestions for, 91, 115, 270, 304-305, 308
  See also Instability
Clarity, 16-17, 79, 81-91, 106-114, 146-148
Clergy, 14-15, 105-106, 125-133, 338-339
Communication
  of dissatisfaction, 270, 304-305
  of evaluations, 155, 164-165, 177
  links in among right holders, 202-204
Competence
  and evaluations, 169-170
  and incompatibility, 294-295, 353
Composition effects, 276, 323
Consensus
  on authority rights, 226-233, 298-299
  and group size, 229
  See also Agreement
Control
  attempts at, 92-93, 192-204, 209-221
  and evaluations, 92-99, 192-204, 340-344
  number exercising, 217-221
  system of, 194-195, 199-204
  task of, 194, 354-357
  See also Authority, Evaluations, Power
Coordination among evaluators, 202-204, 252
Criteria-setting, 137-140, 158-161, 214-215, 221-226
  conflicts in, 248-250, 286
  for exercises, 217-221
  misunderstanding of, 258-259, 288
  and standards, 139-140
  and task properties, 138
  and weights, 138-139

D

Delegation, 71-76, 106-114, 158, 356-357. *See also* Allocating
Differentiation
  of control system, 203-204
  of leadership, 47-48

of positions of performer and evaluator, 193-194
of power in informal groups, 35
of status in informal groups, 45-49
Directives, 71-76, 106-114, 158, 356-357. *See also* Allocating
Disciplines, academic and agreement among evaluators, 172-173
and granting agencies, 241-242
Dissatisfaction. *See* Instability, Satisfaction

E

Efficacy, 16-17, 79, 80-91, 106-114
Effort and evaluations, 235-237, 339-340, 354-356
Electronics firm, 7, 102
Evaluation process
components of, 136-145, 158-162, 194-204, 210-217
model of, 135-145, 195
theory of, 332-358
See also Evaluations, Evaluators
Evaluations
acceptance level for, 243-247
central, 94-95, 337-338, 352, 356
communication of, 155, 164-165, 177
and competence, 169-170
contradictory, 248-252, 285-287
and control, 92-99, 192-204, 340-344, 354-357
and effort, 235-237, 339-341, 354-356
and esteem, 96
frequency of, 167-169, 171, 189, 266, 296-298
importance of, 20, 94-97, 117-119, 179-185, 196-197, 318-320, 337-345, 356
low, 327-329
nonperformance bases of, 187-188
peer, 10, 20, 121, 238
of performance, 99, 134-135, 196-197, 254-256
of qualities vs. activities, 97-99

and sanctions, 91-99, 195-197, 336-339
and self-concept, 96-97
soundly based, 95, 154, 176-185, 342-347, 349-353, 355-356
specific vs. general, 145-146, 235
unattainable, 259-262, 288-291
uncontrollable, 252-257, 287
unpredictable, 257-259, 288
See also Standards
Evaluators
as administrators, 16-17
agreement among, 172-173
conflicts among, 251-252
and control tasks, 354-357
coordination among, 202-204, 252
distance of from task, 23, 89, 111
importance of, 94-95, 117-122, 240-242, 336-345, 352
influence of over sanctions, 94-97, 117-119, 336-339
nonorganizational, 120-122, 240-242
number of, 217-221
organizational, 94, 119-122, 195-196
and task, 237-242
Expectations, performance, 2

F

Faculty, 12-14, 103, 172-173, 182, 232-242, 353-354
Feedback loop, 144
Five Organizations study, 3-9, 99-103, 119-122, 165-168, 170, 187, 209-232, 283-331
of electronics firm, 7, 102
of football team, 8, 102, 117-119, 170, 182-183, 317-320
of hospital, 5, 101, 229-231
of newspaper, 7-8, 102, 117-119, 317-320
positions studied in, 5-9
of research facility, 6-7, 101-102, 121-122
tasks studied in, 99-106
Football team, 8, 102, 117-119, 170, 182-183, 317-320

Formalization, 30
  of authority rights, 206-207, 346-347, 354, 356-357
  and tasks, 82-85, 348-349
Freedom, 107-116, 348-349

G

Gamma, 27-28
Goal assignment. *See* Allocating
Goal setting, 69-71
Goals, 65-71
  cognitive vs. cathectic, 65-66
  commitment to, 95-96
  defined, 66
  displacement of, 147-148, 358
  organizational, 69
  specificity of, 67-68, 146-148
  See also Allocating, Tasks

H

Hierarchy, 59
  experience in, 129-130
  as power system, 36
  status in, 278-279, 308
  as structural element, 55
Hospitals, 5, 101, 229-231

I

Ideologies
  managerial, 50-51
  and task conceptions, 24
Incompatibility, 246-331, 349-353, 356
  and active tasks, 254-256, 260, 265, 287, 299-300
  and age of system, 266-267
  and complexity of authority system, 265, 295-298
  and consensus on authority rights, 298-299
  contagion of, 276, 323
  cost of, 272-273, 316-320
  criteria for, 285, 291
  defined, 247, 351
  distribution of, 292-295
  and evaluation frequency, 266, 296-298
  and instability, 308-331
  and interdependence, 265-266, 295-298
  positional, 320-323

and propriety, 325-326
  resolution of, 268-272, 305, 307-308
  summary measures of, 291-292
  types of, 247-262, 351
Influence on sanctions
  and evaluations, 20, 94-97, 117-119, 179-185, 196-197, 318-320, 337-345, 356
  and evaluators, 119-122, 126-127, 179-185, 237-242, 337-345
  preferred vs. actual, 123-124
  and tasks, 122-125, 127-132, 233-234, 337-345
  See also Sanctions
Informal groups
  and authority, 45-49
  and power, 35-36, 57-58
Instability
  acts of, 304-307
  amount and type of, 273-279, 350-351
  of control systems, 37, 47-49
  defined, 267
  dissatisfaction indicating, 300-304
  effects of, 307-308
  and incompatibility, 268, 272-331, 349-353
  indicators of, 270-271, 300-307
  and power, 185-187
  and propriety, 90-91, 114-116, 349-351
  and status in hierarchy, 308
  summary measures of, 303-307
Interdependence, 156, 205
  and incompatibility, 252-254, 266, 295-298, 350, 352-353

J

Japanese firms, 93-94

L

Laboratory research team, 2
Leadership
  emergence of, 45-49
  formal vs. informal, 52
  strategies of, 50-52
  studies of, 51-52, 54
Legitimacy, 37-42, 56-64
  and authority, 37, 56-59, 192-204

and dramaturgical techniques, 53
and status differentiation, 45-49
and subordinate beliefs, 49-53

M

Motivation, 91-93, 196-197
and incompatibility, 246

N

Newspaper, 7-8, 102, 117-119, 317-320
Nigerian organizations, 188
Noncompliance, 270-271
to allocating, 270-271, 304-305
to sampling, 116, 304-305
Norms
regulating power, 37-42, 48, 56-63, 192-204, 210
supporting power, 49-52, 198-199
and visibility, 149-150
Nurses, 5, 20-23, 104-105, 106-114, 122-125, 173, 185, 338-339, 343, 347

O

Organizations
authority systems in, 49-64, 192-242
defined, 29-30
environment of, 254
formal vs. informal, 29-31
power systems in, 36-37
selection of for study, 3-4, 9-12, 25-26
structure of, 55-56, 77-79, 83-84

P

Performance value, 139
Positional authority, 43-44, 205-207, 226-233
Positional incompatibility, 276-279, 292-294
Positions
selected for study, 4, 5-9, 12-25
time in, 296-298, 323-325, 354
Power
and authority, 29-64, 192-208
authorized, 17, 40-42, 58-64, 192-204, 209-217, 221-226, 346
bases of, 32-33

defined, 33
and dependence, 31-33, 36, 57
endorsed, 40-42, 58-64, 207, 217
in formal organizations, 36-37
in informal groups, 35-36
and motivation of participants, 91-99
regulation of, 37-42, 48, 56-61, 192-204, 210
and work arrangements, 17, 90, 157, 185-187, 189-190, 357
See also Authority, Control, Sanctions
Predictability, 16-17, 79-91, 106-114, 148-149, 160
Principals, 18-20, 111, 171, 188-191
Professional organization studies, 9-26, 103-106
of alternative school teachers, 23-25, 109-110, 169, 338-339, 353
of clergy, 14-15, 105-106, 125-133, 338-339
of faculty, 12-14, 103, 172-173, 182, 232-242, 353-354
of nurses, 20-23, 104-105, 106-114, 122-125, 173-185, 338-339, 343, 347
of principals, 18-20, 111, 171, 188-191
of public school teachers, 15-18, 23-25, 103-104, 106-114, 168-169, 185-187, 188-191, 338-339, 347, 353
tasks in, 102-106
Professional organizations, 10
autonomous vs. heteronomous, 11-12, 15, 21-22, 86-87, 89
and evaluation of qualities, 99
Professionals
and bureaucratic tasks, 127-132
characteristics of, 10
commitments of to goals, 96, 339
and evaluations of qualities, 99
and norms restricting visibility, 150
in organizations, 10-11
and performance evaluations, 254-256
and task dimensions, 85-87, 254-256

Propriety, 17, 217, 345-347, 349-353
and authorization, 221-226, 345-347
for control tasks, 355-357
and incompatibility, 325-326, 356
and instability, 87-91, 114-116
and role distance, 225-226
and validity, 38-40, 345

R

Rationality
assumption of, 87-88
defined, 30
Research facility, 6-7, 101-102, 121-122
Responsibility, 257, 262
Rewards. *See* Sanctions
Role ambiguity, 263-265
Role conflict, 262-263
Role distance, 225-226

S

Sampling, 140-142, 161, 215-216, 221-226
bias in, 152, 259
exercisers, 217-221
conflicts in, 250-251
frequency of, 153, 165-169
indicators for, 141, 161
noncompliance with, 116, 304-305
of performances vs. outcomes, 141-142
techniques for, 142
Sanctions
and control, 92-99
defined, 34
and evaluations, 91-99, 337-339
and task effort, 235-237
See also Influence on sanctions
Satisfaction
absolute vs. relative, 300-301
and acceptance level, 244-245
and agreement among evaluators, 172-173
and agreement on task importance, 130-132
and evaluation frequency, 167-169, 189

and perceived agreement on task importance, 131-132
and power, 185-187, 189-190
and propriety, 114-116
right-specific vs. general, 301-302
and sampling frequency, 167-169
with specific and overall evaluations, 235
summary measures of, 303-304
See also Instability
Schools
alternative, 23-25, 109-110, 169, 338-339, 353
public, 15-20, 23-25, 103-104, 106-114, 168-169, 171, 185-191, 338-339, 347, 353
Scope conditions, 195-197, 335-337
Specialization and active and inert tasks, 82-85, 348-349, 354, 356-357
Standards, evaluation, 12, 139-140, 158-161
and acceptance level, 245-246
for active tasks, 160-161, 260-261
application of, 143
conflicting, 248-250, 286
inappropriately high, 260, 289
knowledge of, 188-189
types of, 159-160
See also Criteria-setting
Stanford Center for Research and Development in Teaching, 15
Status
differentiation of in informal groups, 45-49
equality of, 47-48
ethnic, 187-188
in hierarchy, 153, 165-167, 278-279, 308
student, 274-276
Status characteristics, 2, 98
Structural authority rights, 206-207, 226-233, 346-347, 354. *See also* Positional authority
Structural elements of organizations, 55-56
Structural problems, 276-279, 320-323. *See also* Positional incompatibility

T

Task conceptions
and distance from task, 23, 89,
111
and ideology, 24
variations in among performers,
23-24
variations in between administrators and performers, 16-17,
19, 89-90
and work arrangements, 16-17,
76-91, 106-116, 347-349
See also Tasks
Tasks
active vs. inert, 78-91, 106-114,
160-161, 254-256, 260-261, 287,
299-300, 348-349, 354, 356-357
allocation of, 69-76, 136-137, 158,
200-202, 211-213, 221-226
appraising of, 142-143, 161-162,
213-214, 221-226
bureaucratic vs. professional, 14,
127-132
complexity of, 145-146
conceptions of, 16-17, 23-24, 76-
91, 106-116, 347-349
conflicts between, 251
criteria-setting for, 137-140, 158-
161, 214-215, 221-226
dimensions of, 16-17, 79
distance from, 23, 89, 111, 225-
226
effort on, 235-237, 339-340
faculty, 233
importance of, 122-125, 127-132,
337-345
interdependence of, 156, 205,
252-254
nursing, 22
performance value on, 139-140
performance vs. outcome, 74-76,
99, 141-142, 149-155, 254-256
properties of, 67, 71-74, 138-140,
250
sampling of, 140-142, 152-153,
161, 165-169, 215-226
teaching, 18

visibility of, 20-21, 149-154, 173-
185, 240-242, 343-345, 356
See also Task conceptions
Teachers
in alternative schools, 23-25, 109-
110, 169, 338-339, 353
in public schools, 15-18, 23-25,
103-104, 106-114, 173-191,
338-339, 347, 353
Teaming
among nurses, 21-23, 173-185
among teachers, 21-23, 173-185
and visibility of tasks, 21-23, 155,
173-185
Technology, 76-77, 87-88. *See also*
Tasks
Tests, statistical, 26-28
Theory of evaluation and authority,
332-358
Turnover, 273-274

U

Unity of command, 249-250

V

Validity
and authorization, 217
and propriety, 38-40
Visibility, 20-23, 343-345, 356
costs of, 151-152
and evaluations, 154-155, 176-
185, 343-345
and evaluators, 240-241
of performances vs. outcomes,
149-155
and power, 157
restrictions on, 149-151
and teaming, 21-23, 155, 173-177

W

Work arrangements
actual vs. preferred, 17, 90
and organizational structure, 77-
79
and power, 17, 90, 157, 185-187,
189-190, 357
and task conceptions, 16-17, 76-
91, 106-116, 348-349